Visitor 1

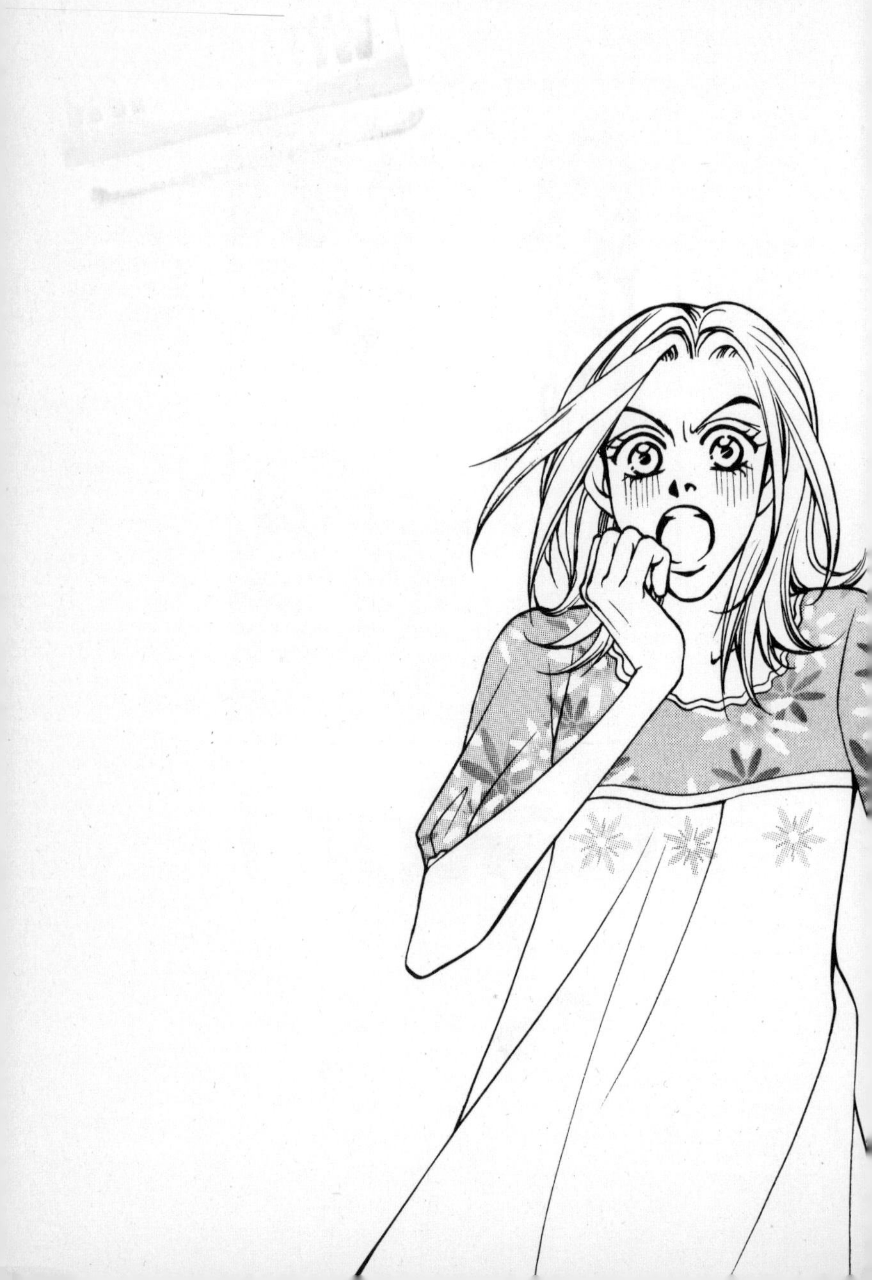

VISITOR

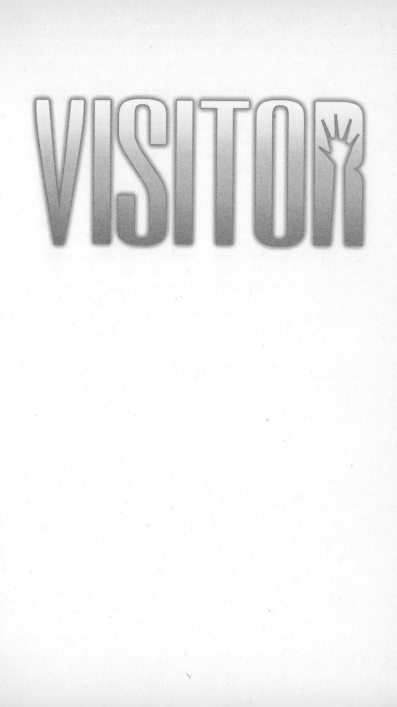

Visitor Vol. 1

created by Yee-Jung No

Translation - Jennifer Hahm
English Adaptation - Jay Antani
Retouch and Lettering - Jeannie Lee
Production Artists - James Lee and James Dashiell
Cover Design - Raymond Makowski

Editor - Tim Beedle
Digital Imaging Manager - Chris Buford
Pre-Press Manager - Antonio DePietro
Production Managers - Jennifer Miller and Mutsumi Miyazaki
Art Director - Matt Alford
Managing Editor - Jill Freshney
VP of Production - Ron Klamert
Editor-in-Chief - Mike Kiley
President and C.O.O. - John Parker
Publisher and C.E.O. - Stuart Levy

A  **TOKYOPOP** Manga

TOKYOPOP Inc.
5900 Wilshire Blvd. Suite 2000
Los Angeles, CA 90036

E-mail: info@TOKYOPOP.com
Come visit us online at www.TOKYOPOP.com

ISBN: 1-59532-342-2

First TOKYOPOP printing: April 2005
10 9 8 7 6 5 4 3 2 1
Printed in the USA

VISITOR

by
Yee-Jung No

Vol. 1

HAMBURG // LONDON // LOS ANGELES // TOKYO

CONTENTS

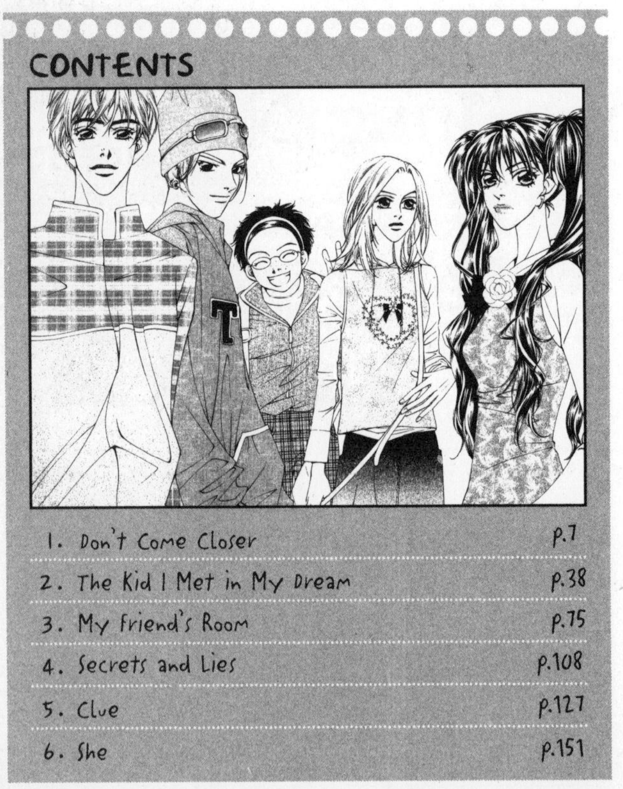

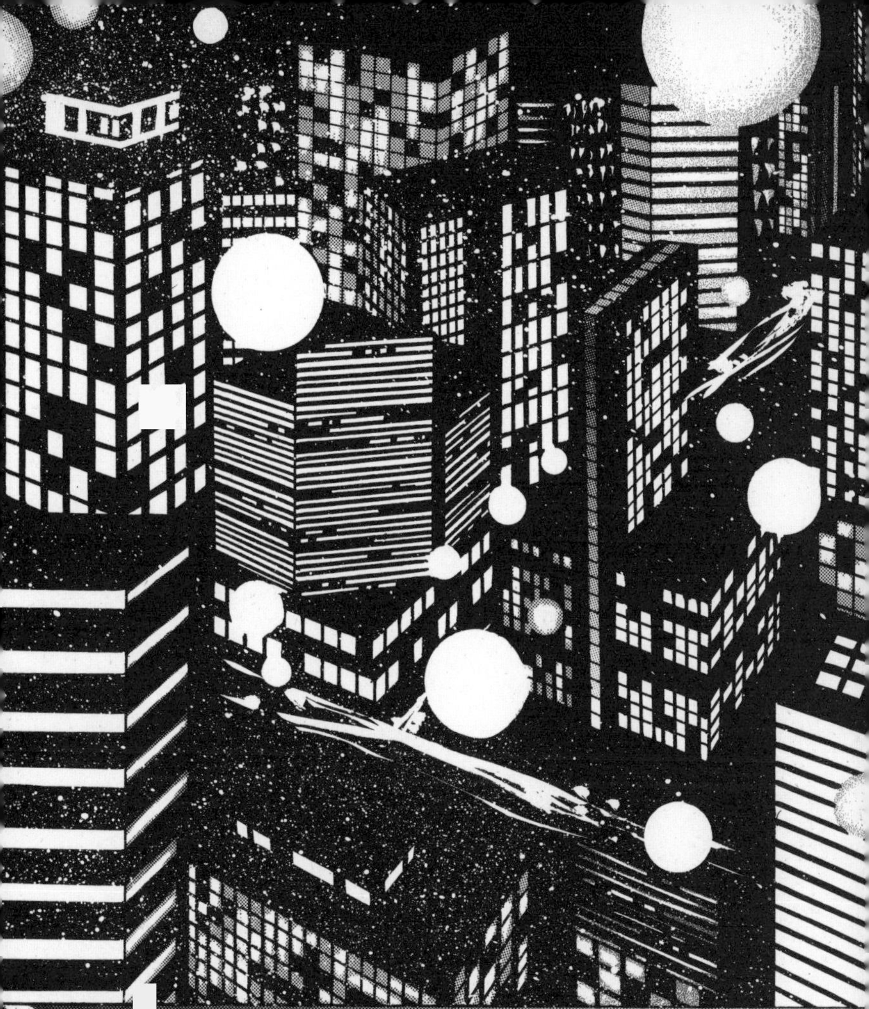

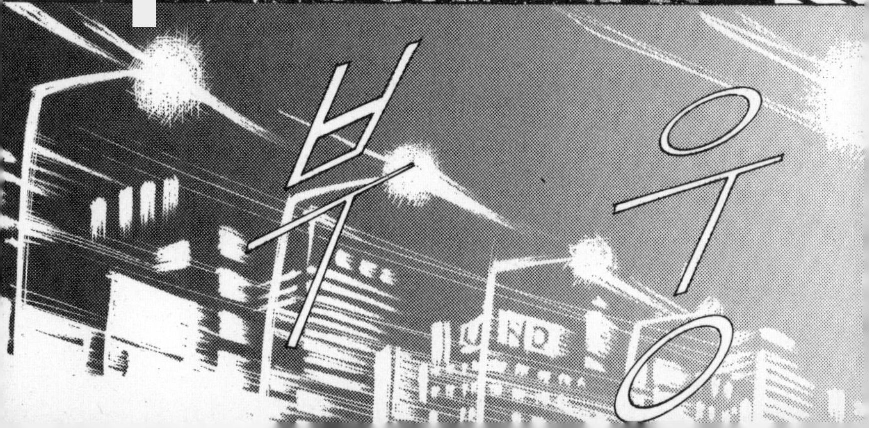
부웅

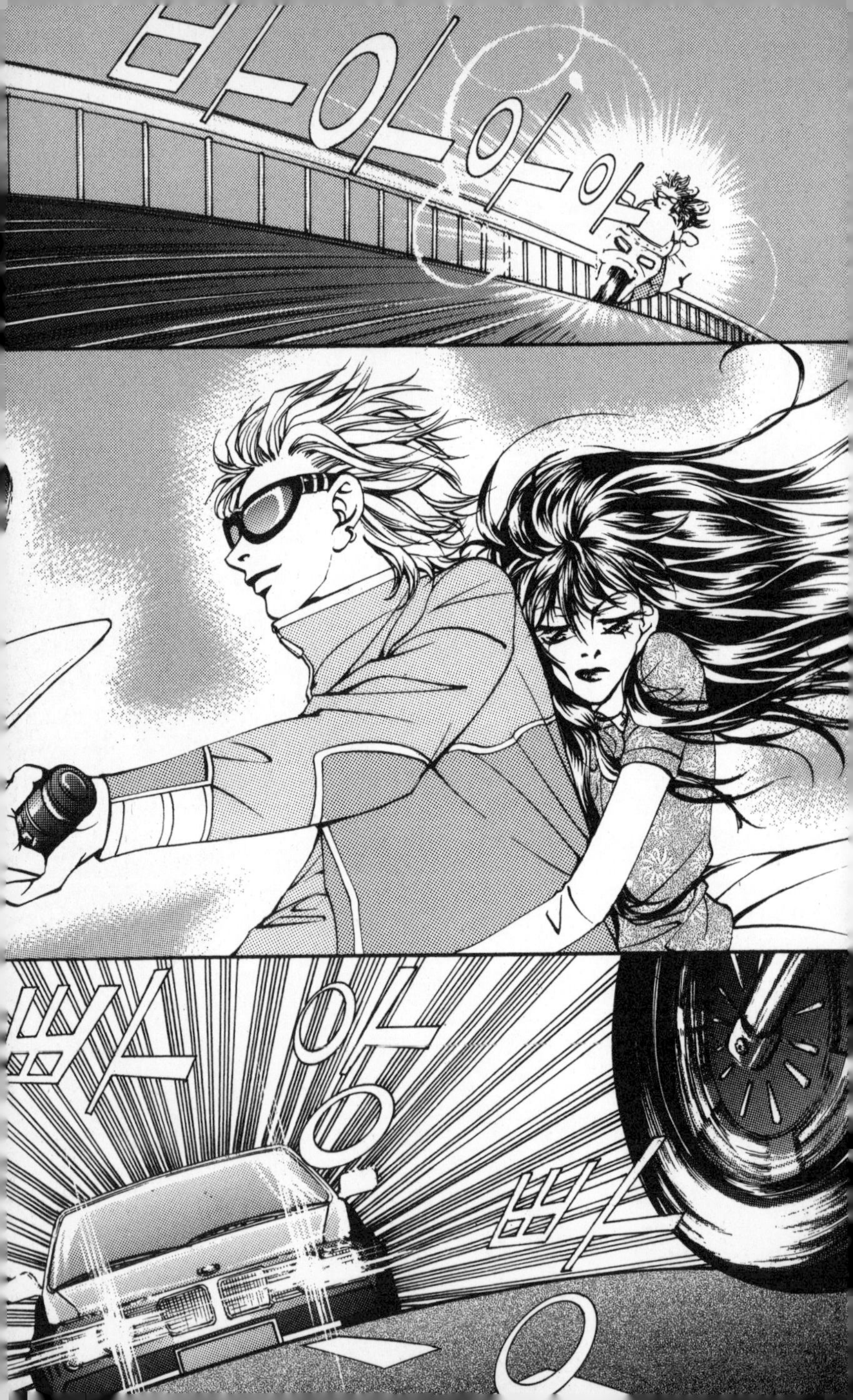
바아아앙
빠앙
빵

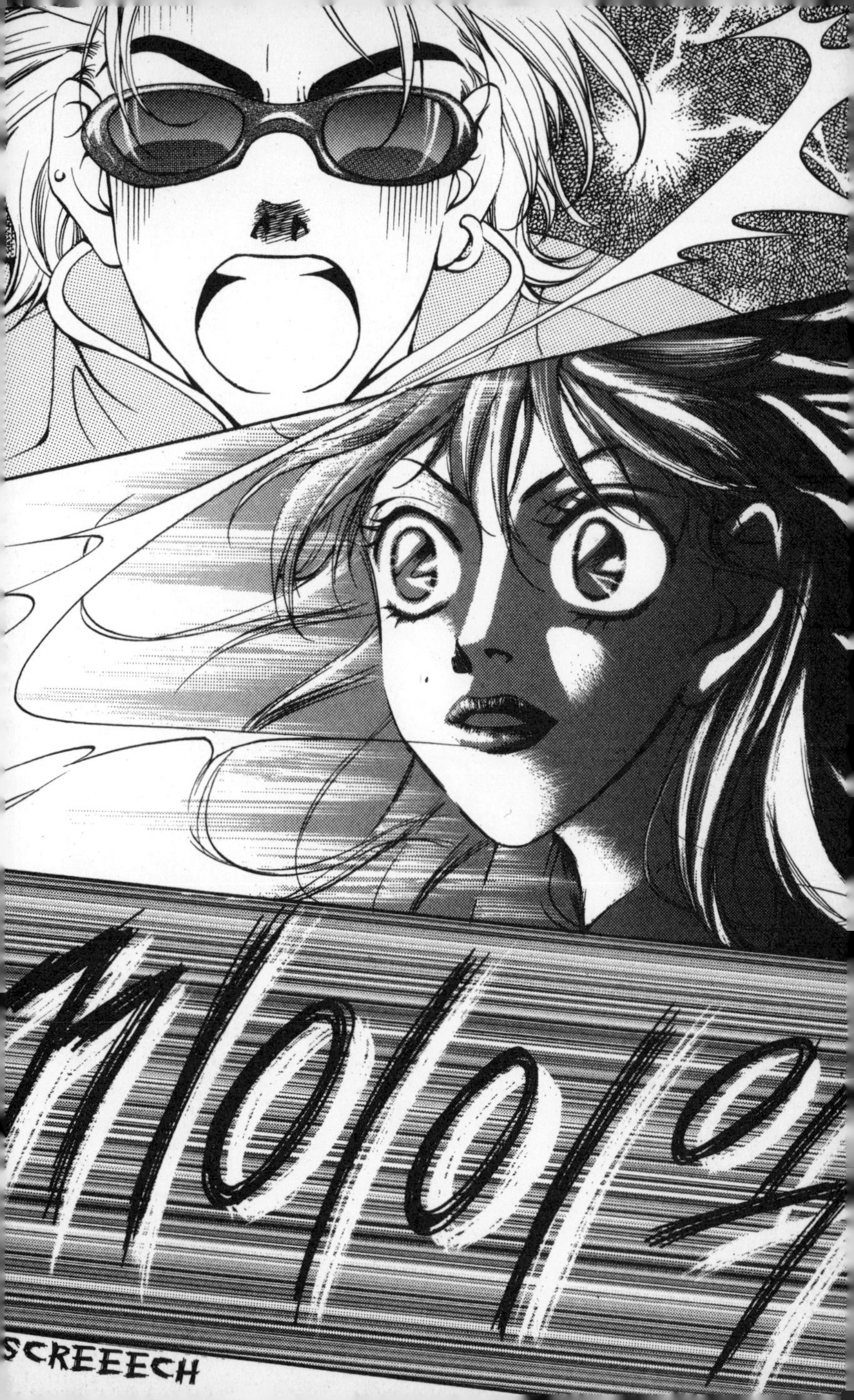
SCREEECH

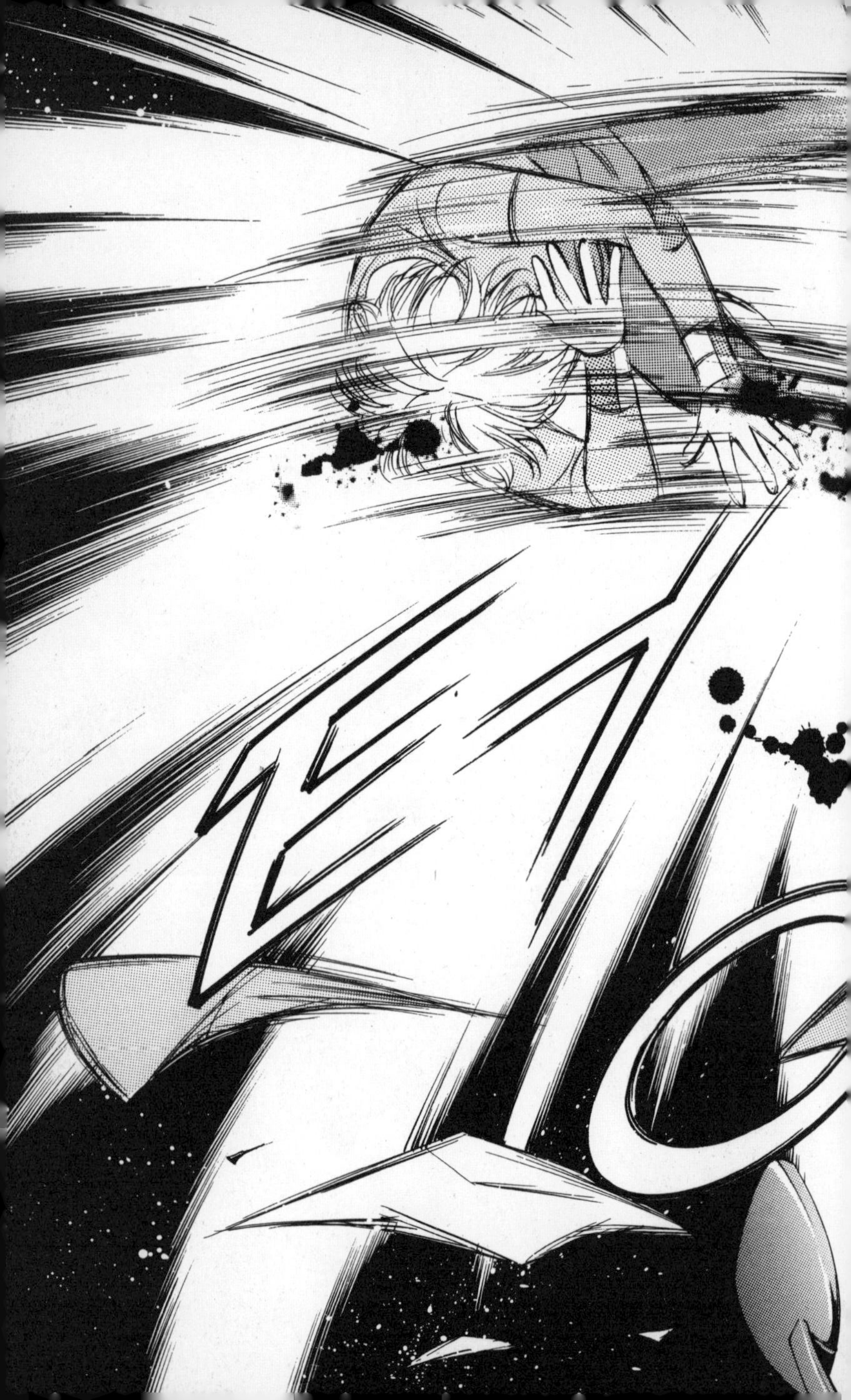

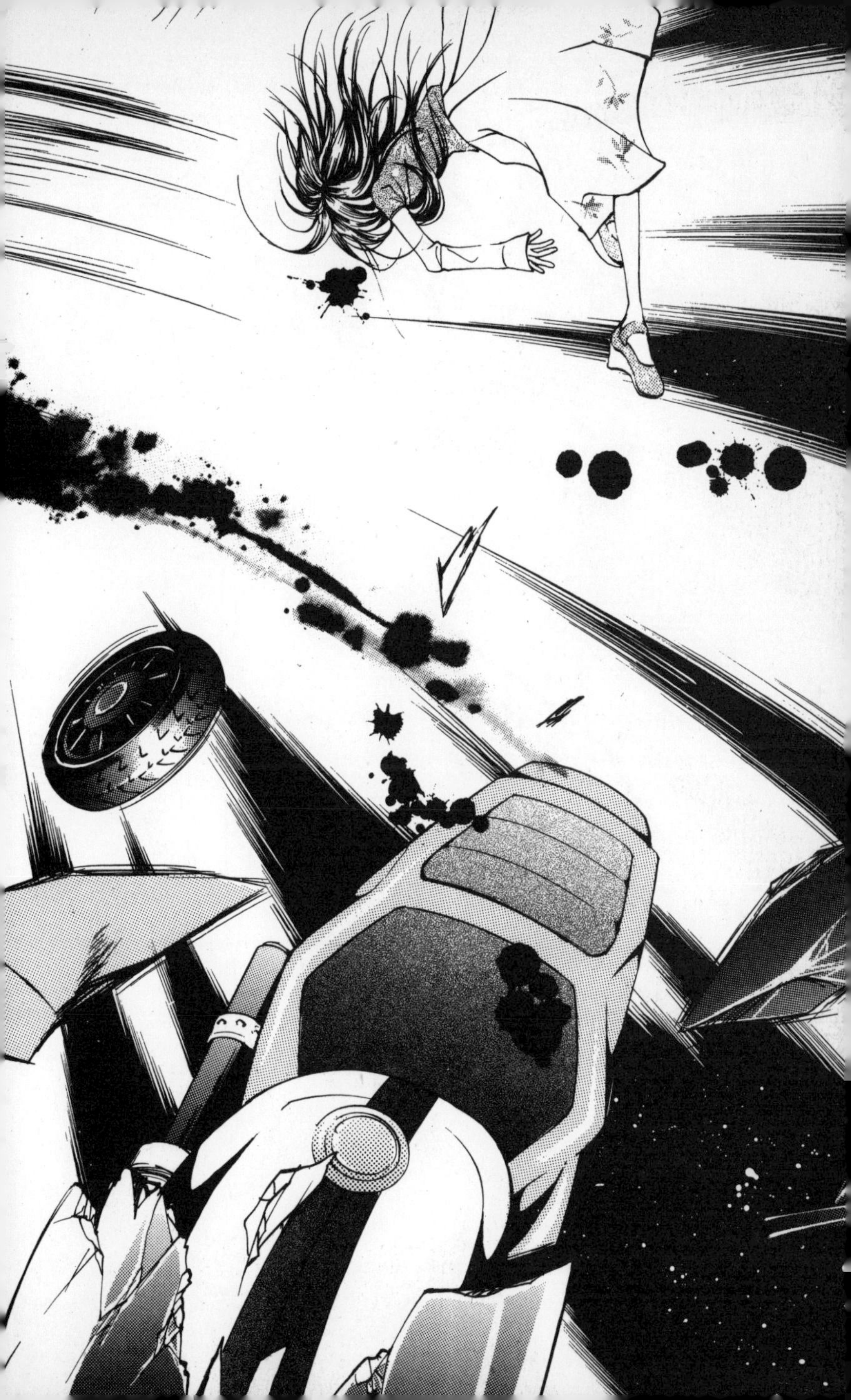

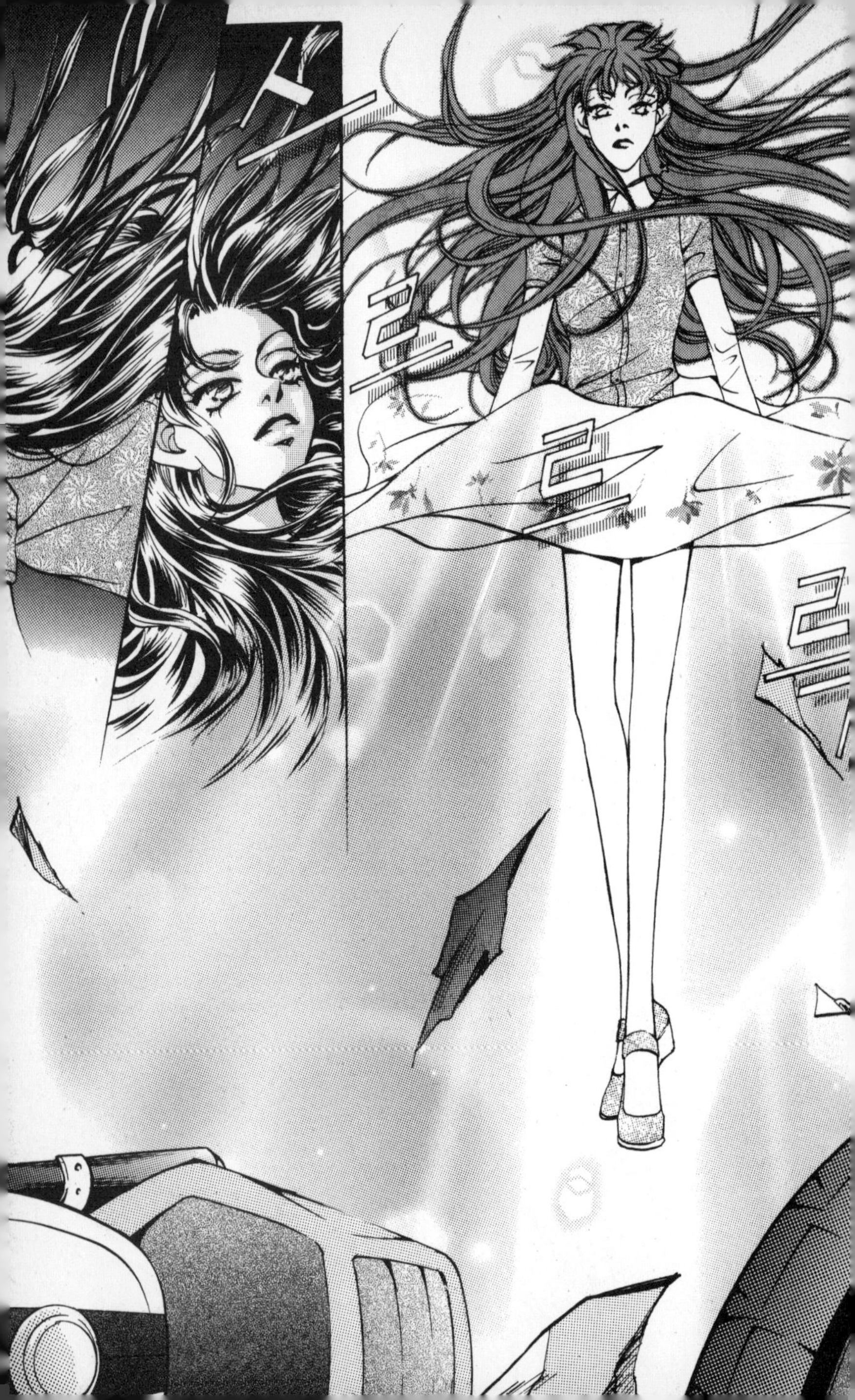

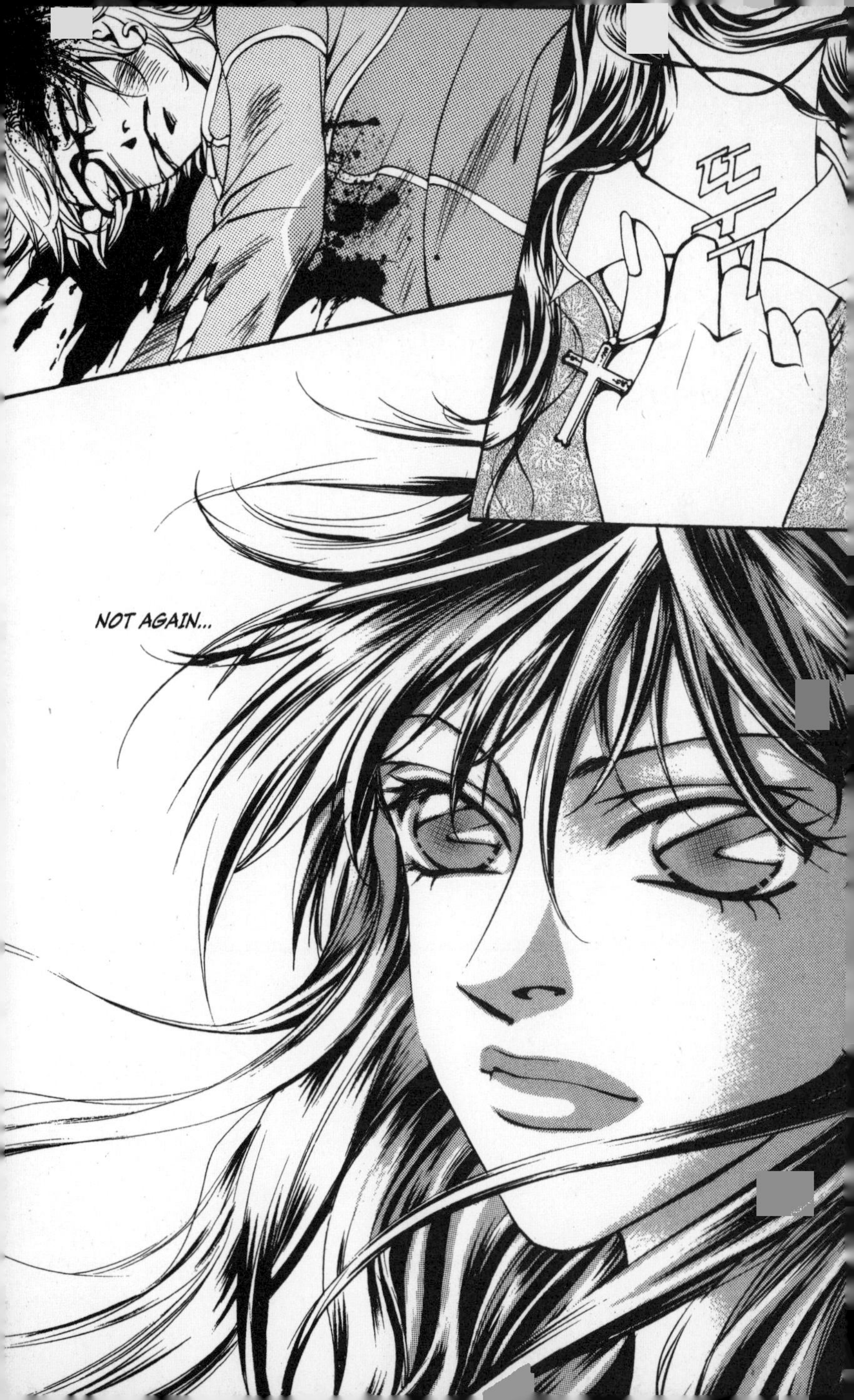
NOT AGAIN...

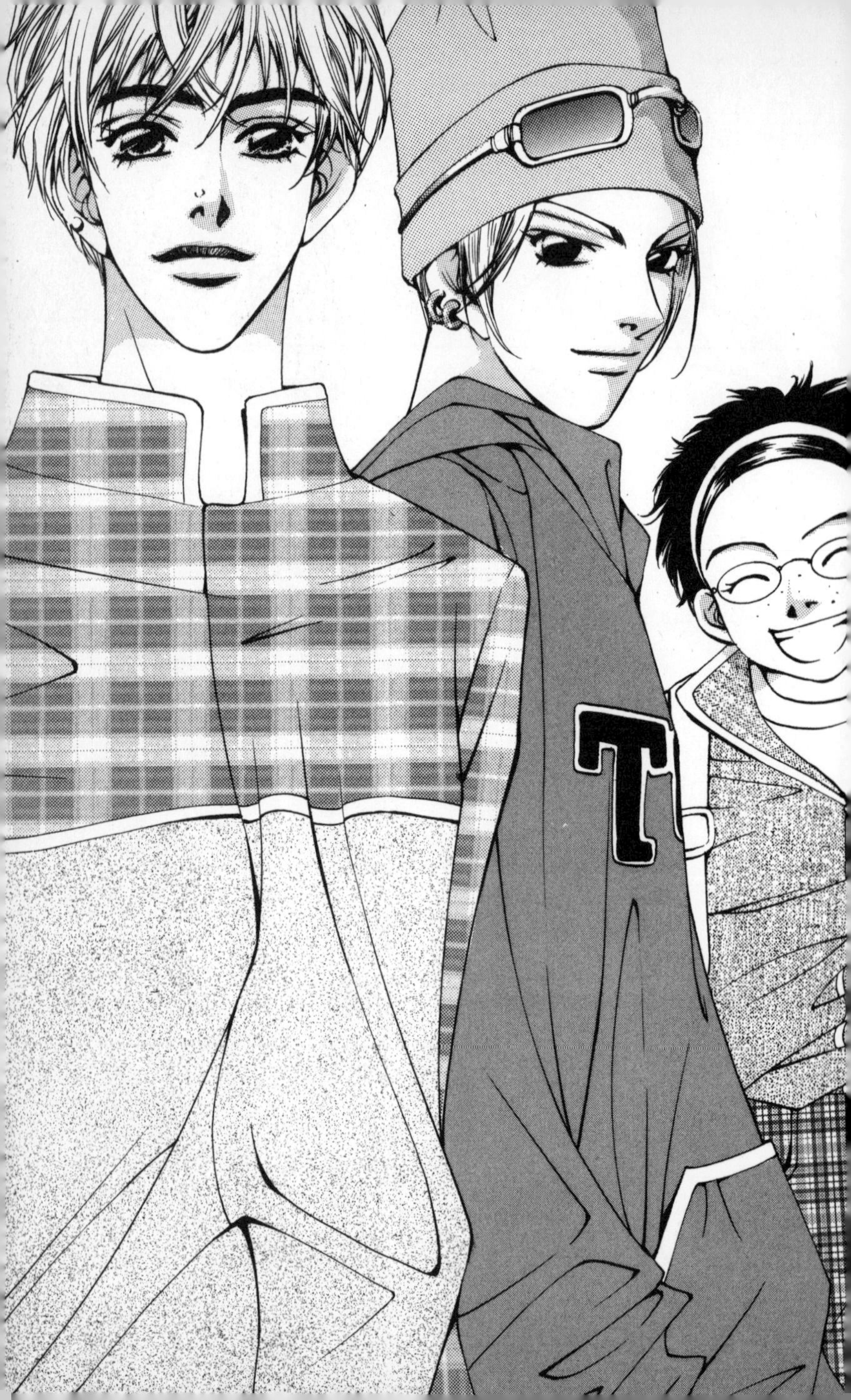
T

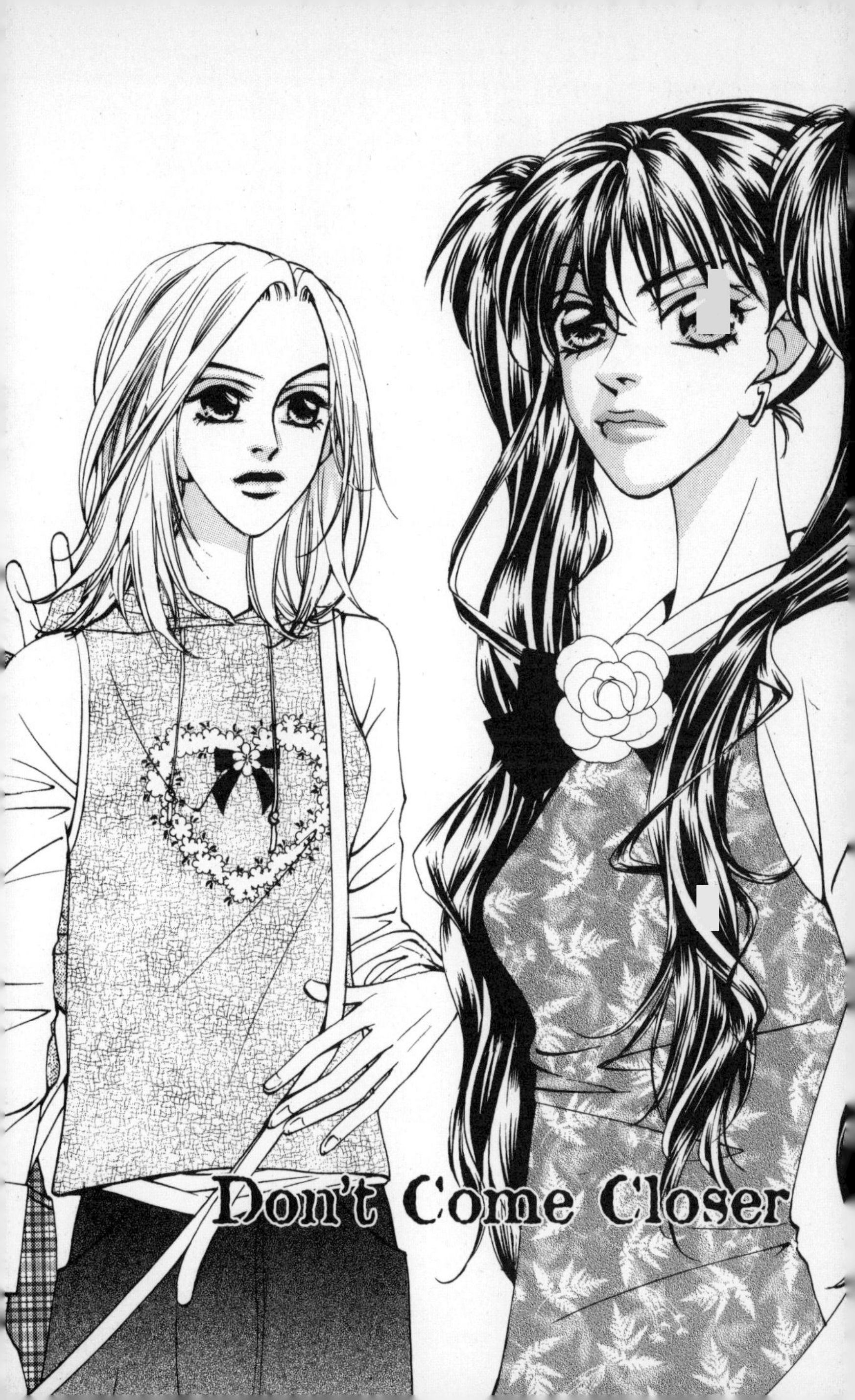
Don't Come Closer

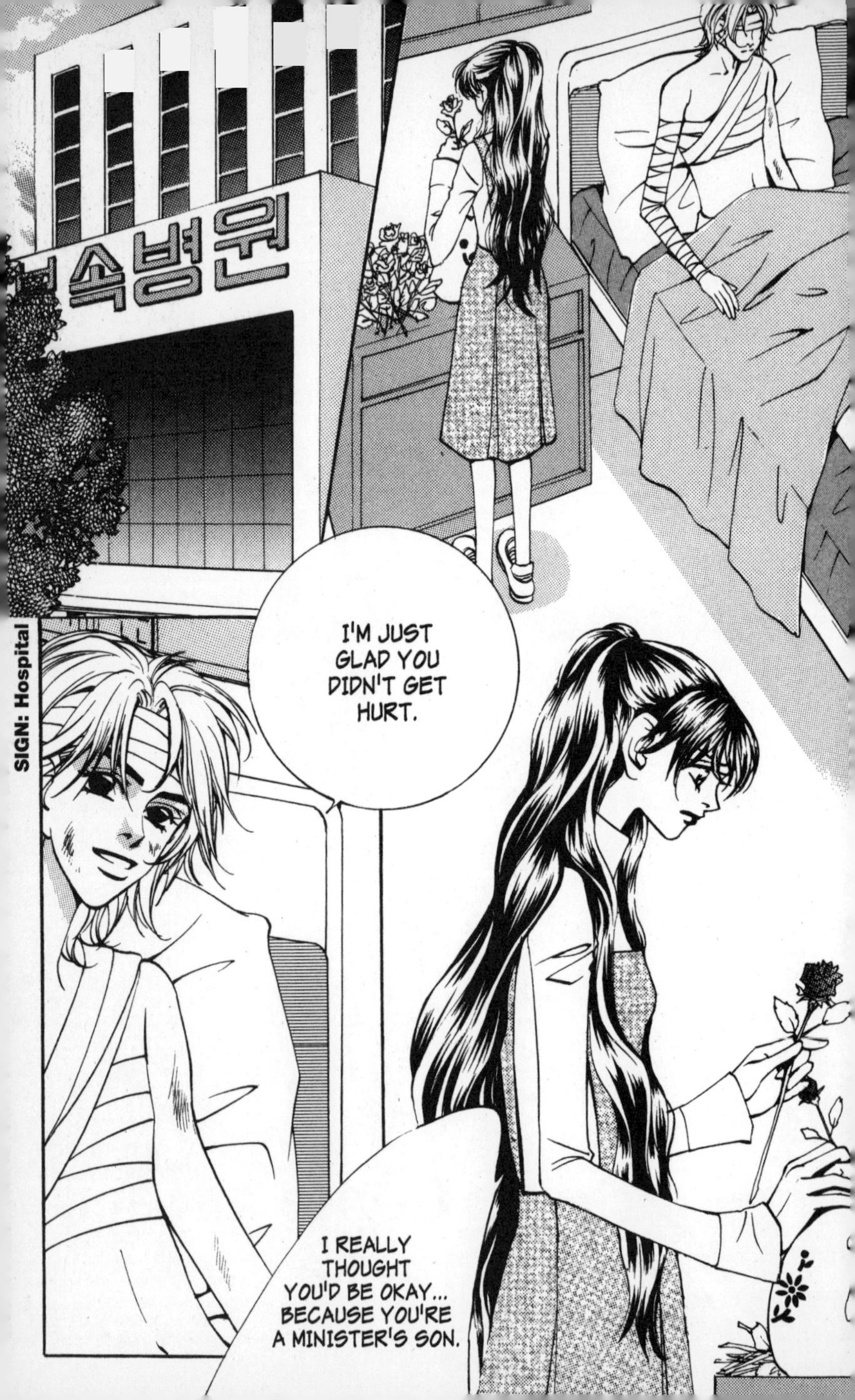
속병원
SIGN: Hospital
I'M JUST GLAD YOU DIDN'T GET HURT.
I REALLY THOUGHT YOU'D BE OKAY... BECAUSE YOU'RE A MINISTER'S SON.

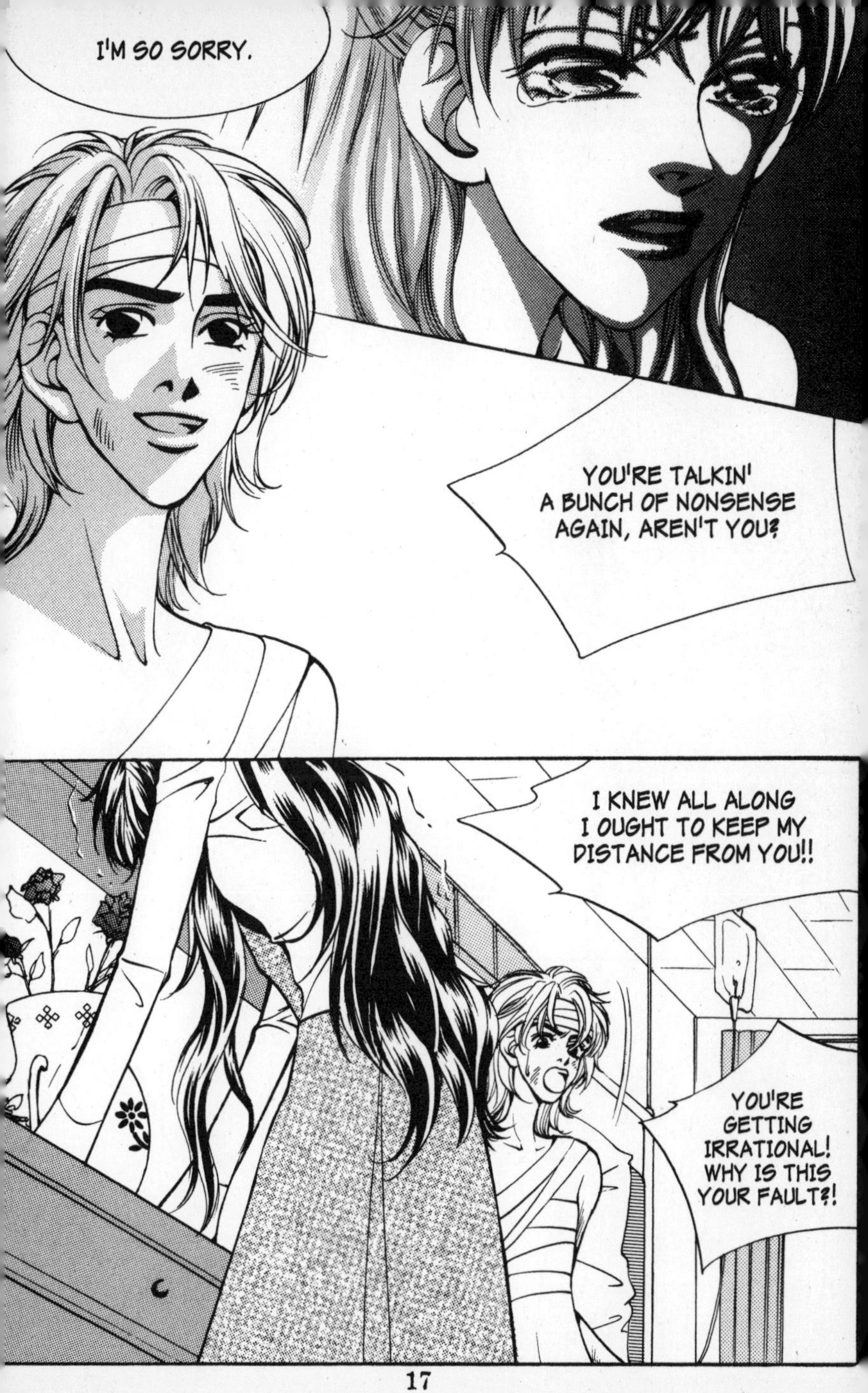

I'M SO SORRY.
YOU'RE TALKIN' A BUNCH OF NONSENSE AGAIN, AREN'T YOU?
I KNEW ALL ALONG I OUGHT TO KEEP MY DISTANCE FROM YOU!!
YOU'RE GETTING IRRATIONAL! WHY IS THIS YOUR FAULT?!

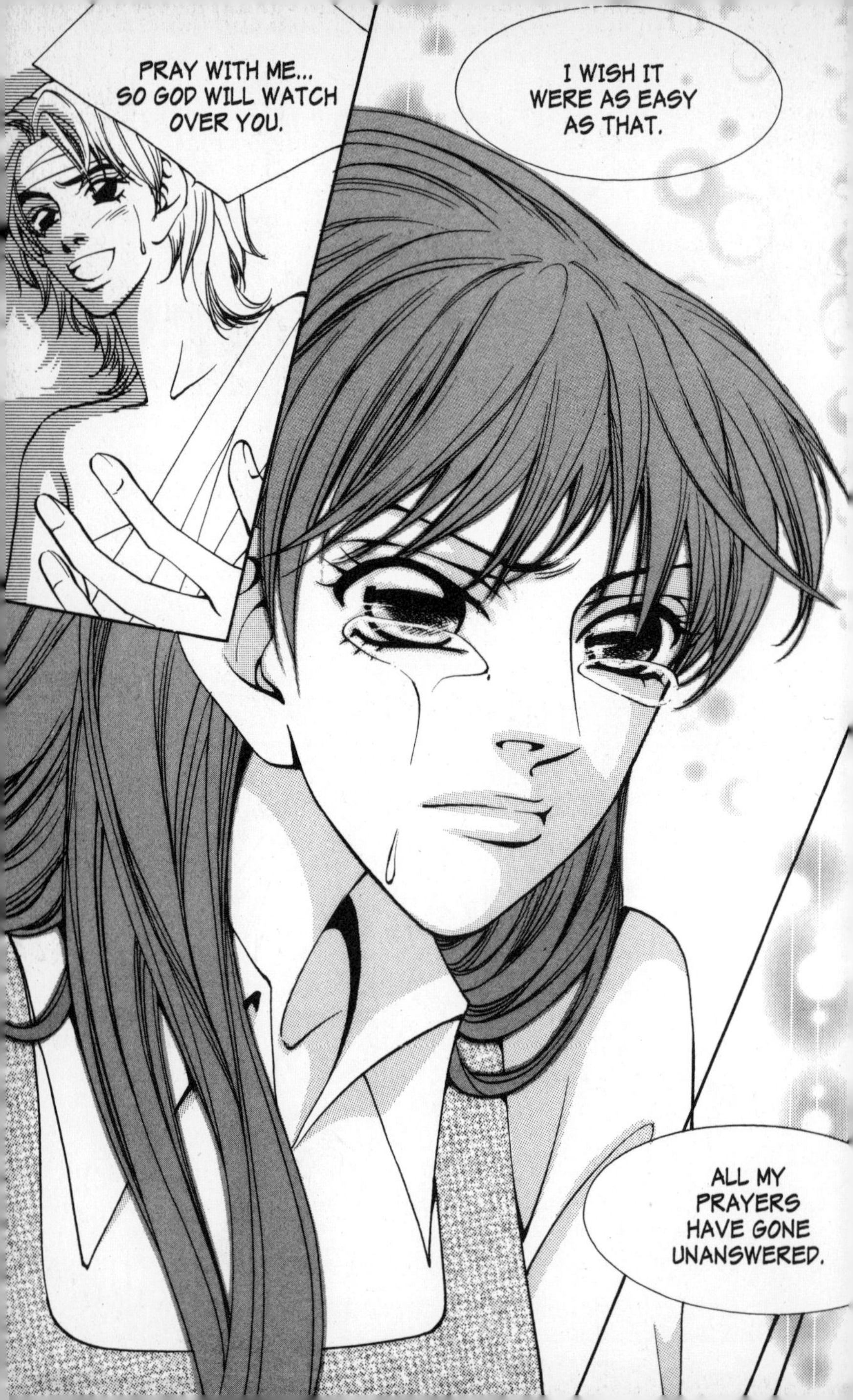
PRAY WITH ME... SO GOD WILL WATCH OVER YOU.
I WISH IT WERE AS EASY AS THAT.
ALL MY PRAYERS HAVE GONE UNANSWERED.

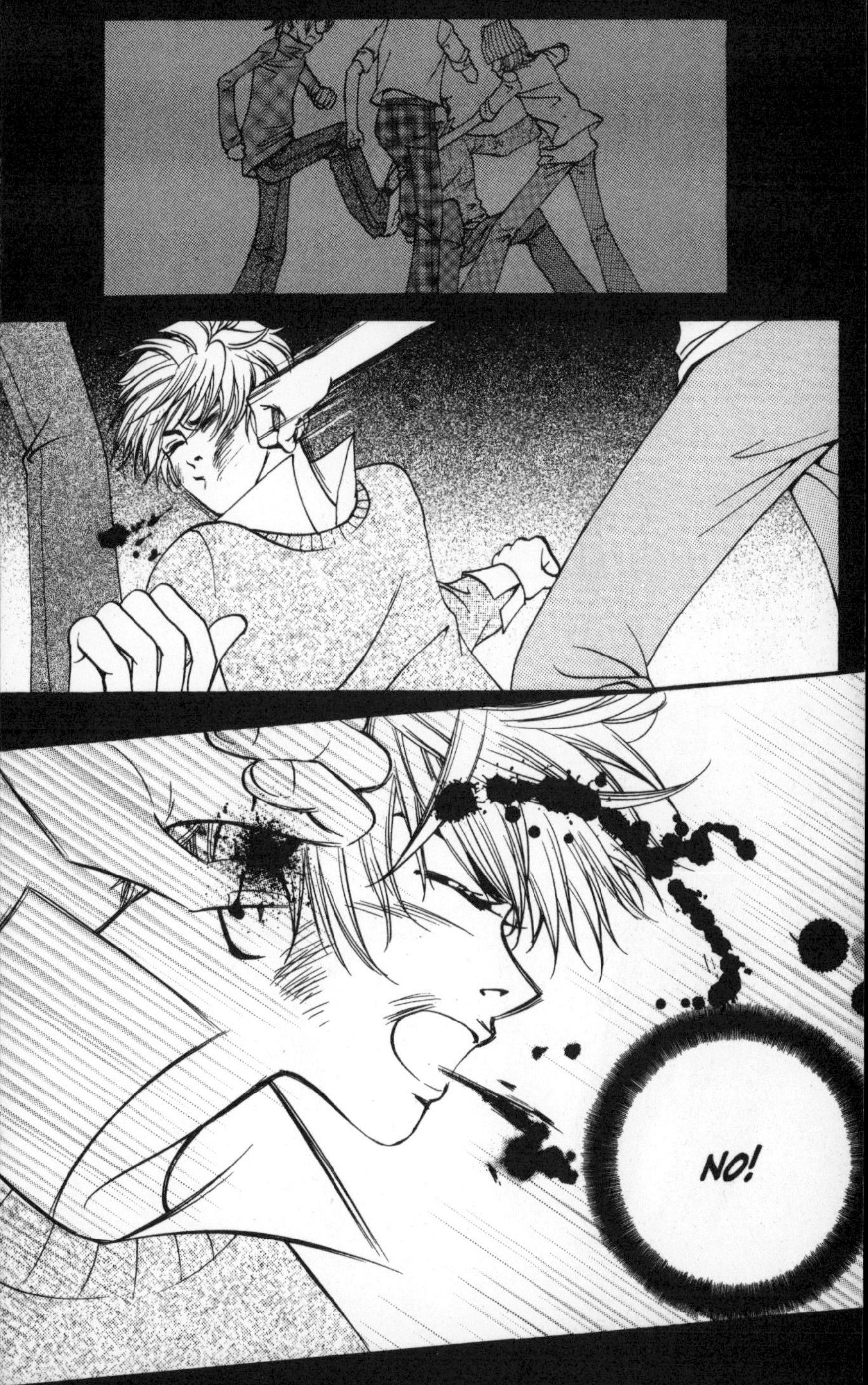
NO!

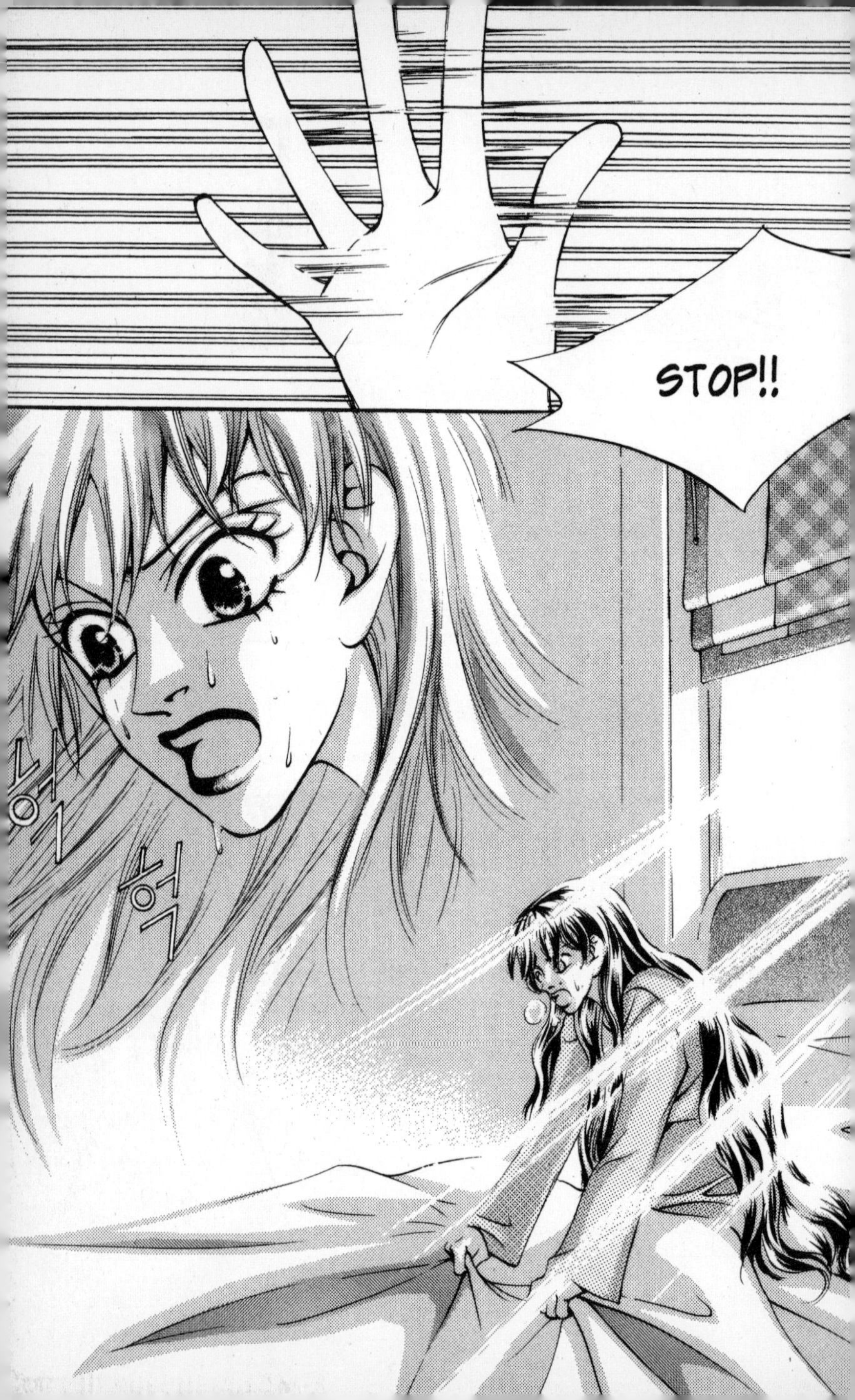
STOP!!
헉 헉

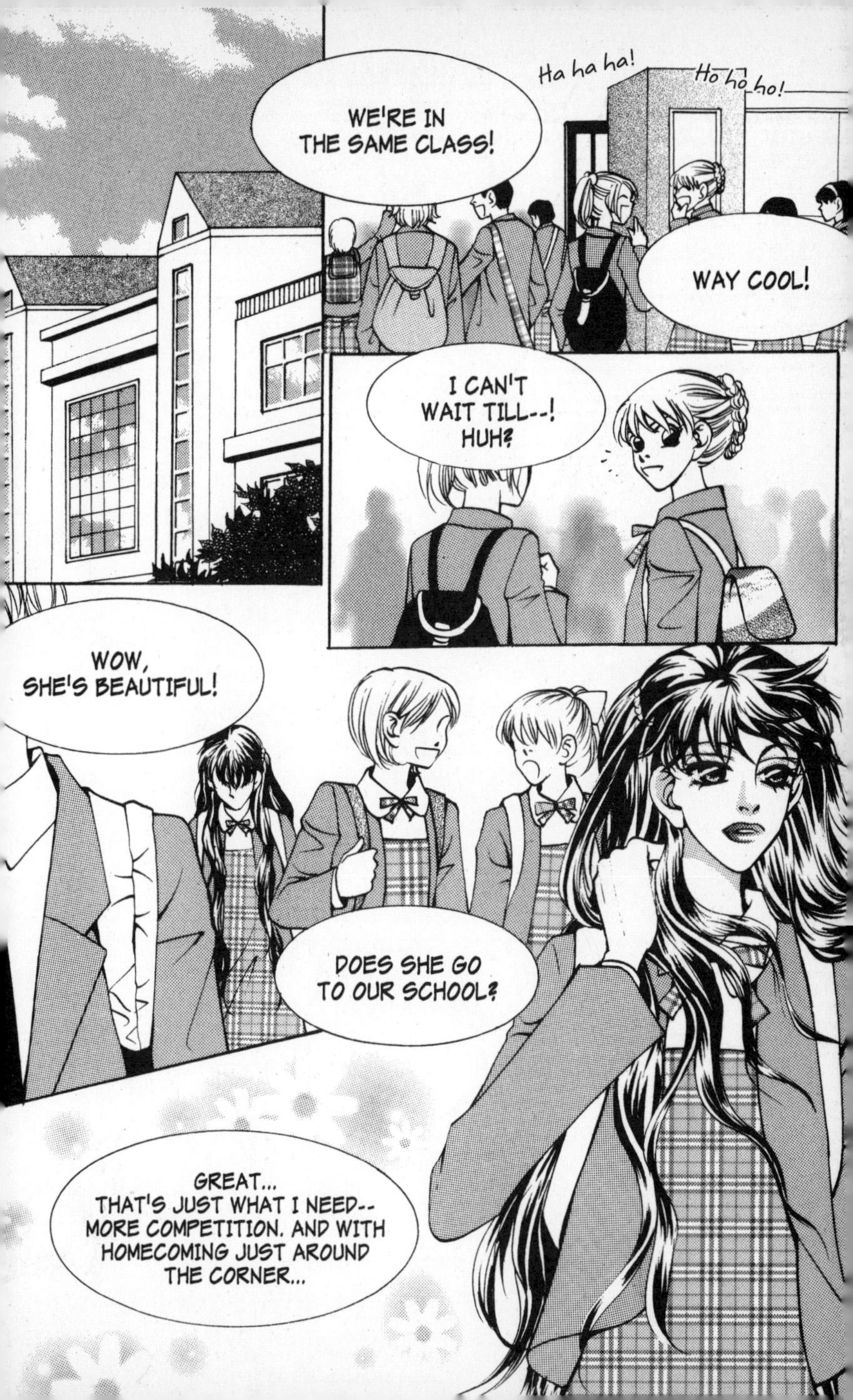
WE'RE IN THE SAME CLASS!
Ha ha ha!
Ho ho ho!
WAY COOL!
I CAN'T WAIT TILL--! HUH?
WOW, SHE'S BEAUTIFUL!
DOES SHE GO TO OUR SCHOOL?
GREAT... THAT'S JUST WHAT I NEED-- MORE COMPETITION. AND WITH HOMECOMING JUST AROUND THE CORNER...

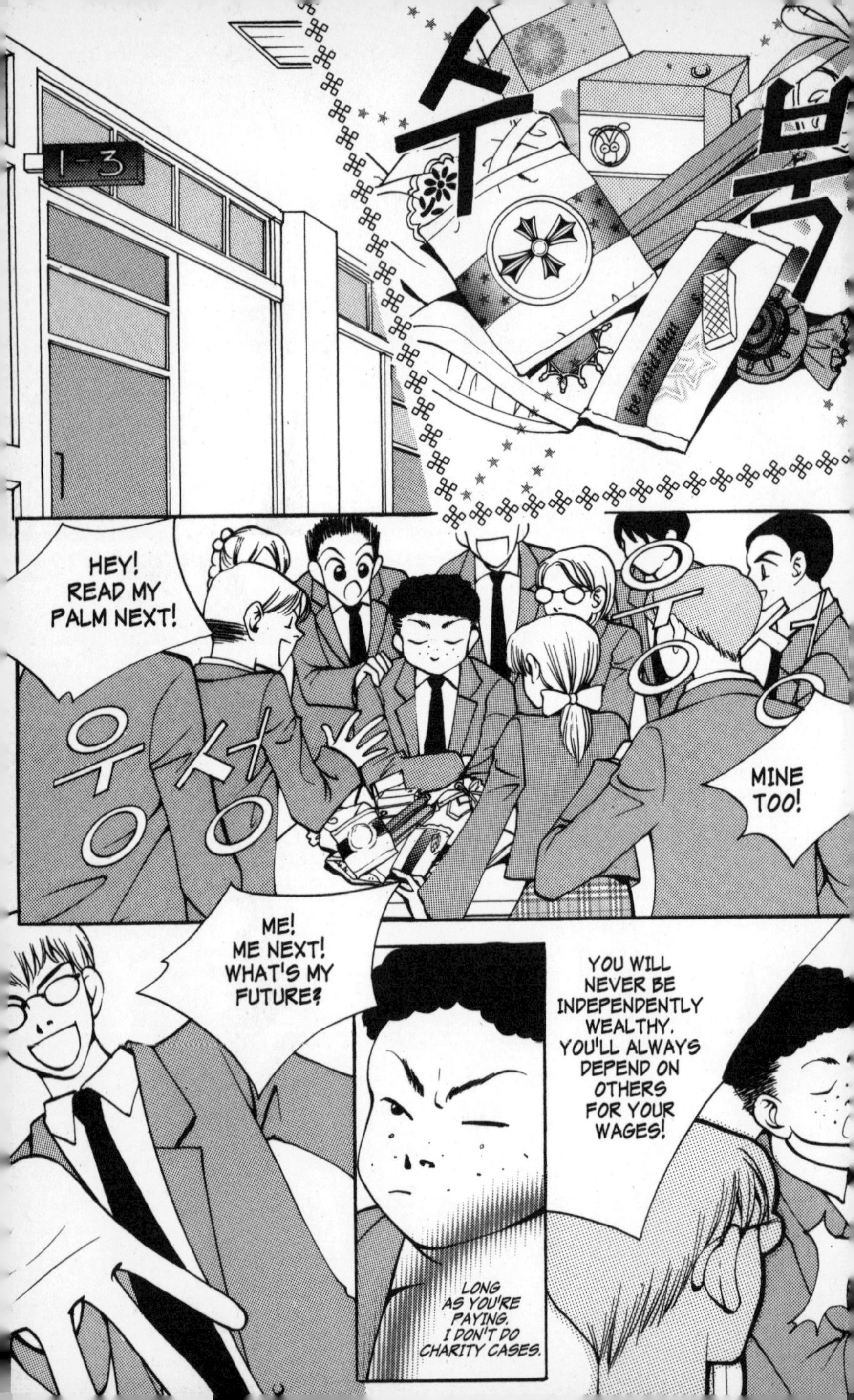
1-3
HEY! READ MY PALM NEXT!
MINE TOO!
ME! ME NEXT! WHAT'S MY FUTURE?
YOU WILL NEVER BE INDEPENDENTLY WEALTHY. YOU'LL ALWAYS DEPEND ON OTHERS FOR YOUR WAGES!
LONG AS YOU'RE PAYING. I DON'T DO CHARITY CASES.

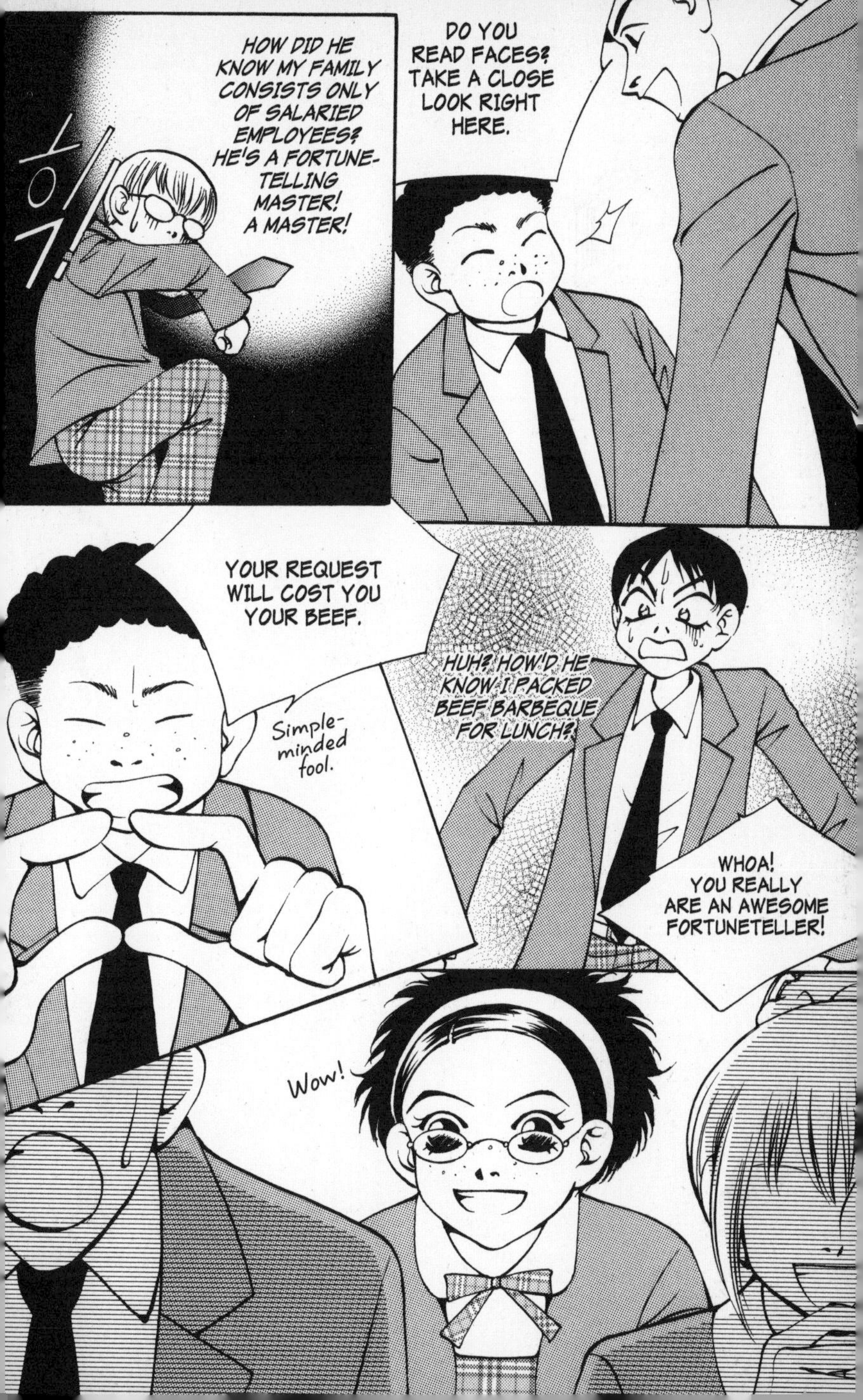
HOW DID HE KNOW MY FAMILY CONSISTS ONLY OF SALARIED EMPLOYEES? HE'S A FORTUNE-TELLING MASTER! A MASTER!
DO YOU READ FACES? TAKE A CLOSE LOOK RIGHT HERE.
YOUR REQUEST WILL COST YOU YOUR BEEF.
Simple-minded fool.
HUH? HOW'D HE KNOW I PACKED BEEF BARBEQUE FOR LUNCH?
WHOA! YOU REALLY ARE AN AWESOME FORTUNETELLER!
Wow!

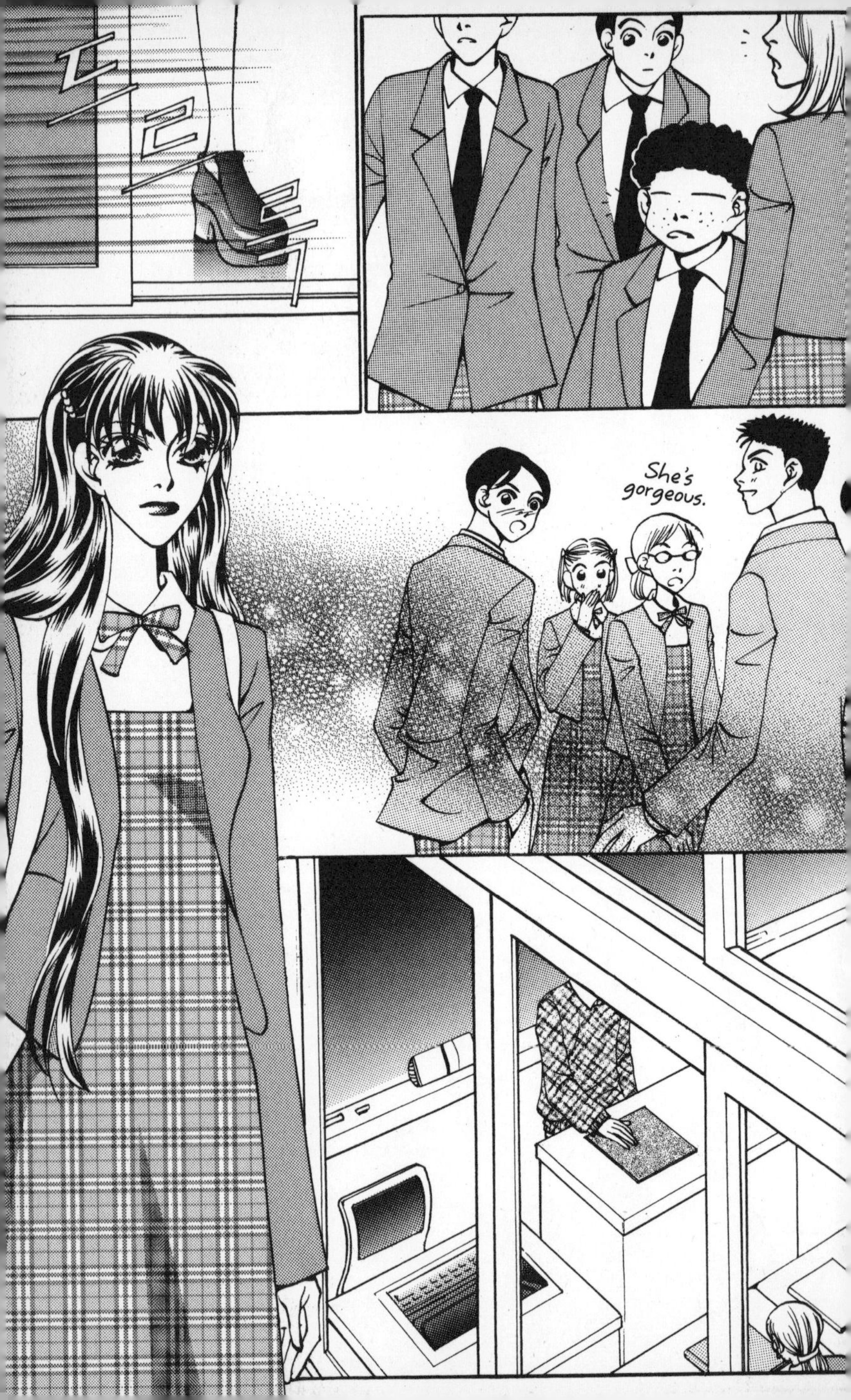
She's gorgeous.

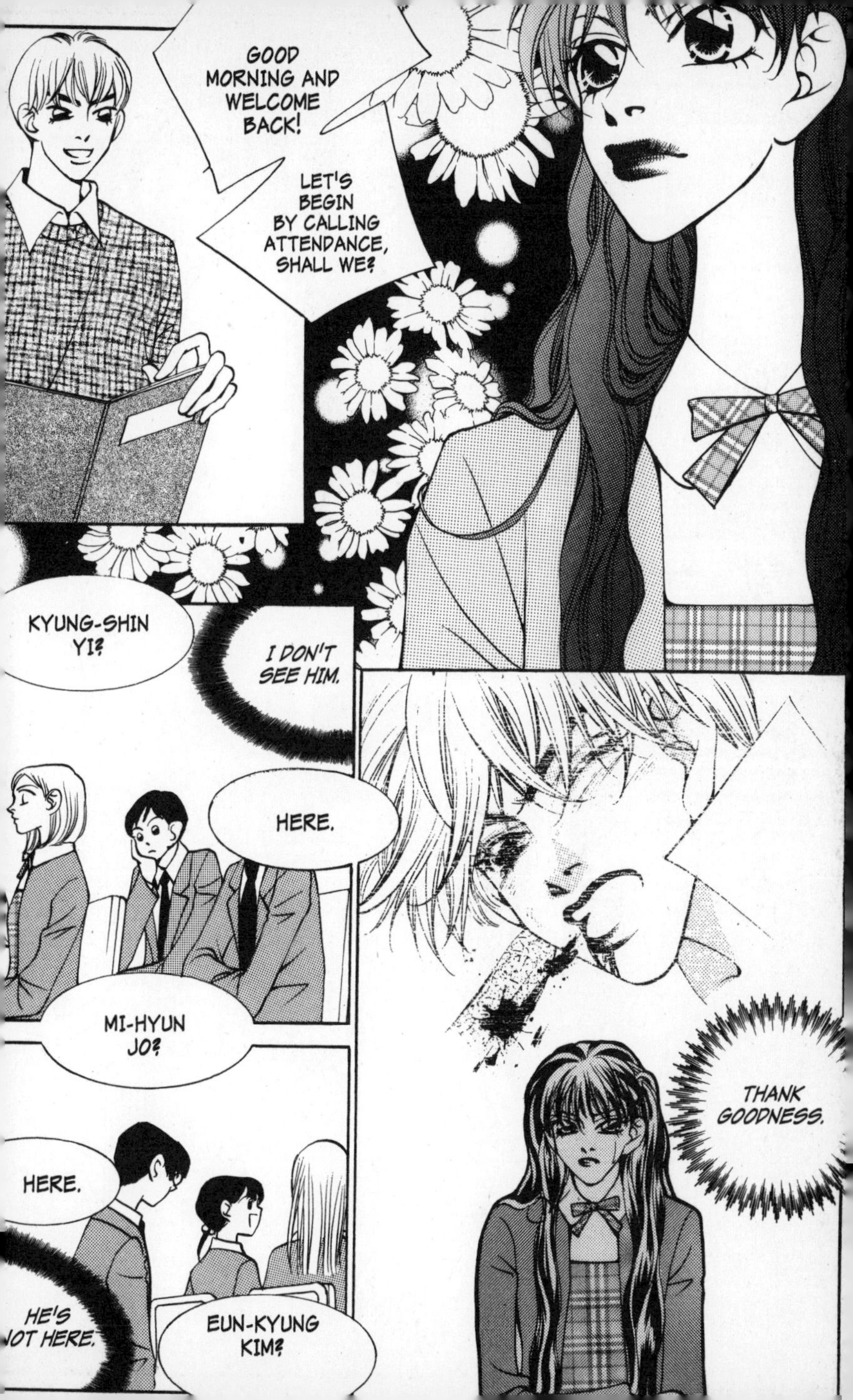
GOOD MORNING AND WELCOME BACK!
LET'S BEGIN BY CALLING ATTENDANCE, SHALL WE?
KYUNG-SHIN YI?
I DON'T SEE HIM.
HERE.
MI-HYUN JO?
HERE.
HE'S OT HERE.
EUN-KYUNG KIM?
THANK GOODNESS.

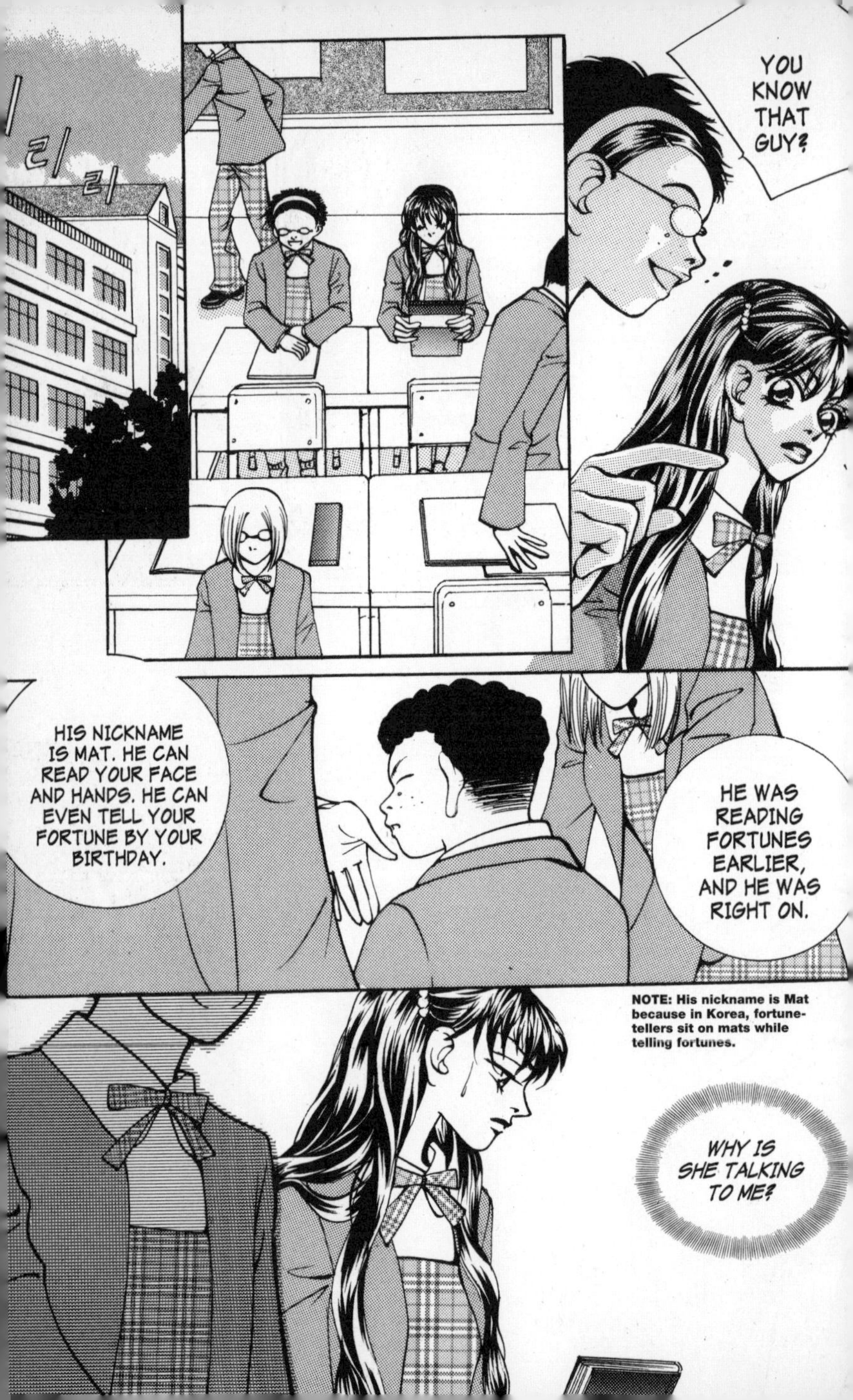

리 리
YOU KNOW THAT GUY?
HIS NICKNAME IS MAT. HE CAN READ YOUR FACE AND HANDS. HE CAN EVEN TELL YOUR FORTUNE BY YOUR BIRTHDAY.
HE WAS READING FORTUNES EARLIER, AND HE WAS RIGHT ON.
NOTE: His nickname is Mat because in Korea, fortune-tellers sit on mats while telling fortunes.
WHY IS SHE TALKING TO ME?

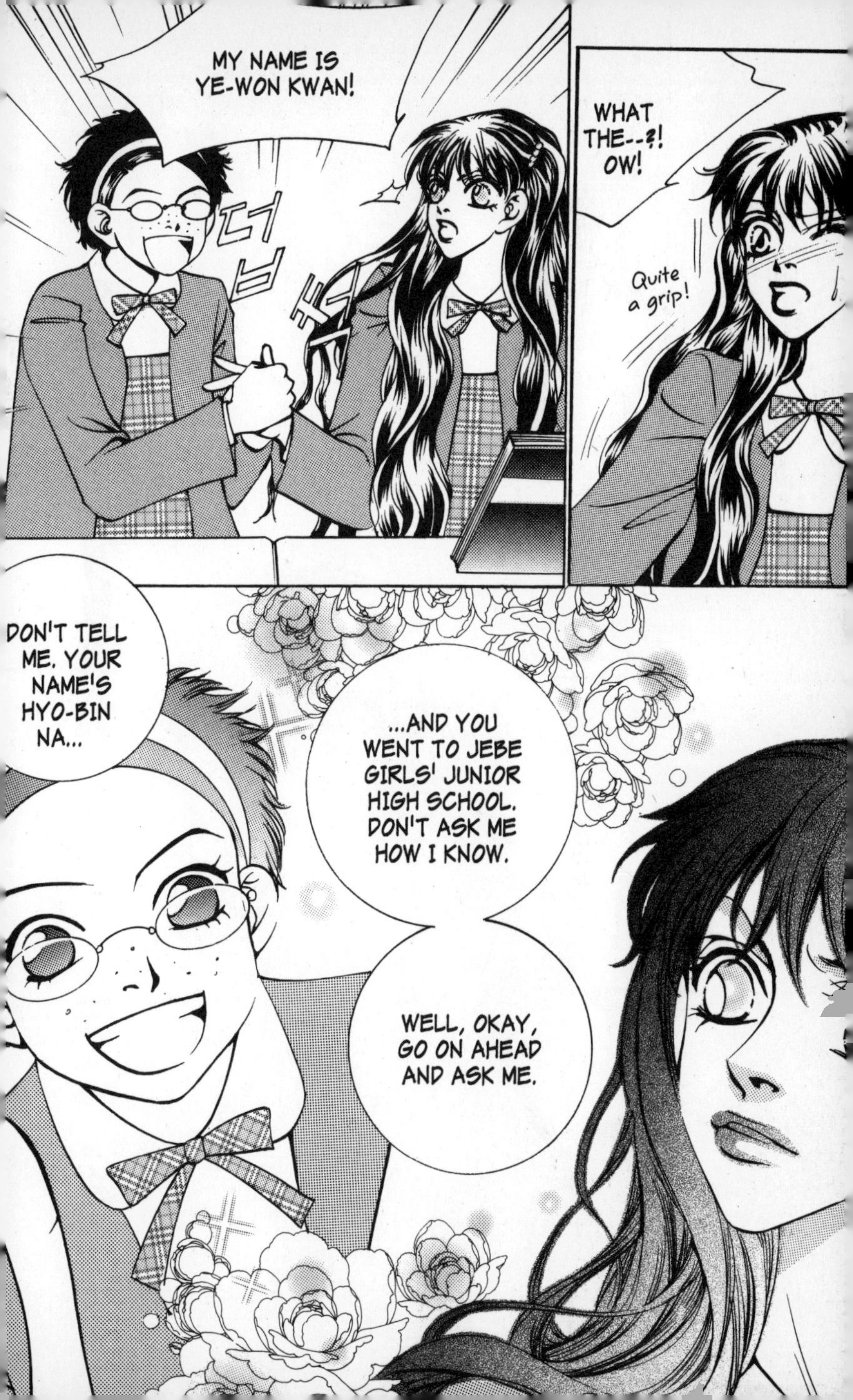
MY NAME IS YE-WON KWAN!
WHAT THE--?! OW!
Quite a grip!
DON'T TELL ME. YOUR NAME'S HYO-BIN NA...
...AND YOU WENT TO JEBE GIRLS' JUNIOR HIGH SCHOOL. DON'T ASK ME HOW I KNOW.
WELL, OKAY, GO ON AHEAD AND ASK ME.

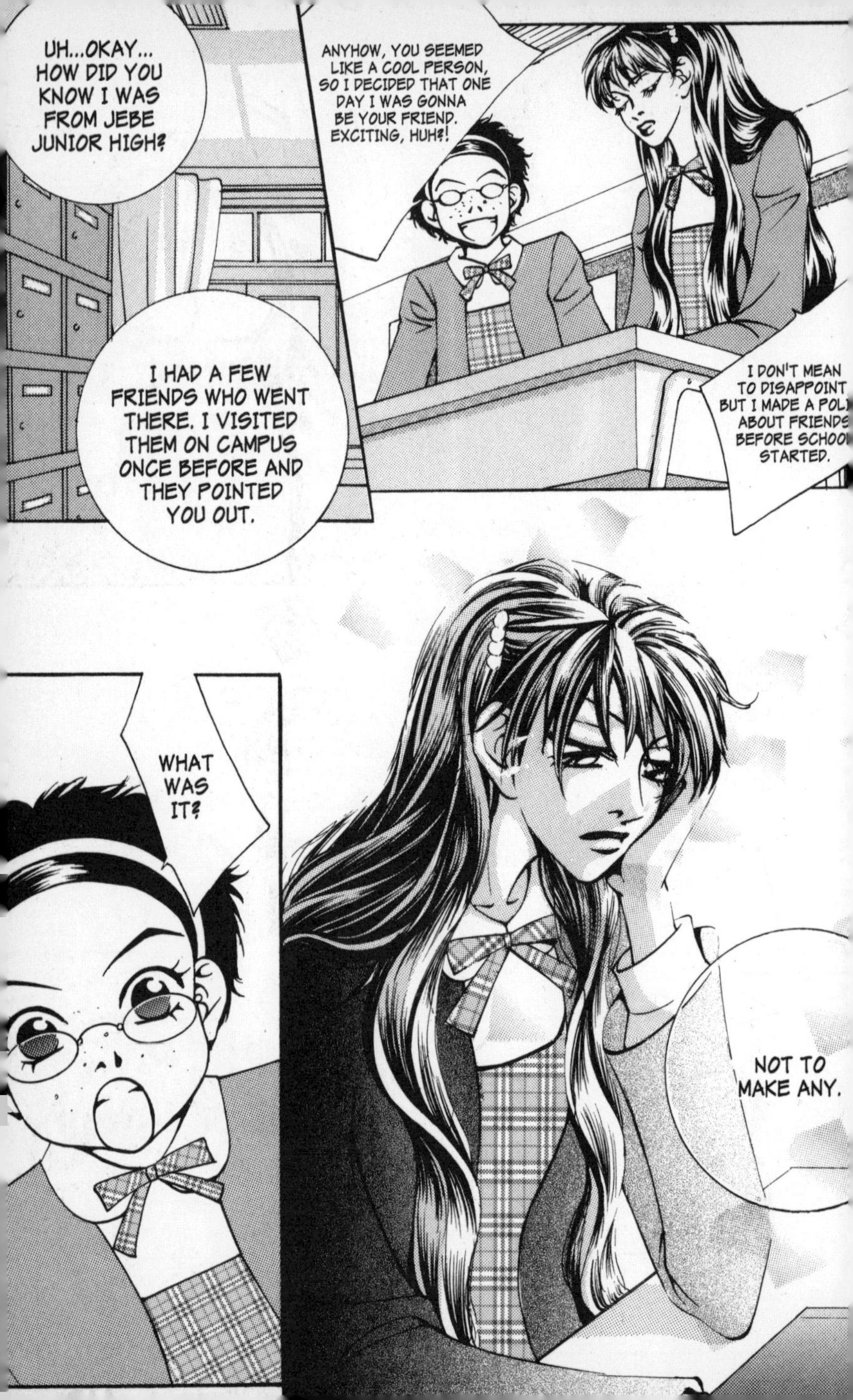
UH...OKAY... HOW DID YOU KNOW I WAS FROM JEBE JUNIOR HIGH?
I HAD A FEW FRIENDS WHO WENT THERE. I VISITED THEM ON CAMPUS ONCE BEFORE AND THEY POINTED YOU OUT.
ANYHOW, YOU SEEMED LIKE A COOL PERSON, SO I DECIDED THAT ONE DAY I WAS GONNA BE YOUR FRIEND. EXCITING, HUH?!
I DON'T MEAN TO DISAPPOINT BUT I MADE A POL ABOUT FRIENDS BEFORE SCHOO STARTED.
WHAT WAS IT?
NOT TO MAKE ANY.

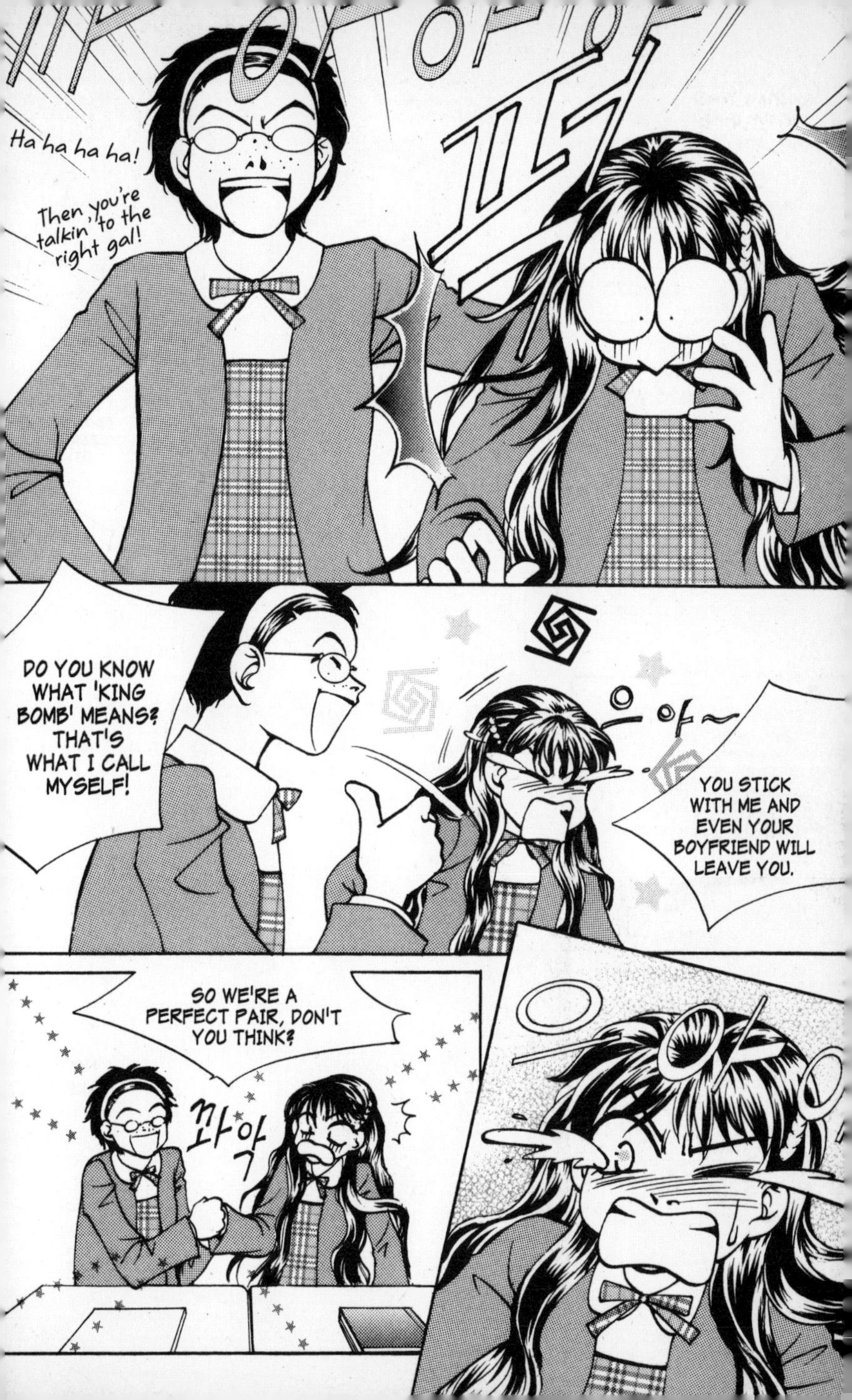
Ha ha ha ha ha!
Then, you're talkin to the right gal!
DO YOU KNOW WHAT 'KING BOMB' MEANS? THAT'S WHAT I CALL MYSELF!
으아~
YOU STICK WITH ME AND EVEN YOUR BOYFRIEND WILL LEAVE YOU.
SO WE'RE A PERFECT PAIR, DON'T YOU THINK?
꽈악

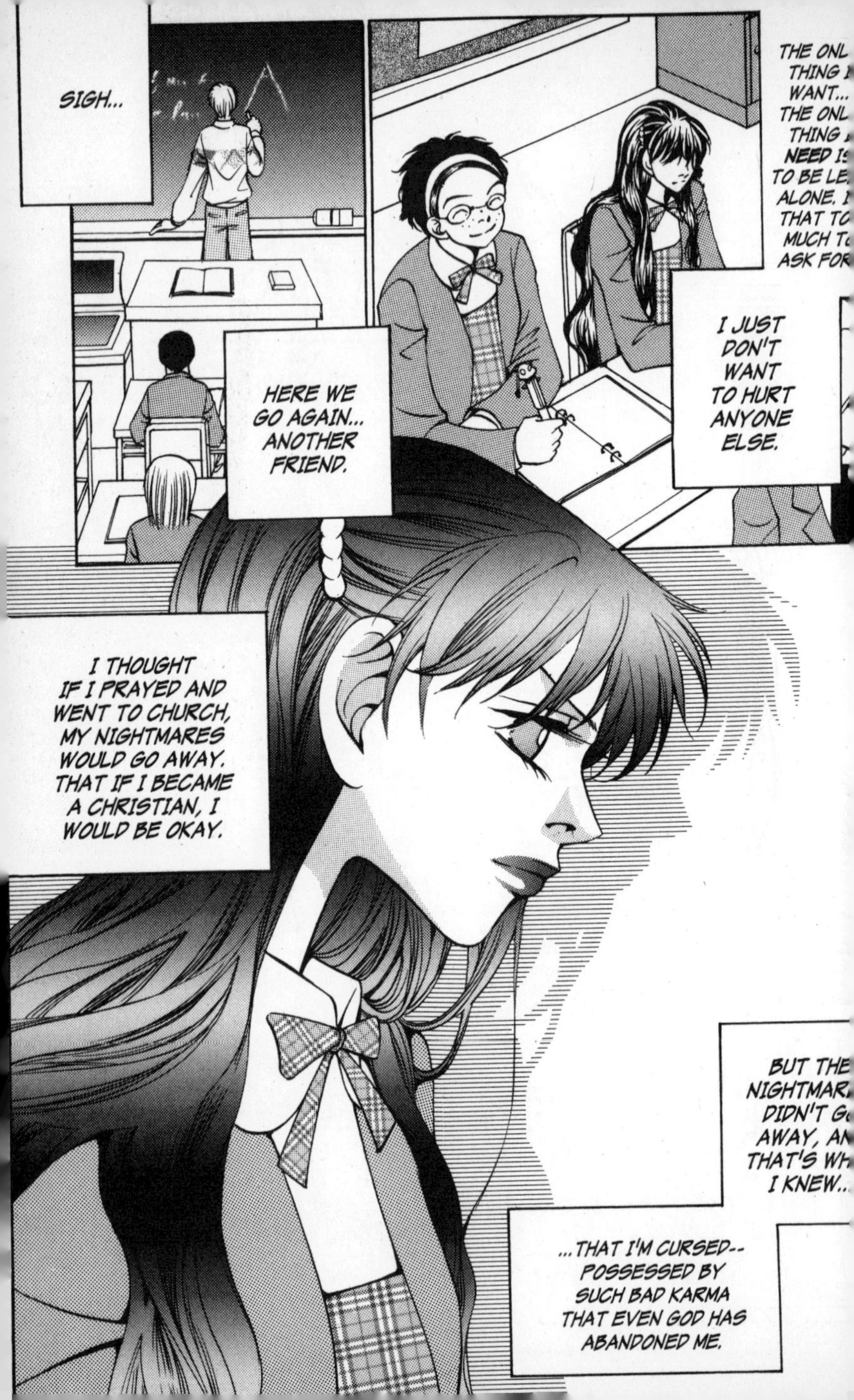
SIGH...
HERE WE GO AGAIN... ANOTHER FRIEND.
THE ONL THING I WANT... THE ONL THING NEED IS TO BE LE ALONE. I THAT TO MUCH TO ASK FOR
I JUST DON'T WANT TO HURT ANYONE ELSE.
I THOUGHT IF I PRAYED AND WENT TO CHURCH, MY NIGHTMARES WOULD GO AWAY. THAT IF I BECAME A CHRISTIAN, I WOULD BE OKAY.
BUT THE NIGHTMAR DIDN'T G AWAY, AN THAT'S WH I KNEW...
...THAT I'M CURSED-- POSSESSED BY SUCH BAD KARMA THAT EVEN GOD HAS ABANDONED ME.

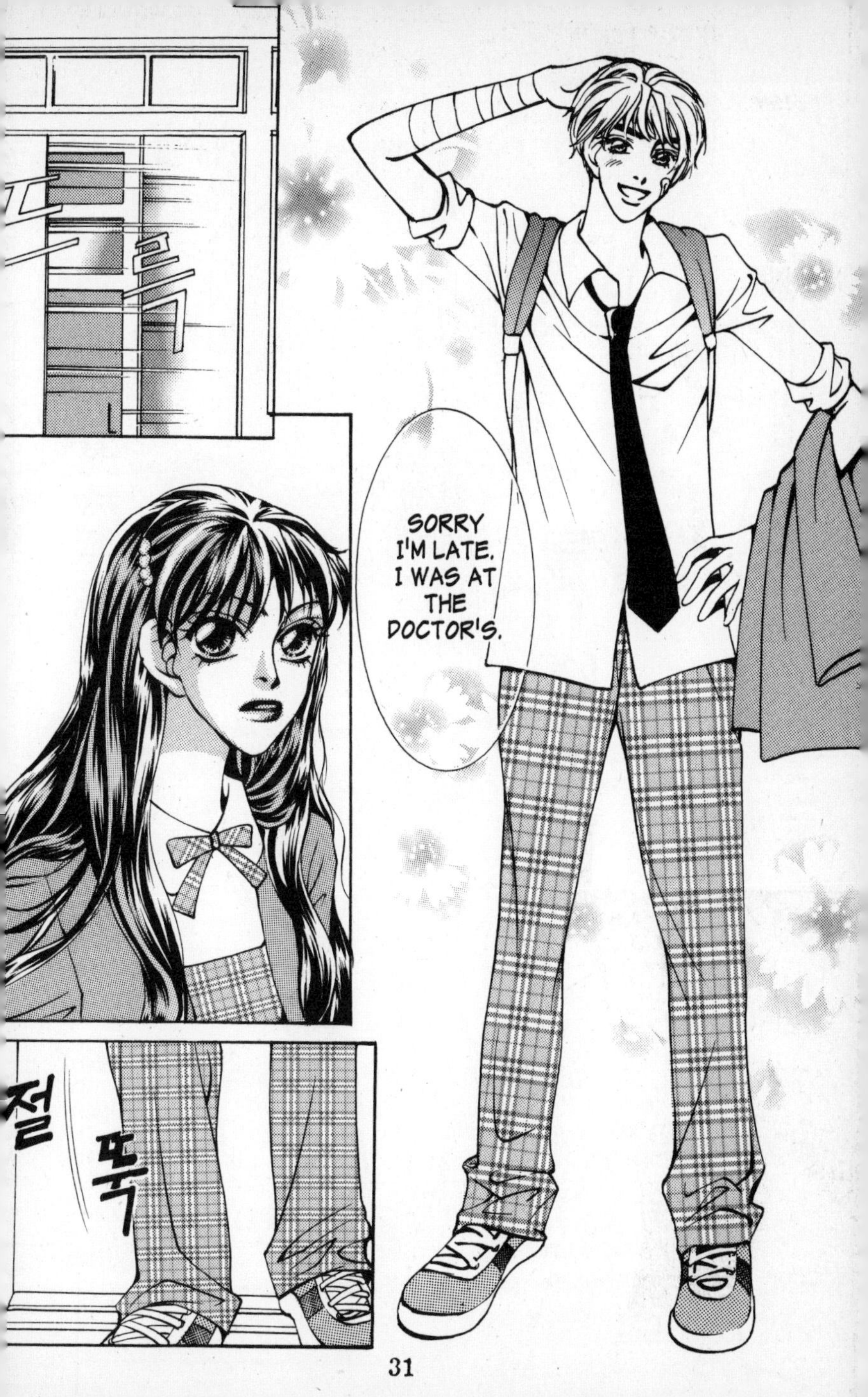
절뚝
SORRY I'M LATE. I WAS AT THE DOCTOR'S.

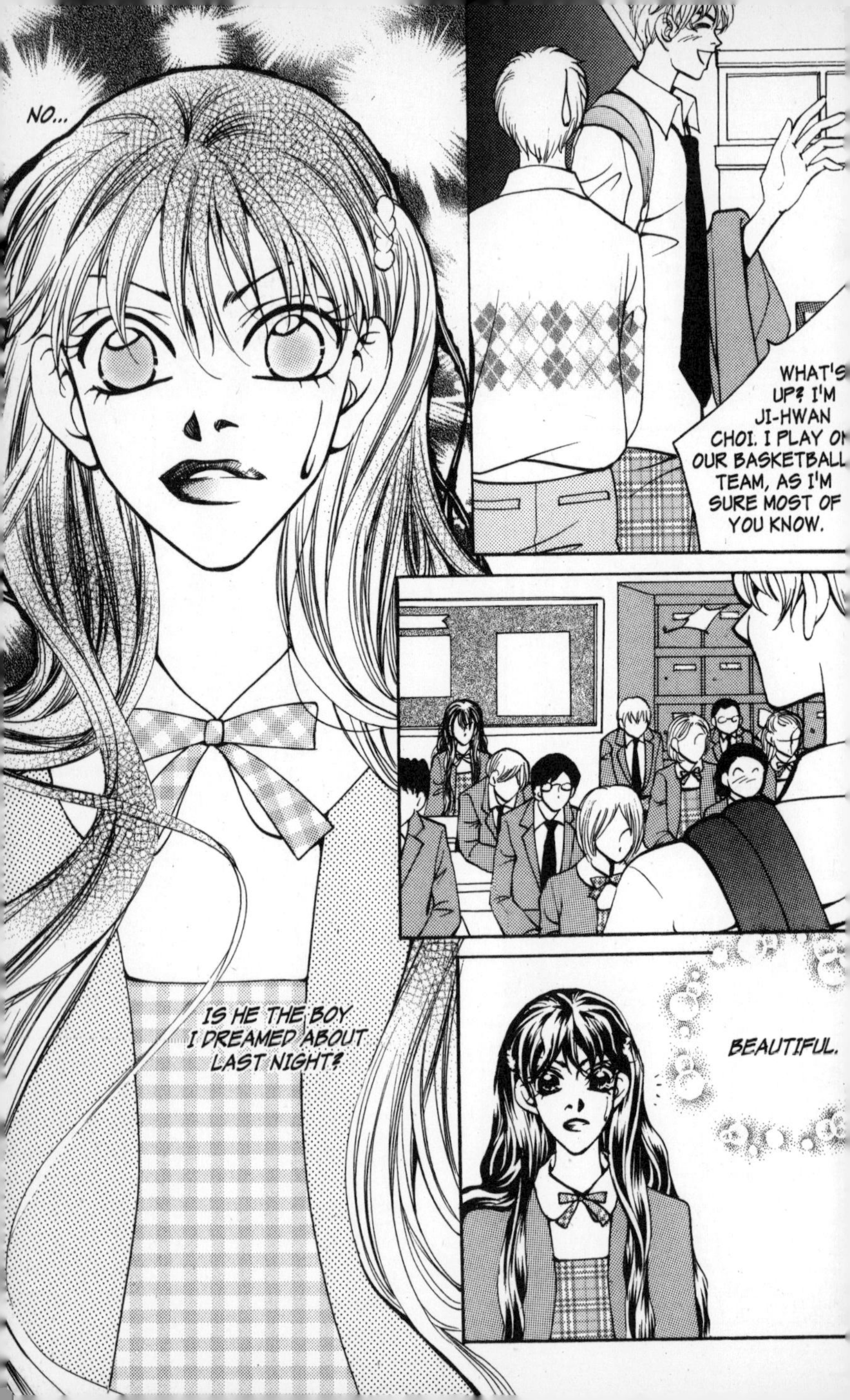
NO...
IS HE THE BOY I DREAMED ABOUT LAST NIGHT?
WHAT'S UP? I'M JI-HWAN CHOI. I PLAY ON OUR BASKETBALL TEAM, AS I'M SURE MOST OF YOU KNOW.
BEAUTIFUL.

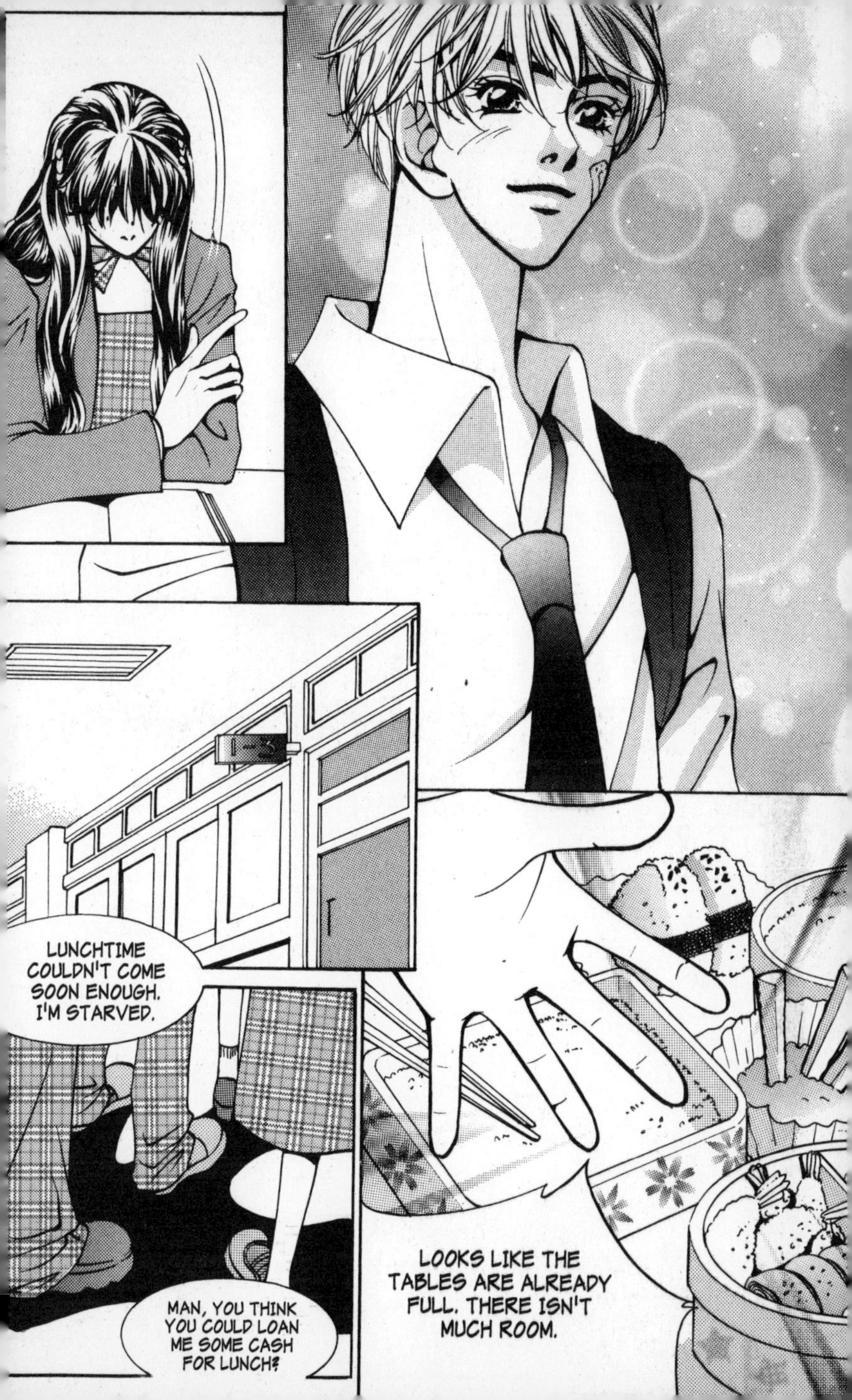
LUNCHTIME COULDN'T COME SOON ENOUGH. I'M STARVED.
MAN, YOU THINK YOU COULD LOAN ME SOME CASH FOR LUNCH?
LOOKS LIKE THE TABLES ARE ALREADY FULL. THERE ISN'T MUCH ROOM.

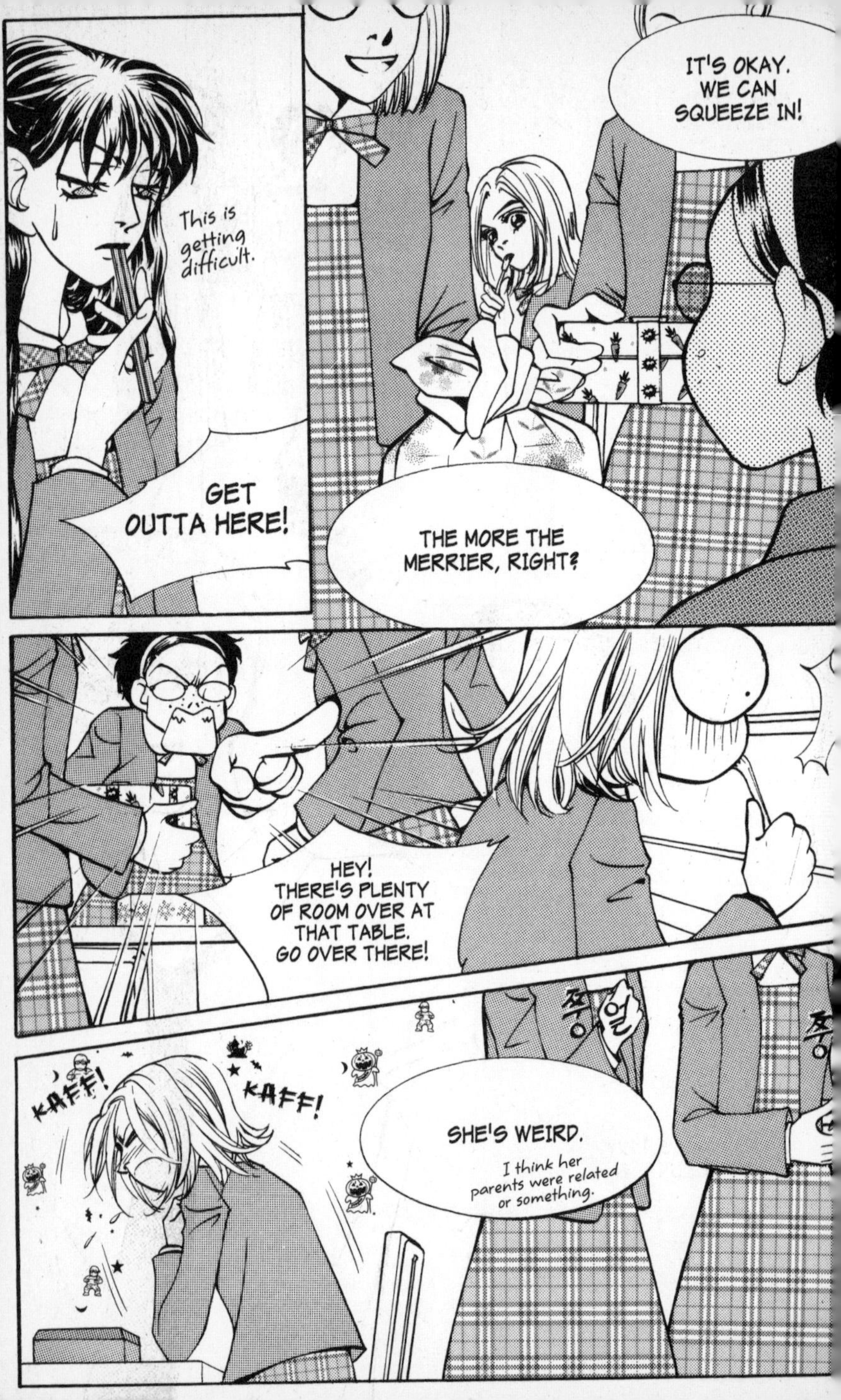
This is getting difficult.
GET OUTTA HERE!
IT'S OKAY. WE CAN SQUEEZE IN!
THE MORE THE MERRIER, RIGHT?
HEY! THERE'S PLENTY OF ROOM OVER AT THAT TABLE. GO OVER THERE!
주얼
주
KAFF!
KAFF!
SHE'S WEIRD.
I think her parents were related or something.

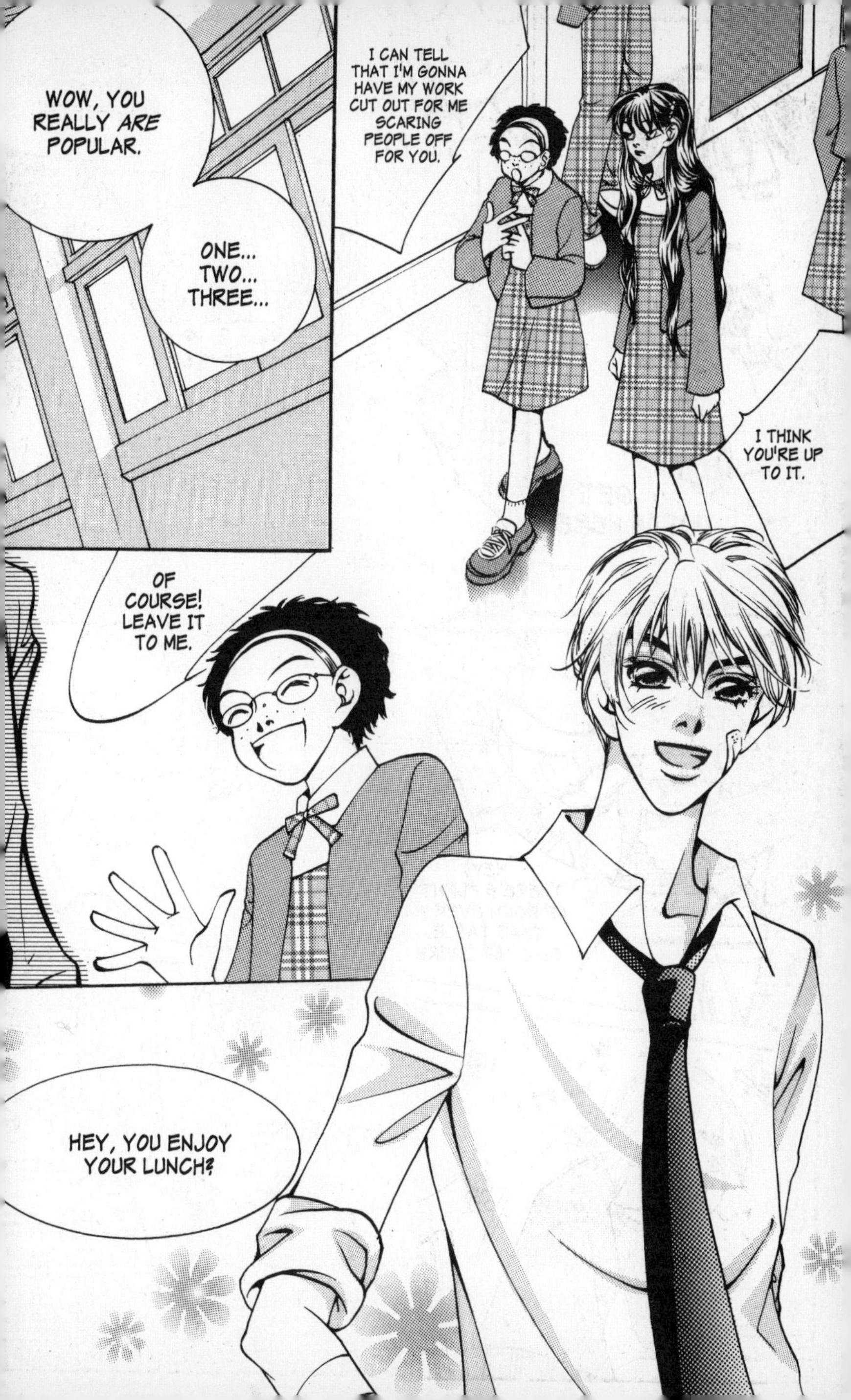
WOW, YOU REALLY *ARE* POPULAR.
ONE... TWO... THREE...
I CAN TELL THAT I'M GONNA HAVE MY WORK CUT OUT FOR ME SCARING PEOPLE OFF FOR YOU.
I THINK YOU'RE UP TO IT.
OF COURSE! LEAVE IT TO ME.
HEY, YOU ENJOY YOUR LUNCH?

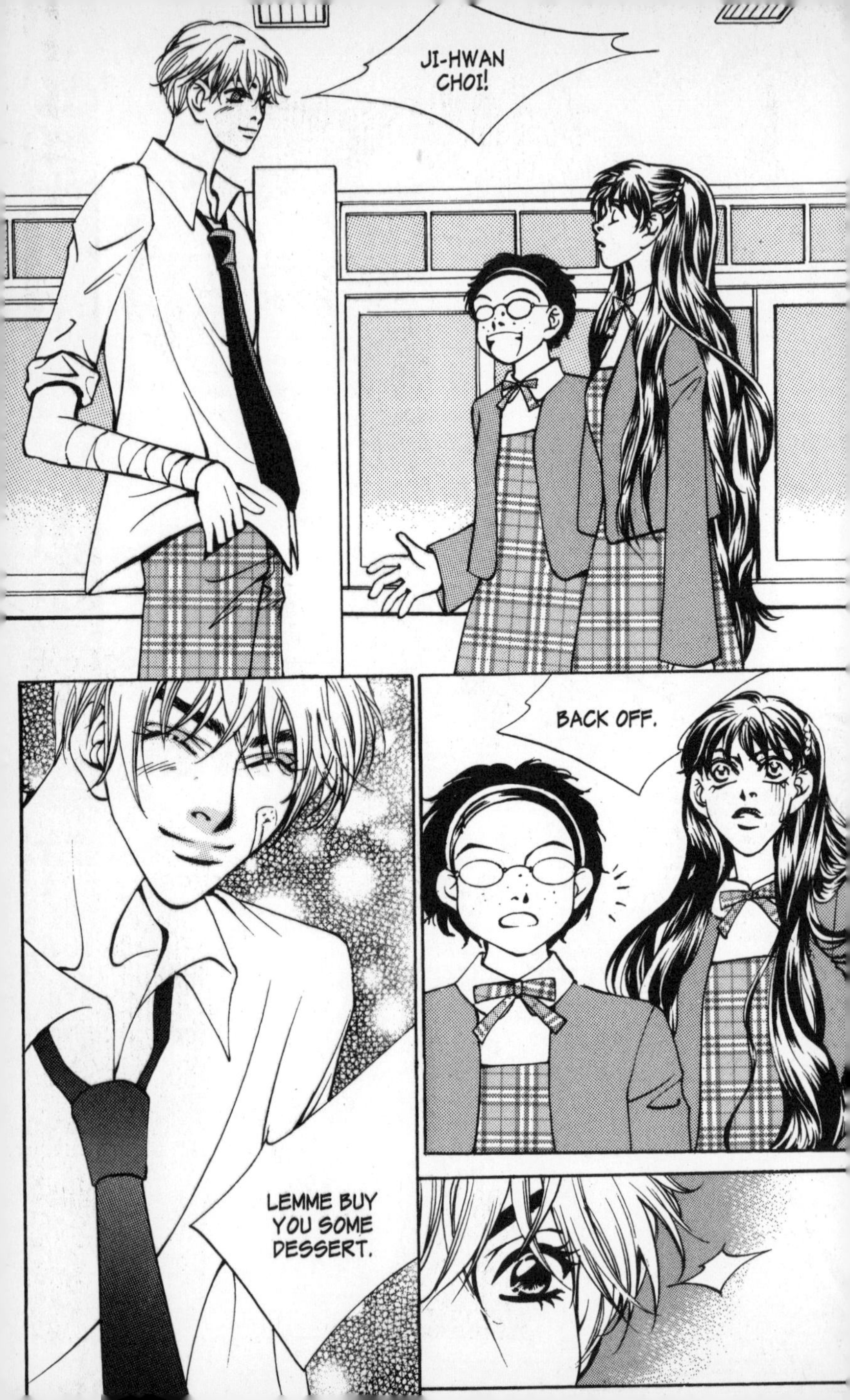
JI-HWAN CHOI!
LEMME BUY YOU SOME DESSERT.
BACK OFF.

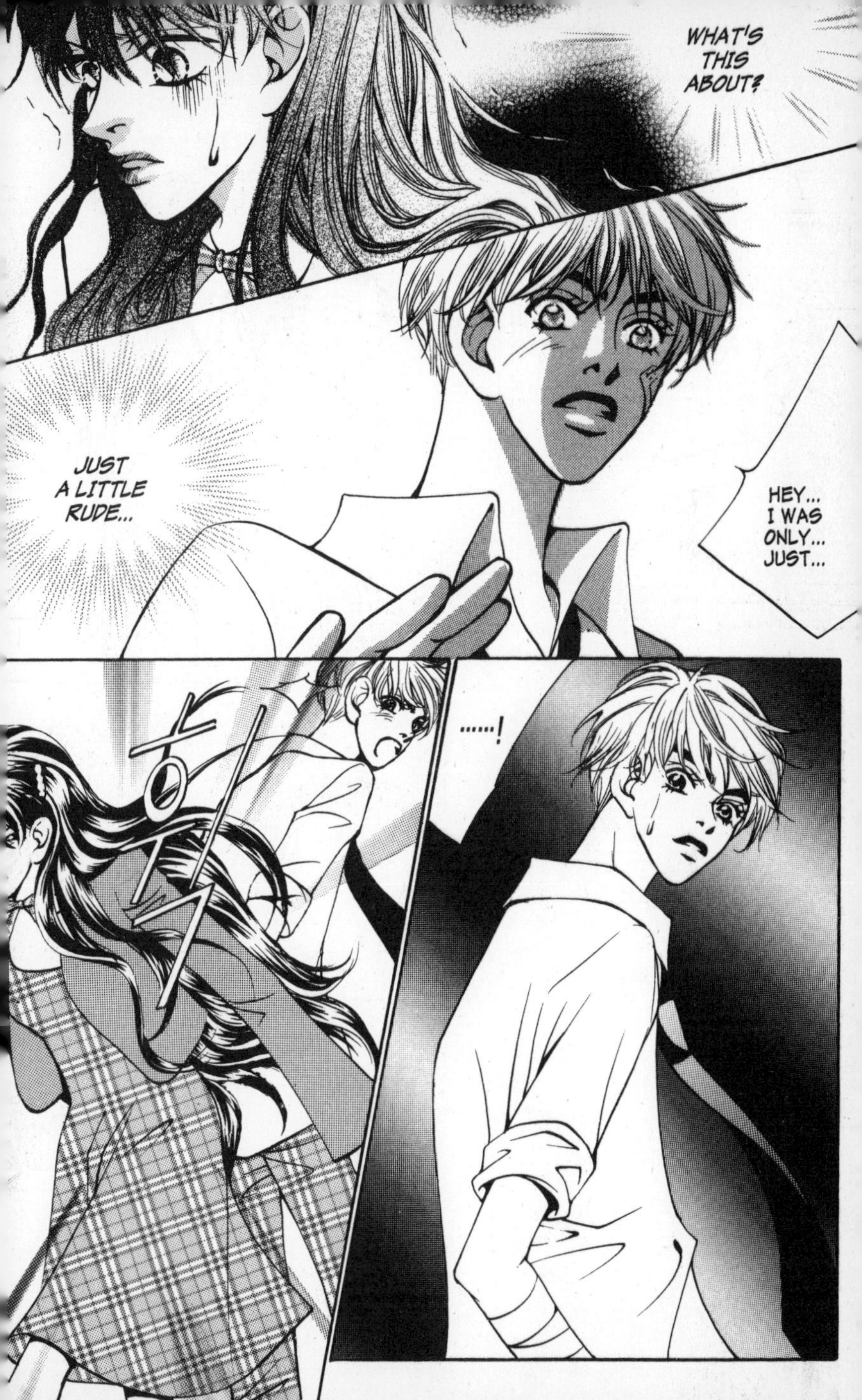
WHAT'S THIS ABOUT?
JUST A LITTLE RUDE...
HEY... I WAS ONLY... JUST...
......!

The Kid I Met in My Dream

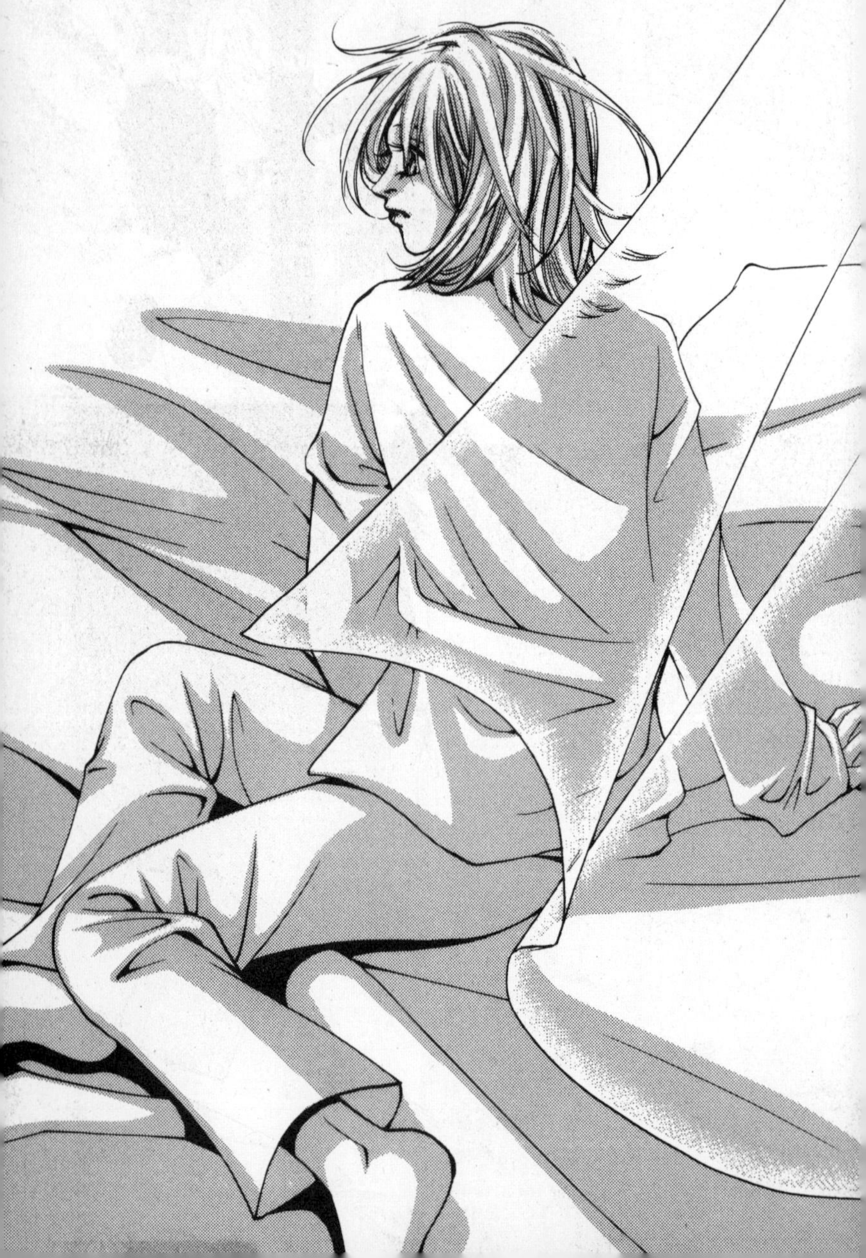

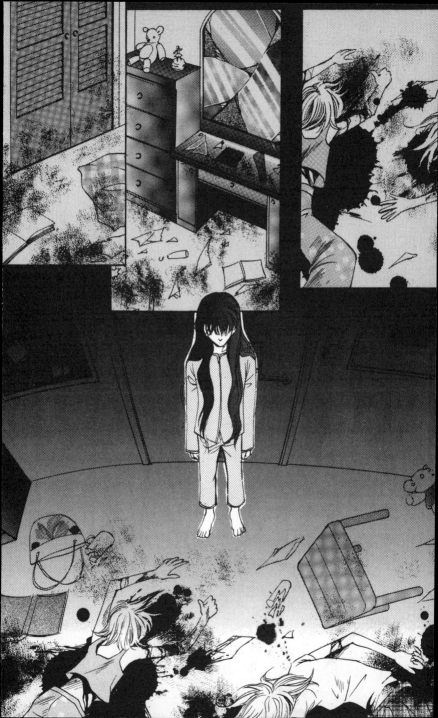

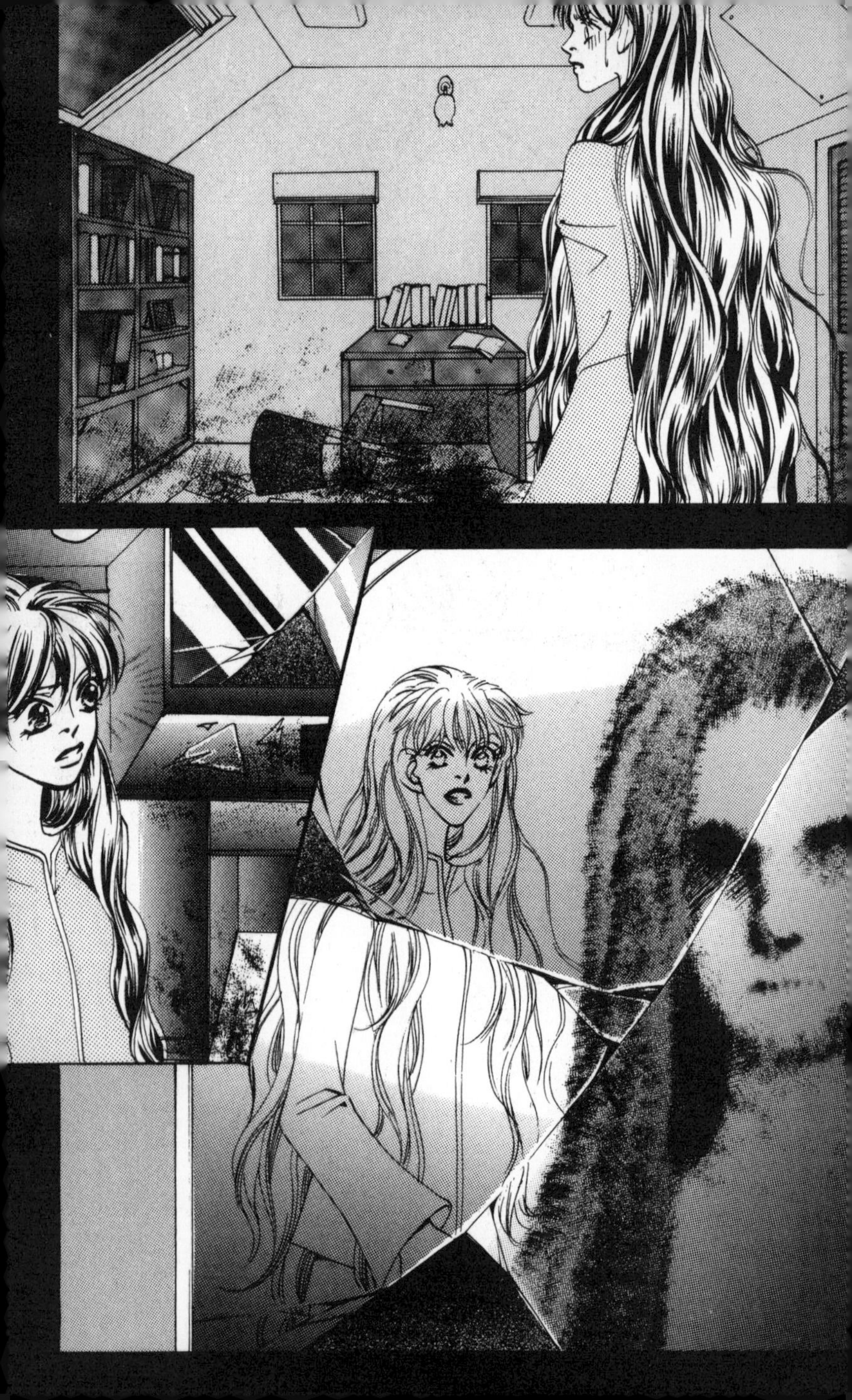

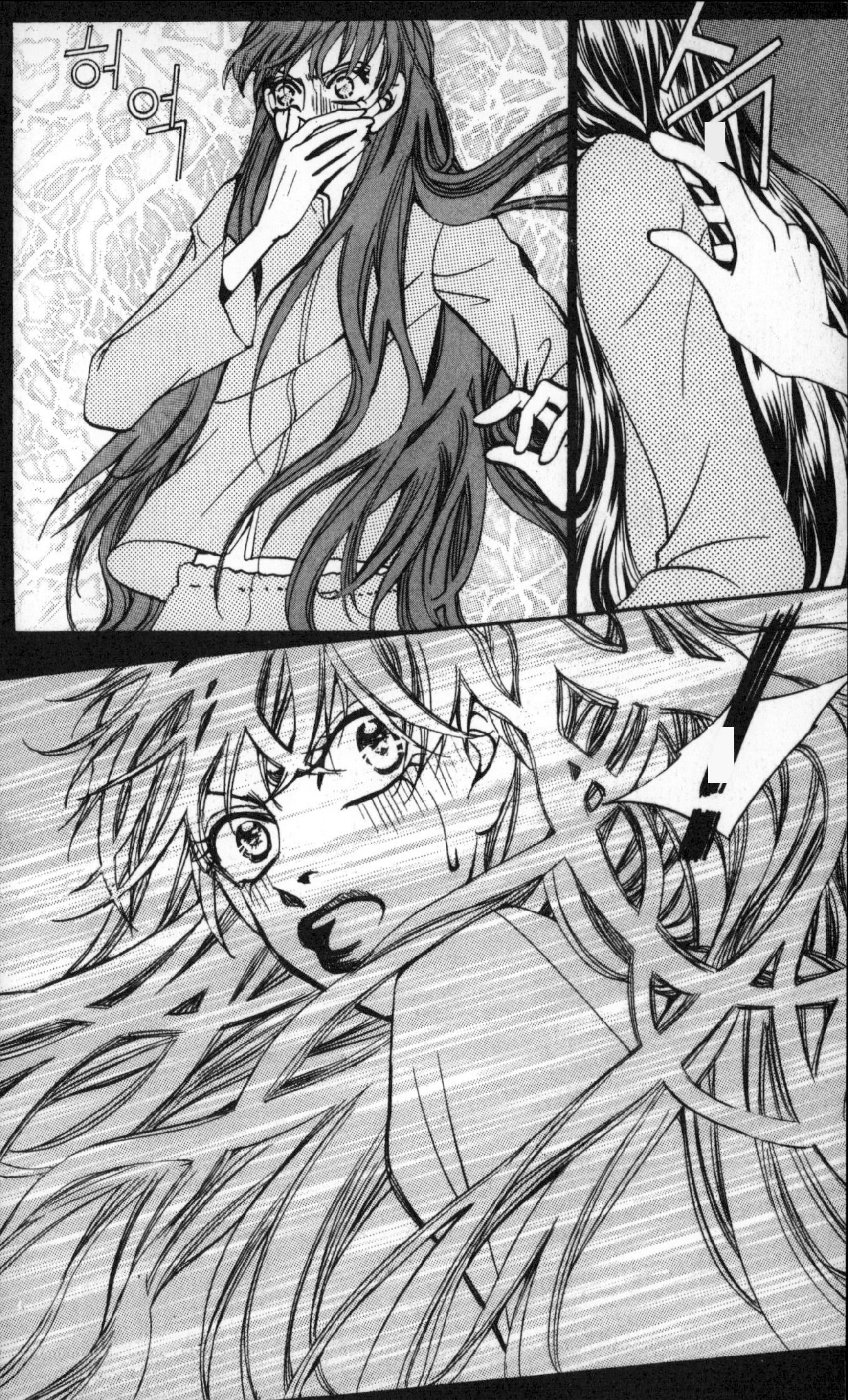
허억

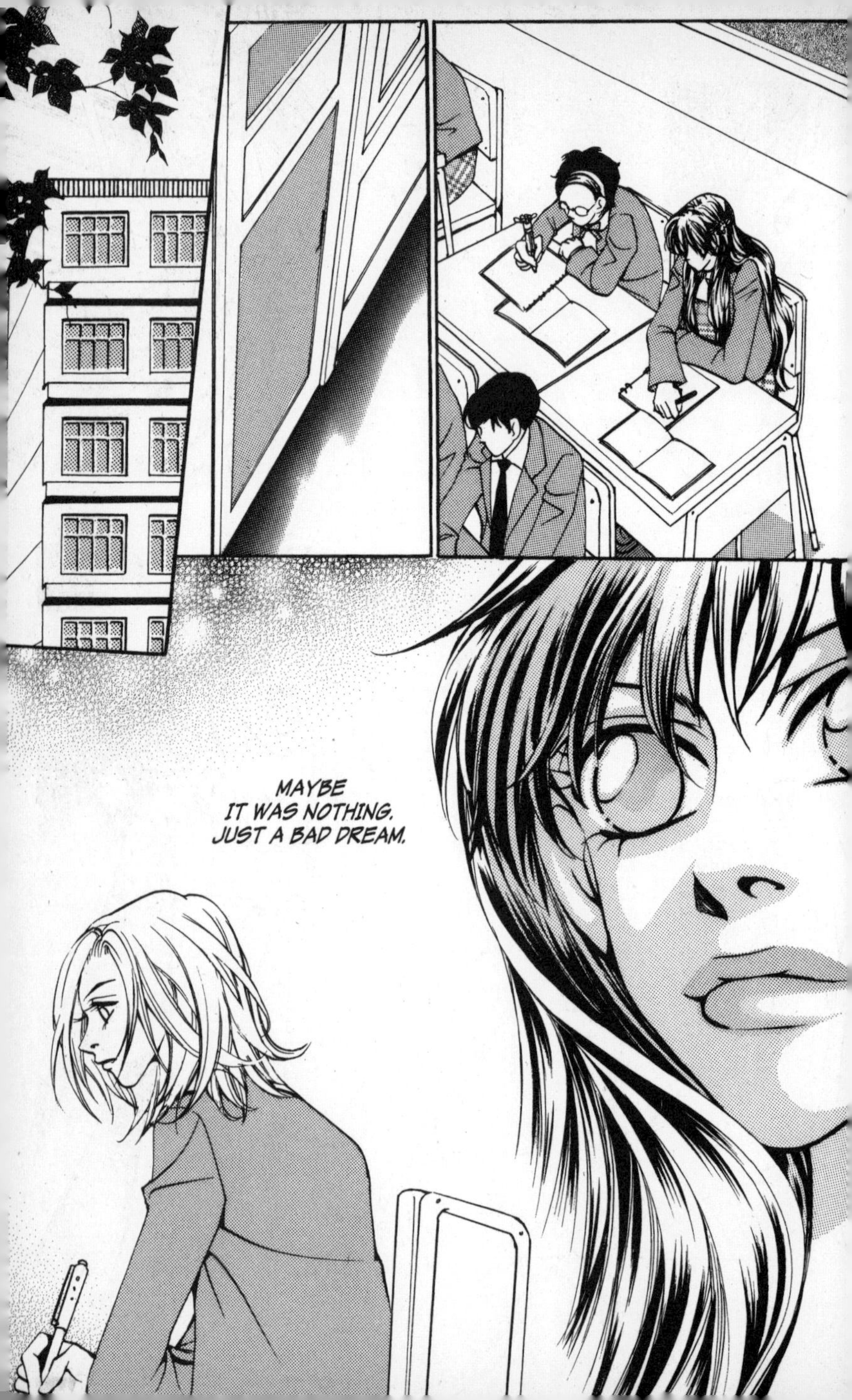
MAYBE
IT WAS NOTHING.
JUST A BAD DREAM.

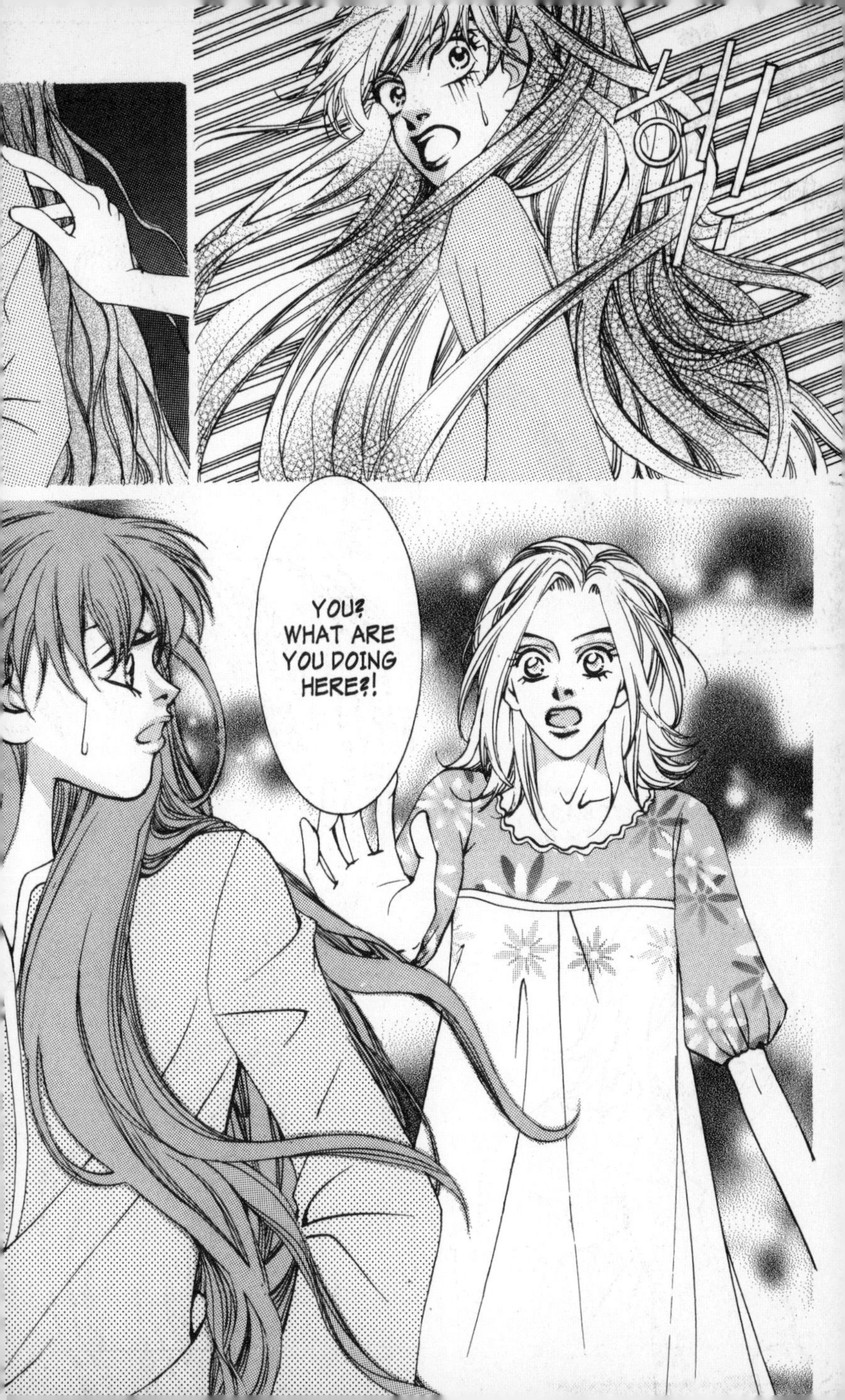
YOU? WHAT ARE YOU DOING HERE?!

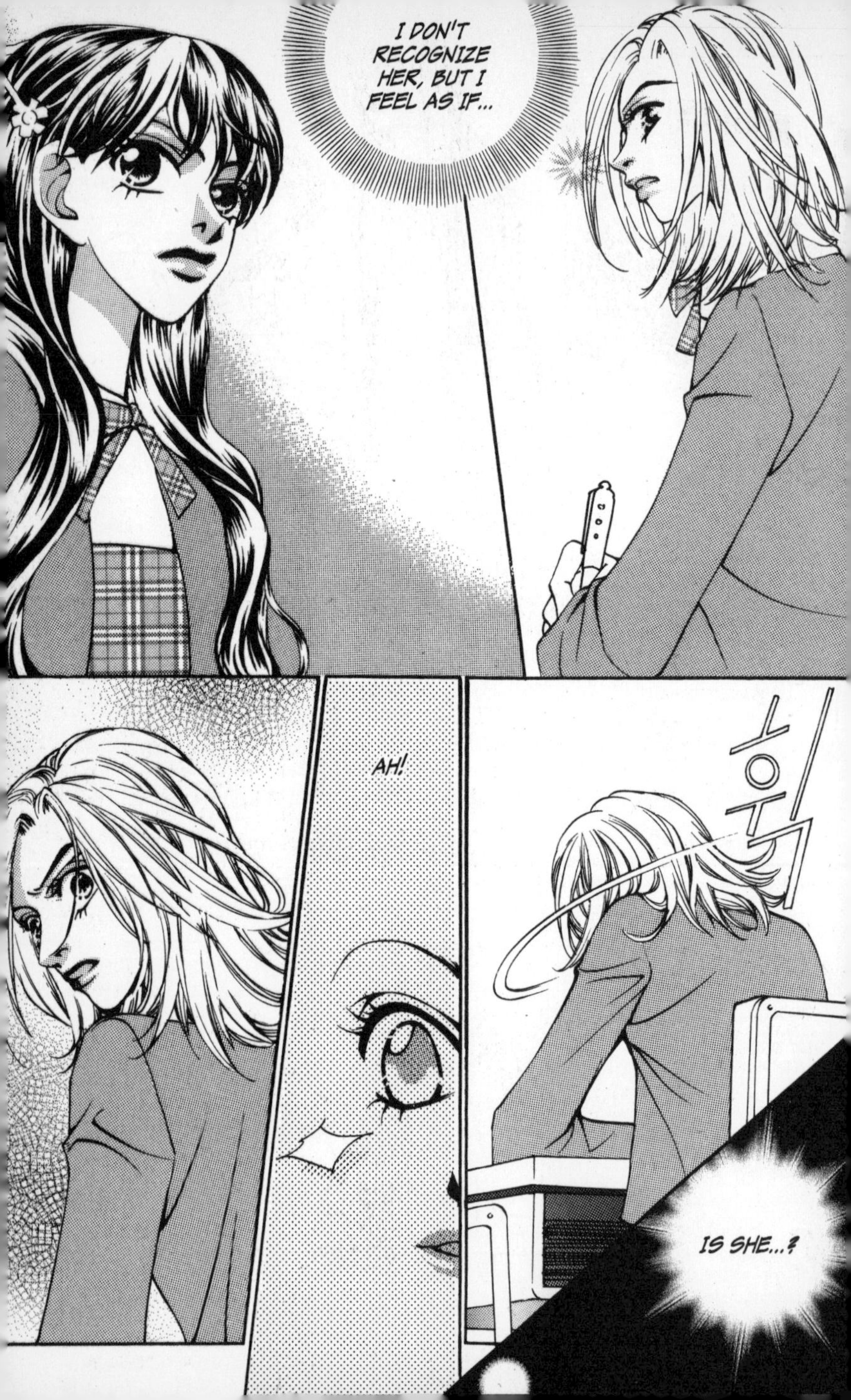
I DON'T RECOGNIZE HER, BUT I FEEL AS IF...
AH!
IS SHE...?

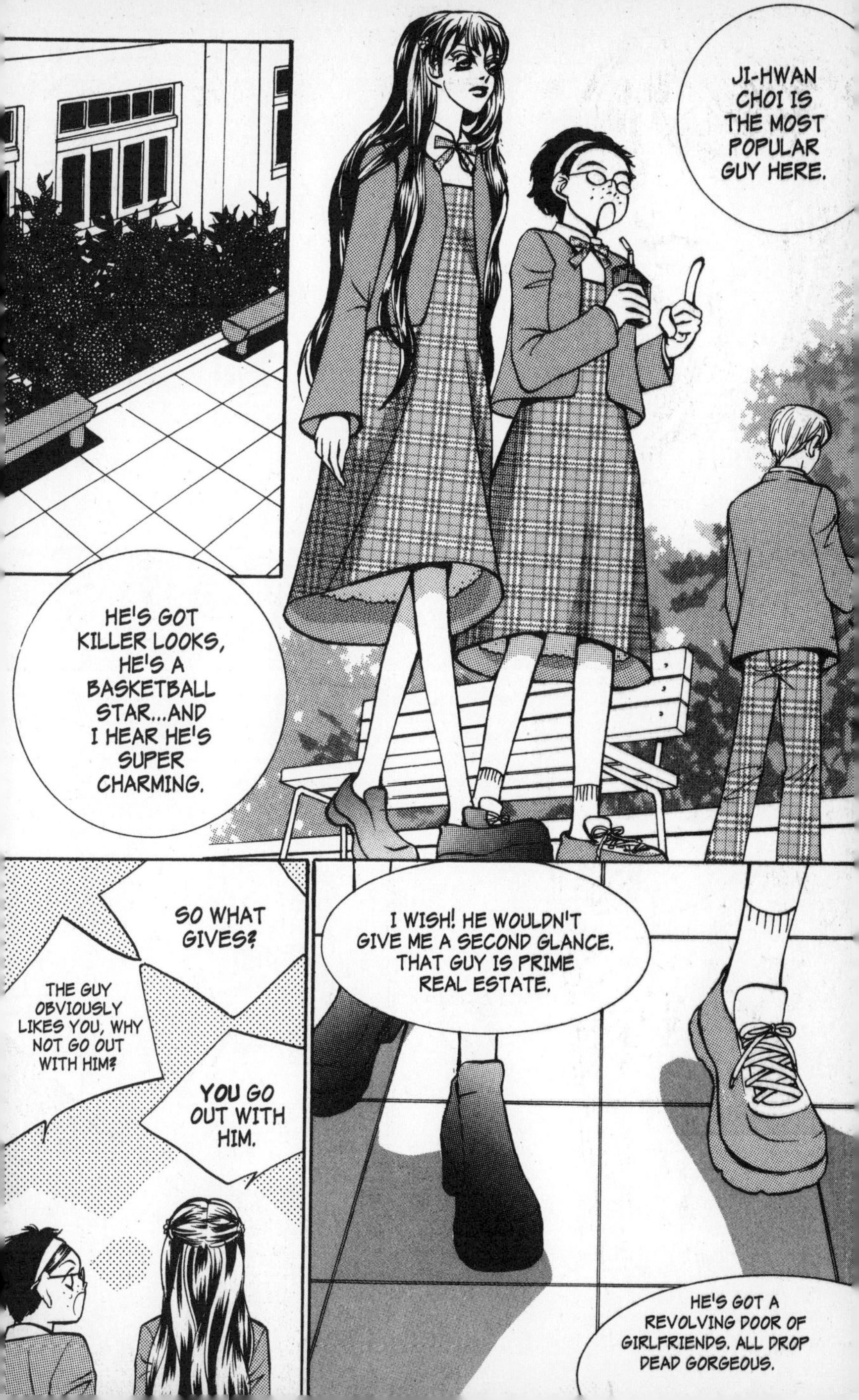
JI-HWAN CHOI IS THE MOST POPULAR GUY HERE.
HE'S GOT KILLER LOOKS, HE'S A BASKETBALL STAR...AND I HEAR HE'S SUPER CHARMING.
SO WHAT GIVES?
THE GUY OBVIOUSLY LIKES YOU, WHY NOT GO OUT WITH HIM?
YOU GO OUT WITH HIM.
I WISH! HE WOULDN'T GIVE ME A SECOND GLANCE. THAT GUY IS PRIME REAL ESTATE.
HE'S GOT A REVOLVING DOOR OF GIRLFRIENDS. ALL DROP DEAD GORGEOUS.

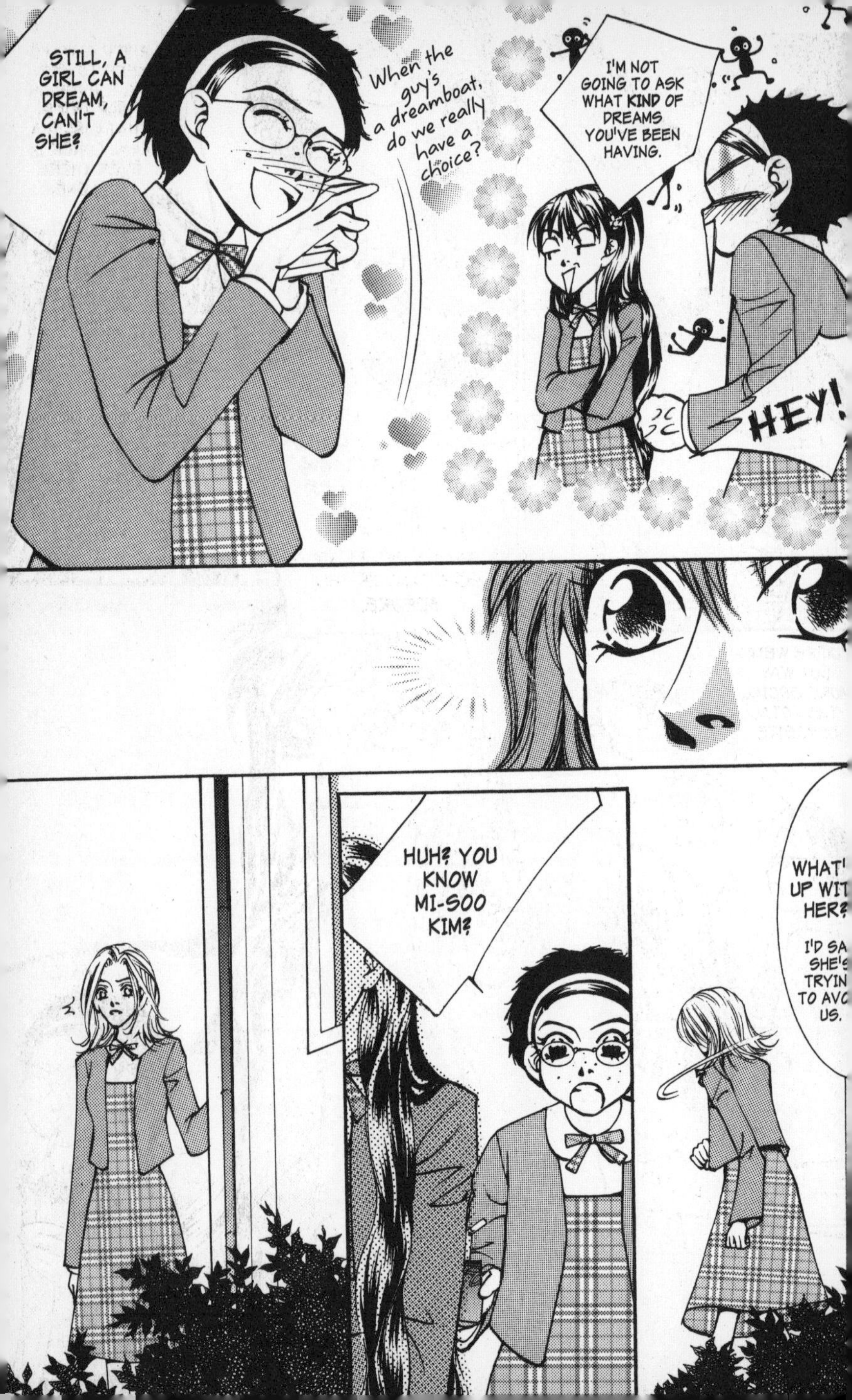
STILL, A GIRL CAN DREAM, CAN'T SHE?
When the guy's a dreamboat, do we really have a choice?
I'M NOT GOING TO ASK WHAT KIND OF DREAMS YOU'VE BEEN HAVING.
HEY!
HUH? YOU KNOW MI-SOO KIM?
WHAT' UP WIT HER?
I'D SA SHE'S TRYIN TO AVC US.

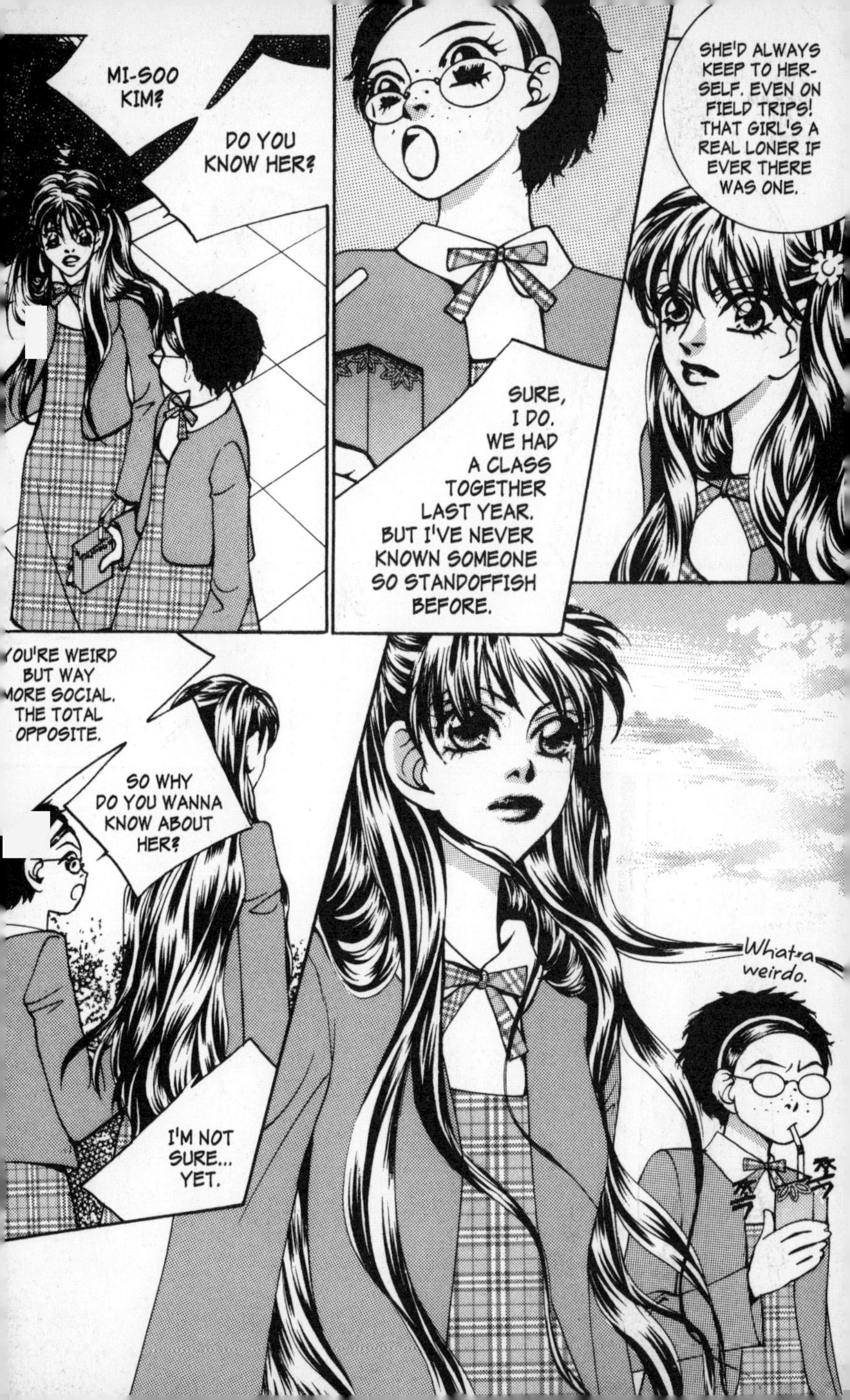

MI-SOO KIM?
DO YOU KNOW HER?
SURE, I DO. WE HAD A CLASS TOGETHER LAST YEAR. BUT I'VE NEVER KNOWN SOMEONE SO STANDOFFISH BEFORE.
SHE'D ALWAYS KEEP TO HER-SELF. EVEN ON FIELD TRIPS! THAT GIRL'S A REAL LONER IF EVER THERE WAS ONE.
OU'RE WEIRD BUT WAY ORE SOCIAL. THE TOTAL OPPOSITE.
SO WHY DO YOU WANNA KNOW ABOUT HER?
I'M NOT SURE... YET.
What a weirdo.

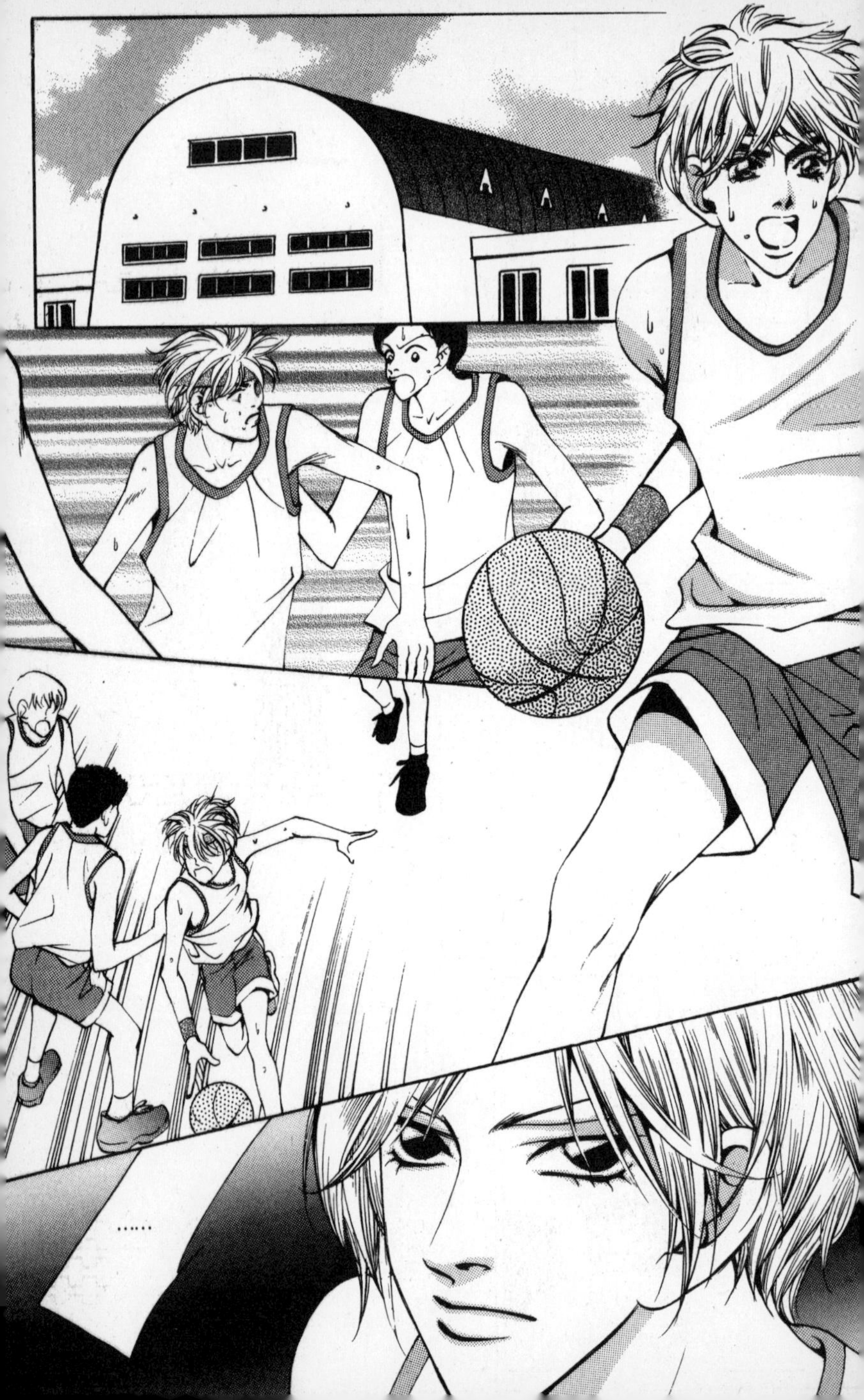
……

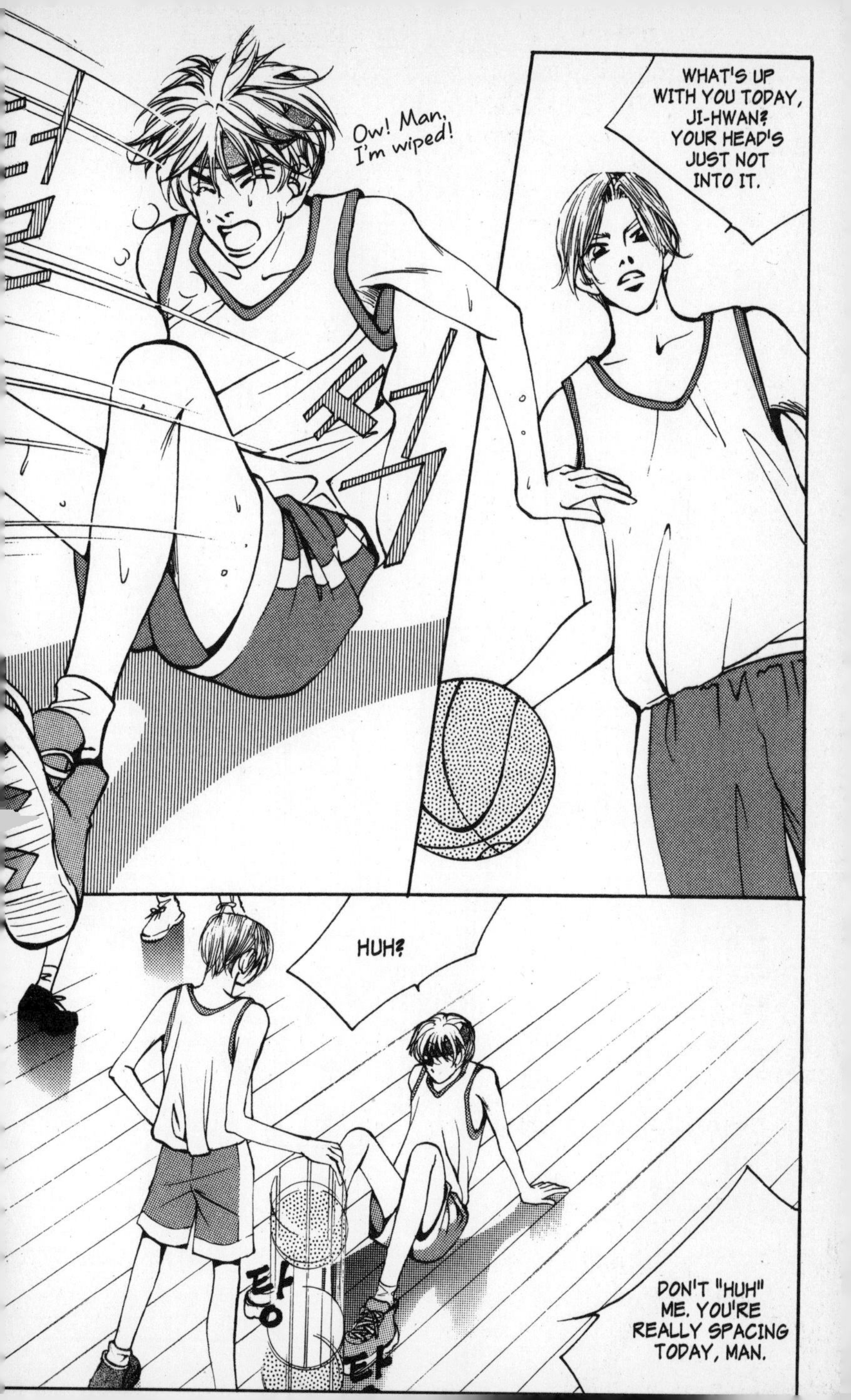
Ow! Man, I'm wiped!
WHAT'S UP WITH YOU TODAY, JI-HWAN? YOUR HEAD'S JUST NOT INTO IT.
HUH?
DON'T "HUH" ME. YOU'RE REALLY SPACING TODAY, MAN.

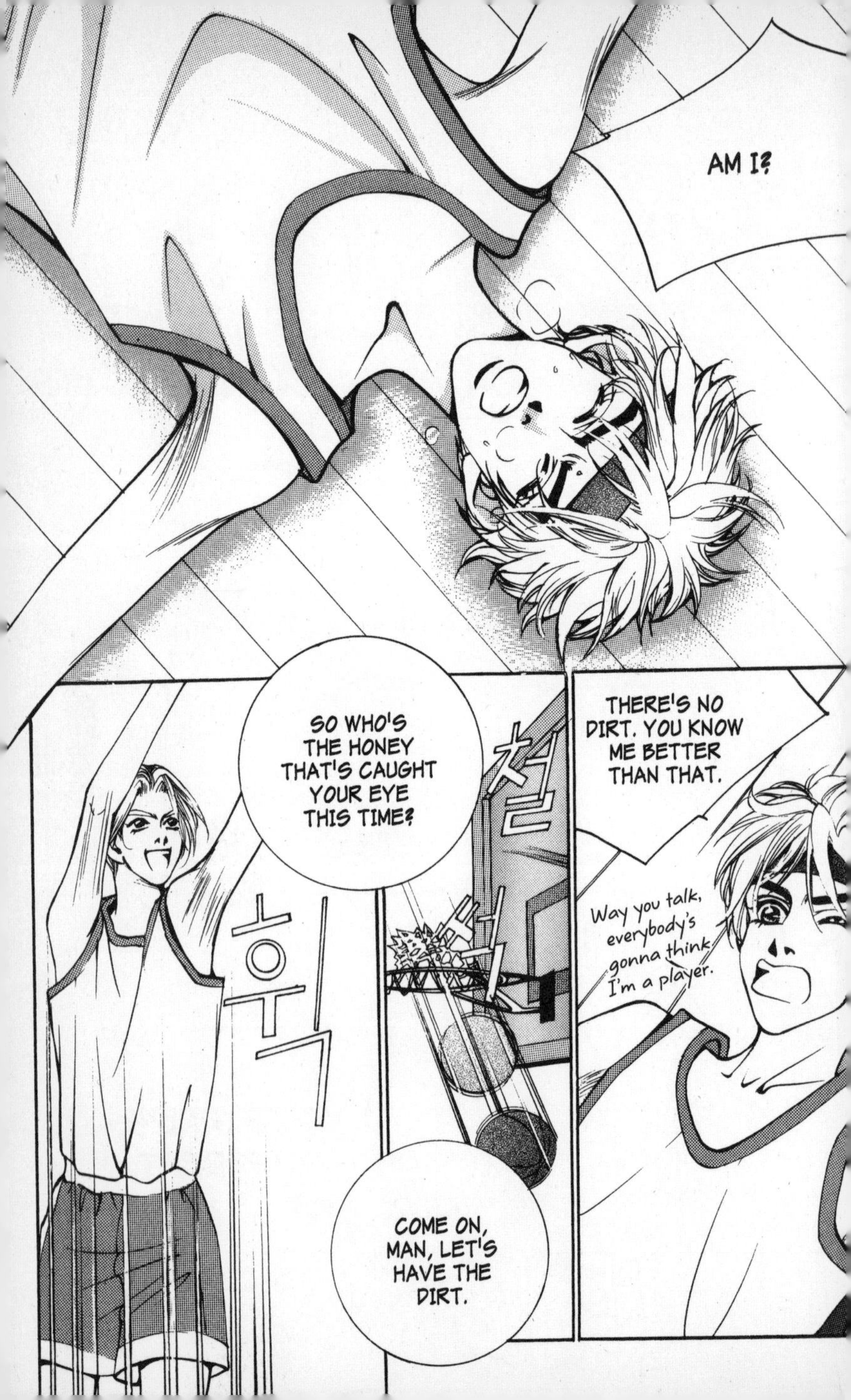
AM I?
SO WHO'S THE HONEY THAT'S CAUGHT YOUR EYE THIS TIME?
휙
COME ON, MAN, LET'S HAVE THE DIRT.
THERE'S NO DIRT. YOU KNOW ME BETTER THAN THAT.
Way you talk, everybody's gonna think I'm a player.

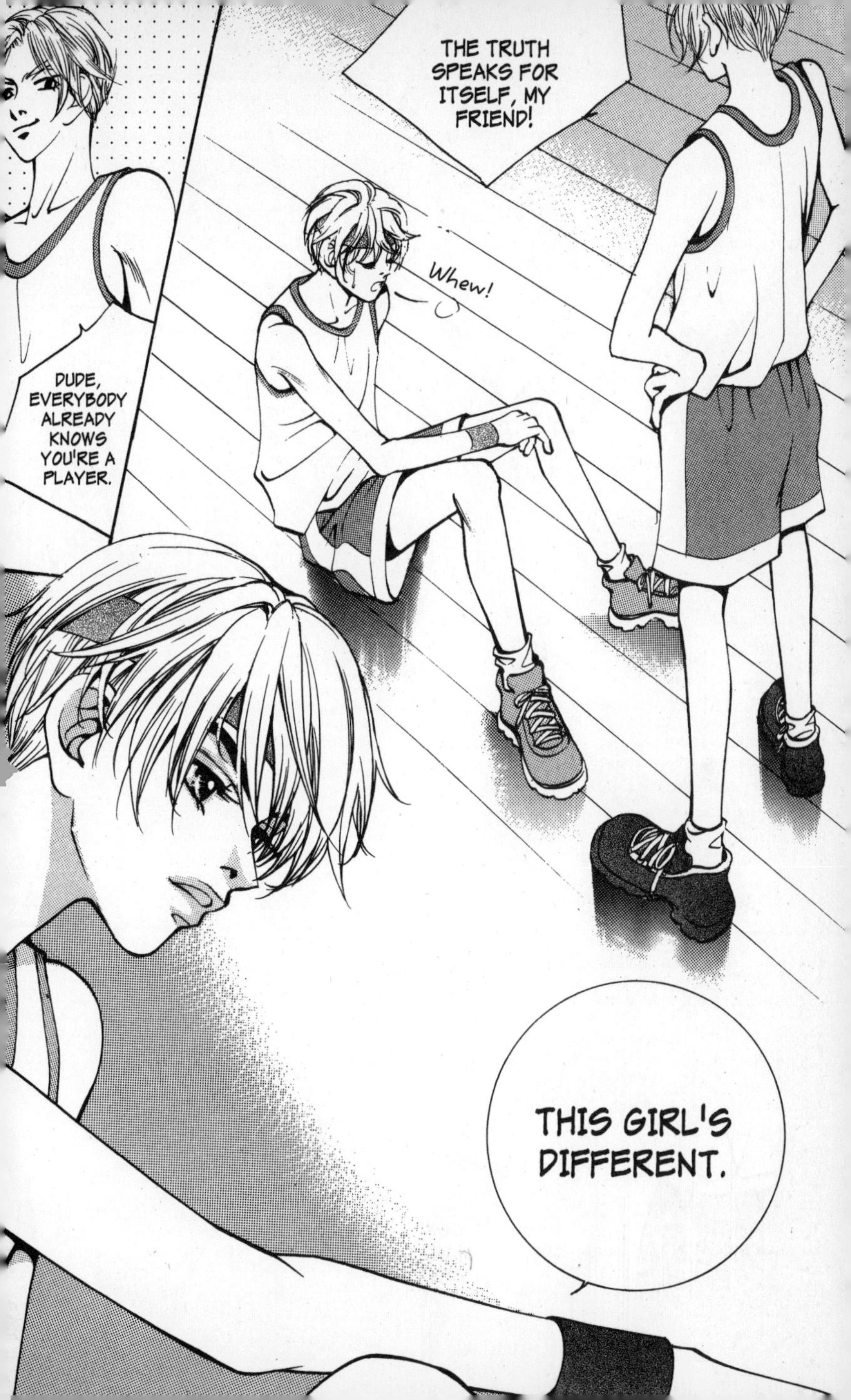
DUDE, EVERYBODY ALREADY KNOWS YOU'RE A PLAYER.
THE TRUTH SPEAKS FOR ITSELF, MY FRIEND!
Whew!
THIS GIRL'S DIFFERENT.

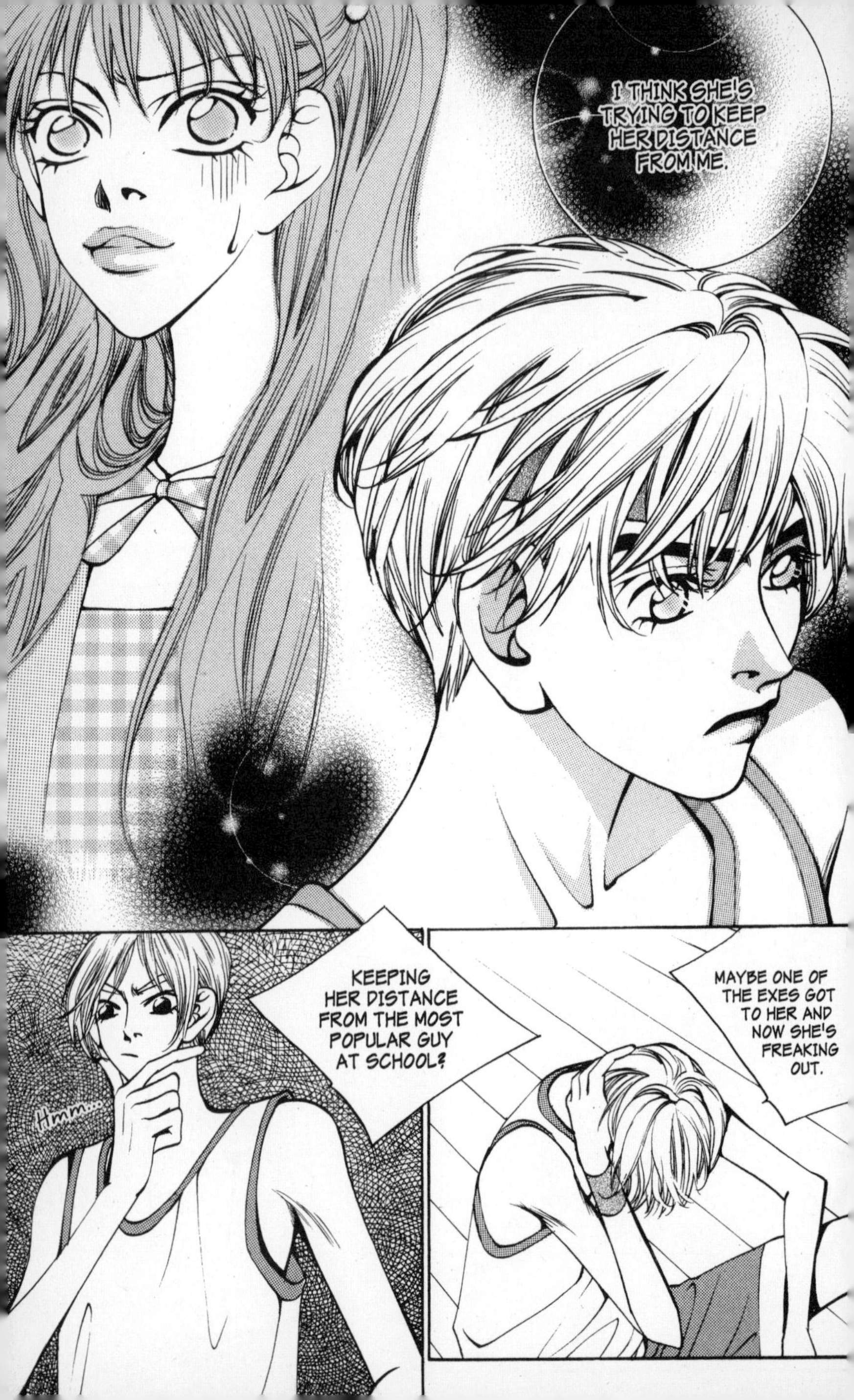
I THINK SHE'S TRYING TO KEEP HER DISTANCE FROM ME.
Hmm...
KEEPING HER DISTANCE FROM THE MOST POPULAR GUY AT SCHOOL?
MAYBE ONE OF THE EXES GOT TO HER AND NOW SHE'S FREAKING OUT.

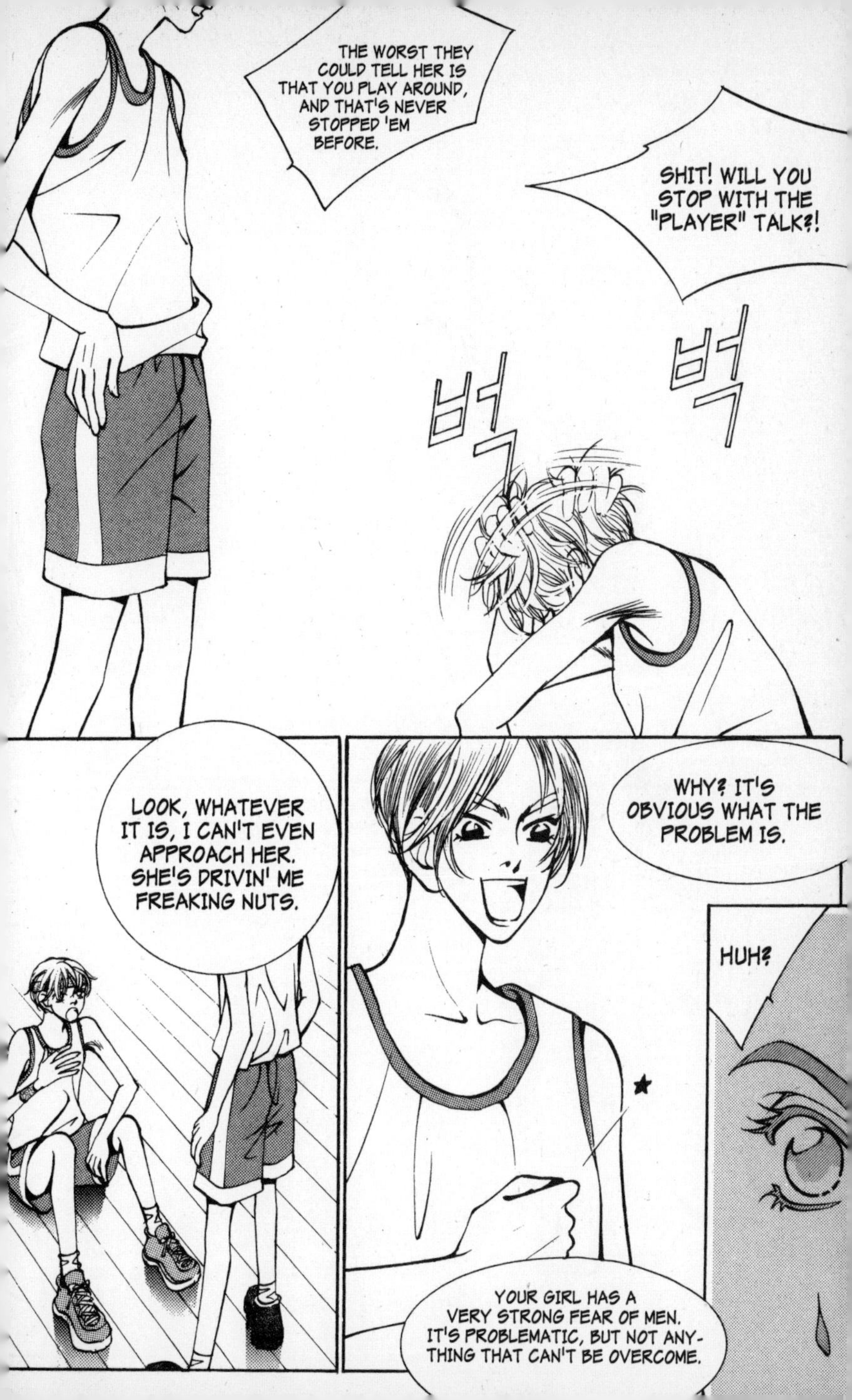
THE WORST THEY COULD TELL HER IS THAT YOU PLAY AROUND, AND THAT'S NEVER STOPPED 'EM BEFORE.
SHIT! WILL YOU STOP WITH THE "PLAYER" TALK?!
벅 벅
LOOK, WHATEVER IT IS, I CAN'T EVEN APPROACH HER. SHE'S DRIVIN' ME FREAKING NUTS.
WHY? IT'S OBVIOUS WHAT THE PROBLEM IS.
HUH?
YOUR GIRL HAS A VERY STRONG FEAR OF MEN. IT'S PROBLEMATIC, BUT NOT ANY-THING THAT CAN'T BE OVERCOME.

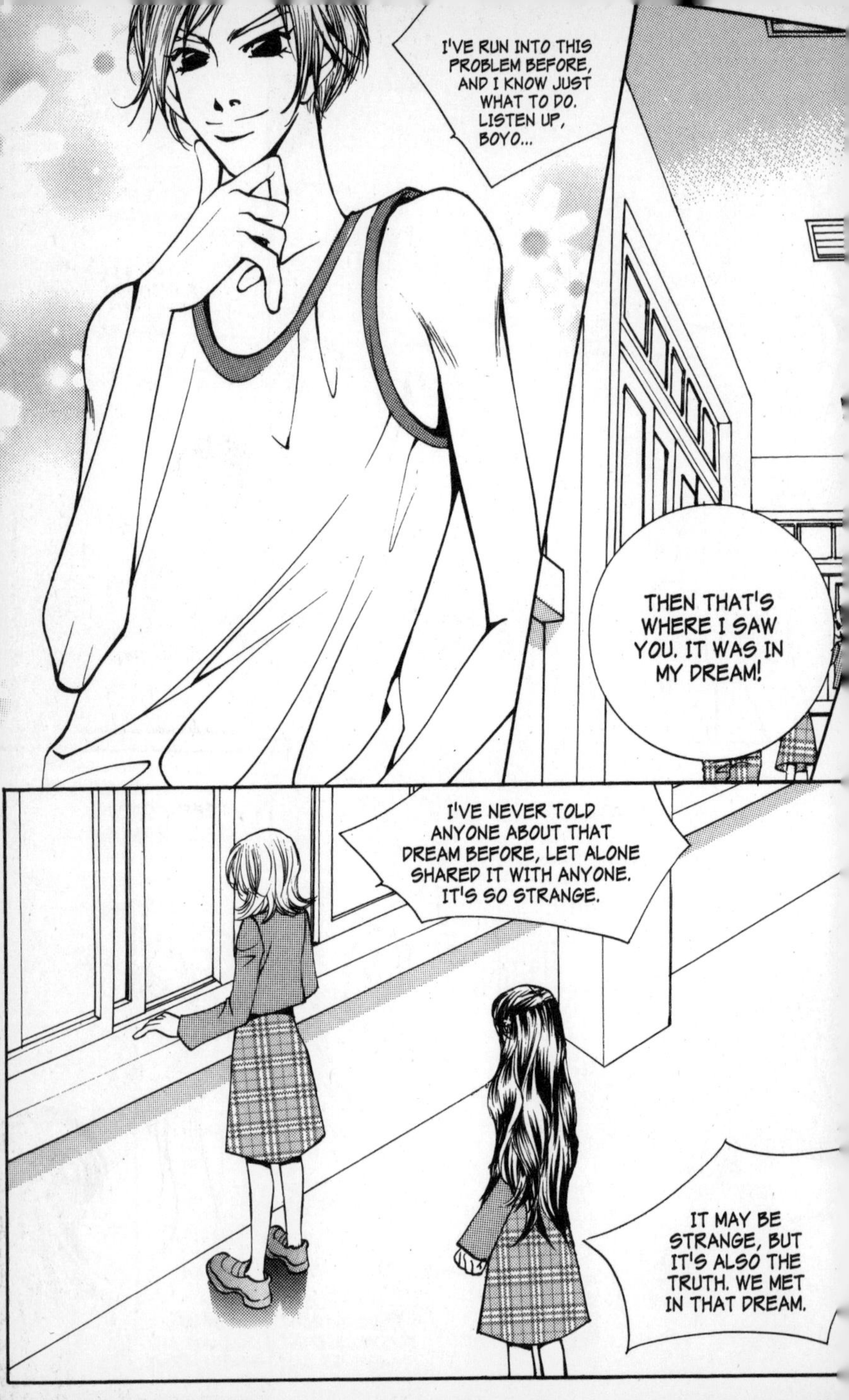
I'VE RUN INTO THIS PROBLEM BEFORE, AND I KNOW JUST WHAT TO DO. LISTEN UP, BOYO...
THEN THAT'S WHERE I SAW YOU. IT WAS IN MY DREAM!
I'VE NEVER TOLD ANYONE ABOUT THAT DREAM BEFORE, LET ALONE SHARED IT WITH ANYONE. IT'S SO STRANGE.
IT MAY BE STRANGE, BUT IT'S ALSO THE TRUTH. WE MET IN THAT DREAM.

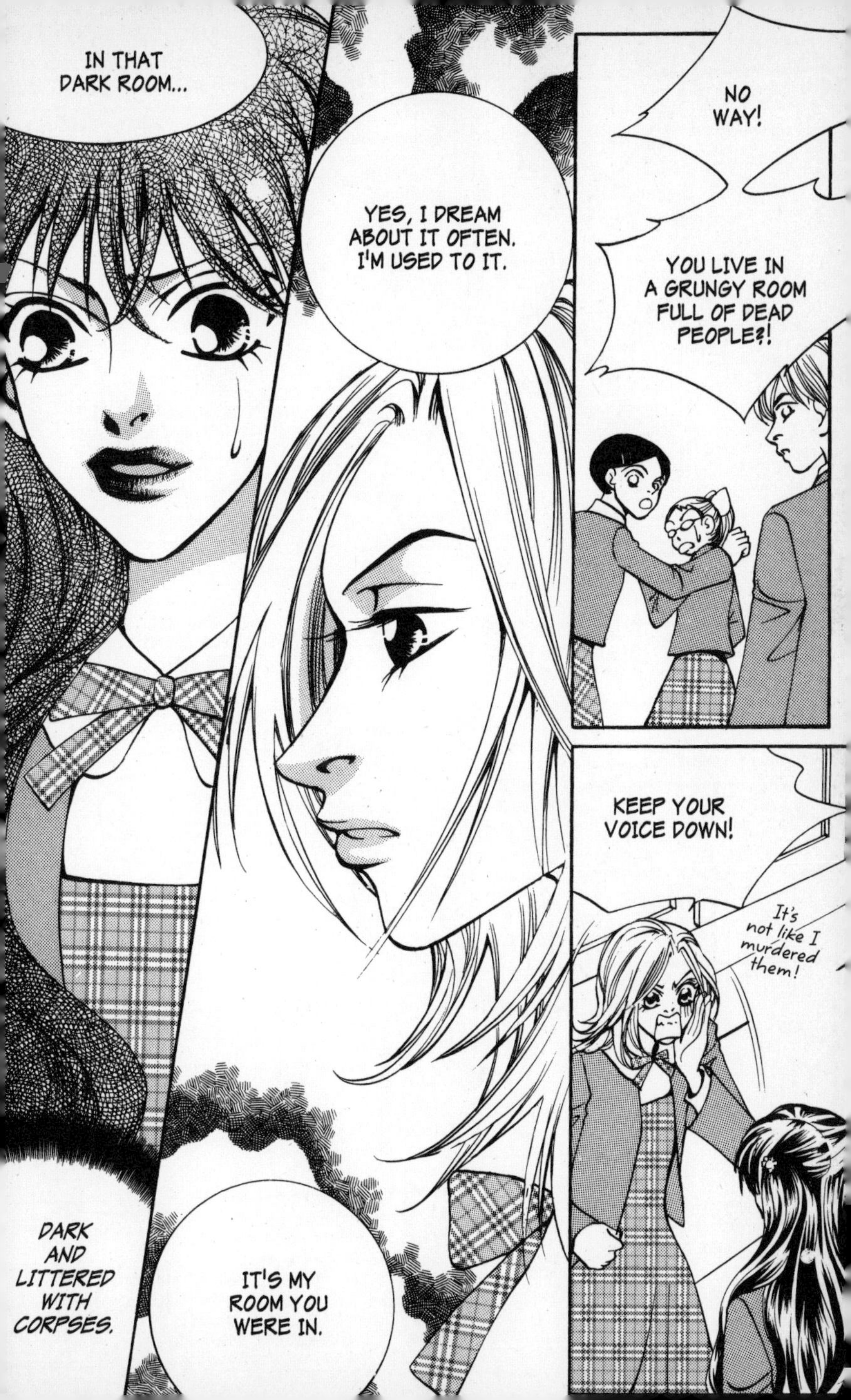
IN THAT DARK ROOM...
DARK AND LITTERED WITH CORPSES.
YES, I DREAM ABOUT IT OFTEN. I'M USED TO IT.
IT'S MY ROOM YOU WERE IN.
NO WAY!
YOU LIVE IN A GRUNGY ROOM FULL OF DEAD PEOPLE?!
KEEP YOUR VOICE DOWN!
It's not like I murdered them!

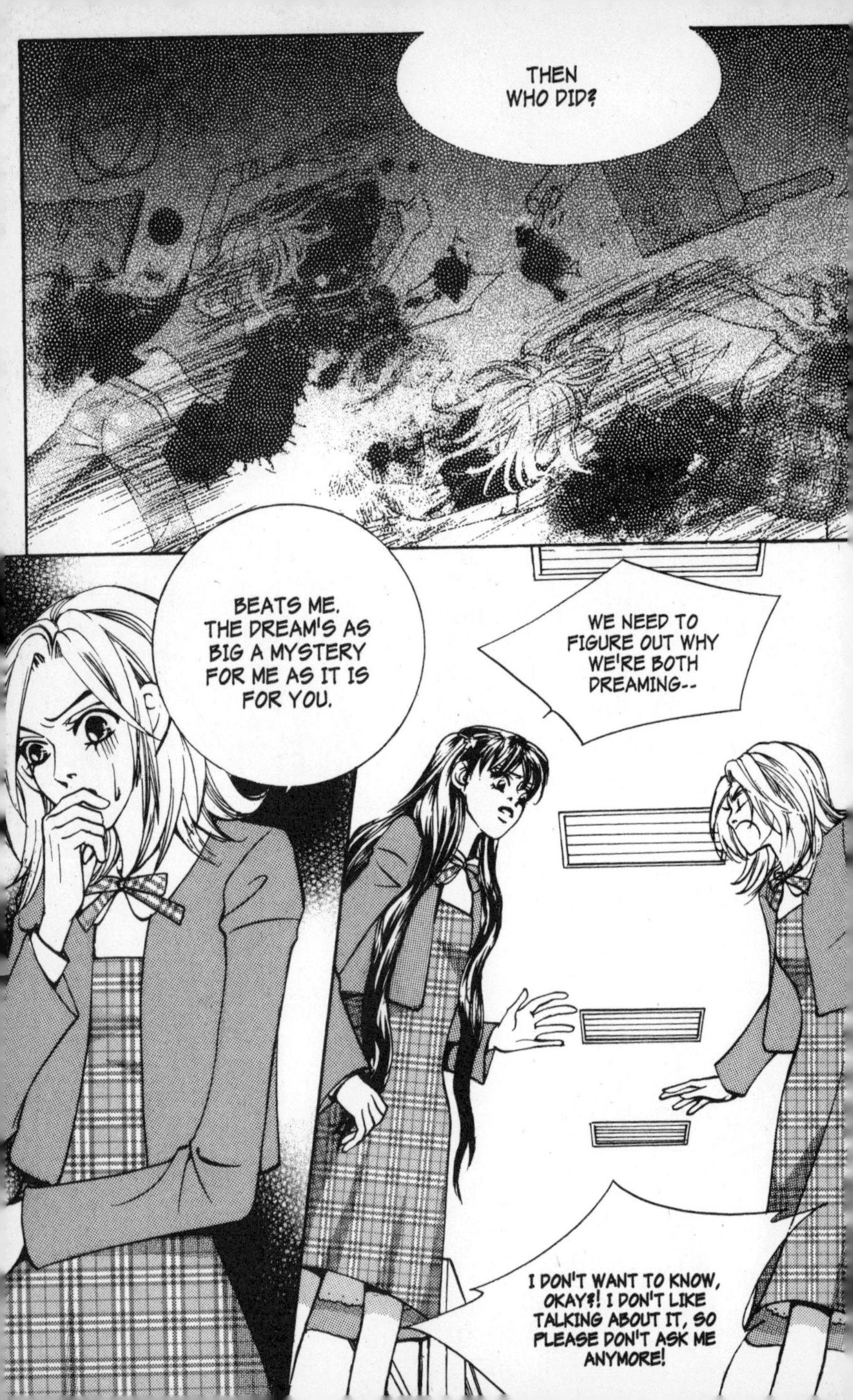
THEN WHO DID?
BEATS ME. THE DREAM'S AS BIG A MYSTERY FOR ME AS IT IS FOR YOU.
WE NEED TO FIGURE OUT WHY WE'RE BOTH DREAMING--
I DON'T WANT TO KNOW, OKAY?! I DON'T LIKE TALKING ABOUT IT, SO PLEASE DON'T ASK ME ANYMORE!

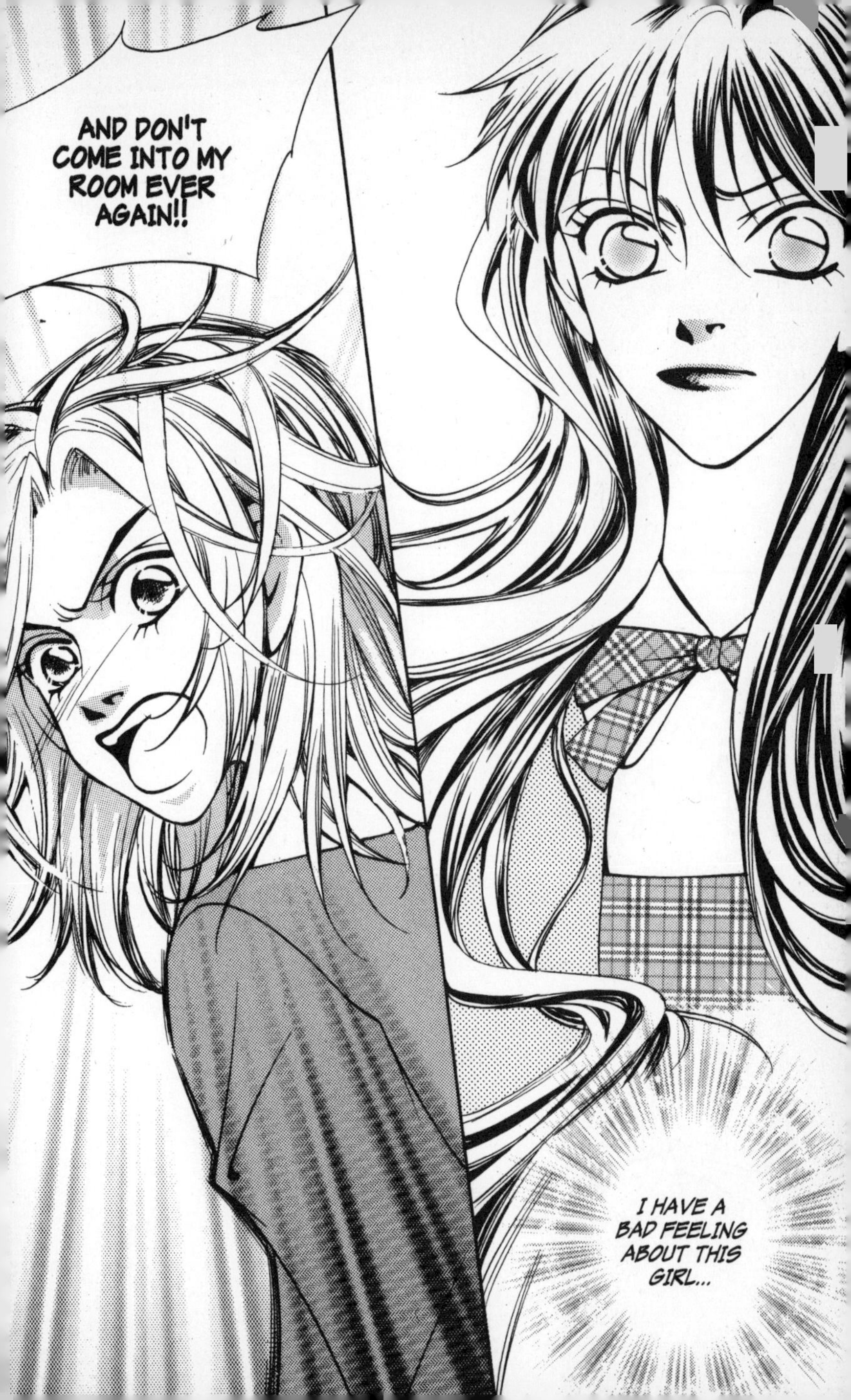
AND DON'T COME INTO MY ROOM EVER AGAIN!!
I HAVE A BAD FEELING ABOUT THIS GIRL...

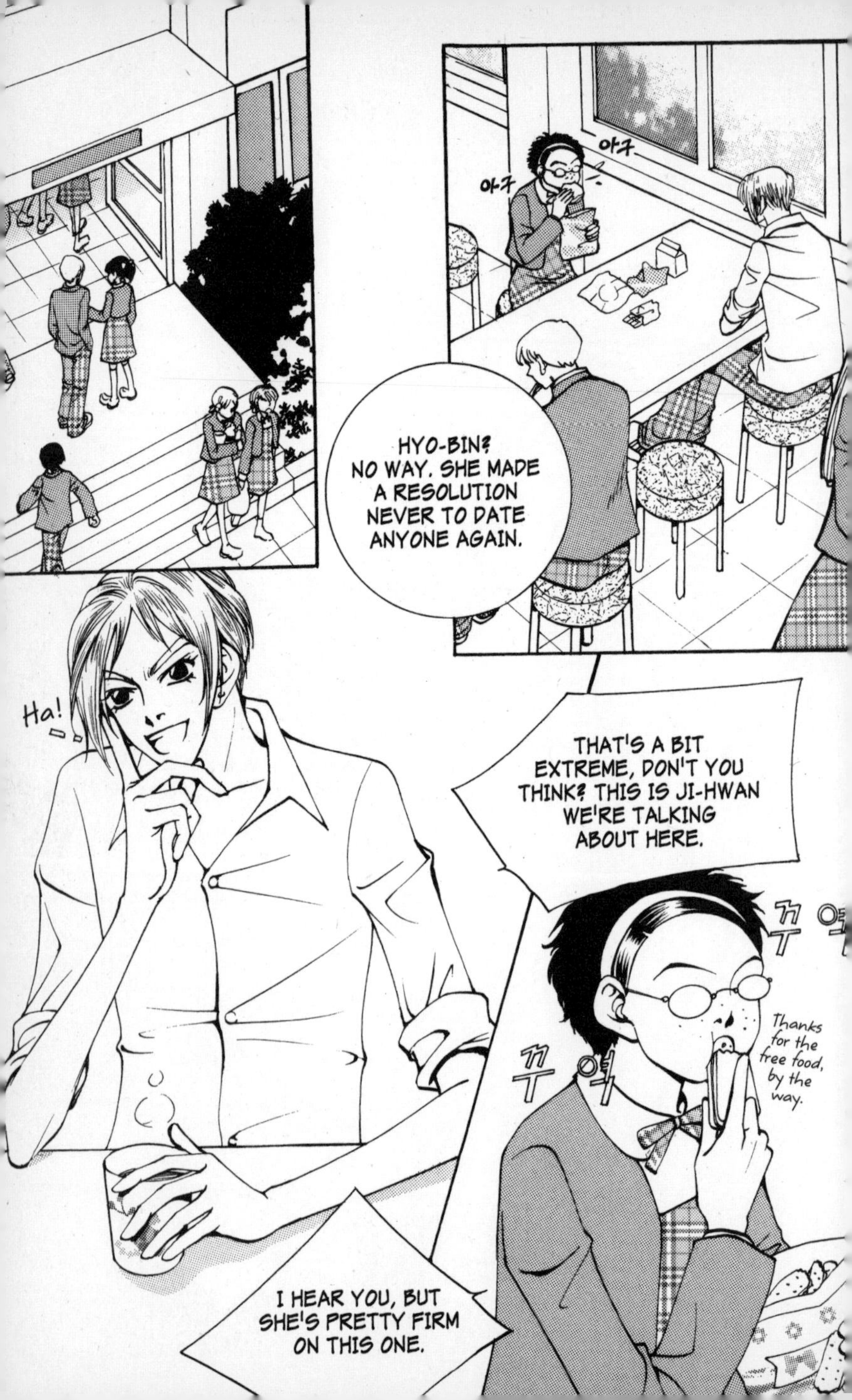
아구
아구
HYO-BIN? NO WAY. SHE MADE A RESOLUTION NEVER TO DATE ANYONE AGAIN.
Ha!
THAT'S A BIT EXTREME, DON'T YOU THINK? THIS IS JI-HWAN WE'RE TALKING ABOUT HERE.
꺼억
꺼억
Thanks for the free food, by the way.
I HEAR YOU, BUT SHE'S PRETTY FIRM ON THIS ONE.

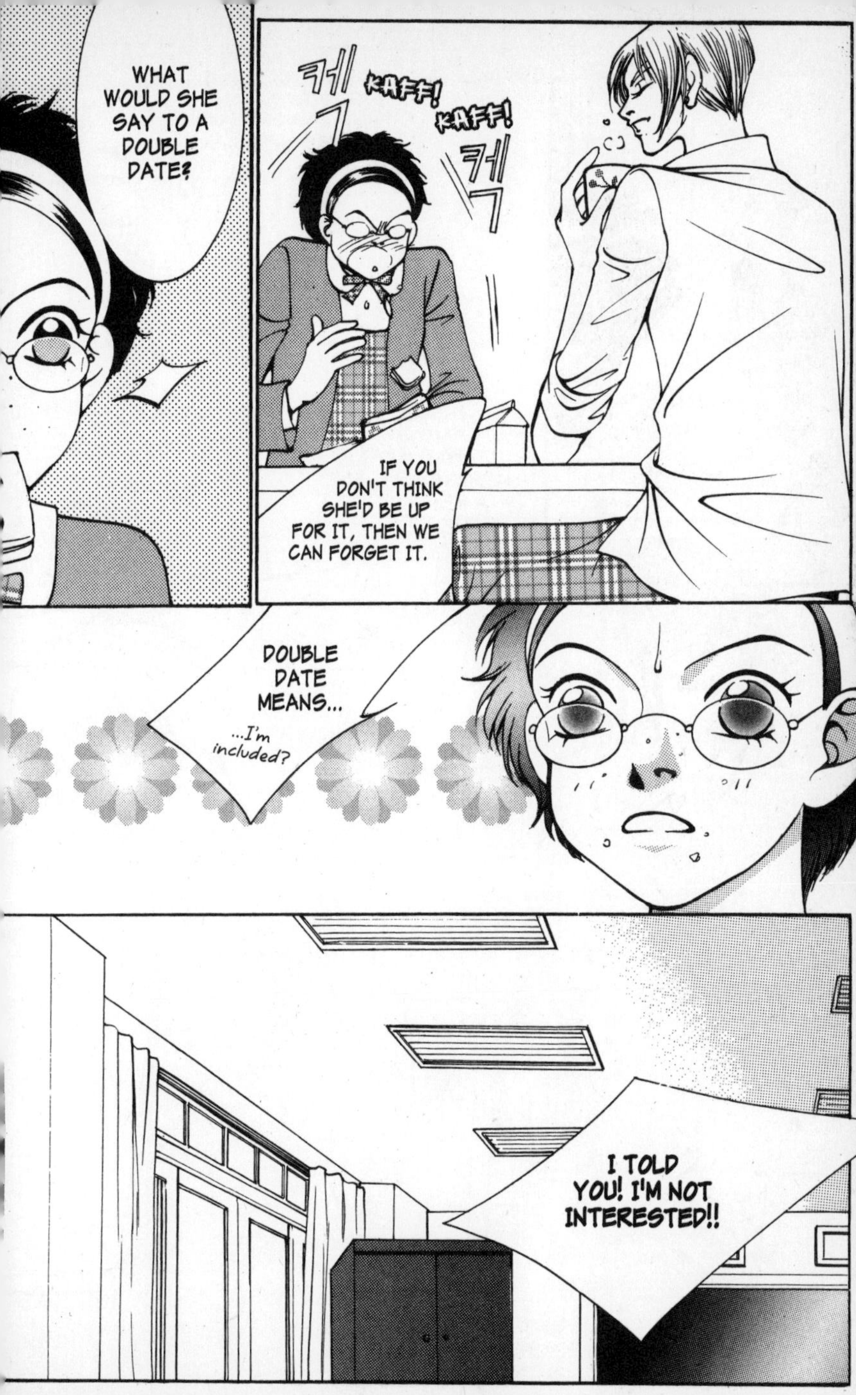
WHAT WOULD SHE SAY TO A DOUBLE DATE?
KAFF!
KAFF!
IF YOU DON'T THINK SHE'D BE UP FOR IT, THEN WE CAN FORGET IT.
DOUBLE DATE MEANS...
...I'm included?
I TOLD YOU! I'M NOT INTERESTED!!

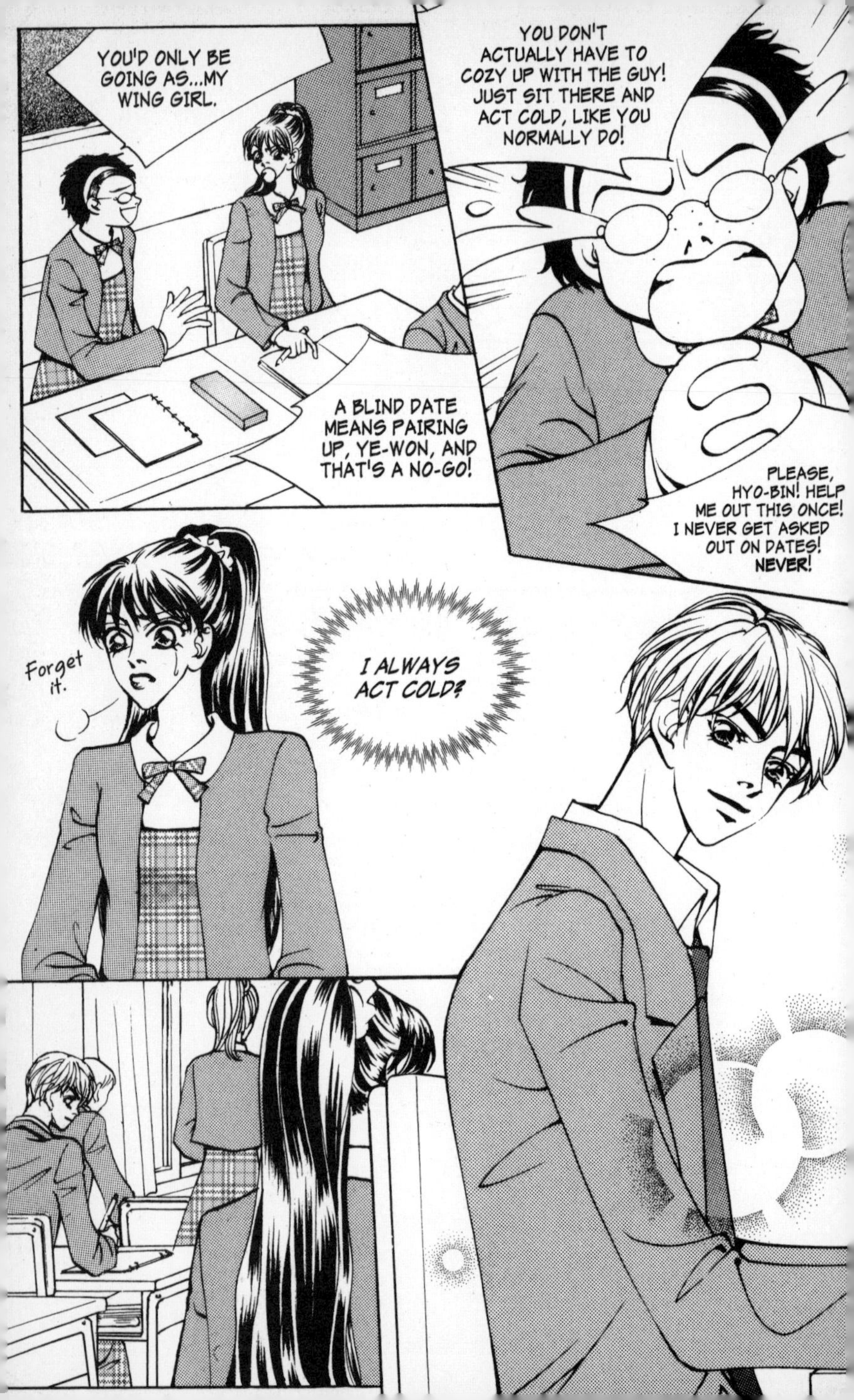
YOU'D ONLY BE GOING AS...MY WING GIRL.
A BLIND DATE MEANS PAIRING UP, YE-WON, AND THAT'S A NO-GO!
YOU DON'T ACTUALLY HAVE TO COZY UP WITH THE GUY! JUST SIT THERE AND ACT COLD, LIKE YOU NORMALLY DO!
PLEASE, HYO-BIN! HELP ME OUT THIS ONCE! I NEVER GET ASKED OUT ON DATES! **NEVER!**
Forget it.
I ALWAYS ACT COLD?

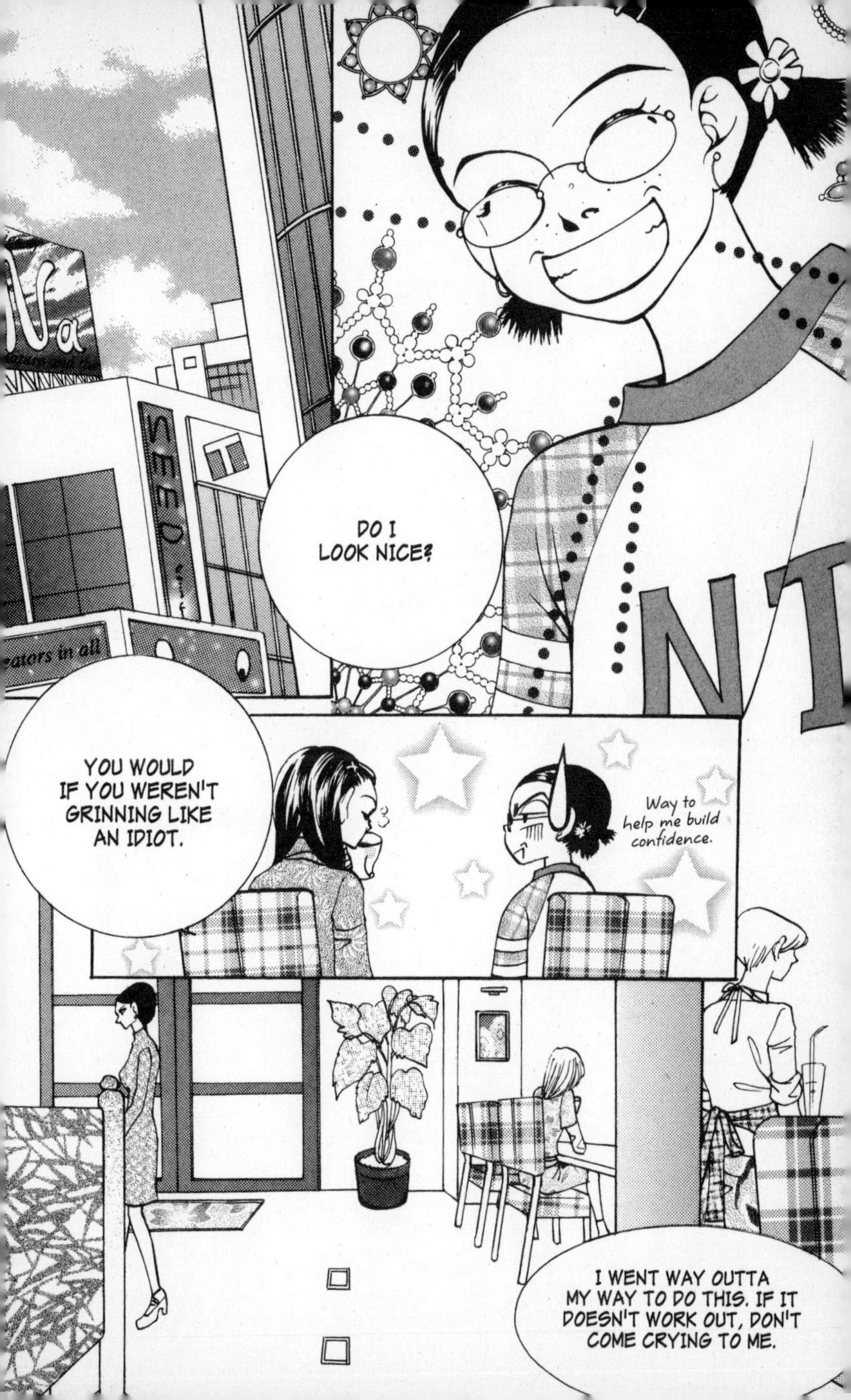
SEED
DO I LOOK NICE?
YOU WOULD IF YOU WEREN'T GRINNING LIKE AN IDIOT.
Way to help me build confidence.
I WENT WAY OUTTA MY WAY TO DO THIS. IF IT DOESN'T WORK OUT, DON'T COME CRYING TO ME.

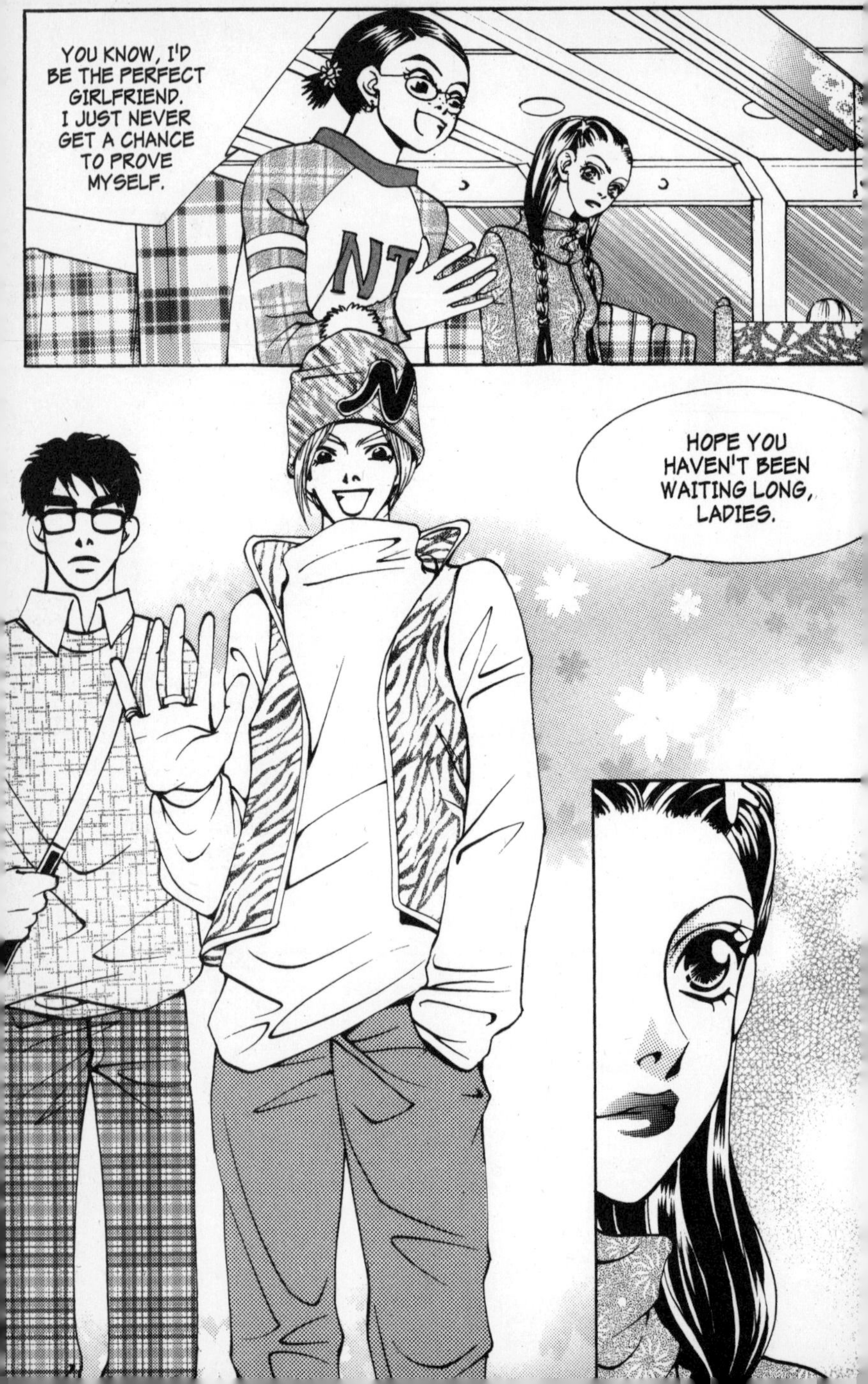
YOU KNOW, I'D BE THE PERFECT GIRLFRIEND. I JUST NEVER GET A CHANCE TO PROVE MYSELF.
HOPE YOU HAVEN'T BEEN WAITING LONG, LADIES.

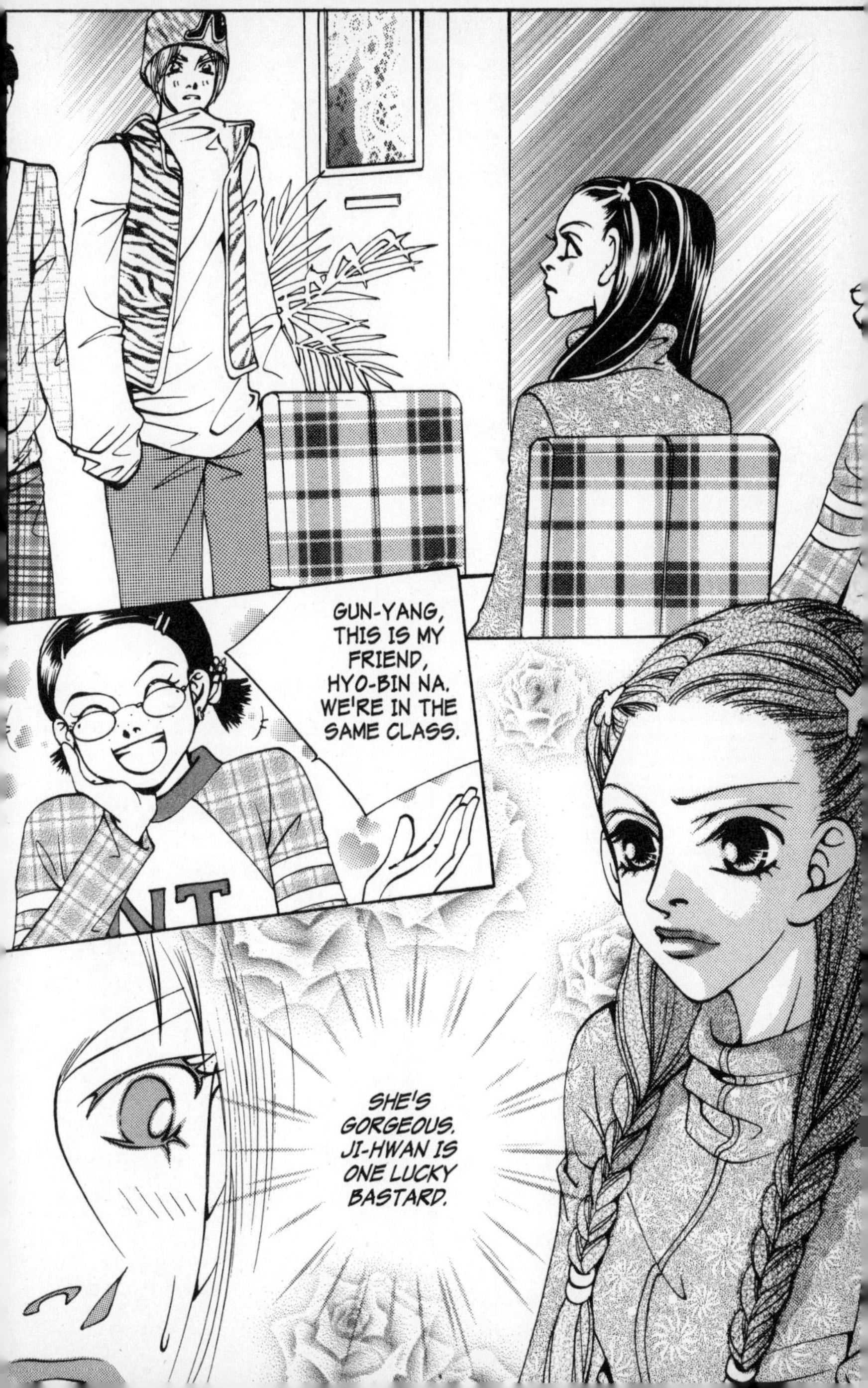
GUN-YANG, THIS IS MY FRIEND, HYO-BIN NA. WE'RE IN THE SAME CLASS.
SHE'S GORGEOUS. JI-HWAN IS ONE LUCKY BASTARD.

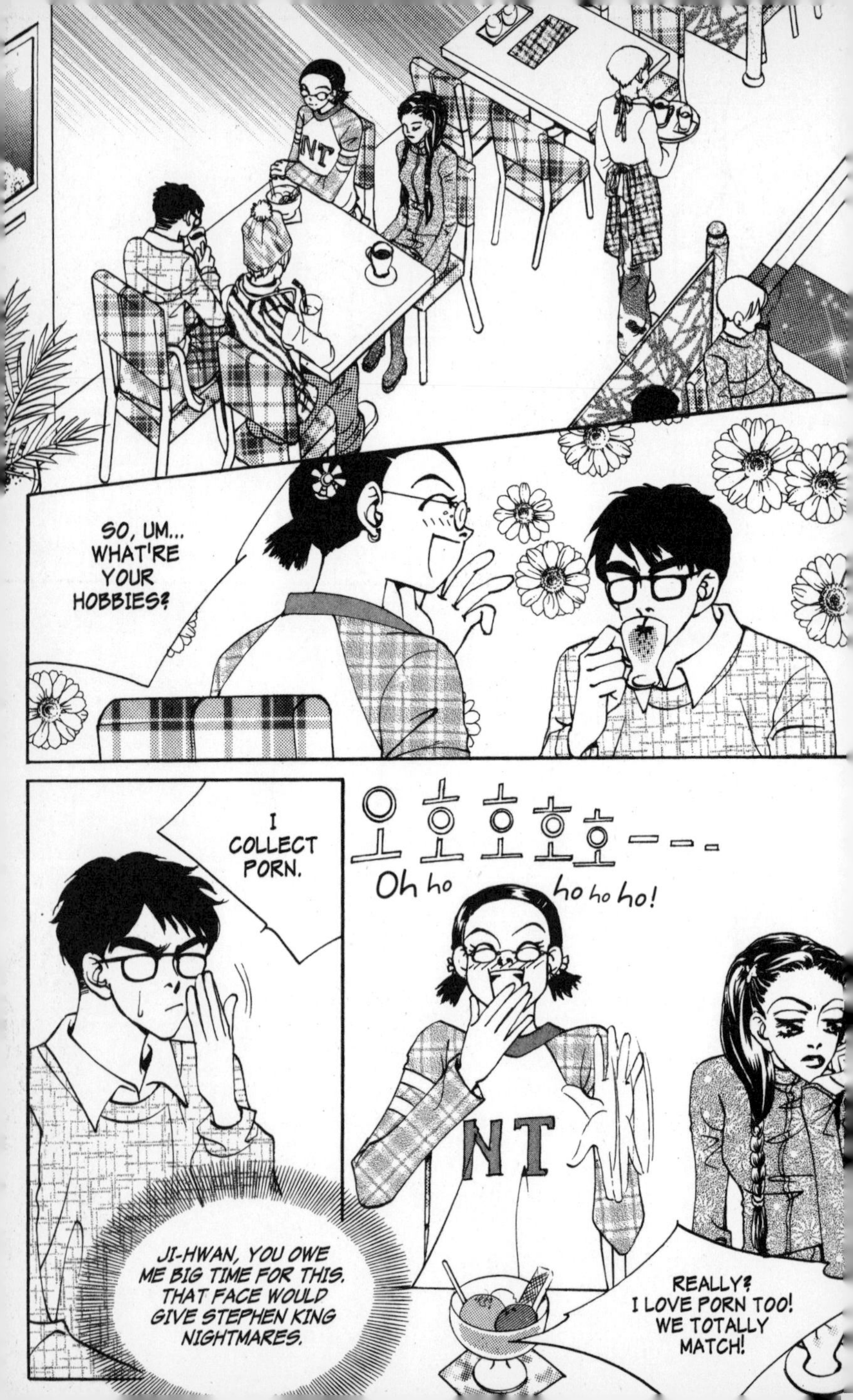
SO, UM... WHAT'RE YOUR HOBBIES?
I COLLECT PORN.
JI-HWAN, YOU OWE ME BIG TIME FOR THIS. THAT FACE WOULD GIVE STEPHEN KING NIGHTMARES.
오호호호호
Oh ho ho ho ho!
REALLY? I LOVE PORN TOO! WE TOTALLY MATCH!

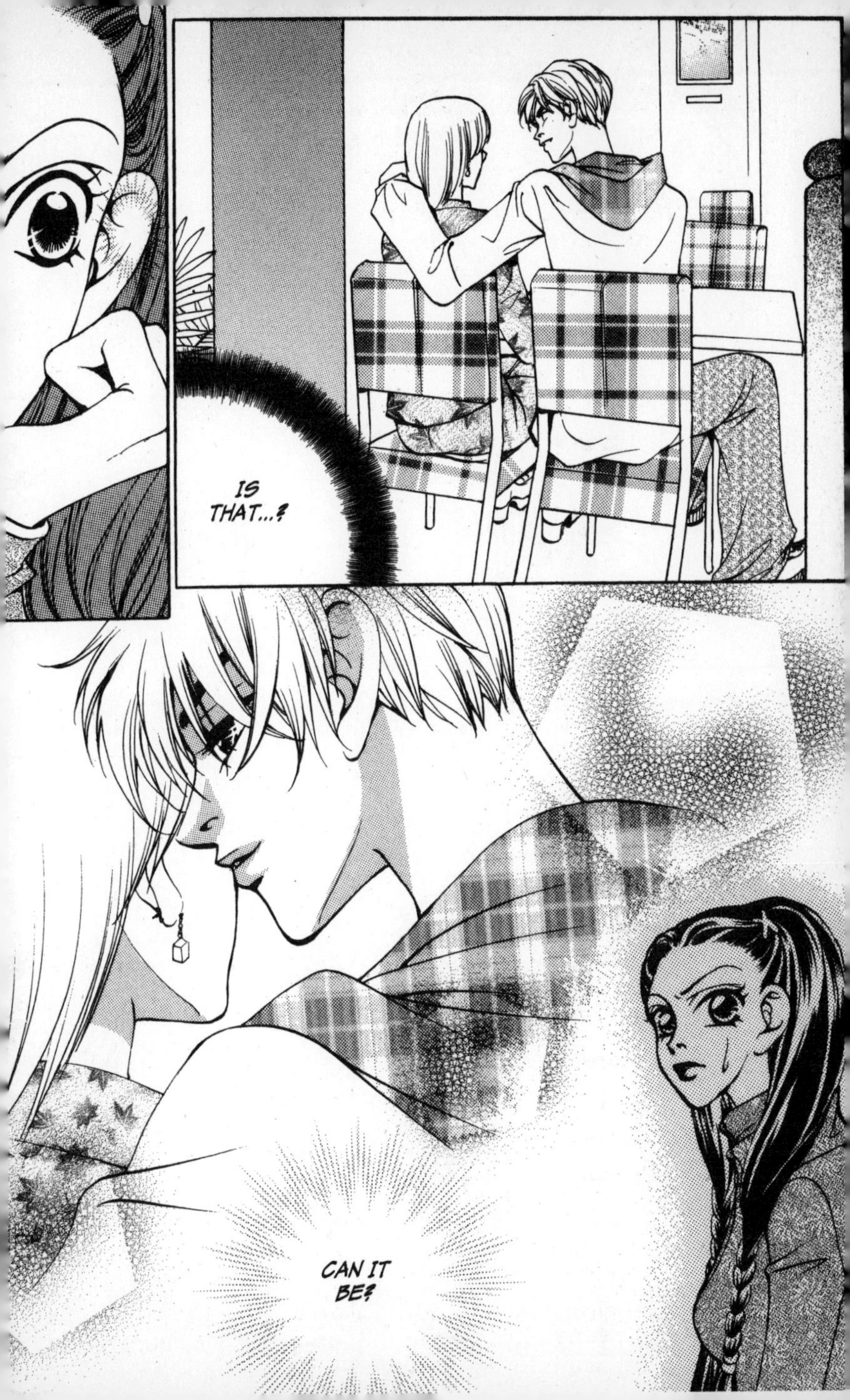
IS THAT...?
CAN IT BE?

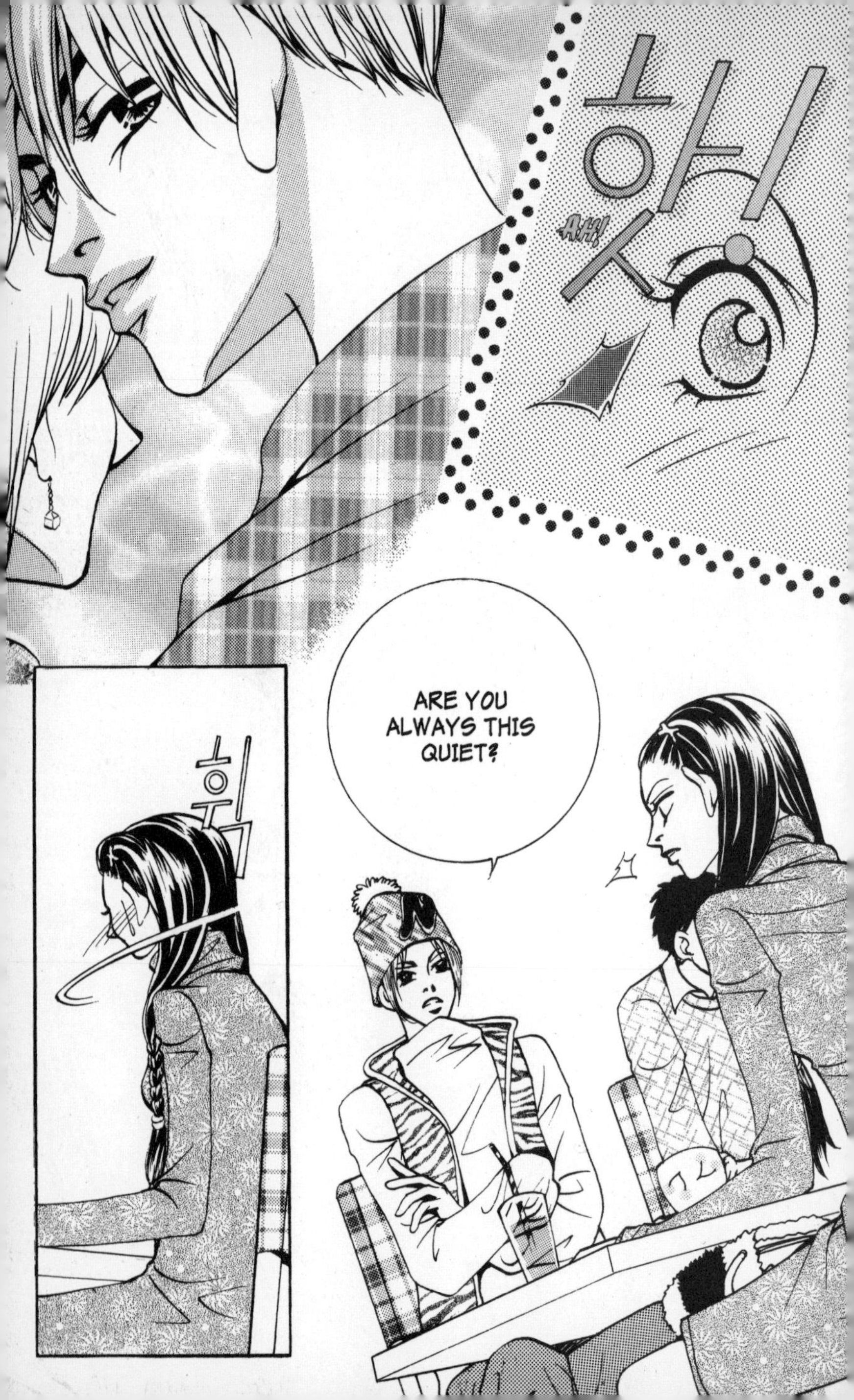
AH!
ARE YOU ALWAYS THIS QUIET?

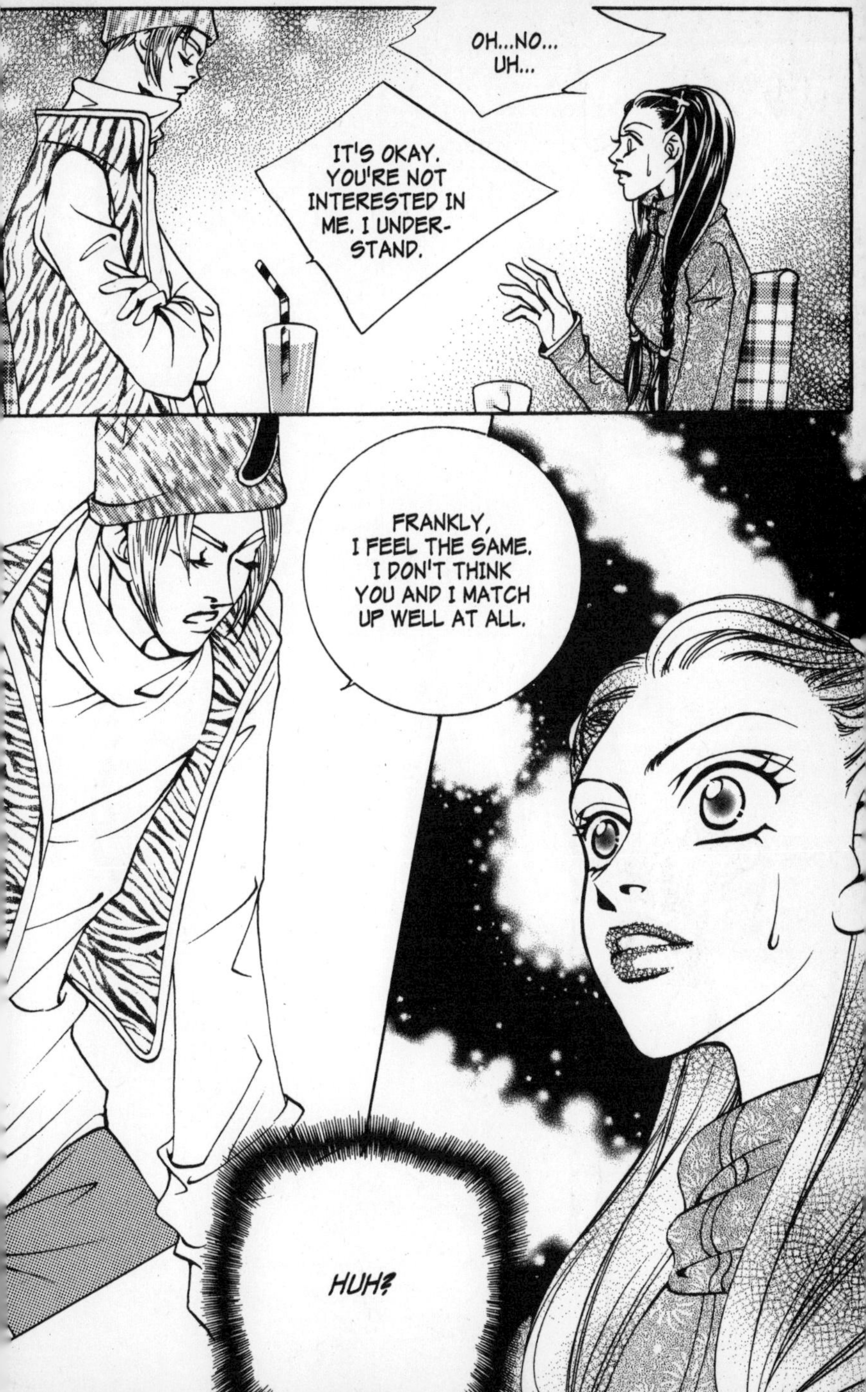
OH...NO... UH...
IT'S OKAY. YOU'RE NOT INTERESTED IN ME. I UNDER-STAND.
FRANKLY, I FEEL THE SAME. I DON'T THINK YOU AND I MATCH UP WELL AT ALL.
HUH?

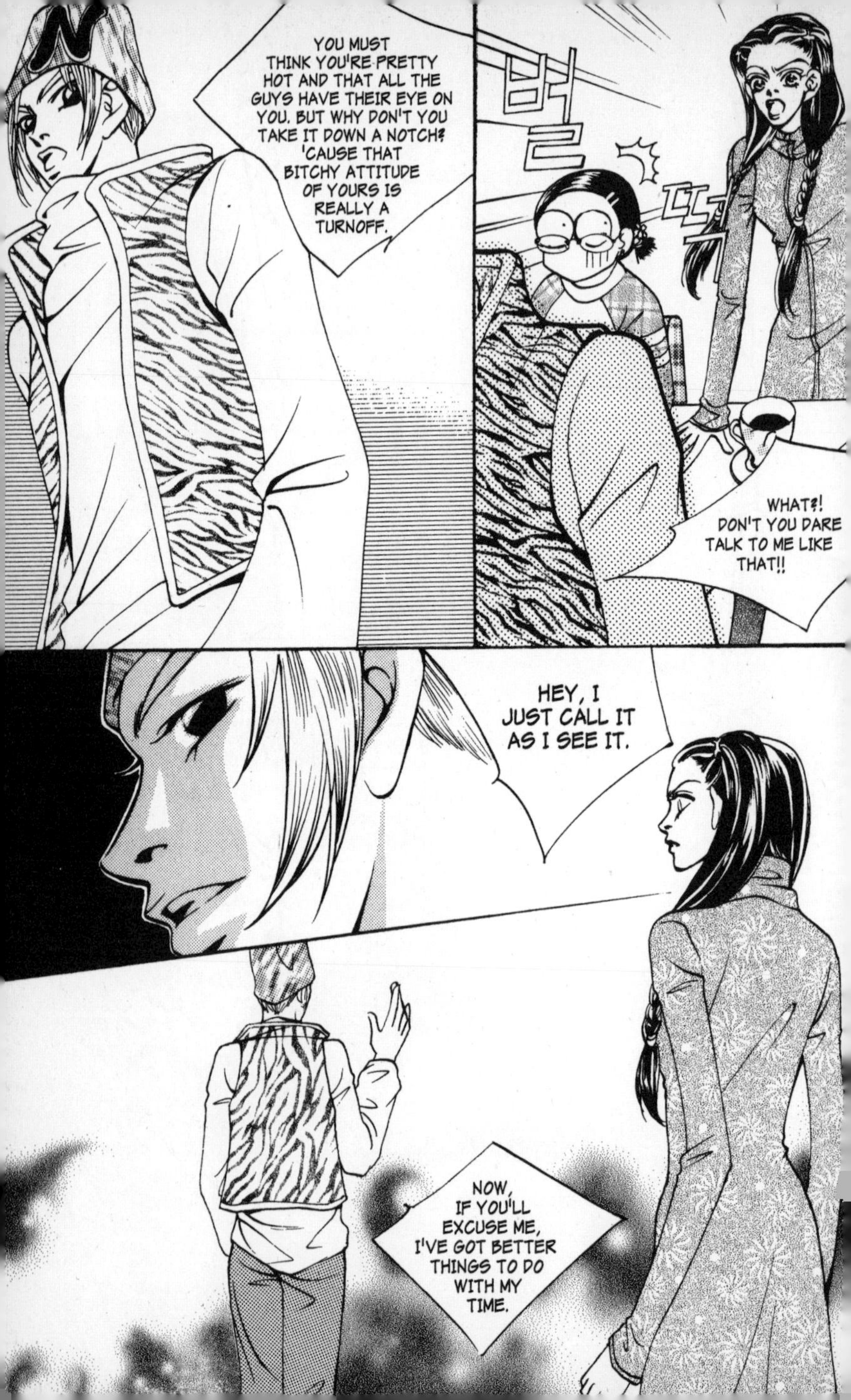
YOU MUST THINK YOU'RE PRETTY HOT AND THAT ALL THE GUYS HAVE THEIR EYE ON YOU. BUT WHY DON'T YOU TAKE IT DOWN A NOTCH? 'CAUSE THAT BITCHY ATTITUDE OF YOURS IS REALLY A TURNOFF.
벌떡
WHAT?! DON'T YOU DARE TALK TO ME LIKE THAT!!
HEY, I JUST CALL IT AS I SEE IT.
NOW, IF YOU'LL EXCUSE ME, I'VE GOT BETTER THINGS TO DO WITH MY TIME.

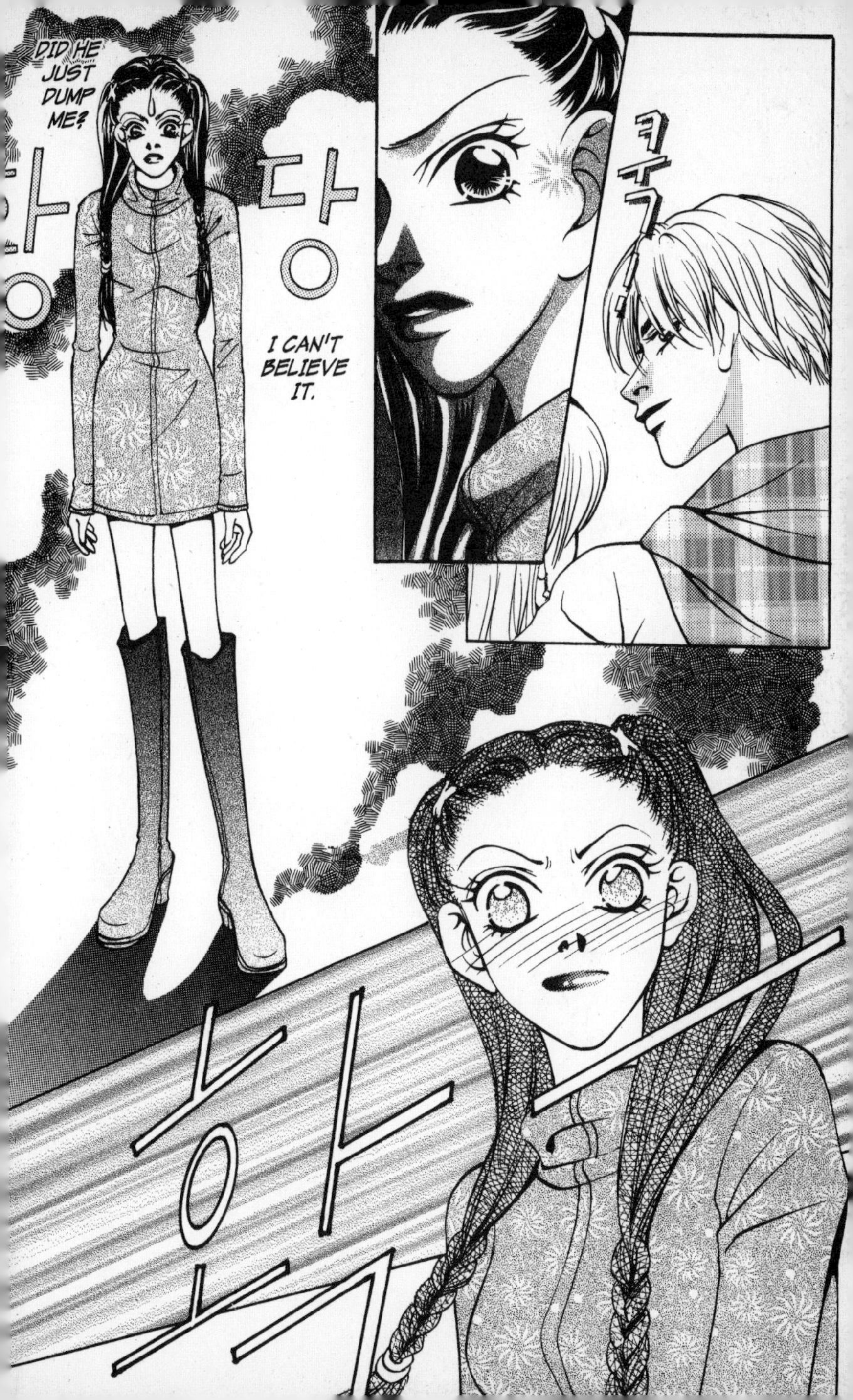
DID HE JUST DUMP ME?
I CAN'T BELIEVE IT.

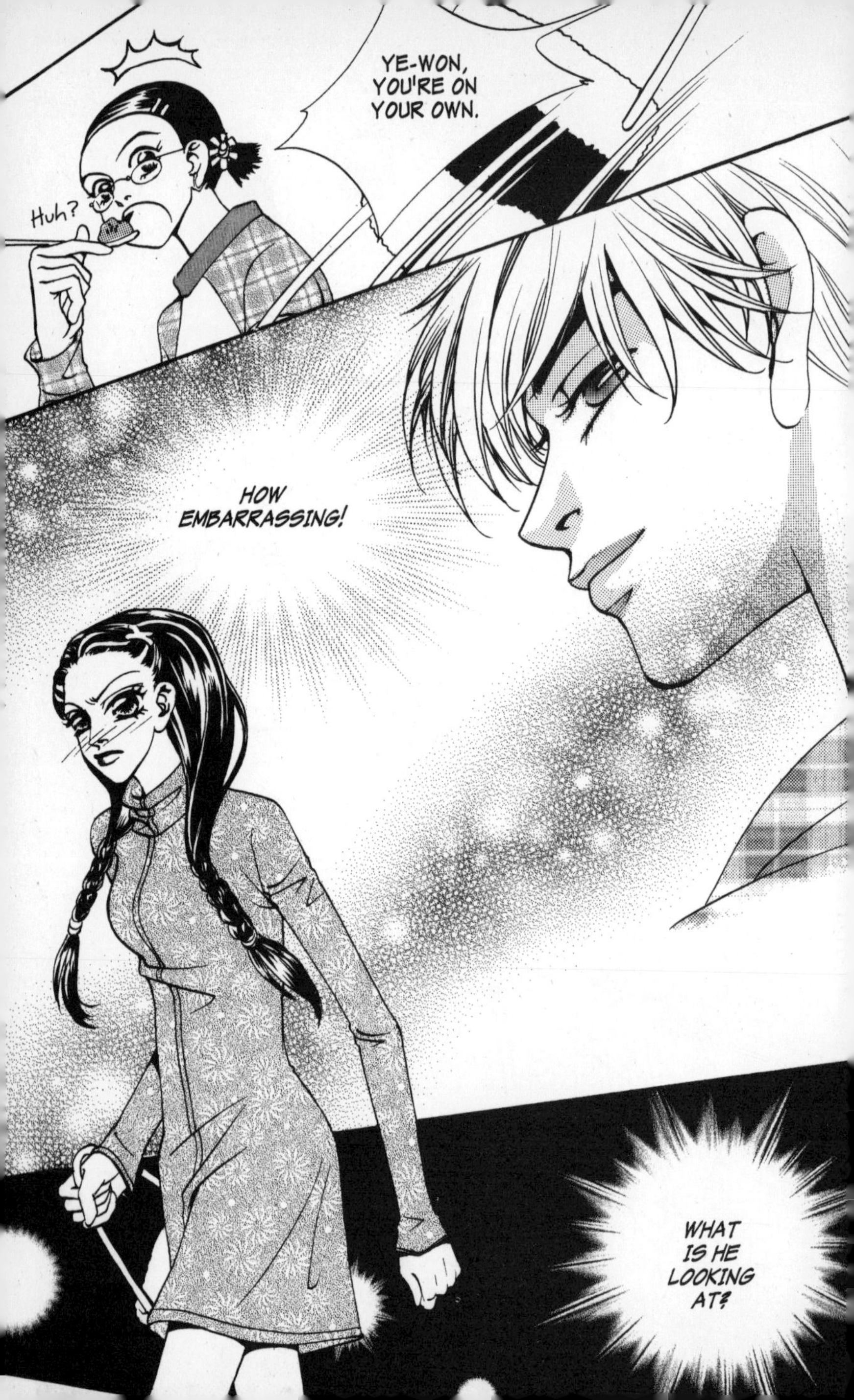
Huh?
YE-WON, YOU'RE ON YOUR OWN.
HOW EMBARRASSING!
WHAT IS HE LOOKING AT?

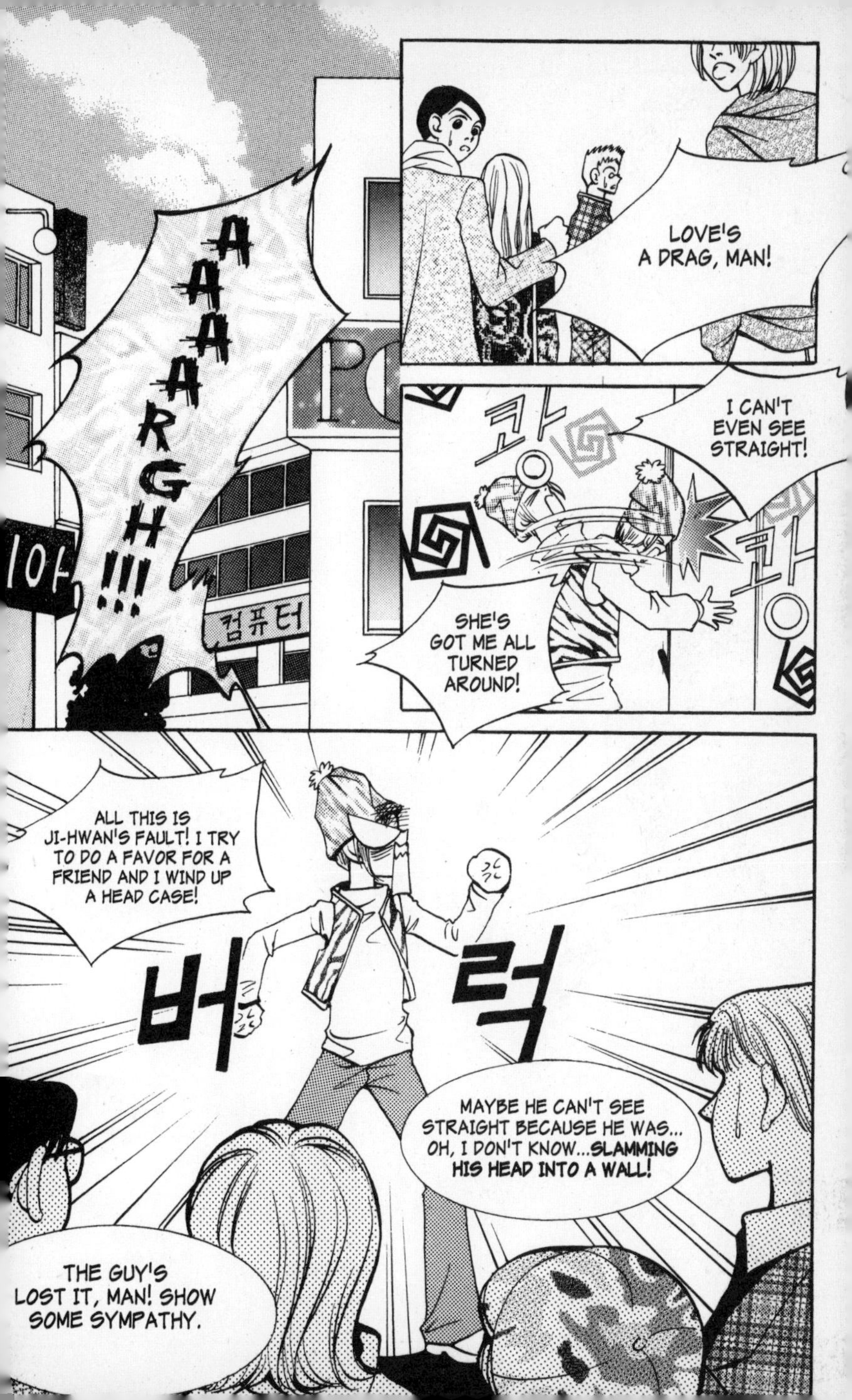

AAAARGH!!!
컴퓨터
LOVE'S A DRAG, MAN!
쾅
I CAN'T EVEN SEE STRAIGHT!
쾅
SHE'S GOT ME ALL TURNED AROUND!
ALL THIS IS JI-HWAN'S FAULT! I TRY TO DO A FAVOR FOR A FRIEND AND I WIND UP A HEAD CASE!
버럭
MAYBE HE CAN'T SEE STRAIGHT BECAUSE HE WAS... OH, I DON'T KNOW...**SLAMMING HIS HEAD INTO A WALL!**
THE GUY'S LOST IT, MAN! SHOW SOME SYMPATHY.

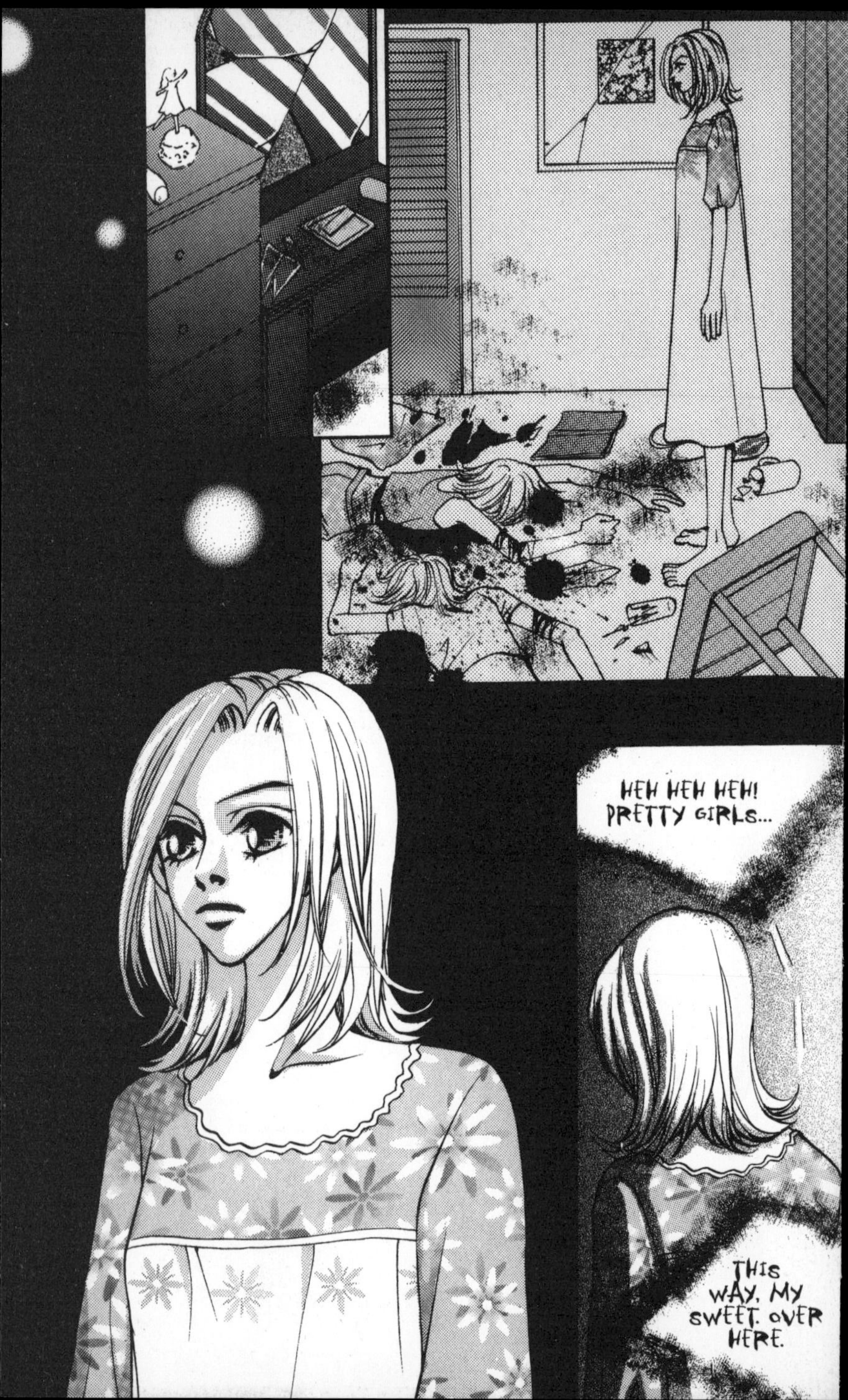
HEH HEH HEH! PRETTY GIRLS...
THIS WAY, MY SWEET. OVER HERE.

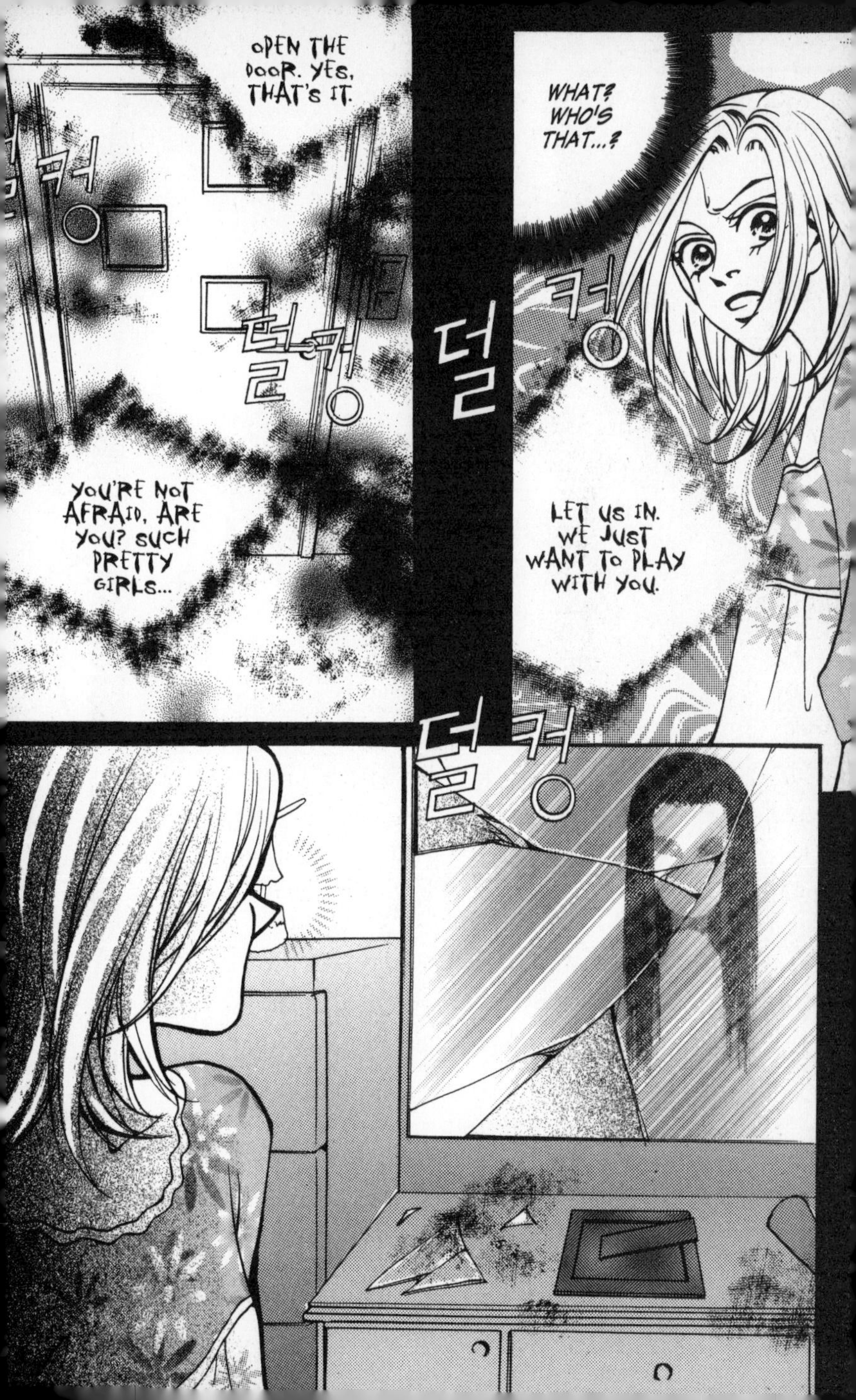
OPEN THE DOOR. YES, THAT'S IT.
덜컹
YOU'RE NOT AFRAID, ARE YOU? SUCH PRETTY GIRLS...
WHAT? WHO'S THAT...?
덜컹
덜컹
LET US IN. WE JUST WANT TO PLAY WITH YOU.
덜컹

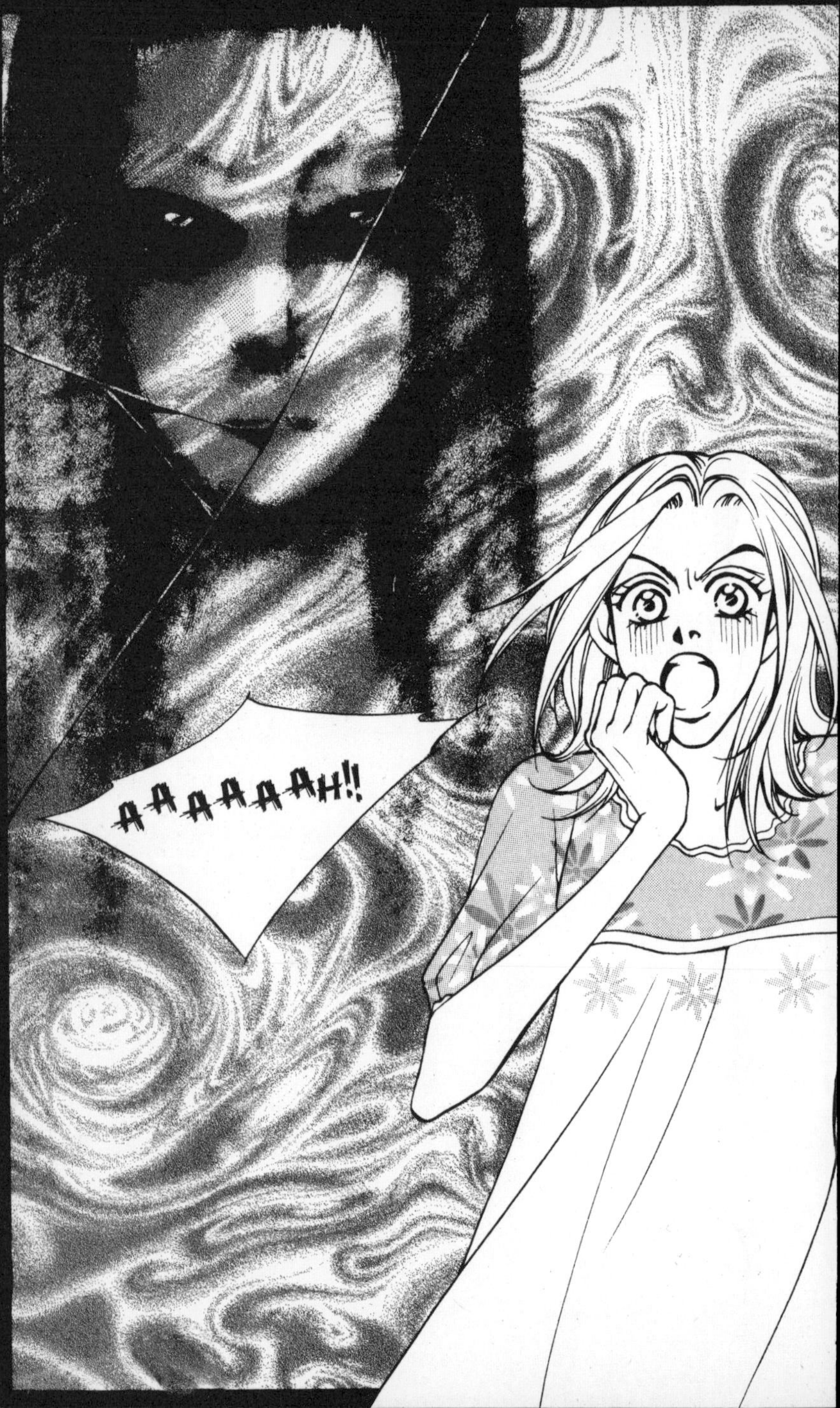
AAAAAAAH!!

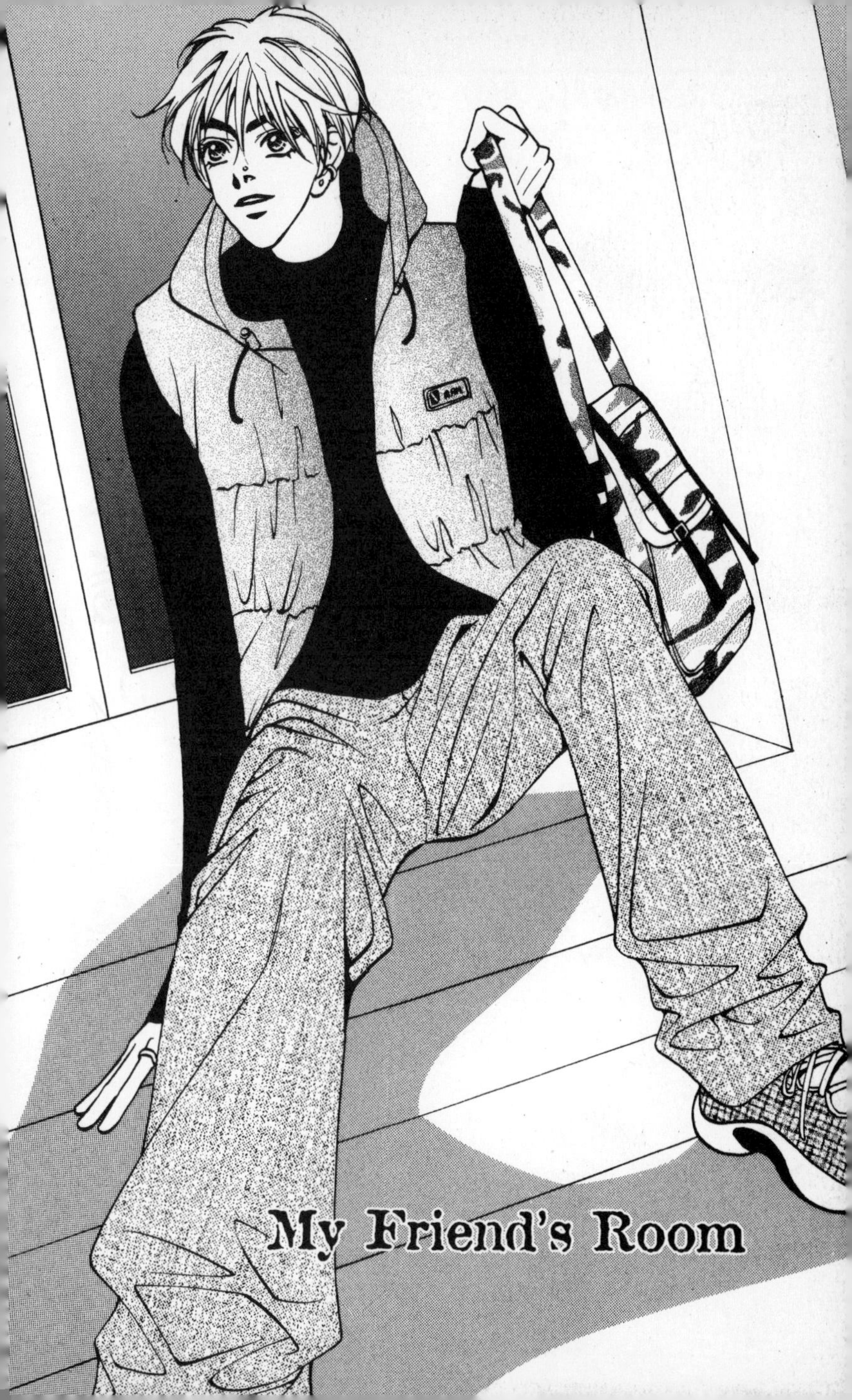

My Friend's Room

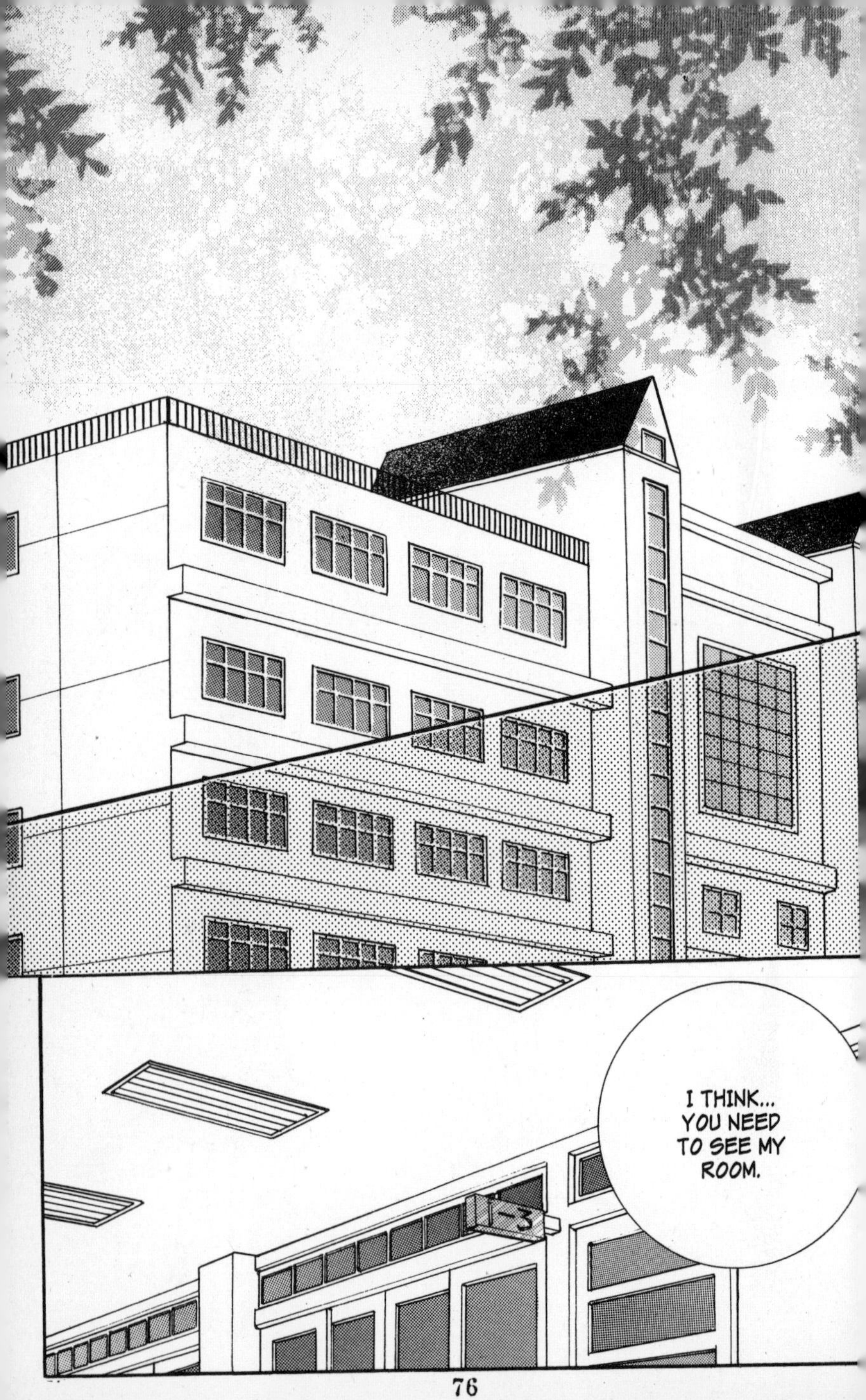
1-3
I THINK... YOU NEED TO SEE MY ROOM.

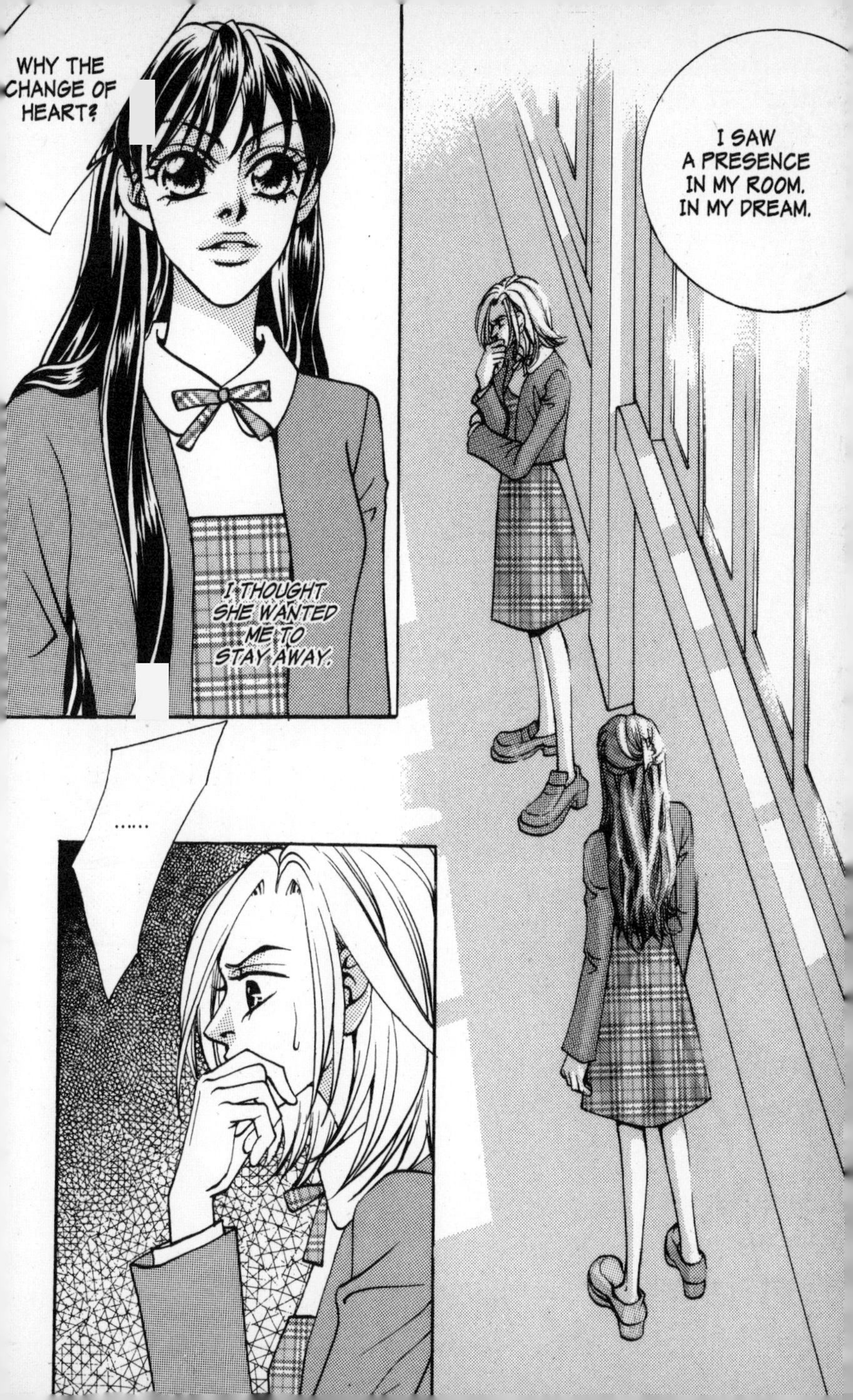
I SAW A PRESENCE IN MY ROOM. IN MY DREAM.
WHY THE CHANGE OF HEART?
I THOUGHT SHE WANTED ME TO STAY AWAY.
......

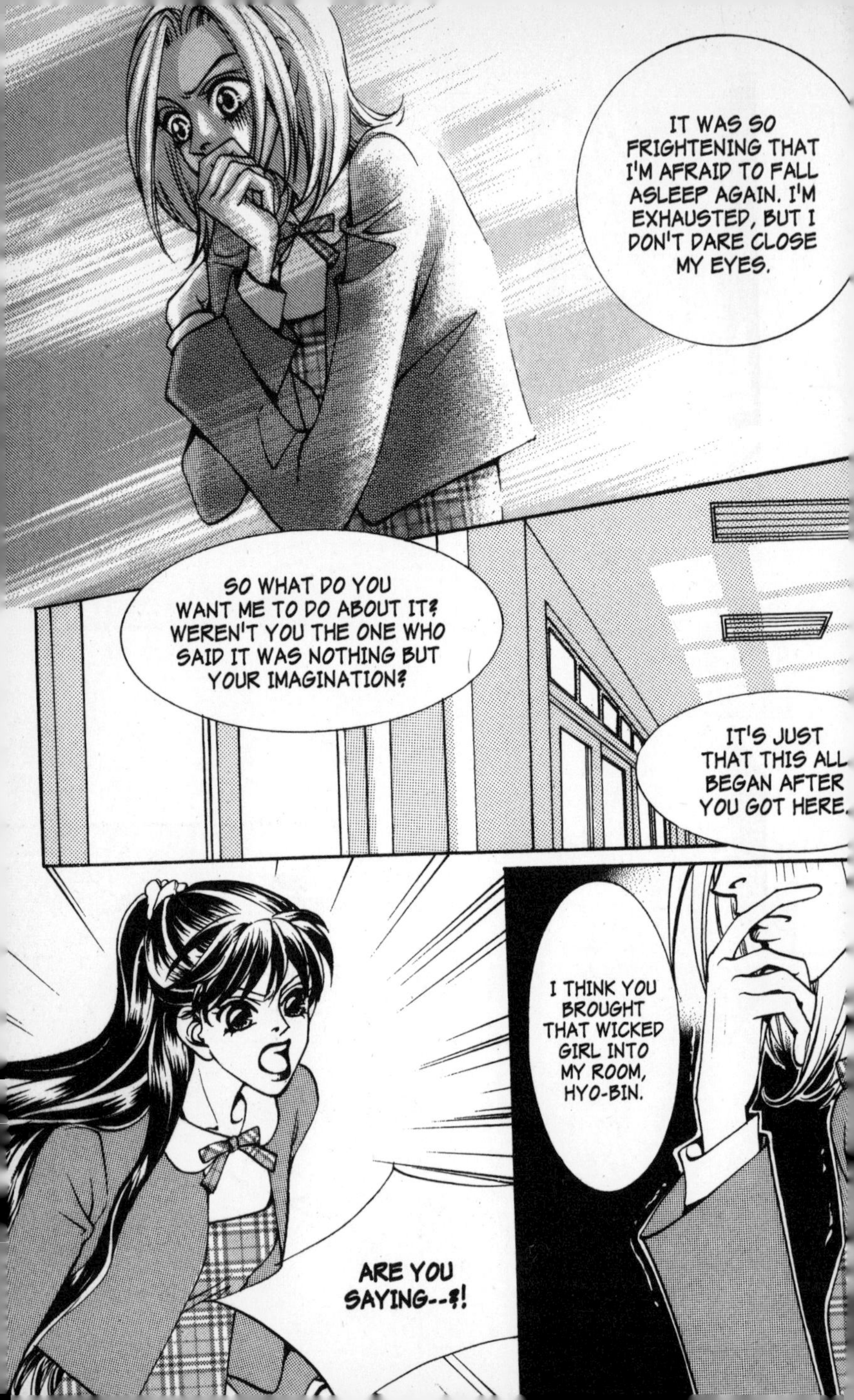
IT WAS SO FRIGHTENING THAT I'M AFRAID TO FALL ASLEEP AGAIN. I'M EXHAUSTED, BUT I DON'T DARE CLOSE MY EYES.
SO WHAT DO YOU WANT ME TO DO ABOUT IT? WEREN'T YOU THE ONE WHO SAID IT WAS NOTHING BUT YOUR IMAGINATION?
IT'S JUST THAT THIS ALL BEGAN AFTER YOU GOT HERE.
ARE YOU SAYING--?!
I THINK YOU BROUGHT THAT WICKED GIRL INTO MY ROOM, HYO-BIN.

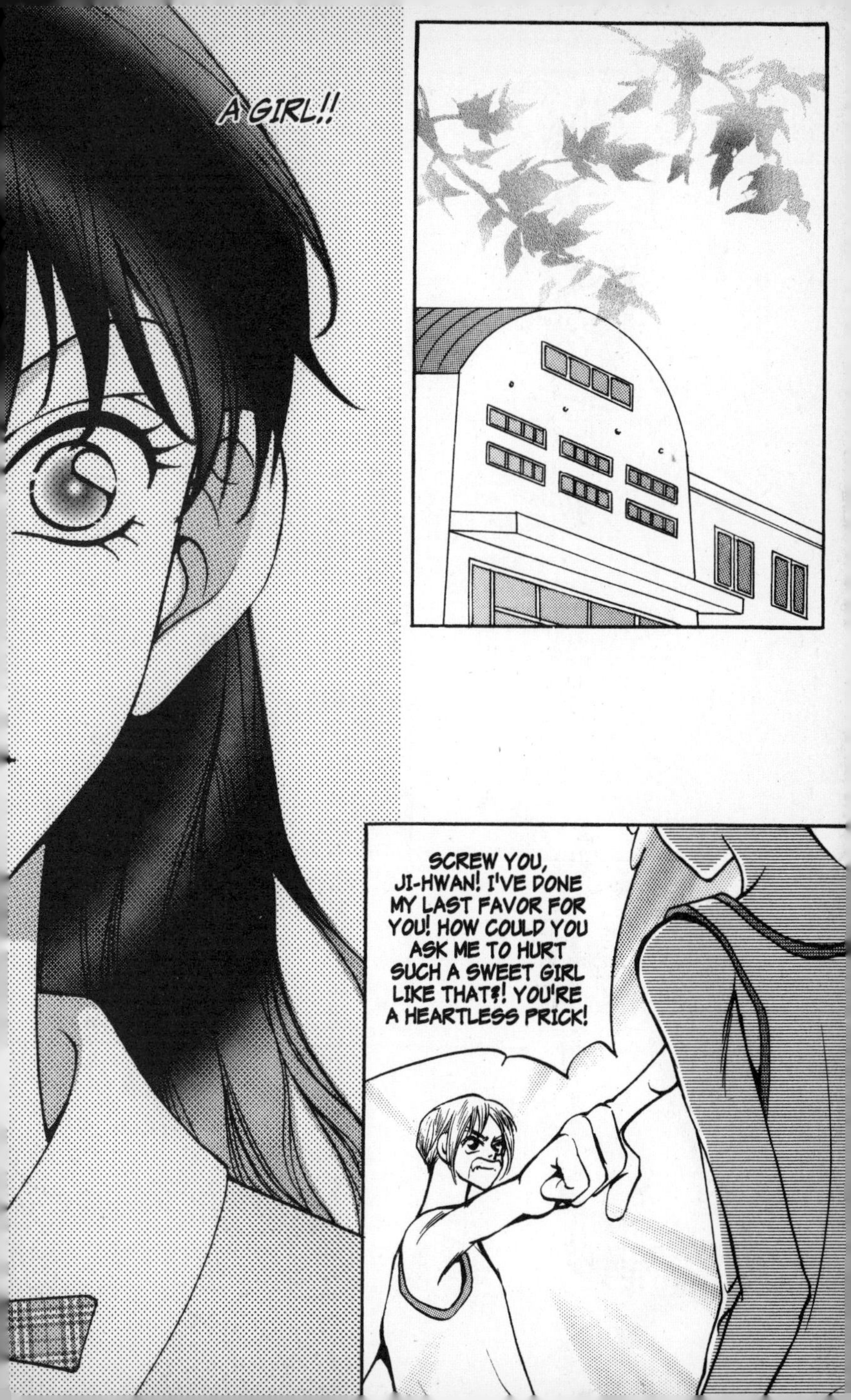
A GIRL!!
SCREW YOU, JI-HWAN! I'VE DONE MY LAST FAVOR FOR YOU! HOW COULD YOU ASK ME TO HURT SUCH A SWEET GIRL LIKE THAT?! YOU'RE A HEARTLESS PRICK!

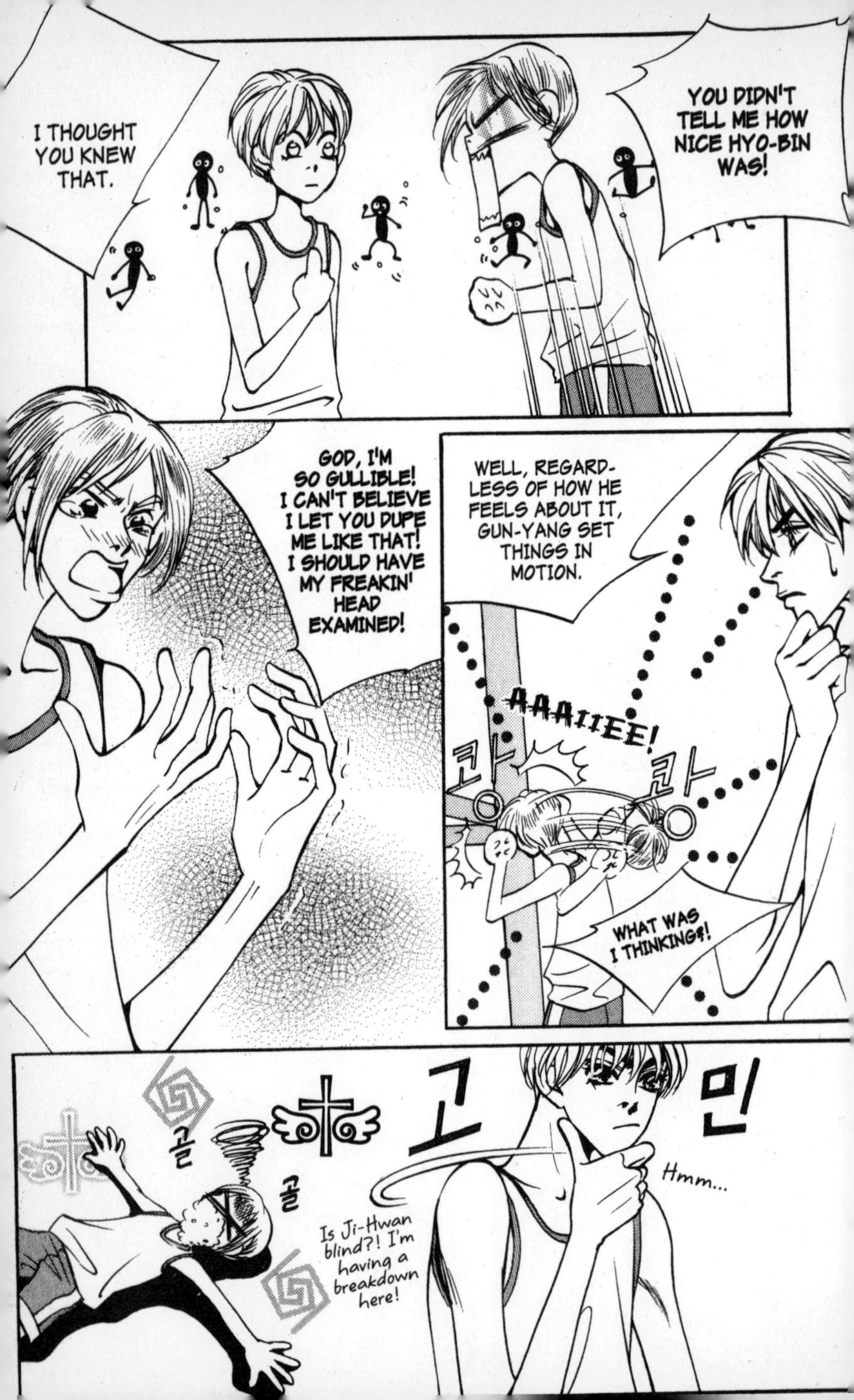

I THOUGHT YOU KNEW THAT.
YOU DIDN'T TELL ME HOW NICE HYO-BIN WAS!
GOD, I'M SO GULLIBLE! I CAN'T BELIEVE I LET YOU DUPE ME LIKE THAT! I SHOULD HAVE MY FREAKIN' HEAD EXAMINED!
WELL, REGARD-LESS OF HOW HE FEELS ABOUT IT, GUN-YANG SET THINGS IN MOTION.
AAAIIEEE!
콰
콰
WHAT WAS I THINKING?!
골
골
Is Ji-Hwan blind?! I'm having a breakdown here!
고민
Hmm...

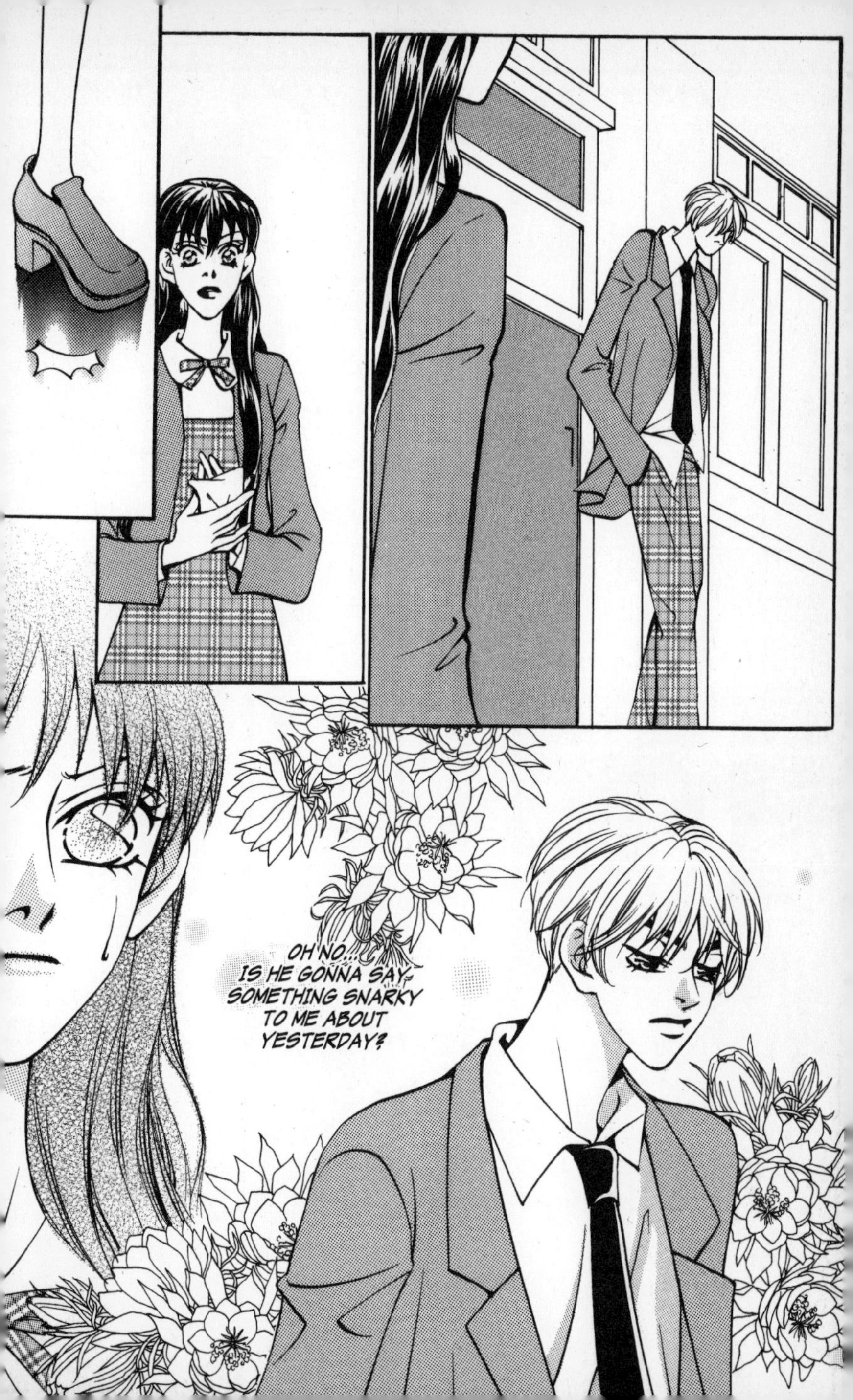
OH NO... IS HE GONNA SAY SOMETHING SNARKY TO ME ABOUT YESTERDAY?

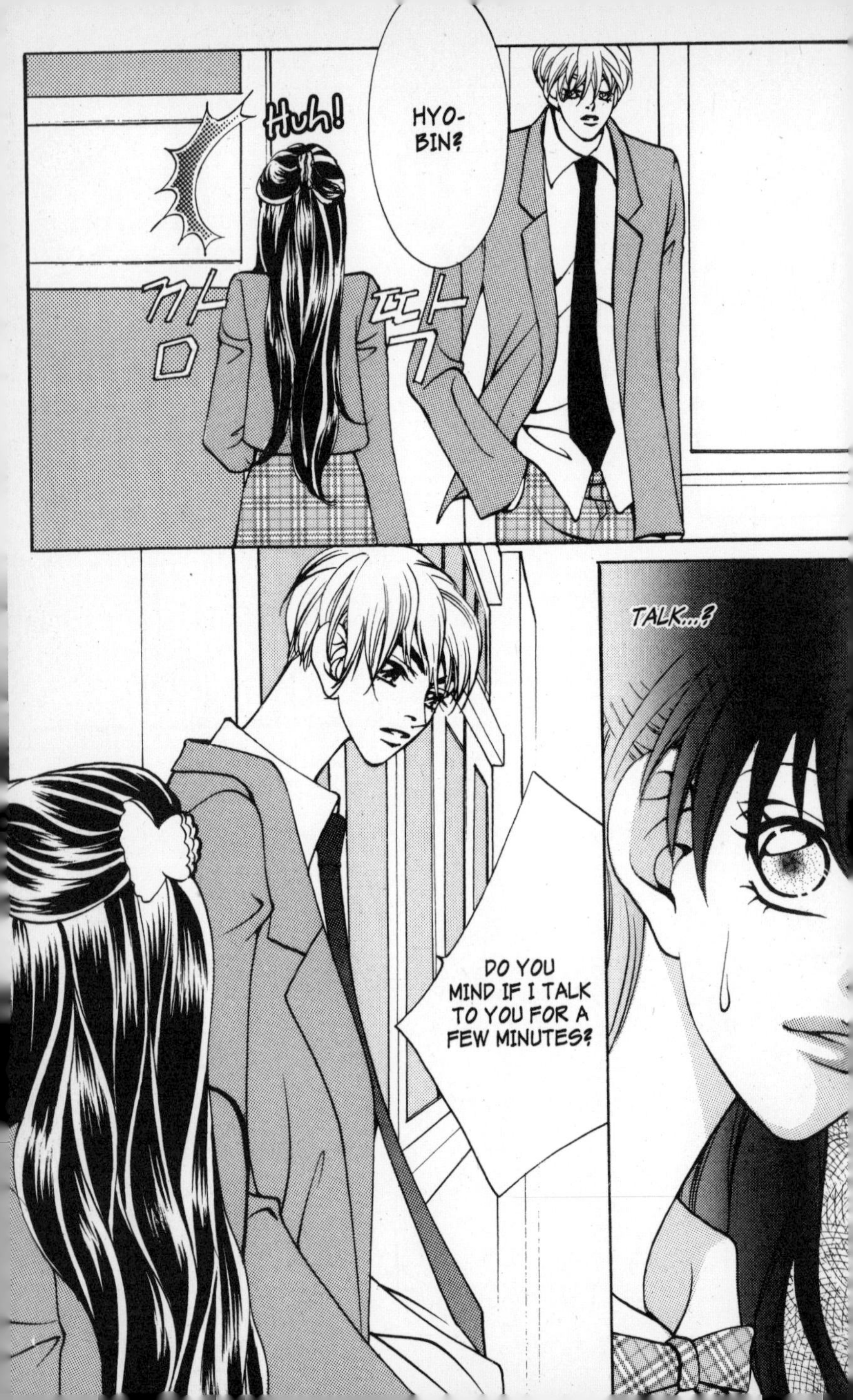
Huh!
HYO-BIN?
깜짝
DO YOU MIND IF I TALK TO YOU FOR A FEW MINUTES?
TALK...?

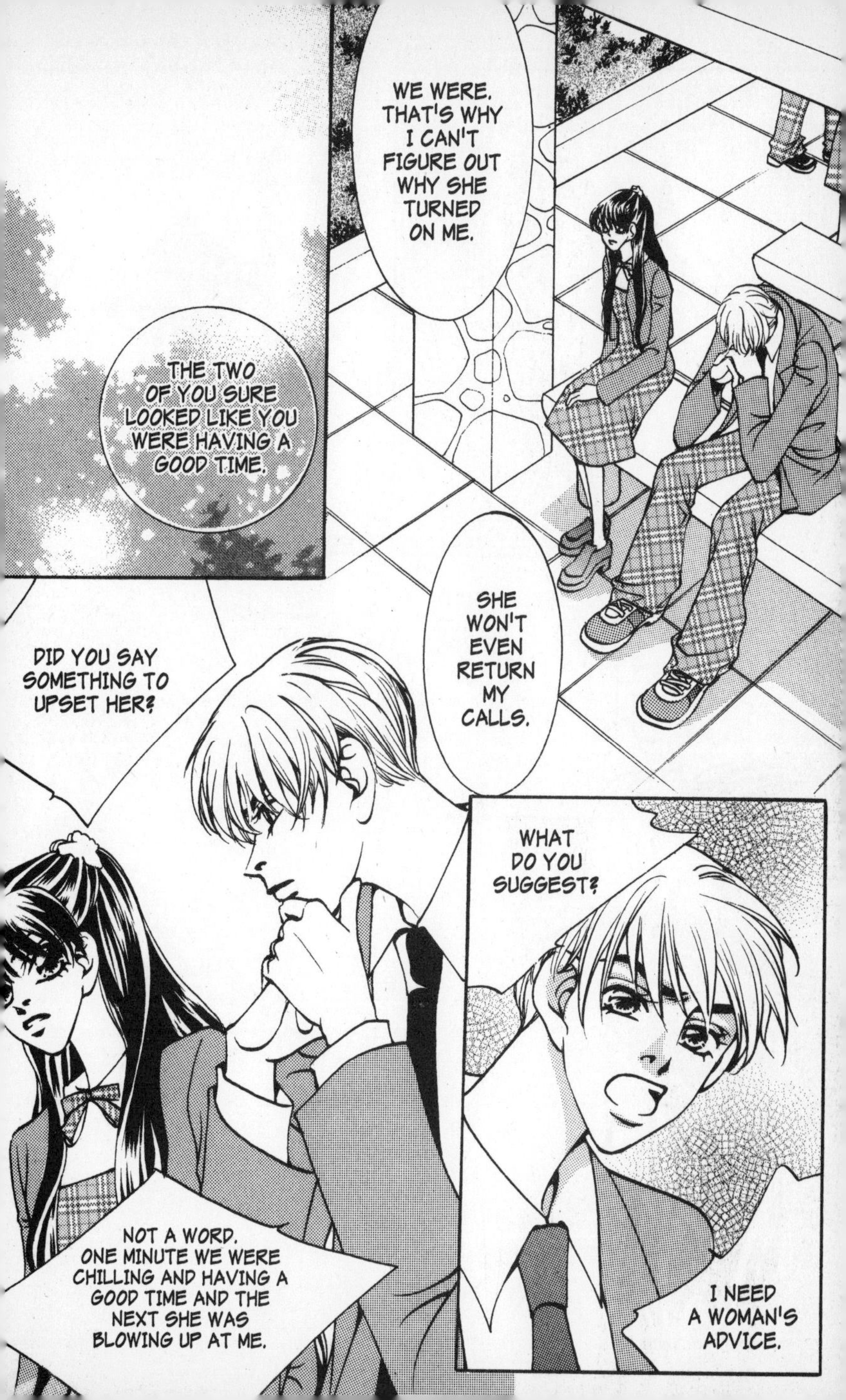
THE TWO OF YOU SURE LOOKED LIKE YOU WERE HAVING A GOOD TIME.
WE WERE. THAT'S WHY I CAN'T FIGURE OUT WHY SHE TURNED ON ME.
SHE WON'T EVEN RETURN MY CALLS.
DID YOU SAY SOMETHING TO UPSET HER?
NOT A WORD. ONE MINUTE WE WERE CHILLING AND HAVING A GOOD TIME AND THE NEXT SHE WAS BLOWING UP AT ME.
WHAT DO YOU SUGGEST?
I NEED A WOMAN'S ADVICE.

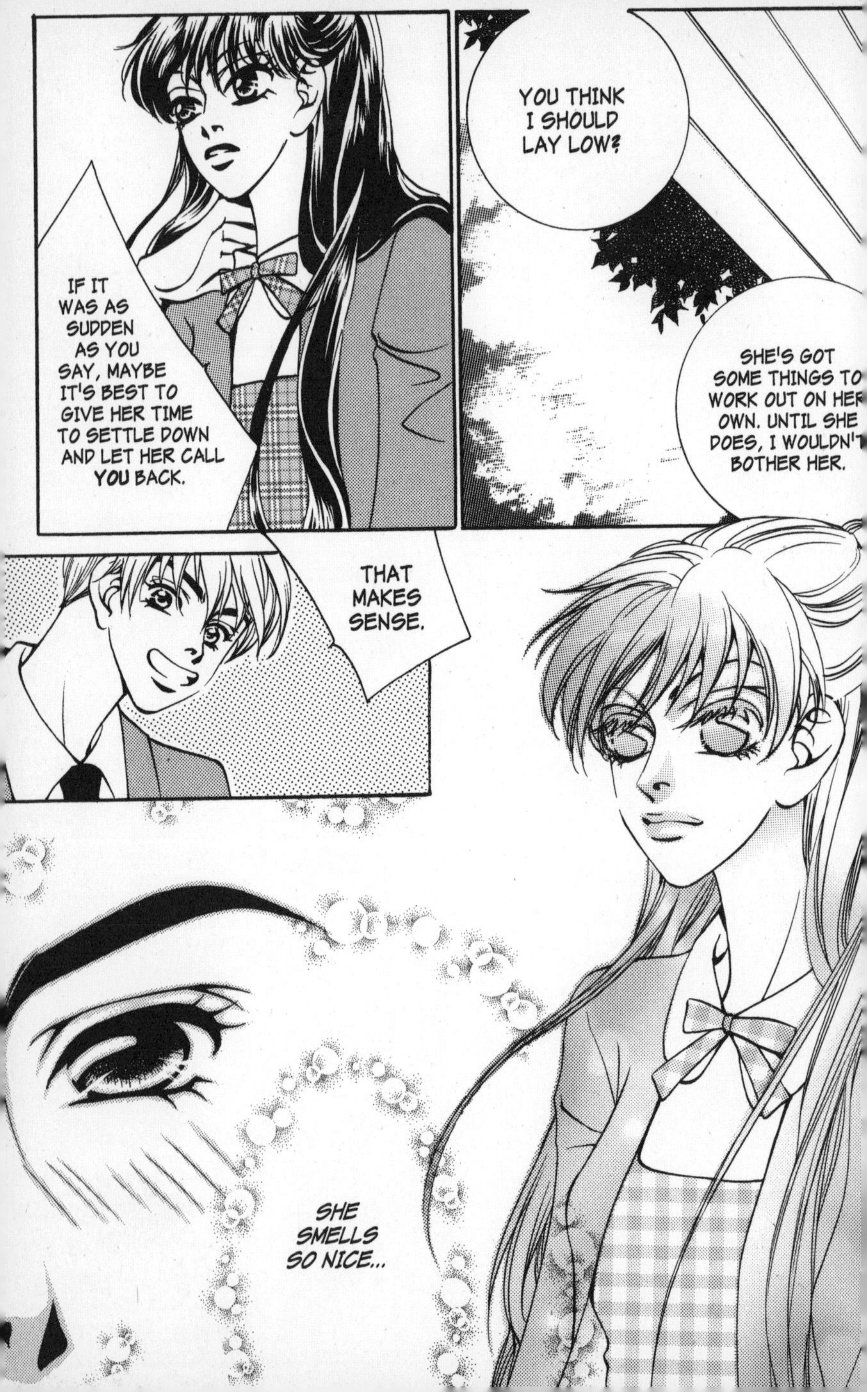
IF IT WAS AS SUDDEN AS YOU SAY, MAYBE IT'S BEST TO GIVE HER TIME TO SETTLE DOWN AND LET HER CALL YOU BACK.
YOU THINK I SHOULD LAY LOW?
SHE'S GOT SOME THINGS TO WORK OUT ON HER OWN. UNTIL SHE DOES, I WOULDN'T BOTHER HER.
THAT MAKES SENSE.
SHE SMELLS SO NICE...

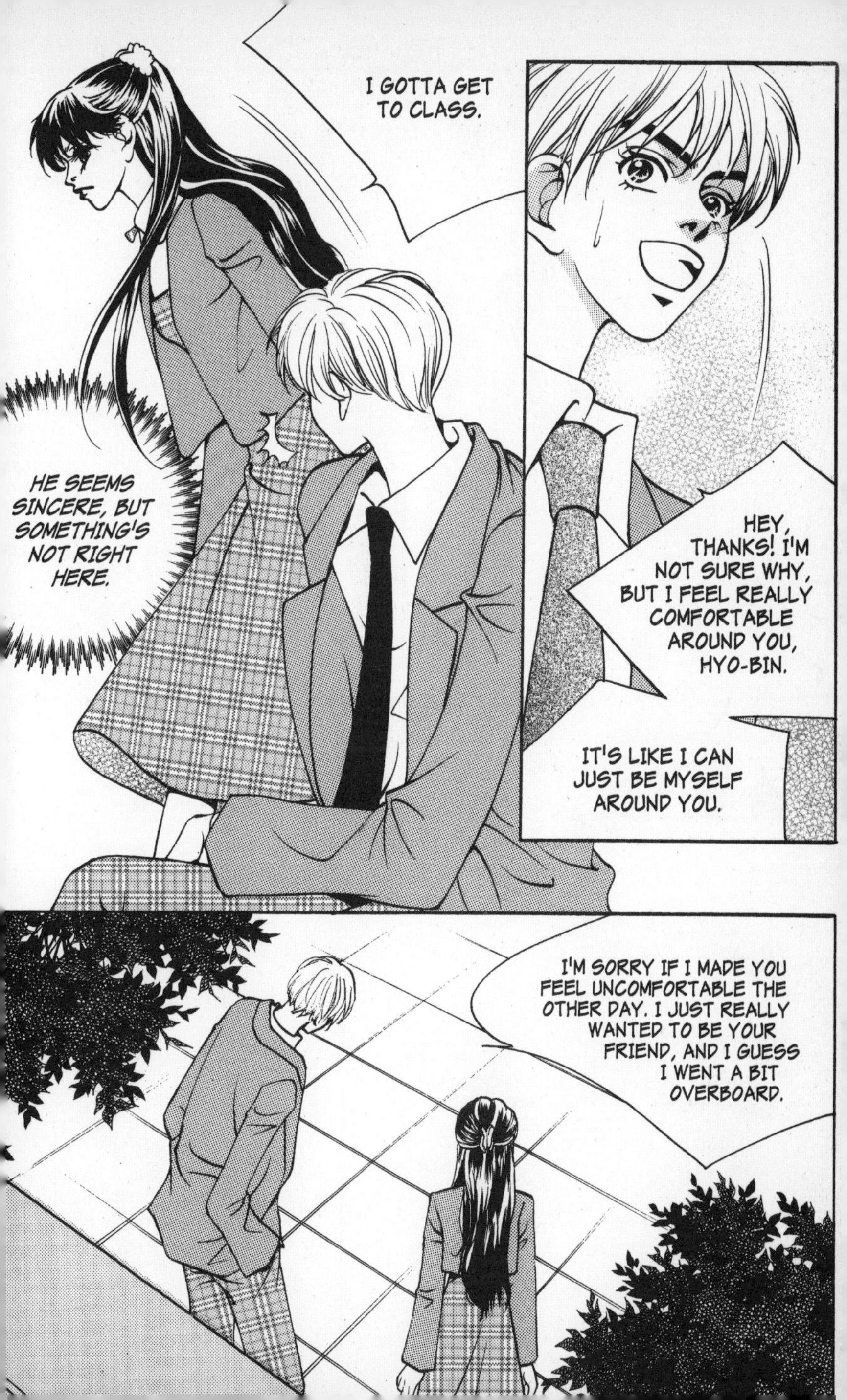
I GOTTA GET TO CLASS.
HE SEEMS SINCERE, BUT SOMETHING'S NOT RIGHT HERE.
HEY, THANKS! I'M NOT SURE WHY, BUT I FEEL REALLY COMFORTABLE AROUND YOU, HYO-BIN.
IT'S LIKE I CAN JUST BE MYSELF AROUND YOU.
I'M SORRY IF I MADE YOU FEEL UNCOMFORTABLE THE OTHER DAY. I JUST REALLY WANTED TO BE YOUR FRIEND, AND I GUESS I WENT A BIT OVERBOARD.

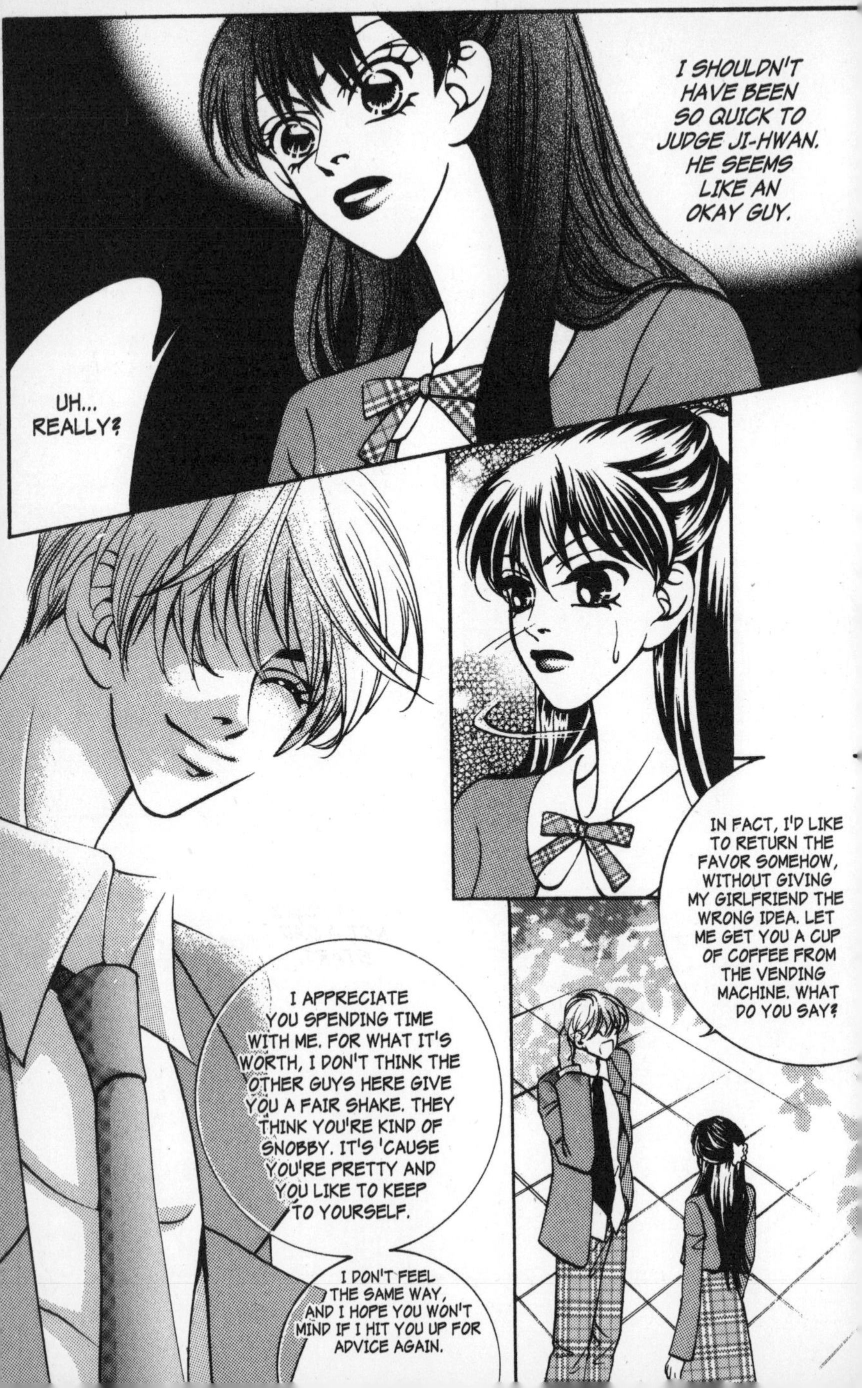
I SHOULDN'T HAVE BEEN SO QUICK TO JUDGE JI-HWAN. HE SEEMS LIKE AN OKAY GUY.
UH... REALLY?
I APPRECIATE YOU SPENDING TIME WITH ME. FOR WHAT IT'S WORTH, I DON'T THINK THE OTHER GUYS HERE GIVE YOU A FAIR SHAKE. THEY THINK YOU'RE KIND OF SNOBBY. IT'S 'CAUSE YOU'RE PRETTY AND YOU LIKE TO KEEP TO YOURSELF.
I DON'T FEEL THE SAME WAY, AND I HOPE YOU WON'T MIND IF I HIT YOU UP FOR ADVICE AGAIN.
IN FACT, I'D LIKE TO RETURN THE FAVOR SOMEHOW, WITHOUT GIVING MY GIRLFRIEND THE WRONG IDEA. LET ME GET YOU A CUP OF COFFEE FROM THE VENDING MACHINE. WHAT DO YOU SAY?

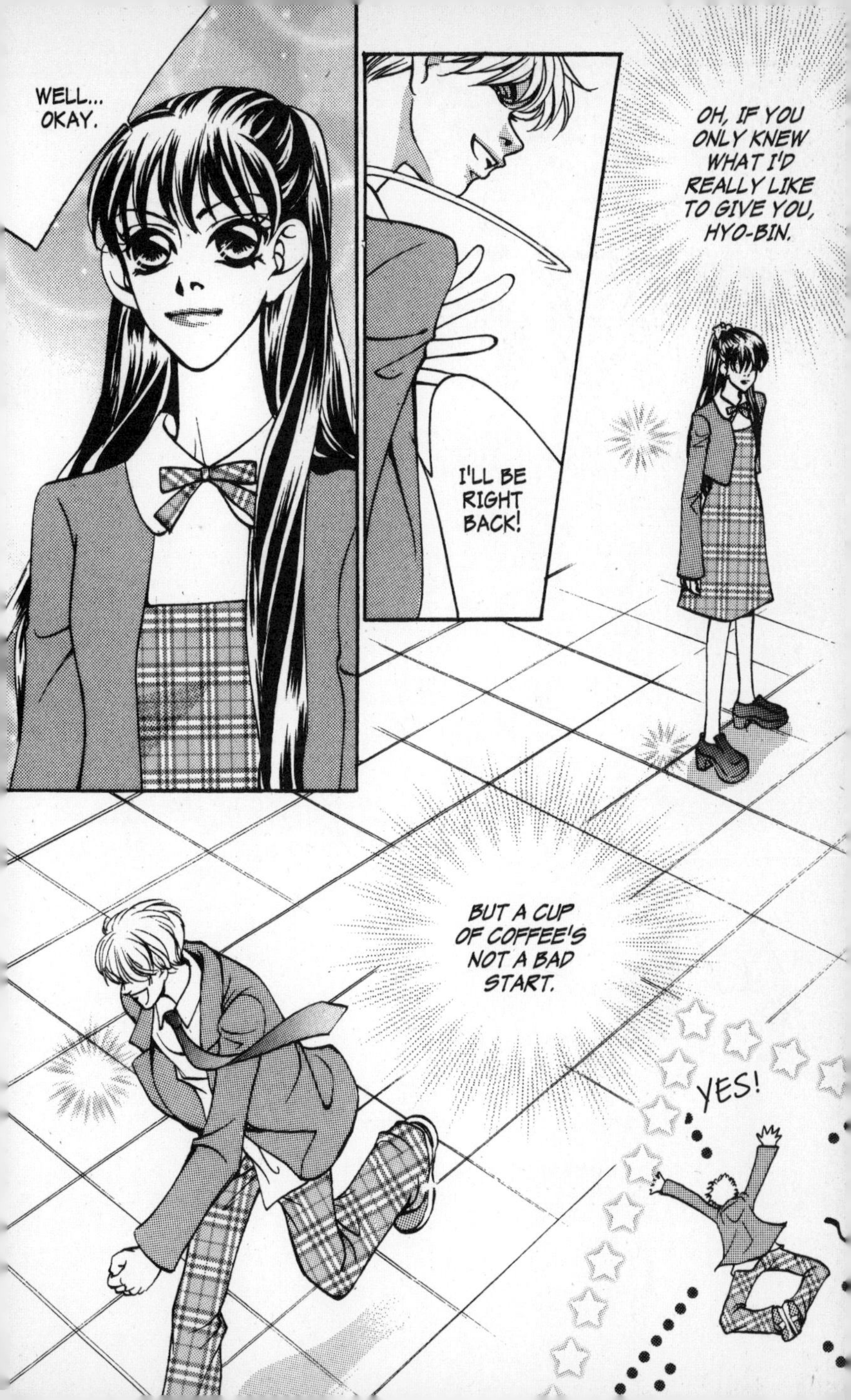
WELL... OKAY.
I'LL BE RIGHT BACK!
OH, IF YOU ONLY KNEW WHAT I'D REALLY LIKE TO GIVE YOU, HYO-BIN.
BUT A CUP OF COFFEE'S NOT A BAD START.
YES!

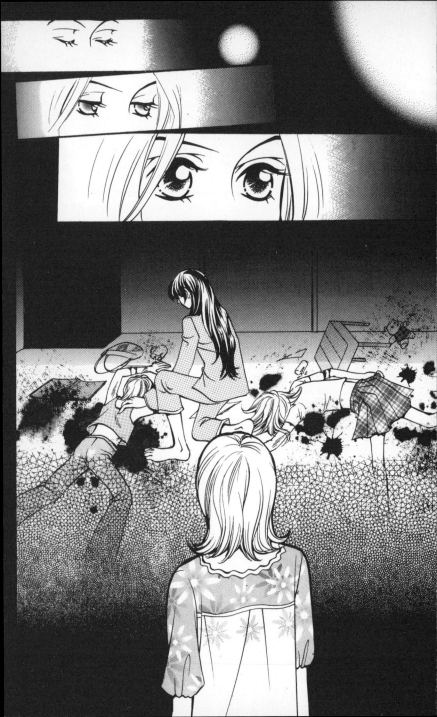

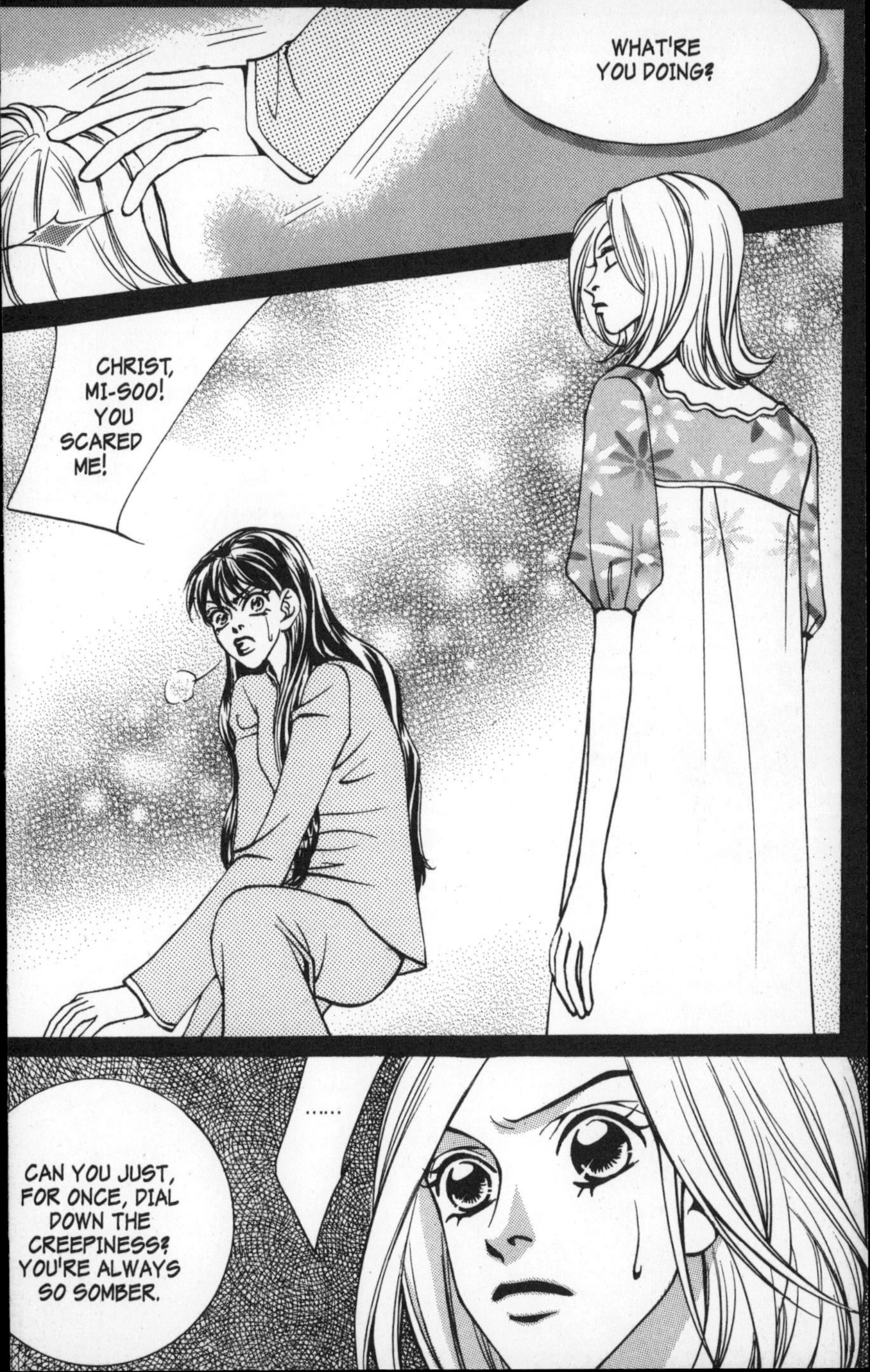
WHAT'RE YOU DOING?
CHRIST, MI-SOO! YOU SCARED ME!
CAN YOU JUST, FOR ONCE, DIAL DOWN THE CREEPINESS? YOU'RE ALWAYS SO SOMBER.
......

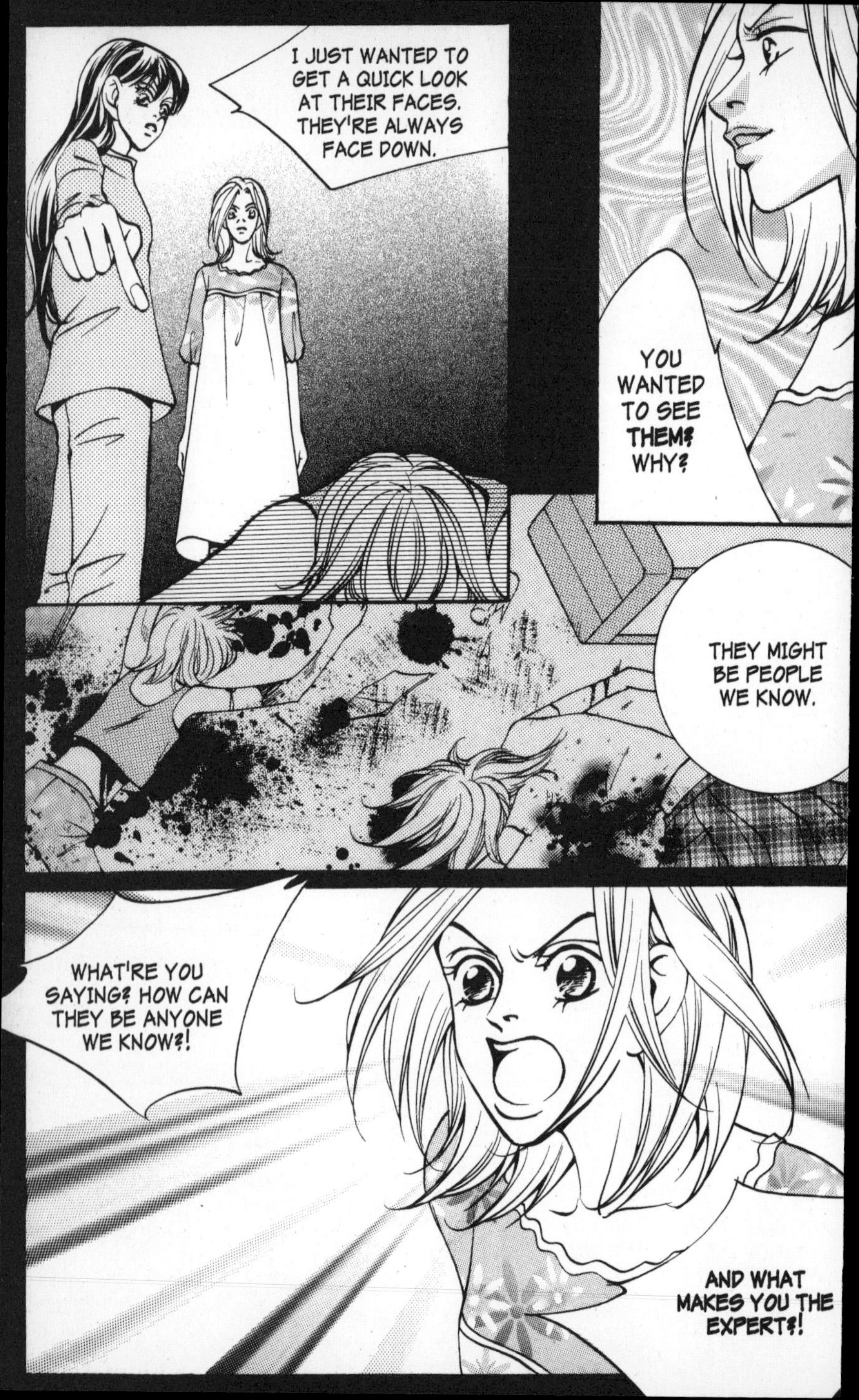
I JUST WANTED TO GET A QUICK LOOK AT THEIR FACES. THEY'RE ALWAYS FACE DOWN.
YOU WANTED TO SEE THEM? WHY?
THEY MIGHT BE PEOPLE WE KNOW.
WHAT'RE YOU SAYING? HOW CAN THEY BE ANYONE WE KNOW?!
AND WHAT MAKES YOU THE EXPERT?!

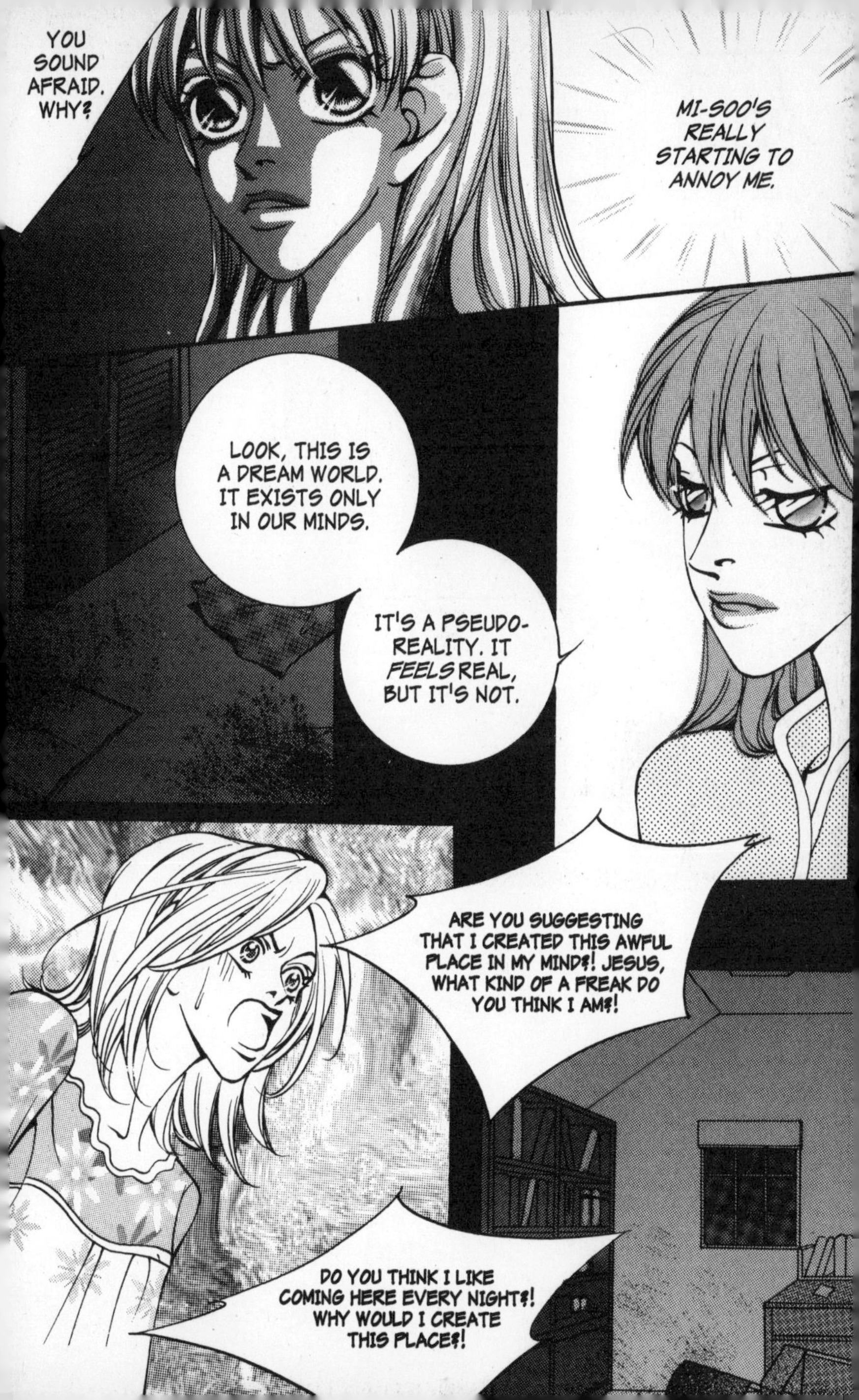
YOU SOUND AFRAID. WHY?
MI-SOO'S REALLY STARTING TO ANNOY ME.
LOOK, THIS IS A DREAM WORLD. IT EXISTS ONLY IN OUR MINDS.
IT'S A PSEUDO-REALITY. IT *FEELS* REAL, BUT IT'S NOT.
ARE YOU SUGGESTING THAT I CREATED THIS AWFUL PLACE IN MY MIND?! JESUS, WHAT KIND OF A FREAK DO YOU THINK I AM?!
DO YOU THINK I LIKE COMING HERE EVERY NIGHT?! WHY WOULD I CREATE THIS PLACE?!

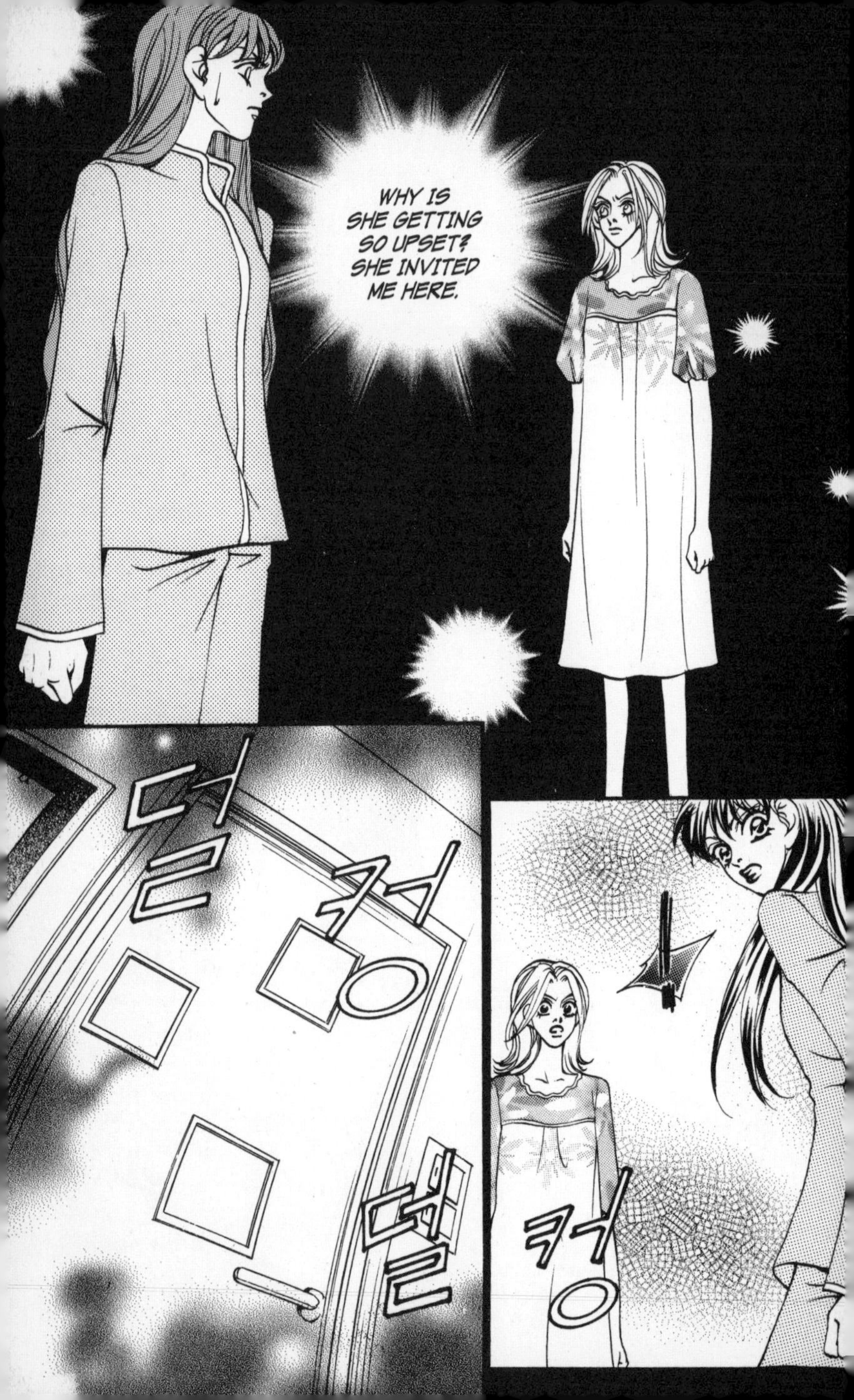
WHY IS SHE GETTING SO UPSET? SHE INVITED ME HERE.

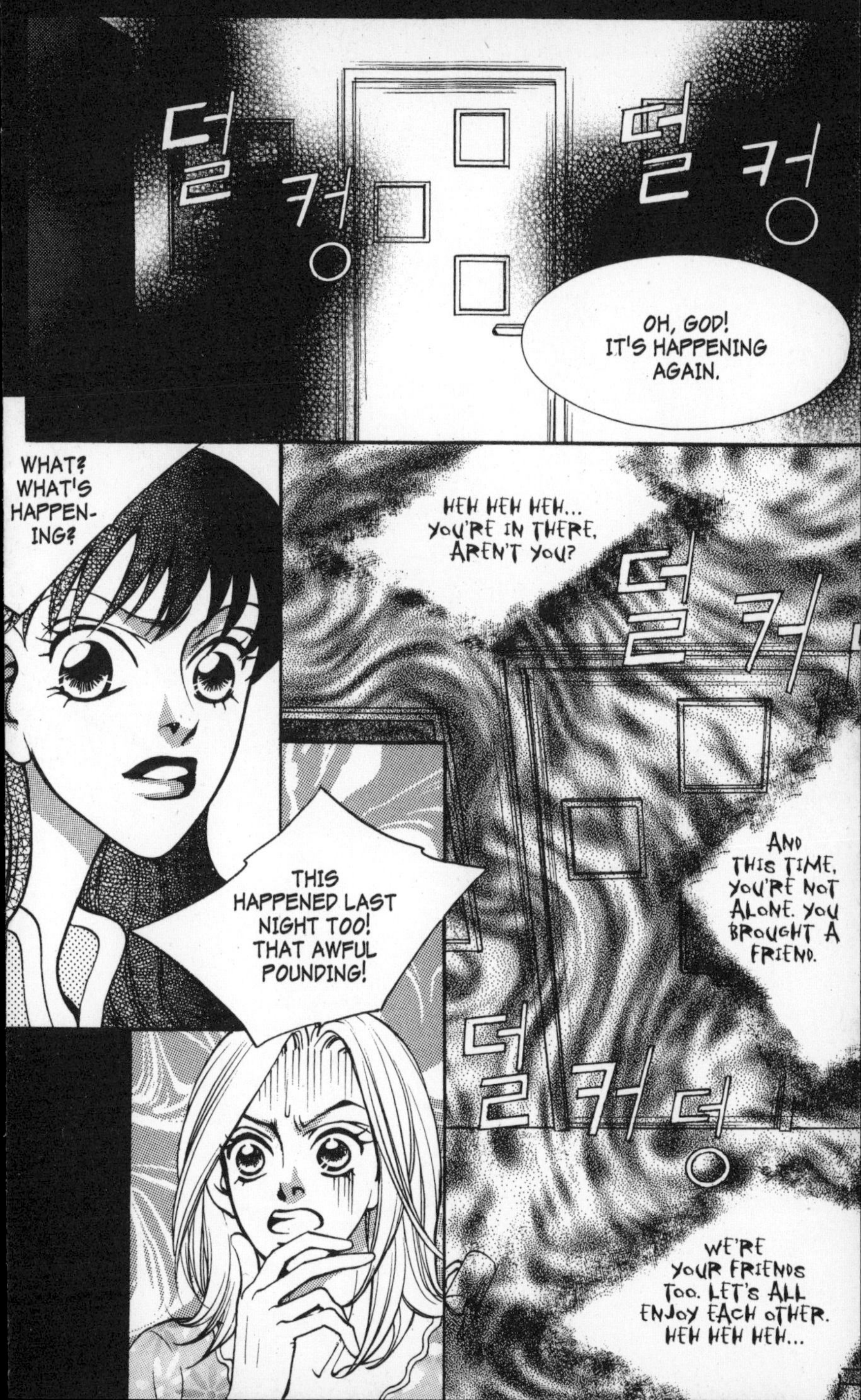
덜컹
덜컹
OH, GOD! IT'S HAPPENING AGAIN.
WHAT? WHAT'S HAPPEN-ING?
THIS HAPPENED LAST NIGHT TOO! THAT AWFUL POUNDING!
HEH HEH HEH... YOU'RE IN THERE, AREN'T YOU?
덜커
AND THIS TIME, YOU'RE NOT ALONE. YOU BROUGHT A FRIEND.
덜커덩
WE'RE YOUR FRIENDS TOO. LET'S ALL ENJOY EACH OTHER. HEH HEH HEH...

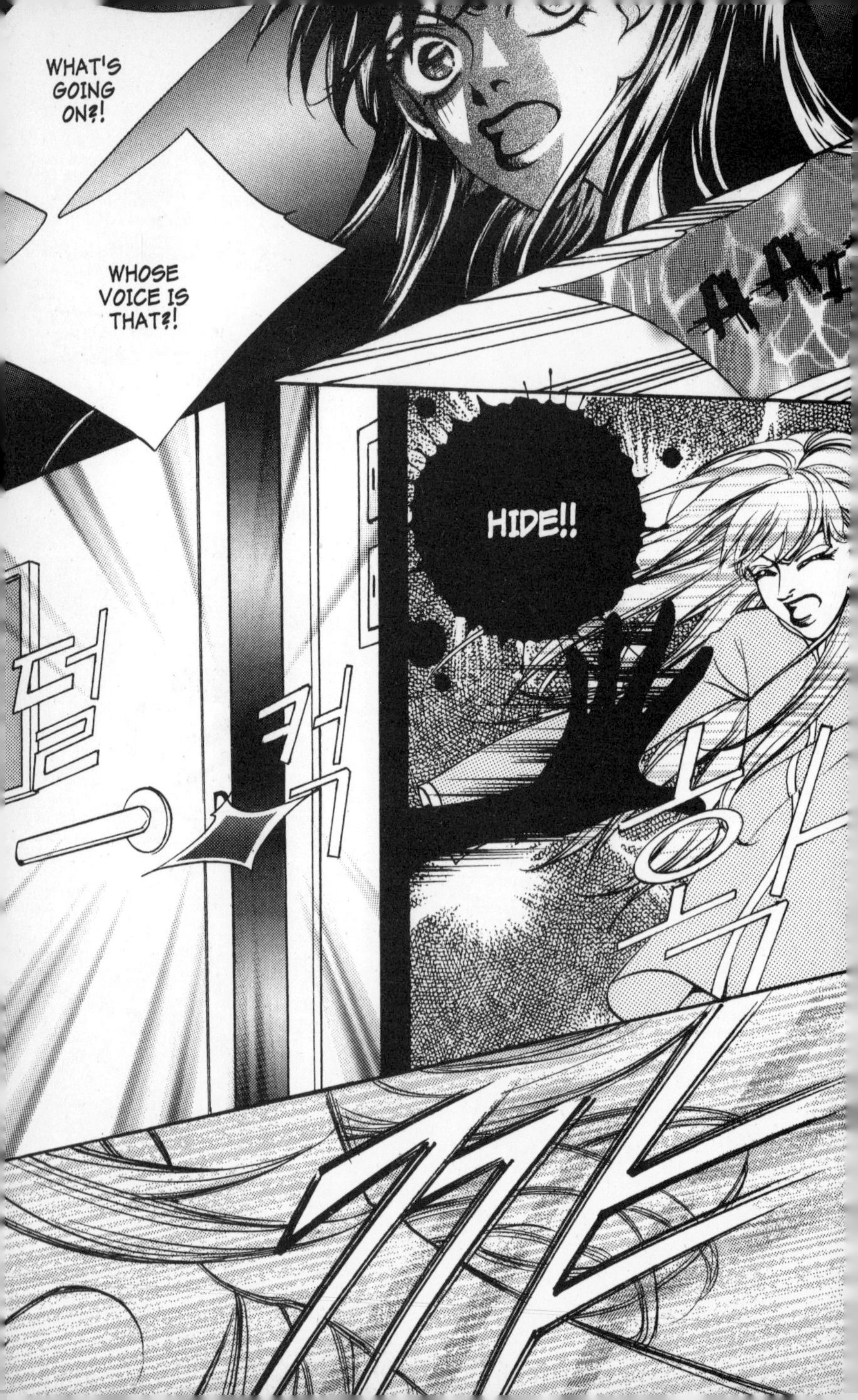
WHAT'S GOING ON?!
WHOSE VOICE IS THAT?!
HIDE!!

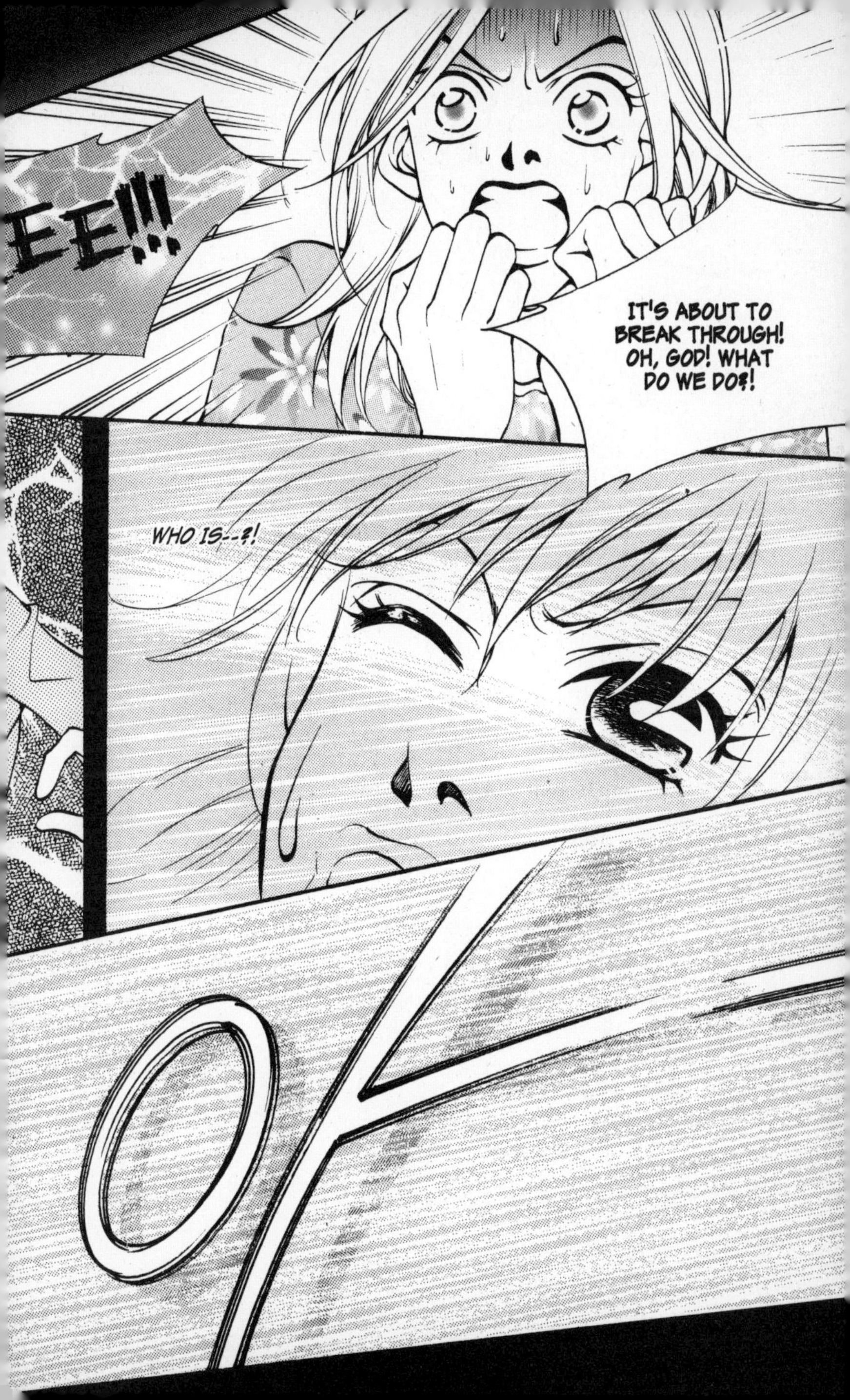
EE!!!
IT'S ABOUT TO BREAK THROUGH! OH, GOD! WHAT DO WE DO?!
WHO IS--?!

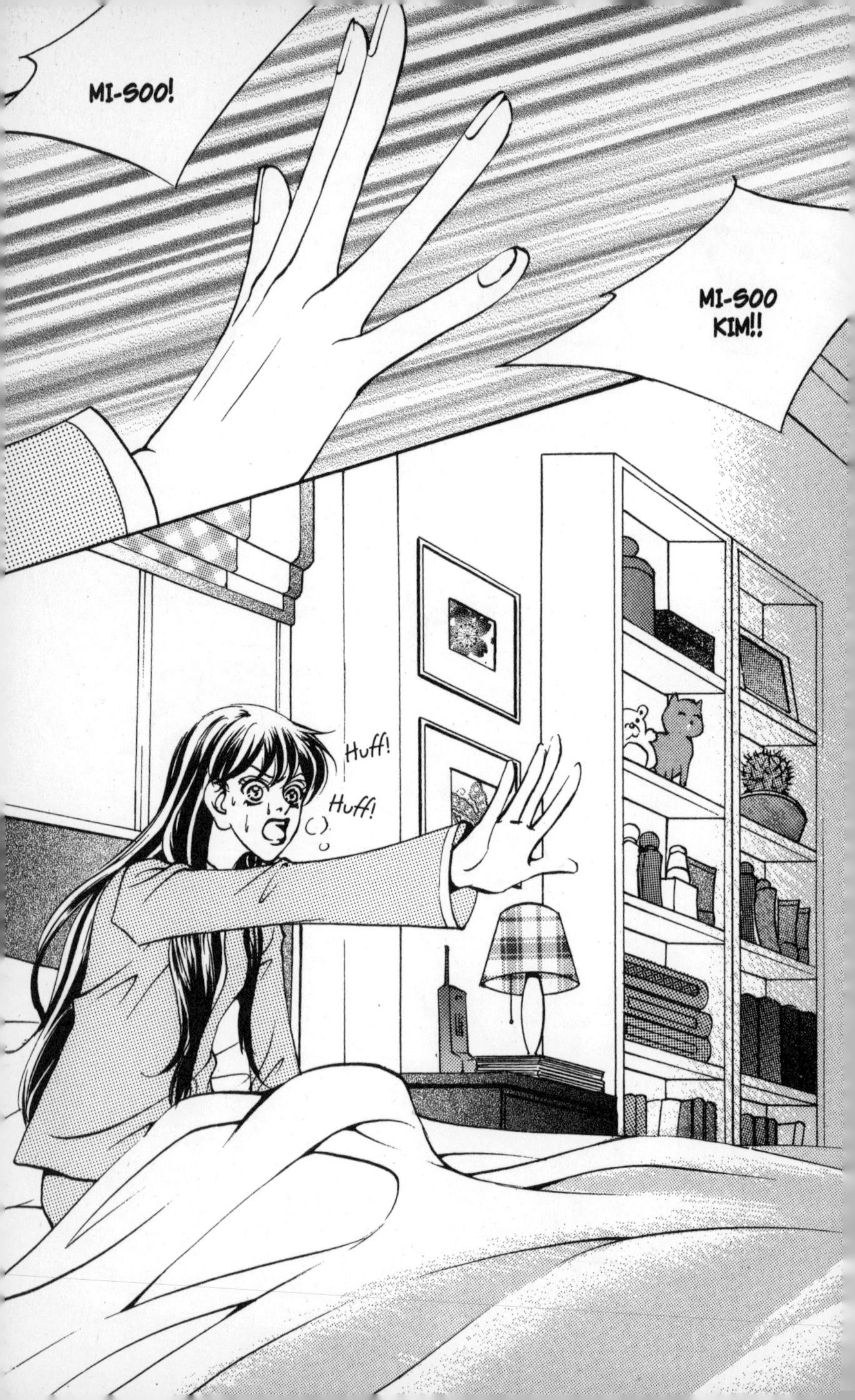
MI-SOO!
MI-SOO KIM!!
Huff!
Huff!

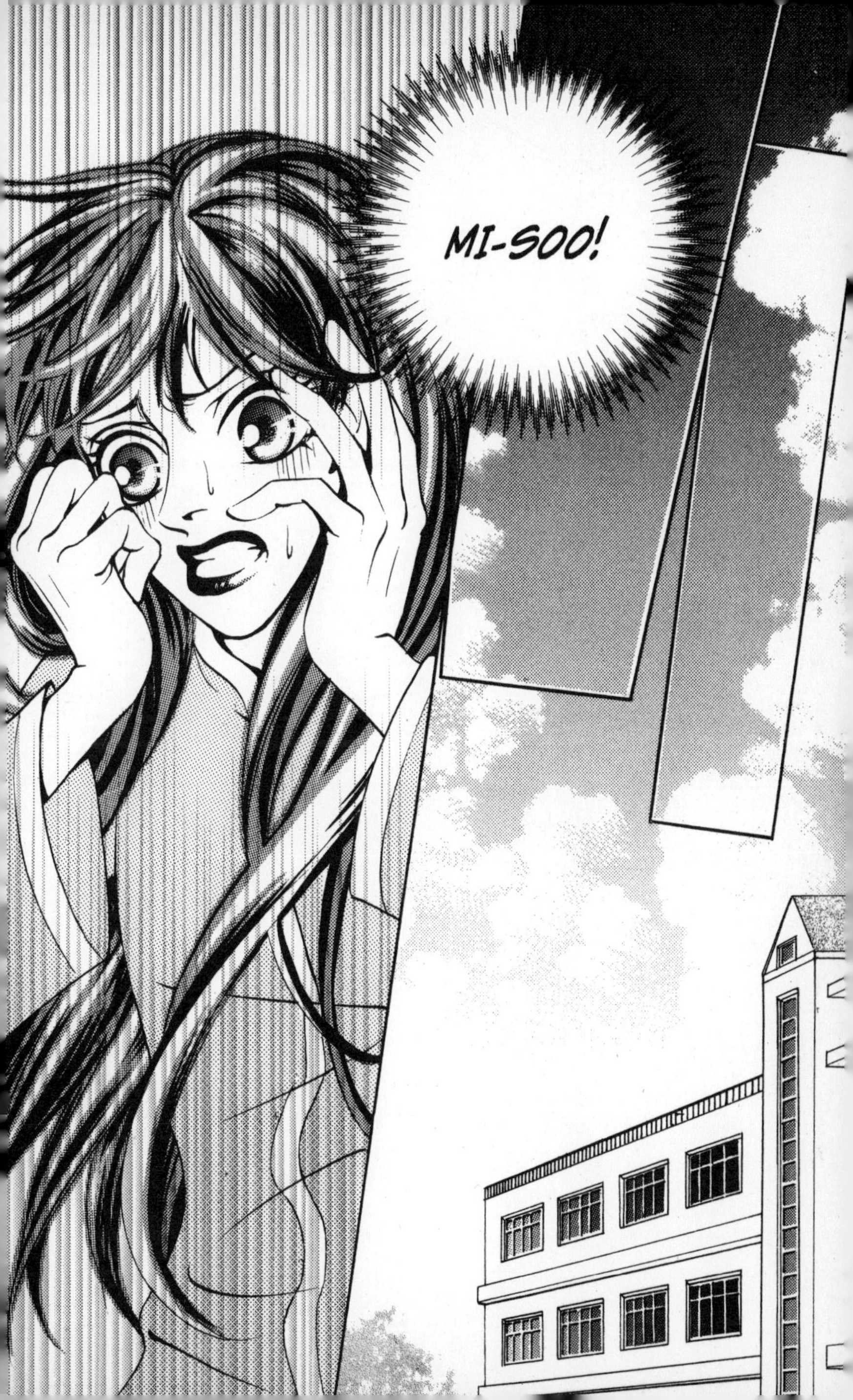
MI-SOO!

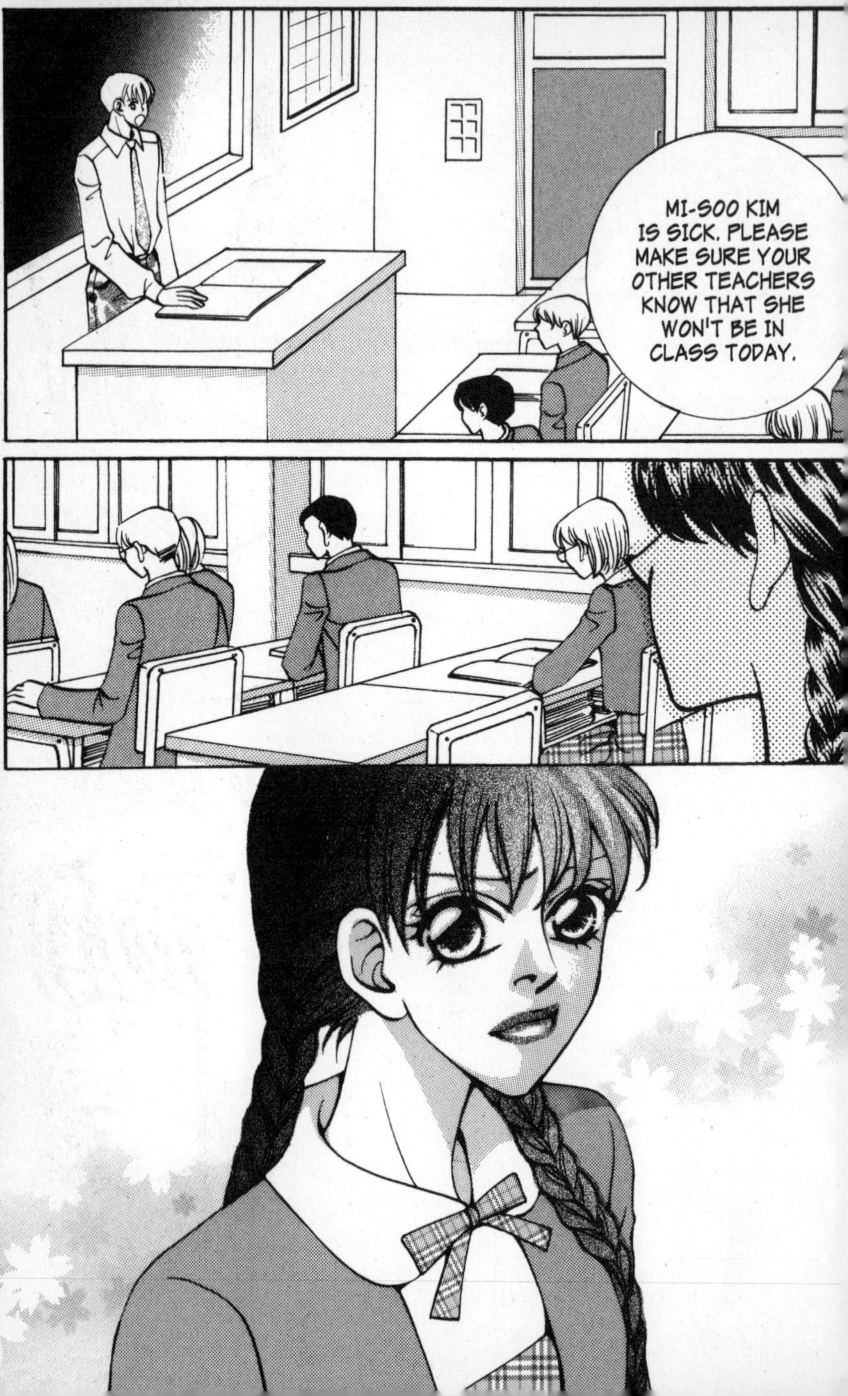
MI-SOO KIM IS SICK. PLEASE MAKE SURE YOUR OTHER TEACHERS KNOW THAT SHE WON'T BE IN CLASS TODAY.

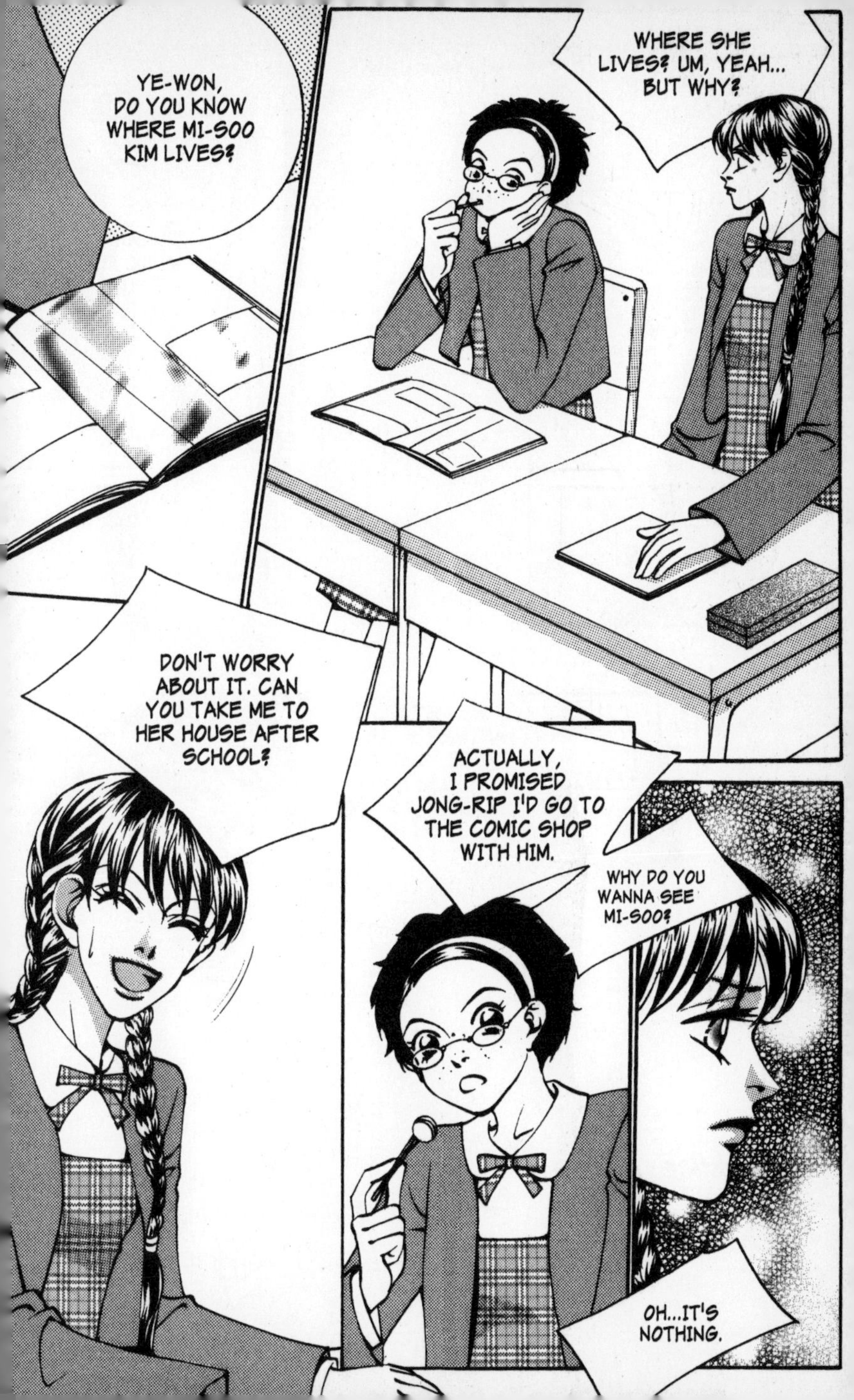
YE-WON, DO YOU KNOW WHERE MI-SOO KIM LIVES?
WHERE SHE LIVES? UM, YEAH... BUT WHY?
DON'T WORRY ABOUT IT. CAN YOU TAKE ME TO HER HOUSE AFTER SCHOOL?
ACTUALLY, I PROMISED JONG-RIP I'D GO TO THE COMIC SHOP WITH HIM.
WHY DO YOU WANNA SEE MI-SOO?
OH...IT'S NOTHING.

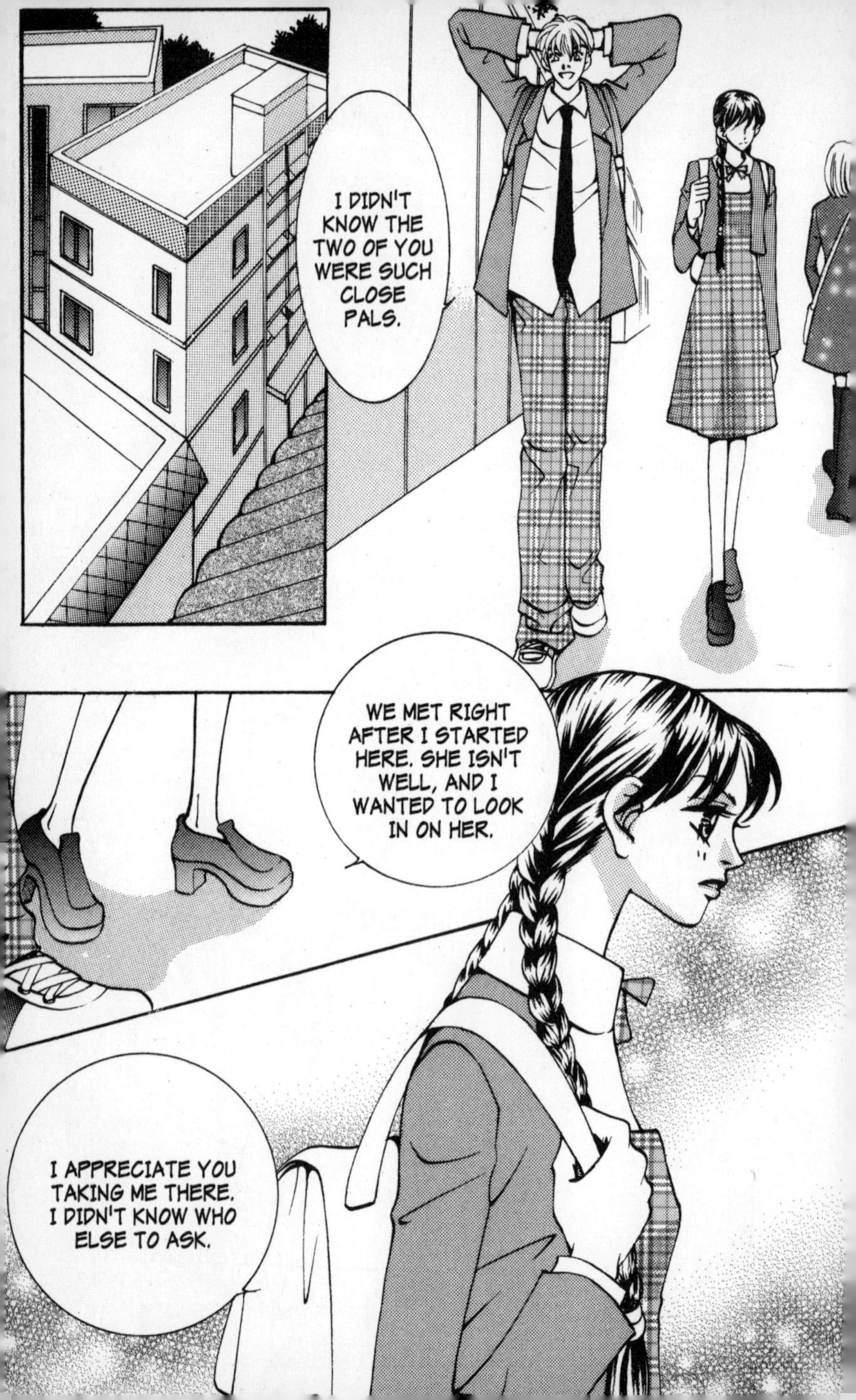
I DIDN'T KNOW THE TWO OF YOU WERE SUCH CLOSE PALS.
WE MET RIGHT AFTER I STARTED HERE. SHE ISN'T WELL, AND I WANTED TO LOOK IN ON HER.
I APPRECIATE YOU TAKING ME THERE. I DIDN'T KNOW WHO ELSE TO ASK.

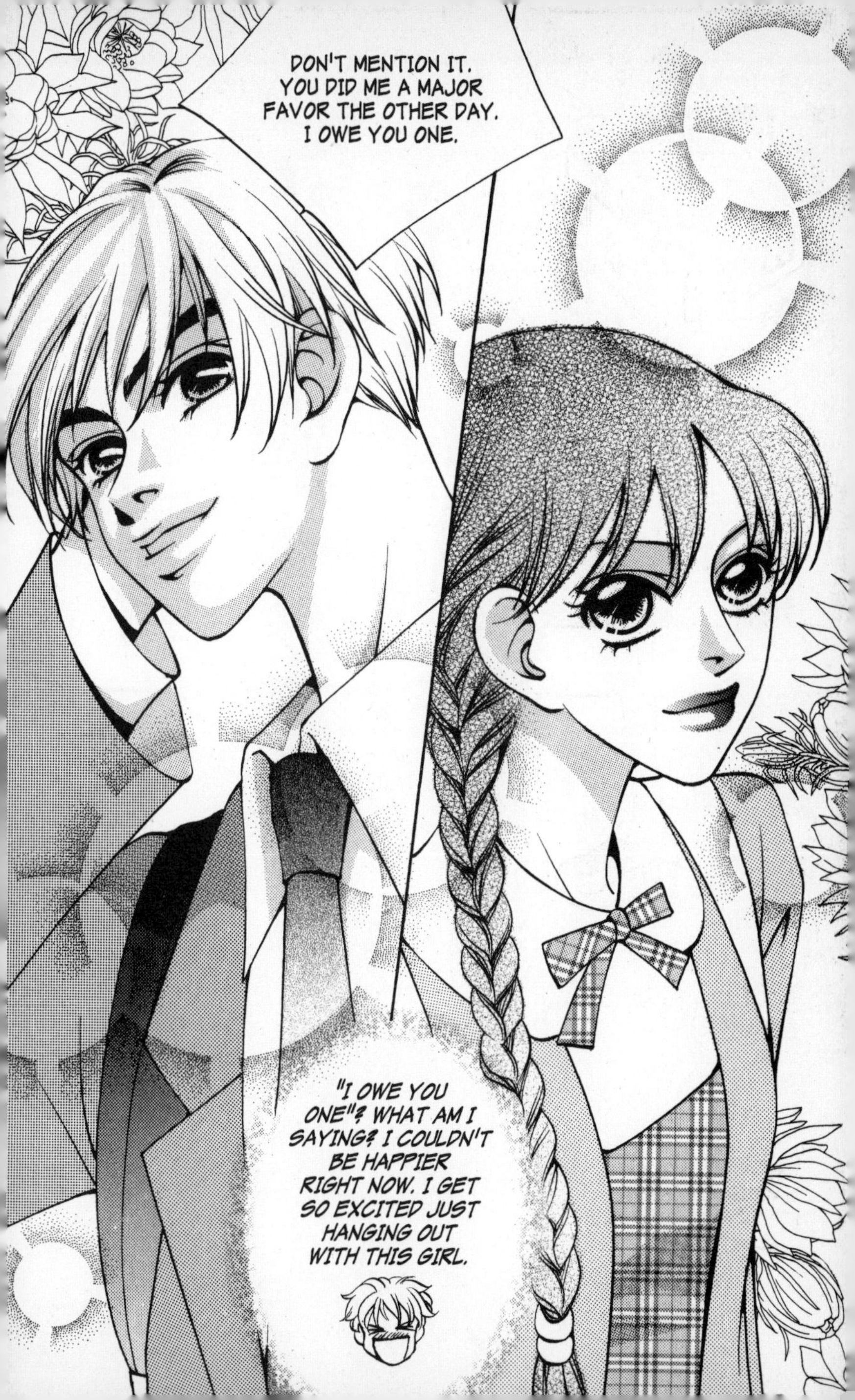
DON'T MENTION IT. YOU DID ME A MAJOR FAVOR THE OTHER DAY. I OWE YOU ONE.
"I OWE YOU ONE"? WHAT AM I SAYING? I COULDN'T BE HAPPIER RIGHT NOW. I GET SO EXCITED JUST HANGING OUT WITH THIS GIRL.

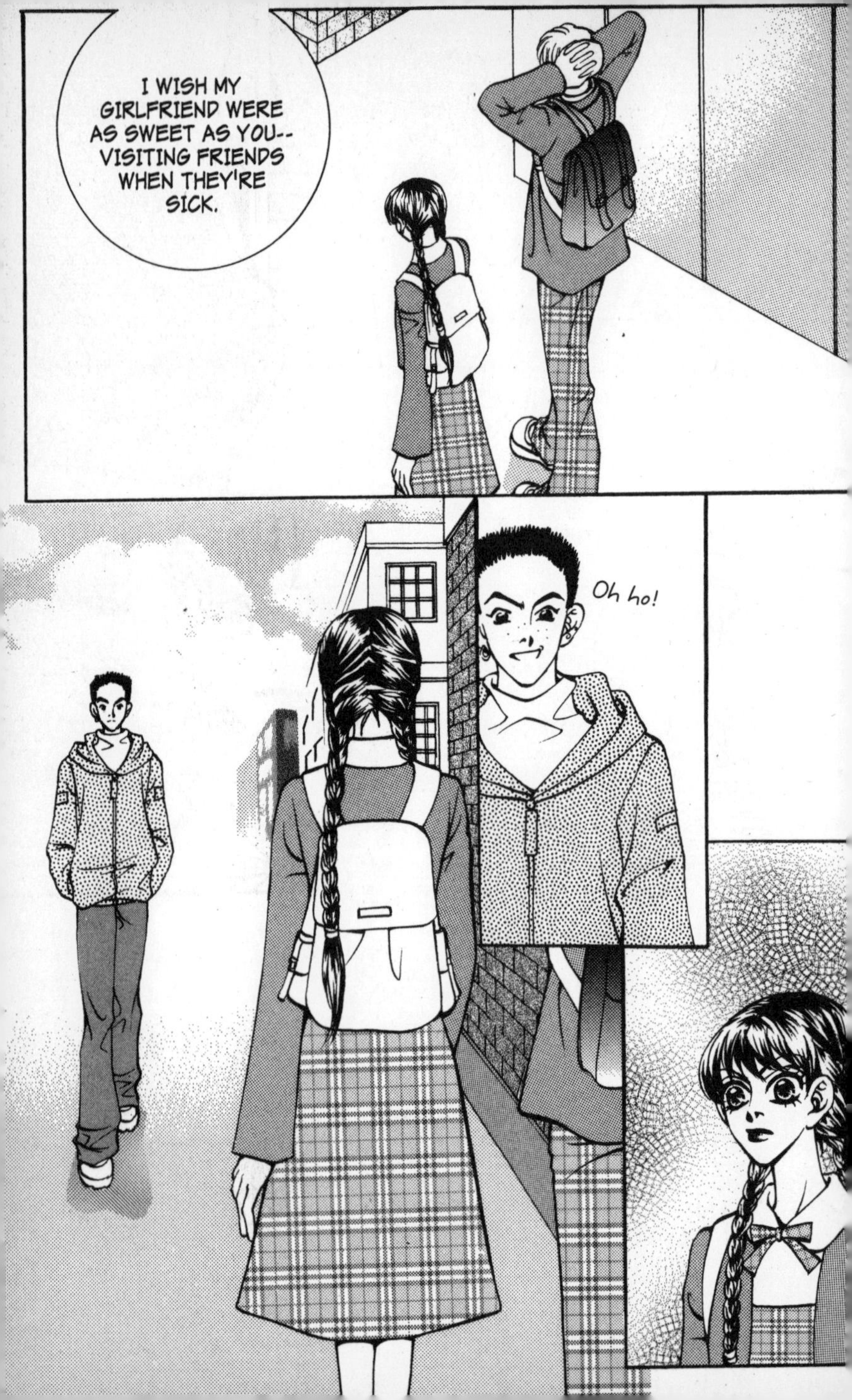
I WISH MY GIRLFRIEND WERE AS SWEET AS YOU--VISITING FRIENDS WHEN THEY'RE SICK.
Oh ho!

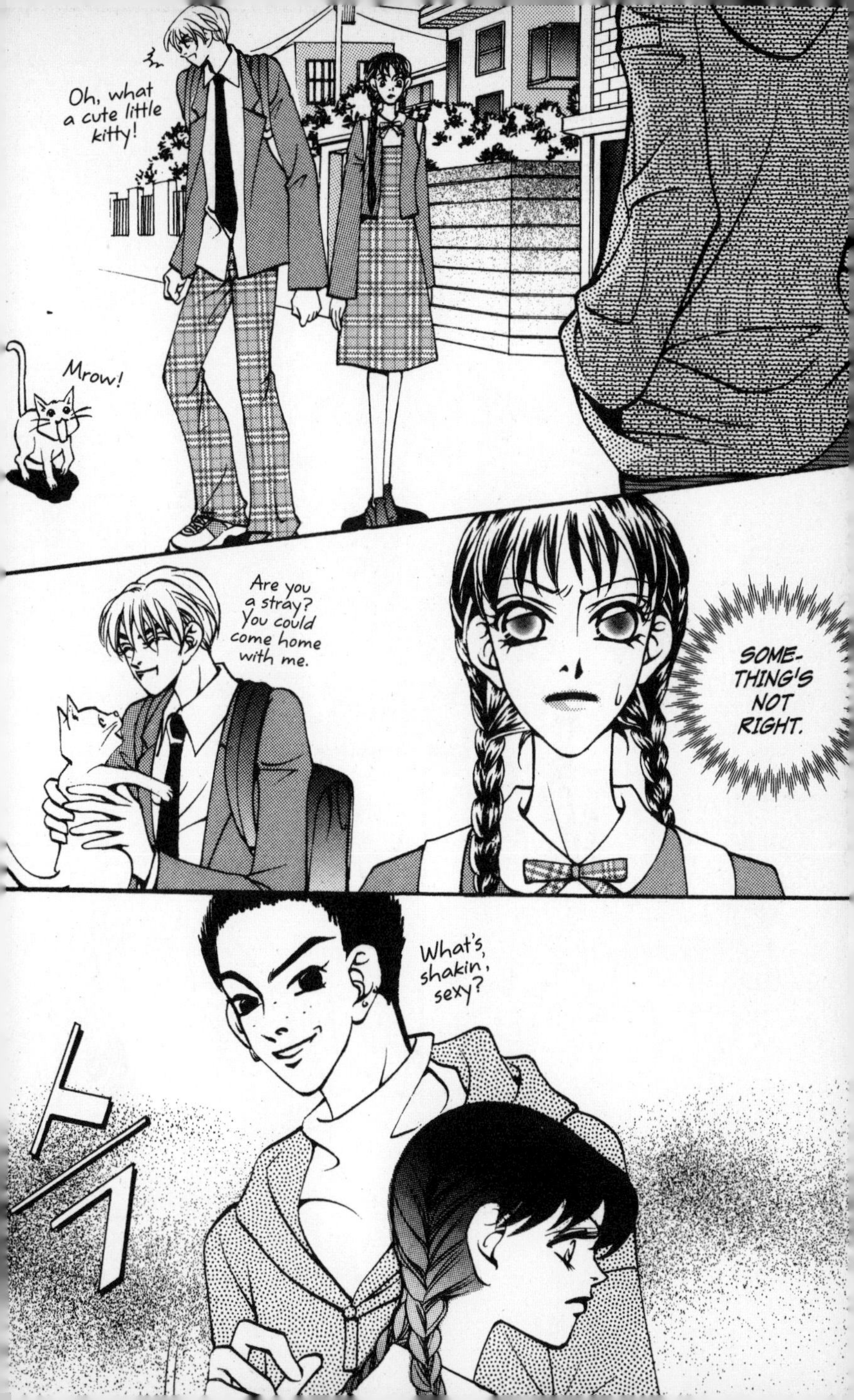
Oh, what a cute little kitty!
Mrow!
Are you a stray? You could come home with me.
SOME-THING'S NOT RIGHT.
What's shakin', sexy?

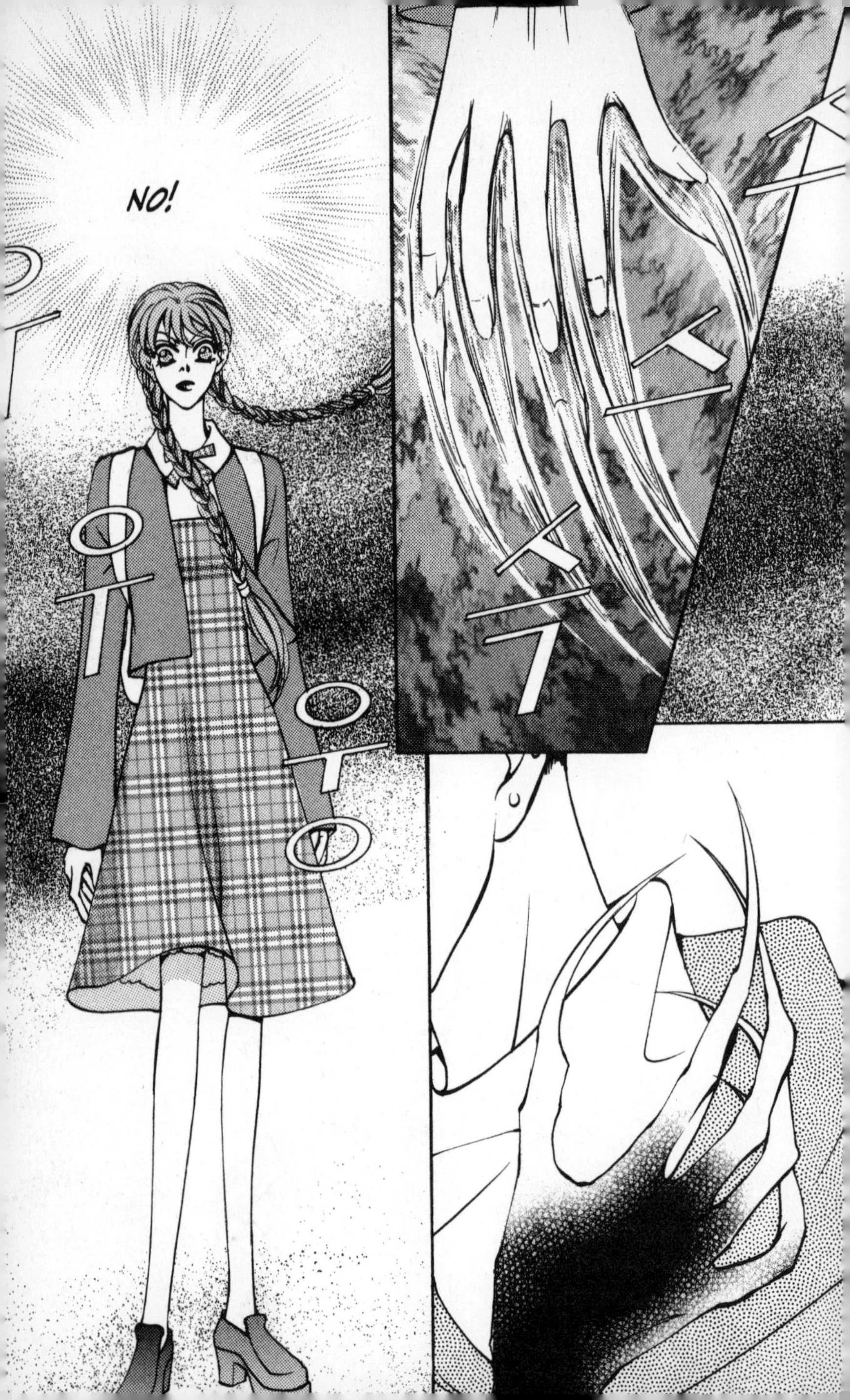
NO!

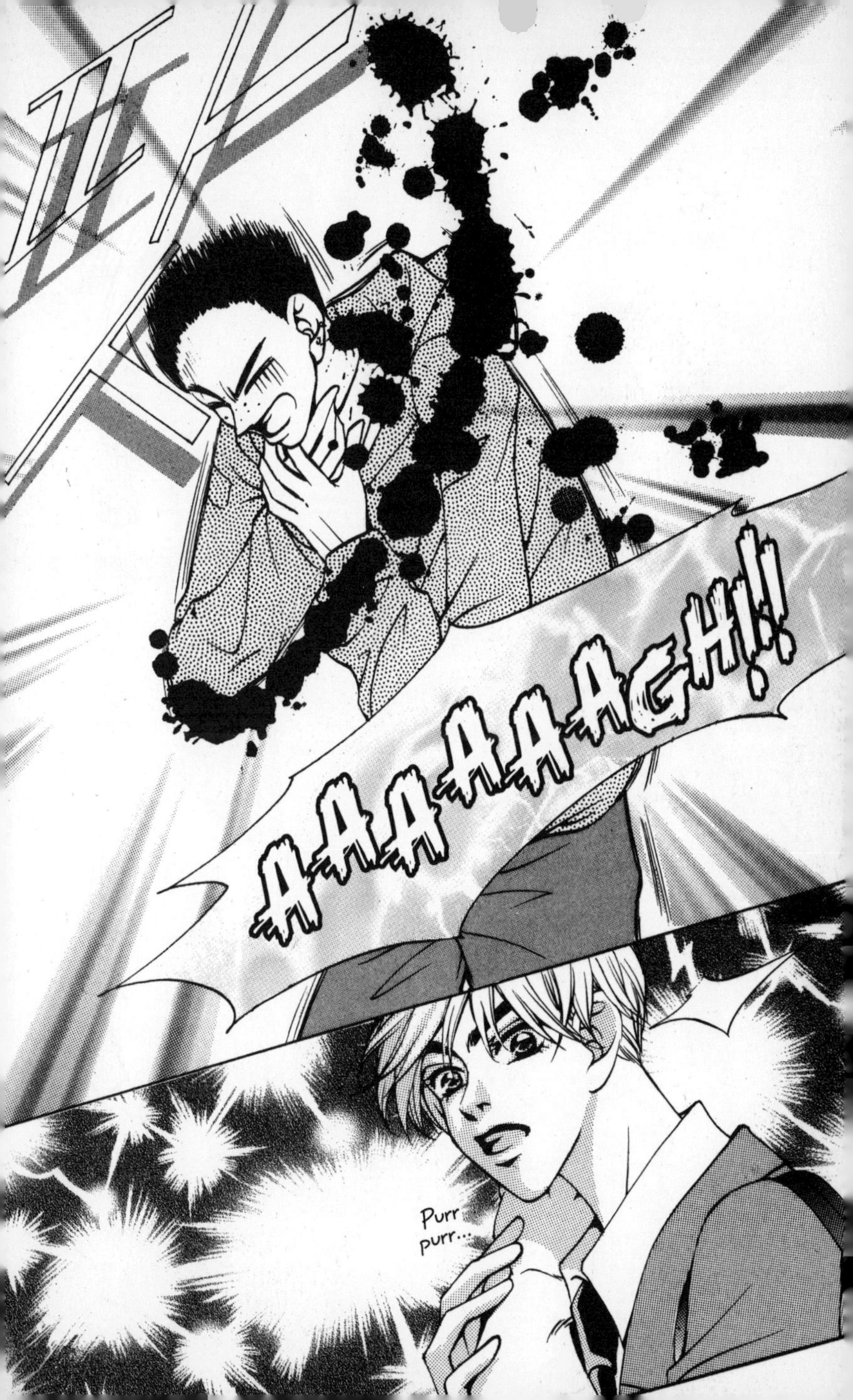
AAAAAAAGH!!
Purr purr...

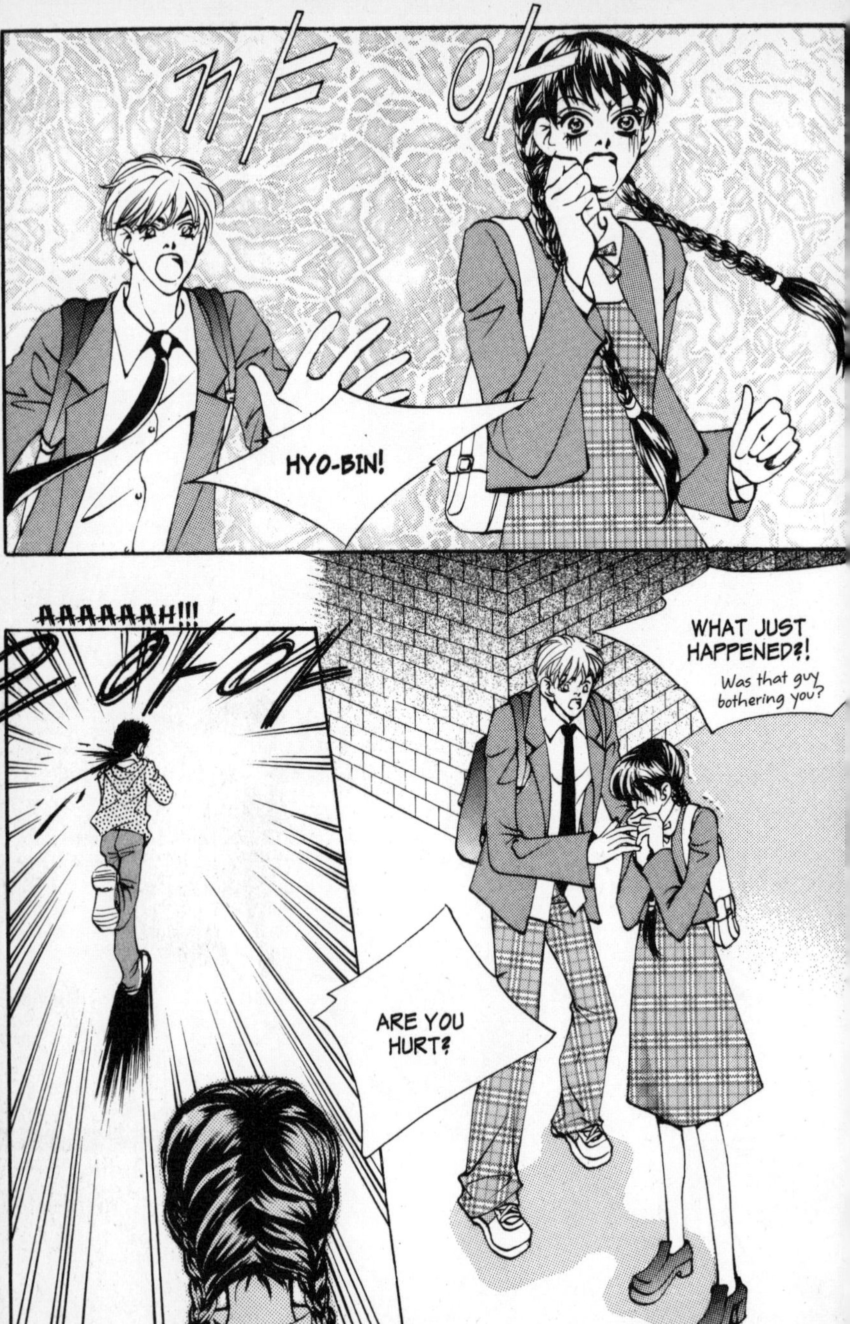
HYO-BIN!
AAAAAAH!!!
WHAT JUST HAPPENED?!
Was that guy bothering you?
ARE YOU HURT?

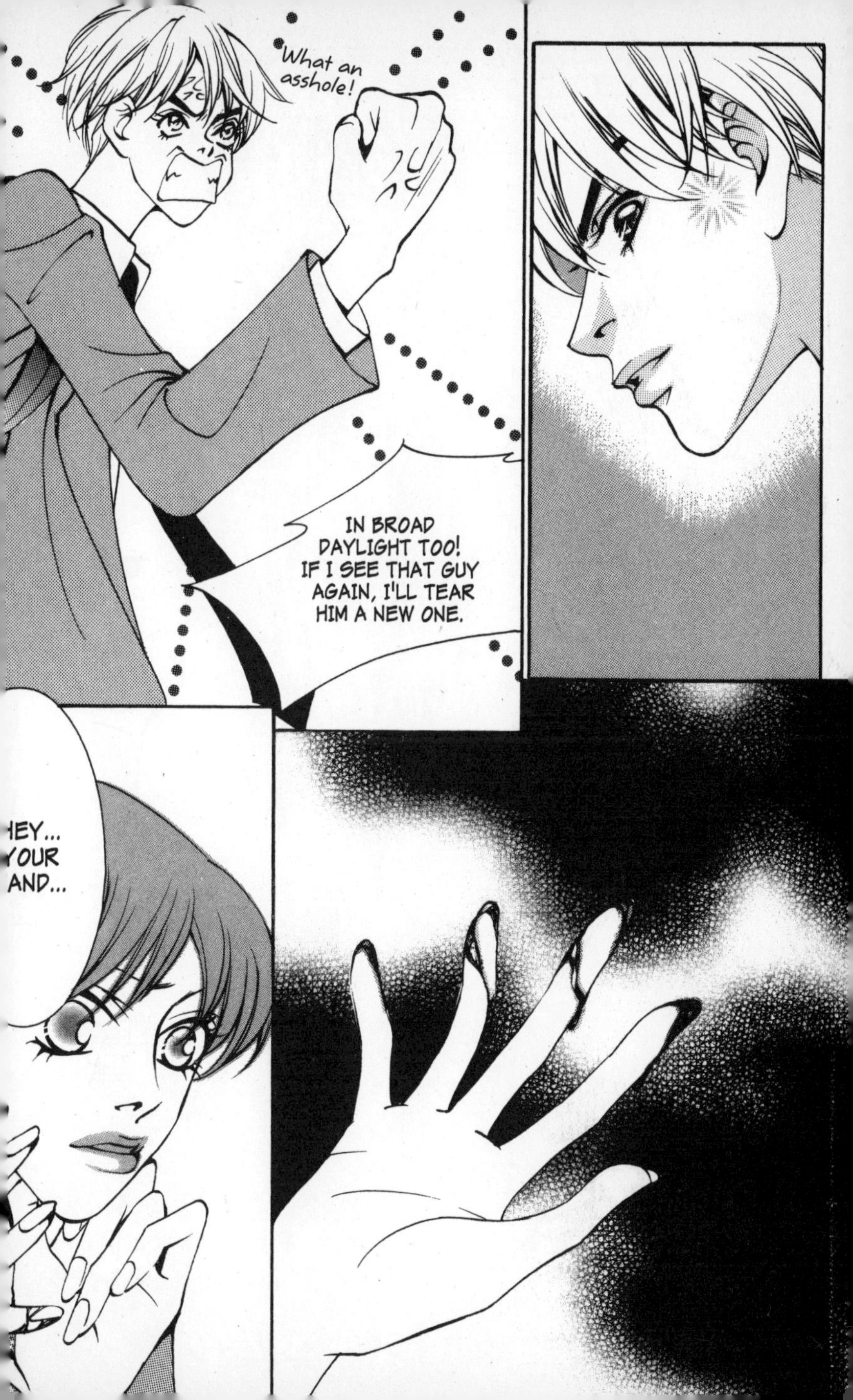
What an asshole!
IN BROAD DAYLIGHT TOO! IF I SEE THAT GUY AGAIN, I'LL TEAR HIM A NEW ONE.
HEY... YOUR AND...

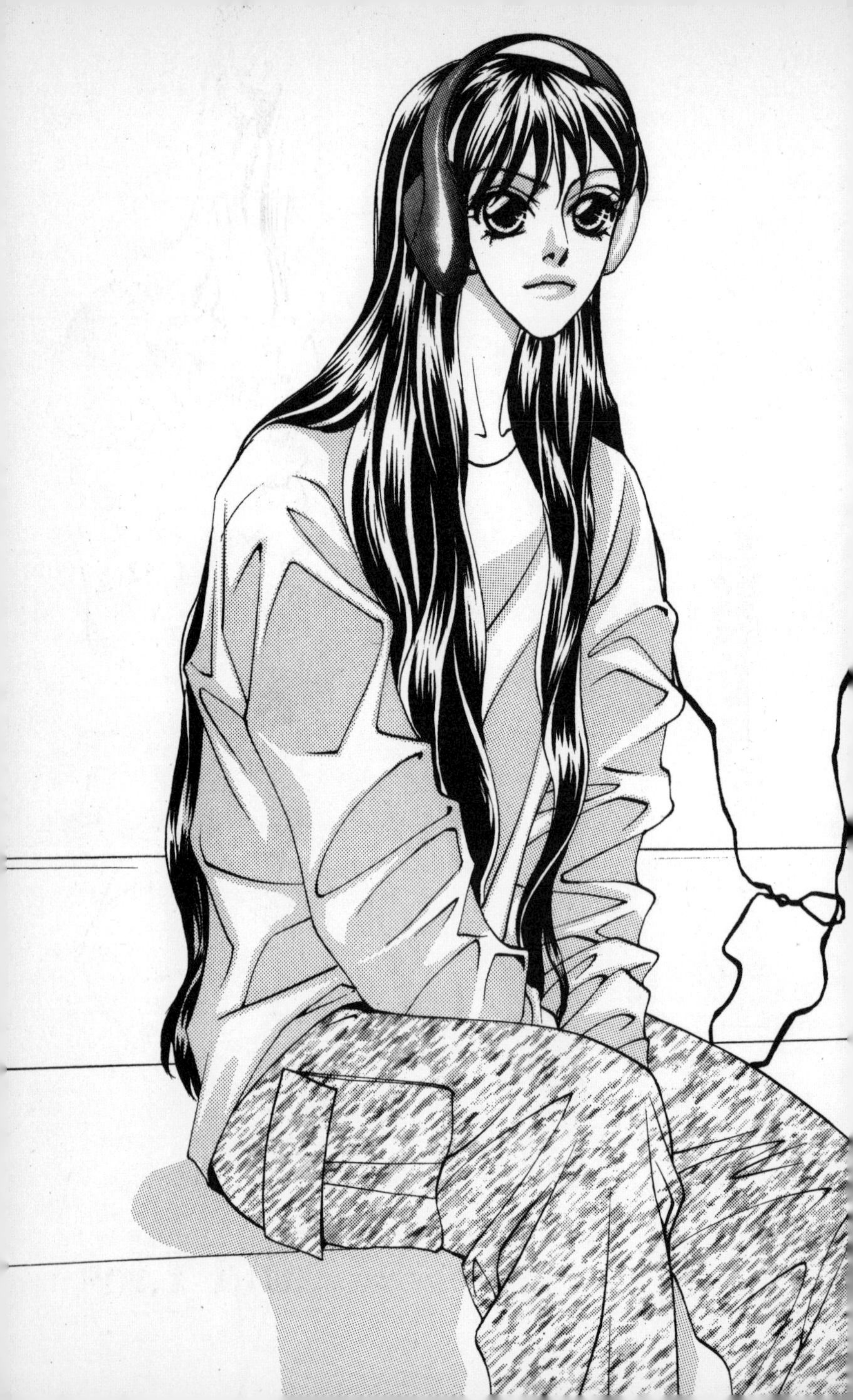

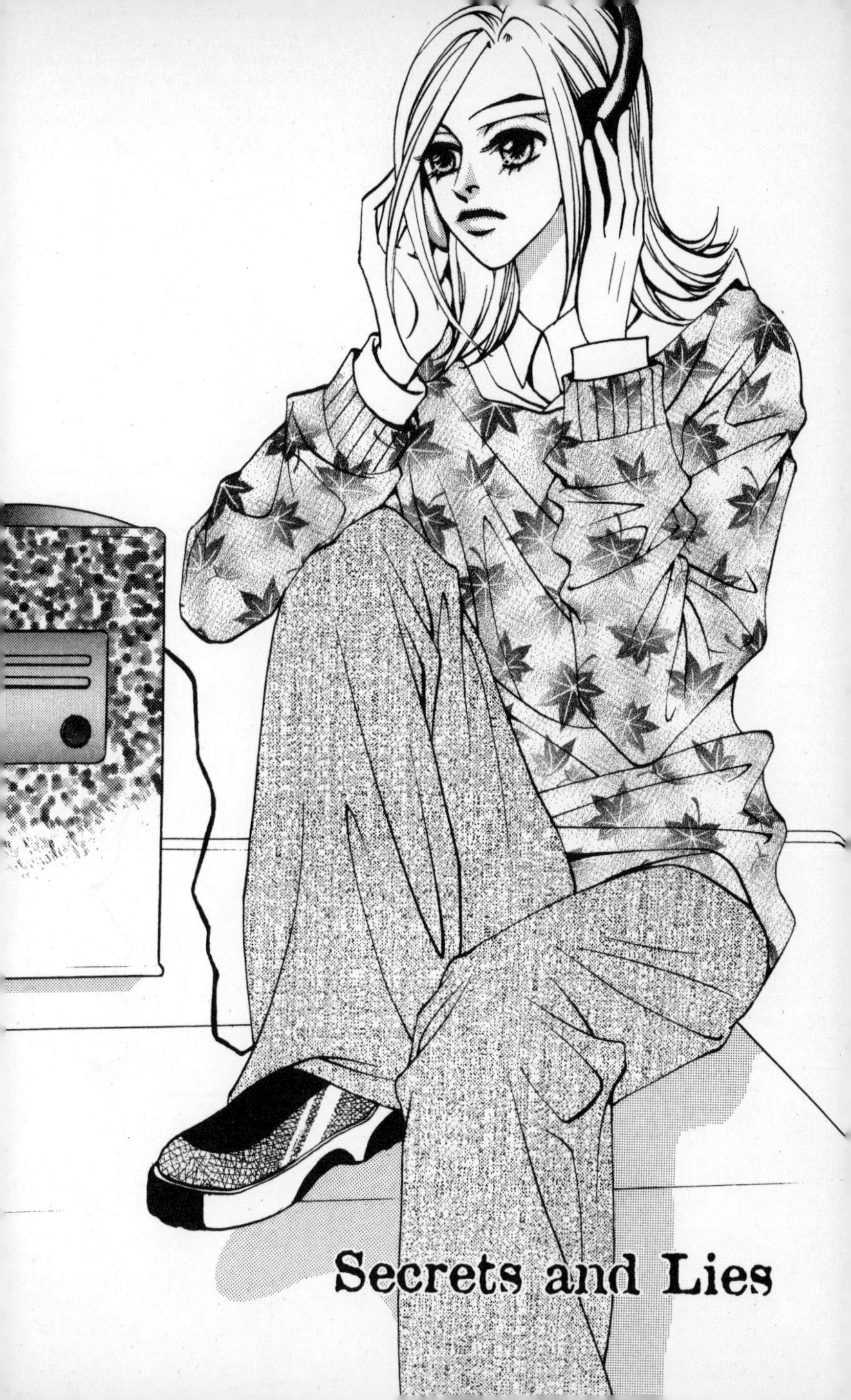
Secrets and Lies

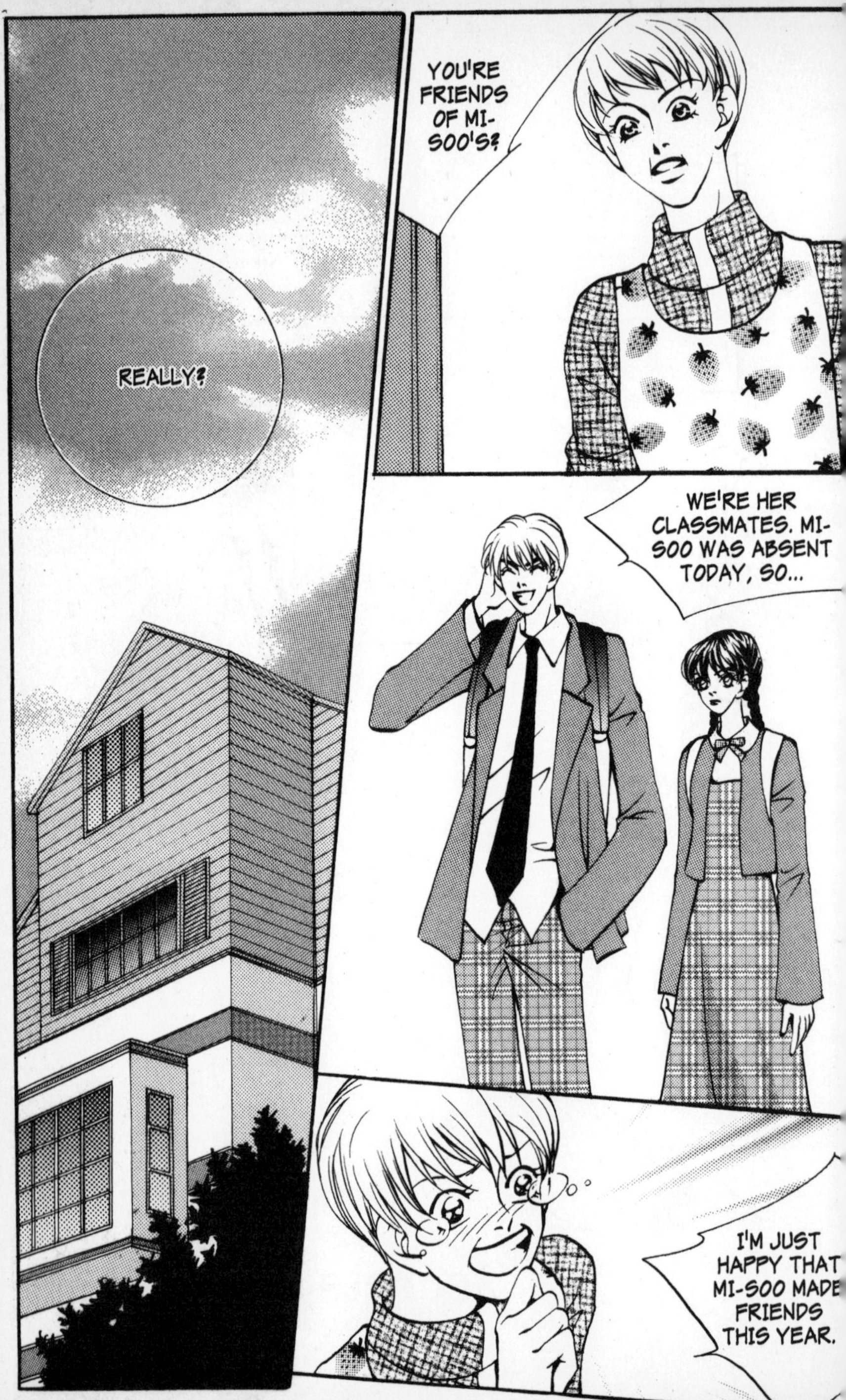
REALLY?
YOU'RE FRIENDS OF MI-SOO'S?
WE'RE HER CLASSMATES. MI-SOO WAS ABSENT TODAY, SO...
I'M JUST HAPPY THAT MI-SOO MADE FRIENDS THIS YEAR.

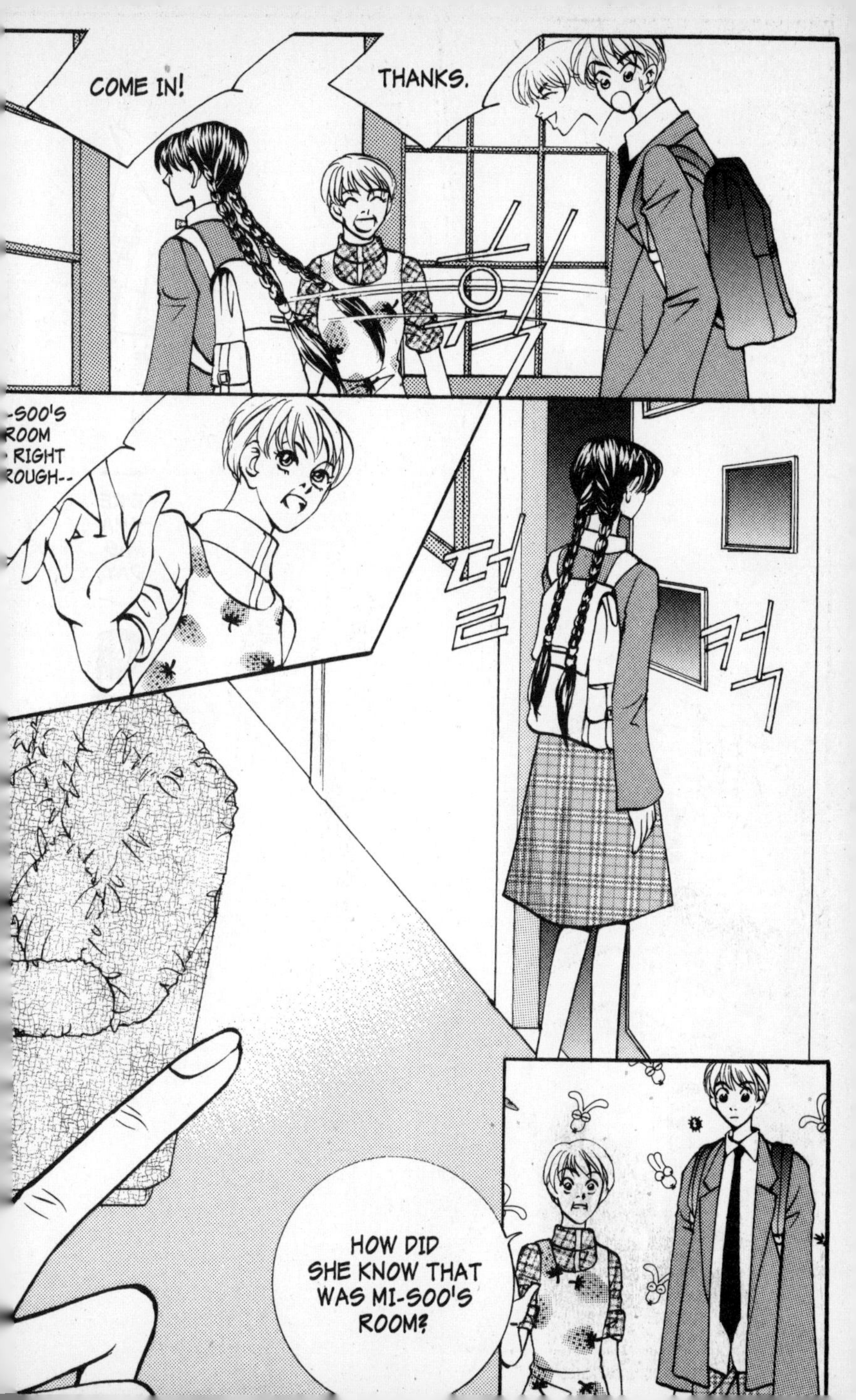
COME IN!
THANKS.
-SOO'S ROOM RIGHT ROUGH--
HOW DID SHE KNOW THAT WAS MI-SOO'S ROOM?

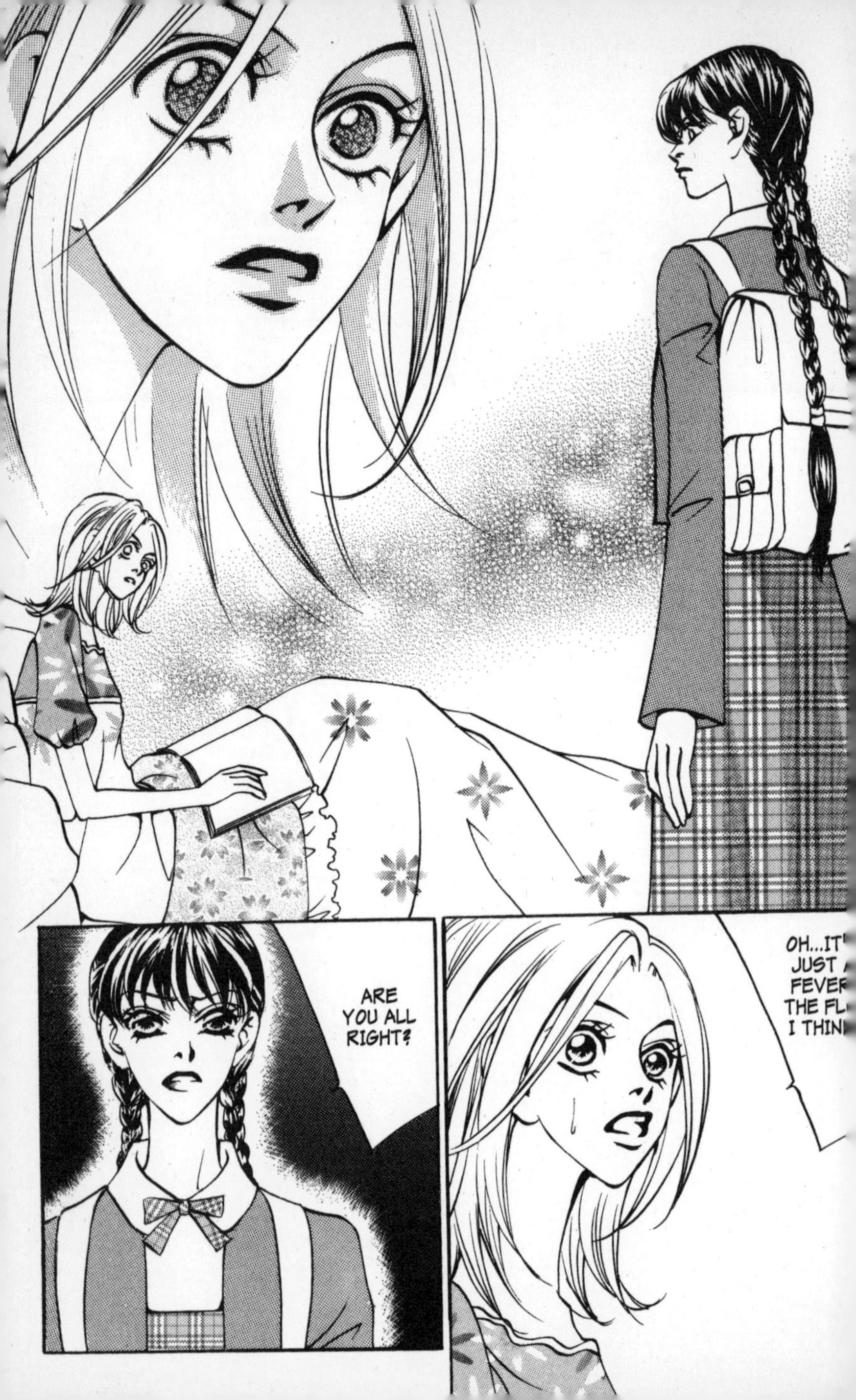
ARE YOU ALL RIGHT?
OH...IT' JUST FEVER THE FL I THIN

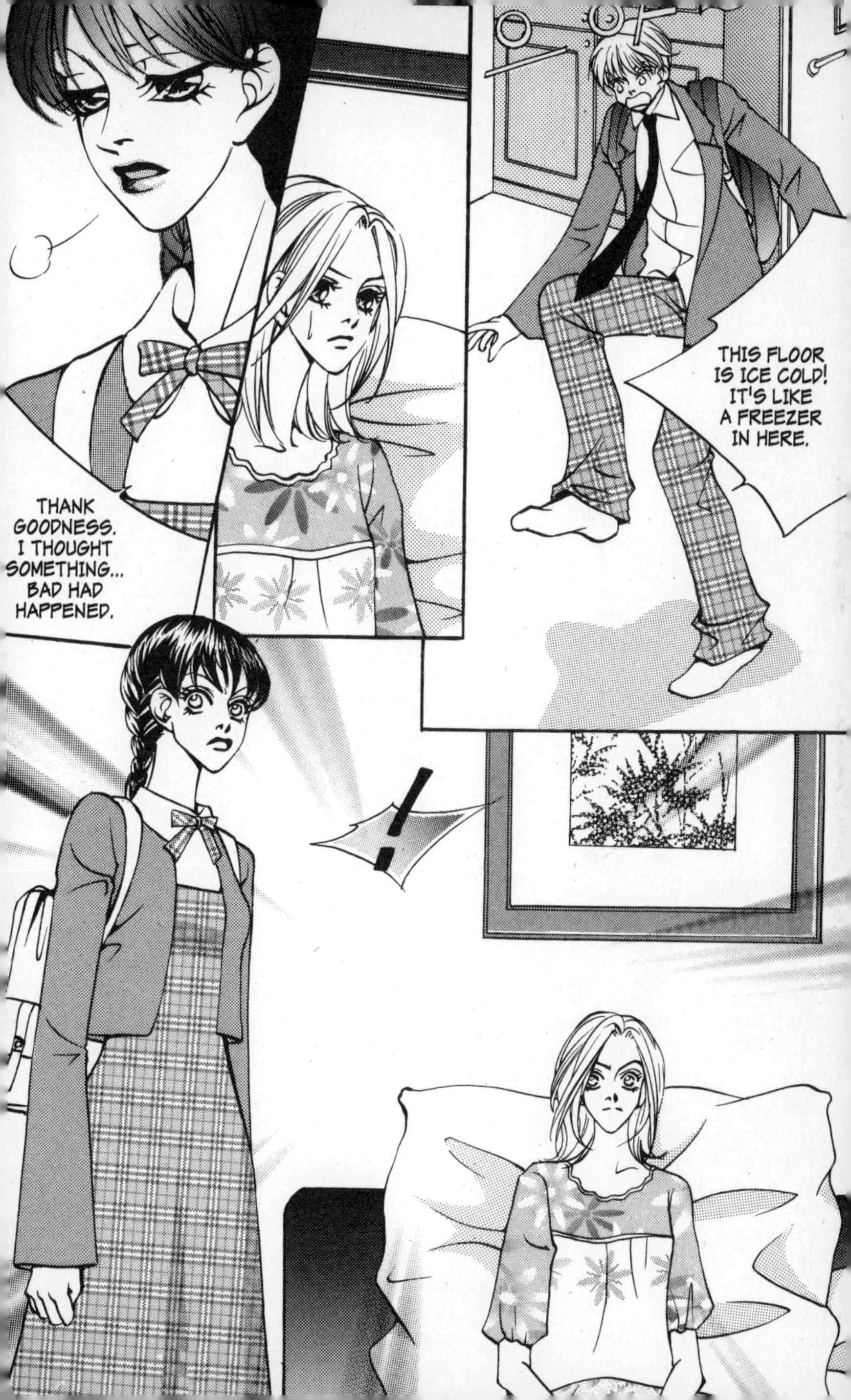
THANK GOODNESS. I THOUGHT SOMETHING... BAD HAD HAPPENED.
THIS FLOOR IS ICE COLD! IT'S LIKE A FREEZER IN HERE.
!

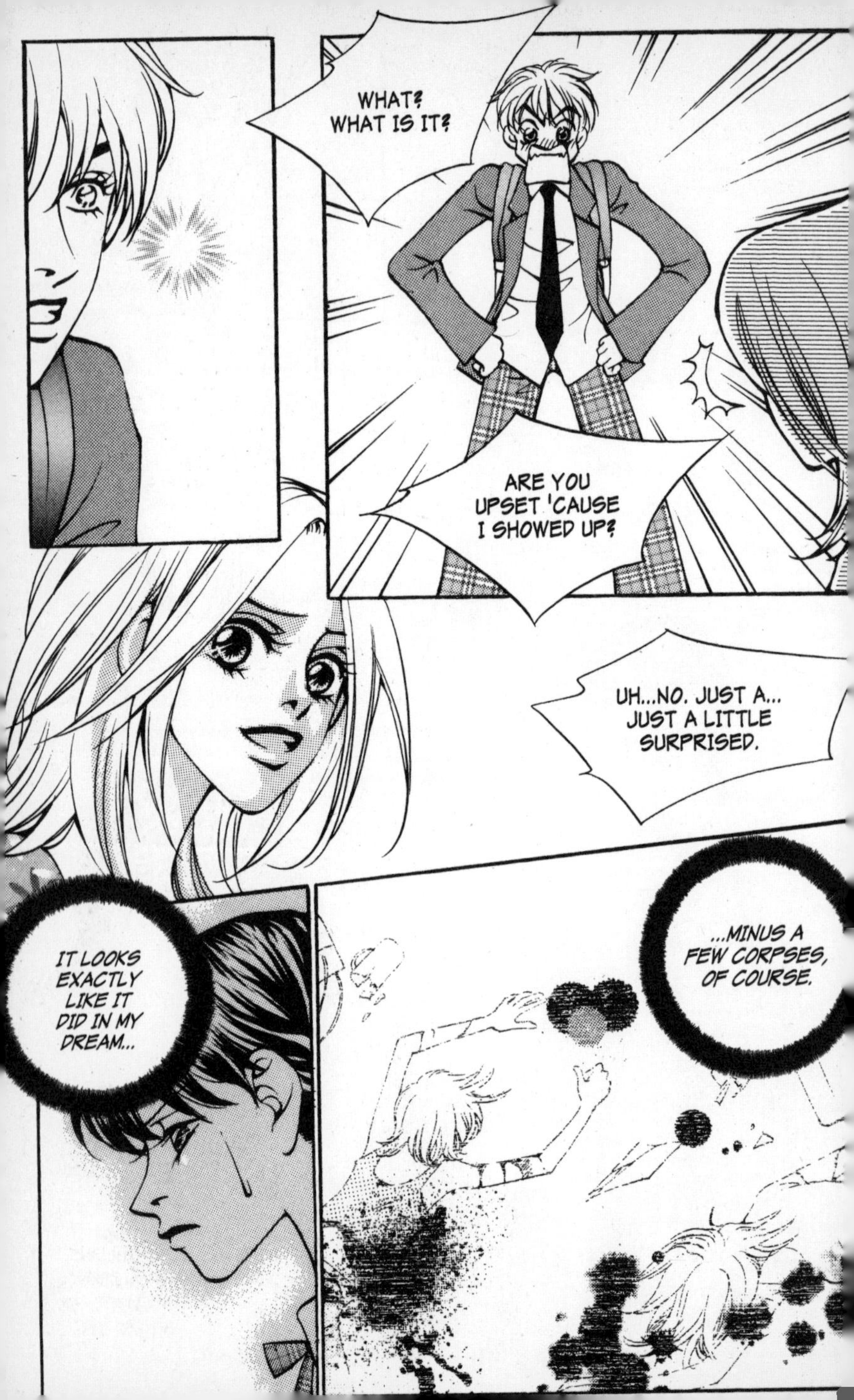
WHAT? WHAT IS IT?
ARE YOU UPSET 'CAUSE I SHOWED UP?
UH...NO. JUST A... JUST A LITTLE SURPRISED.
IT LOOKS EXACTLY LIKE IT DID IN MY DREAM...
...MINUS A FEW CORPSES, OF COURSE.

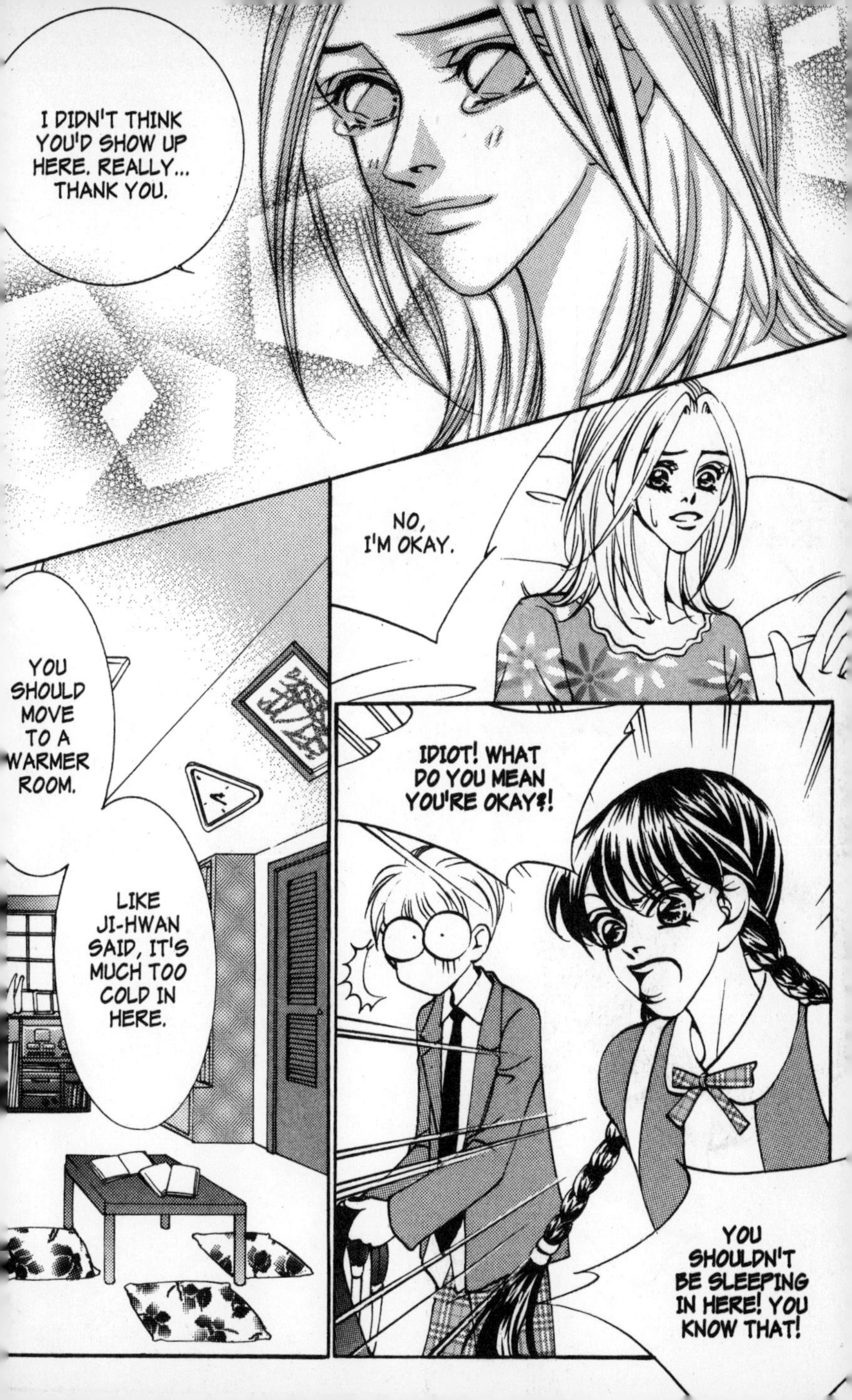
I DIDN'T THINK YOU'D SHOW UP HERE. REALLY... THANK YOU.
NO, I'M OKAY.
YOU SHOULD MOVE TO A WARMER ROOM.
LIKE JI-HWAN SAID, IT'S MUCH TOO COLD IN HERE.
IDIOT! WHAT DO YOU MEAN YOU'RE OKAY?!
YOU SHOULDN'T BE SLEEPING IN HERE! YOU KNOW THAT!

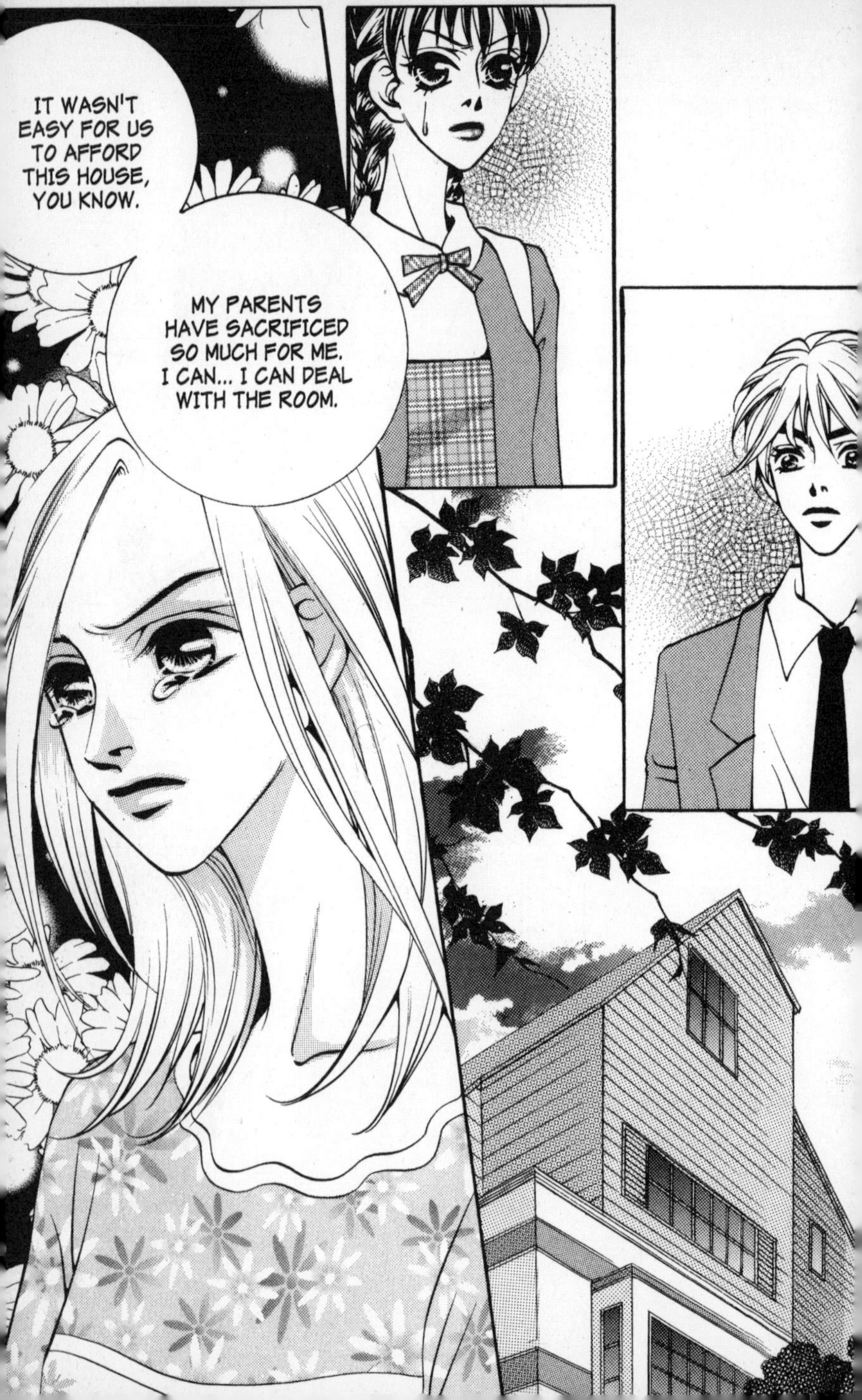
IT WASN'T EASY FOR US TO AFFORD THIS HOUSE, YOU KNOW.
MY PARENTS HAVE SACRIFICED SO MUCH FOR ME. I CAN... I CAN DEAL WITH THE ROOM.

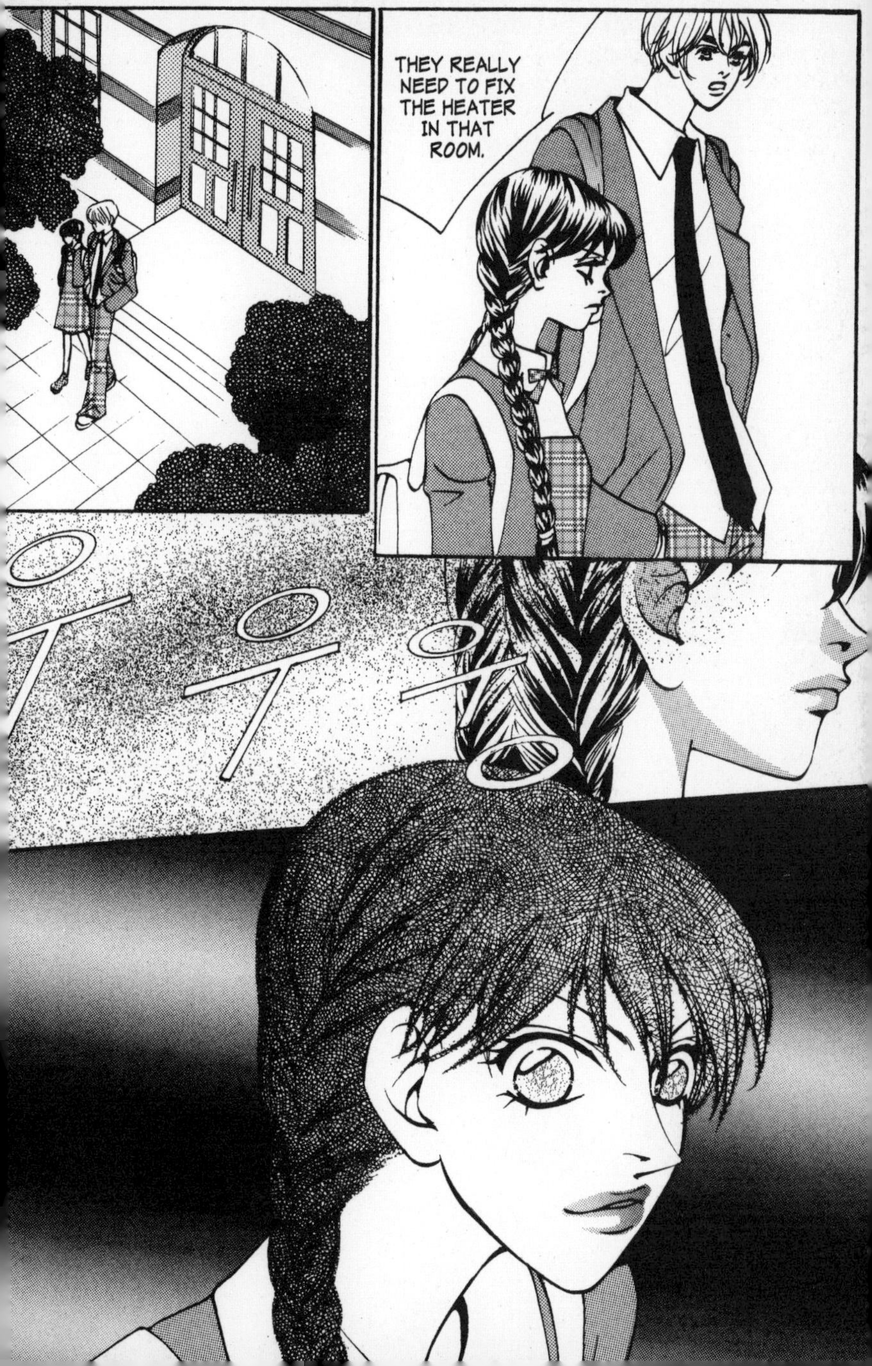
THEY REALLY NEED TO FIX THE HEATER IN THAT ROOM.

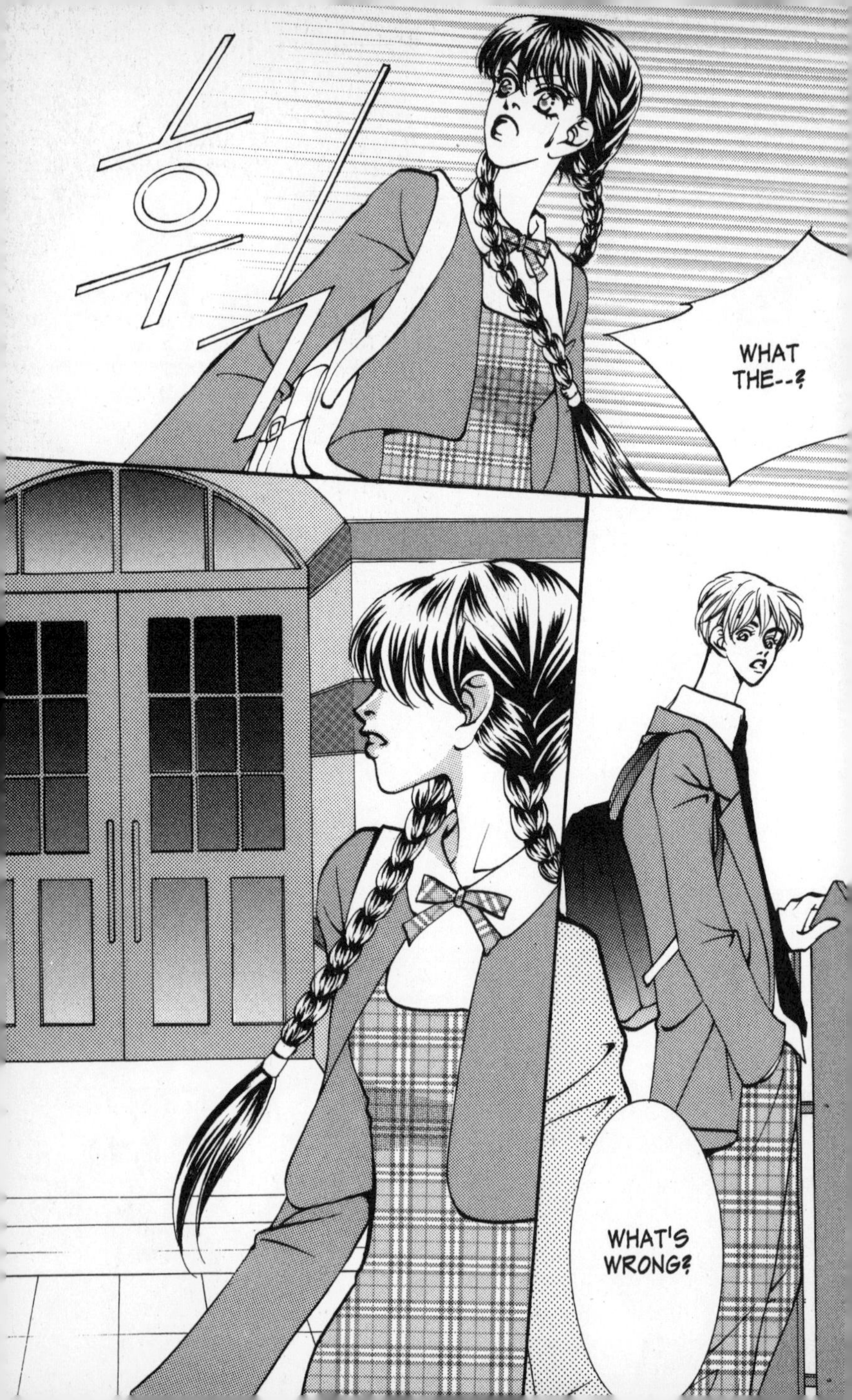
WHAT THE--?
WHAT'S WRONG?

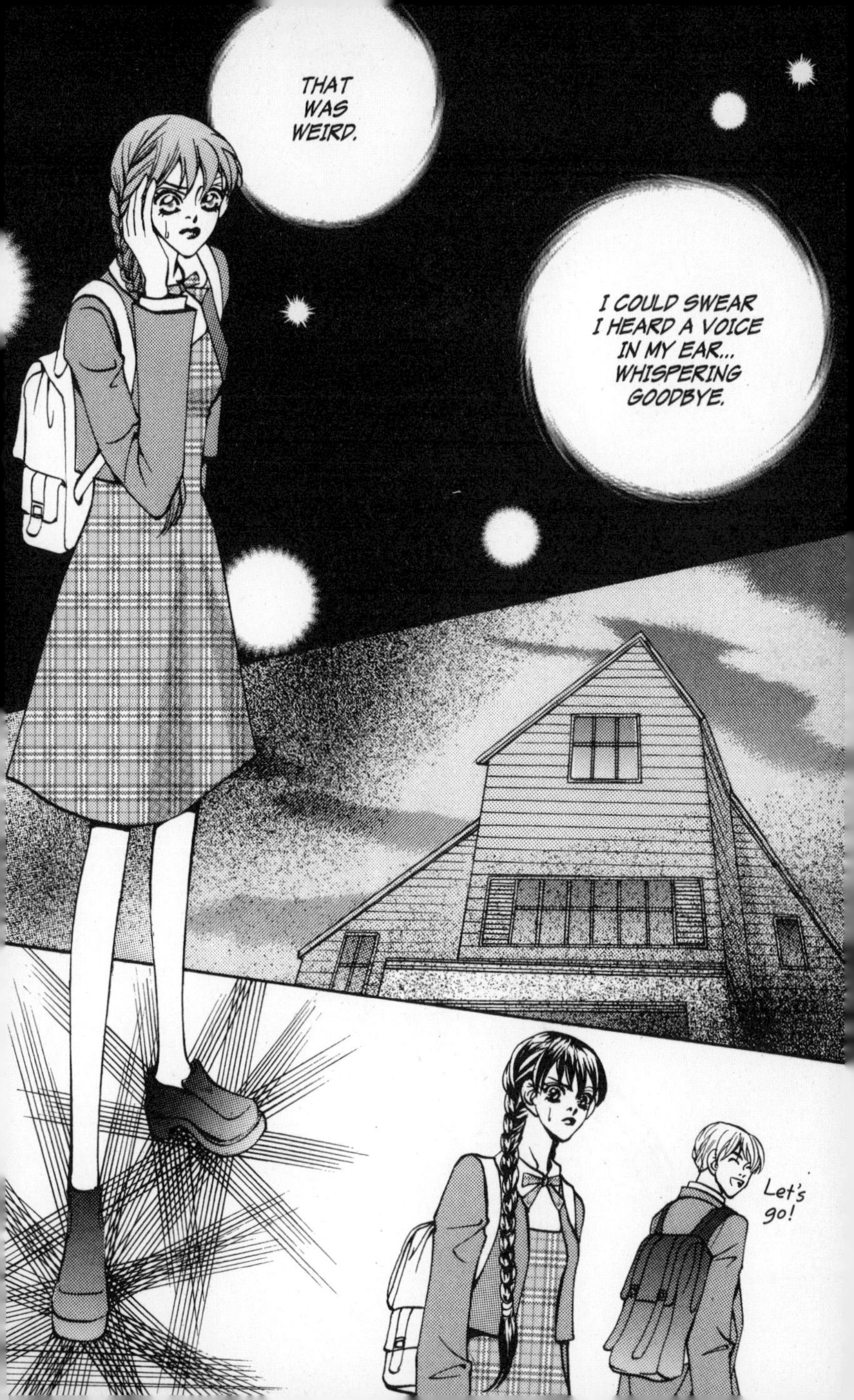
THAT WAS WEIRD.
I COULD SWEAR I HEARD A VOICE IN MY EAR... WHISPERING GOODBYE.
Let's go!

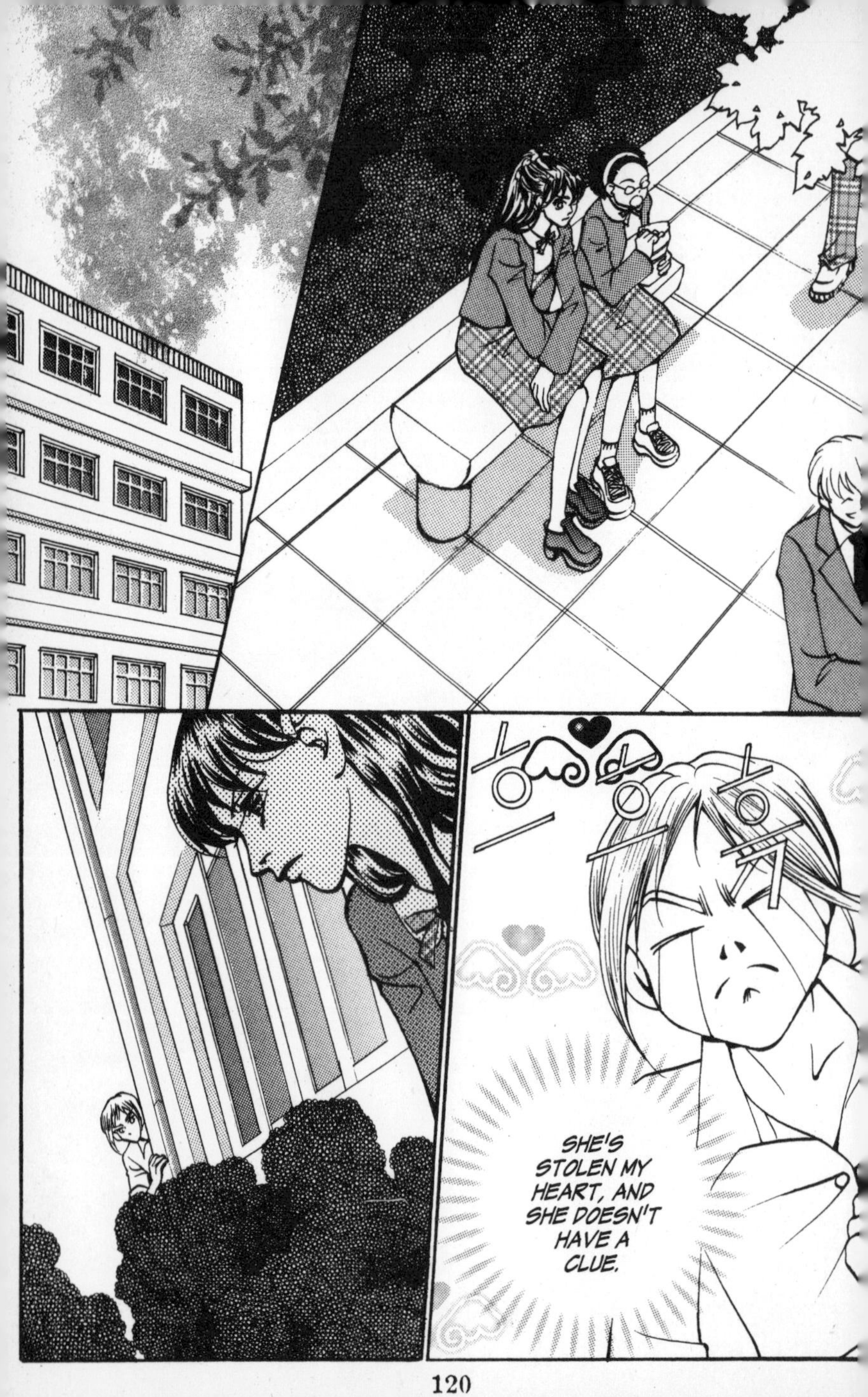
SHE'S STOLEN MY HEART, AND SHE DOESN'T HAVE A CLUE.

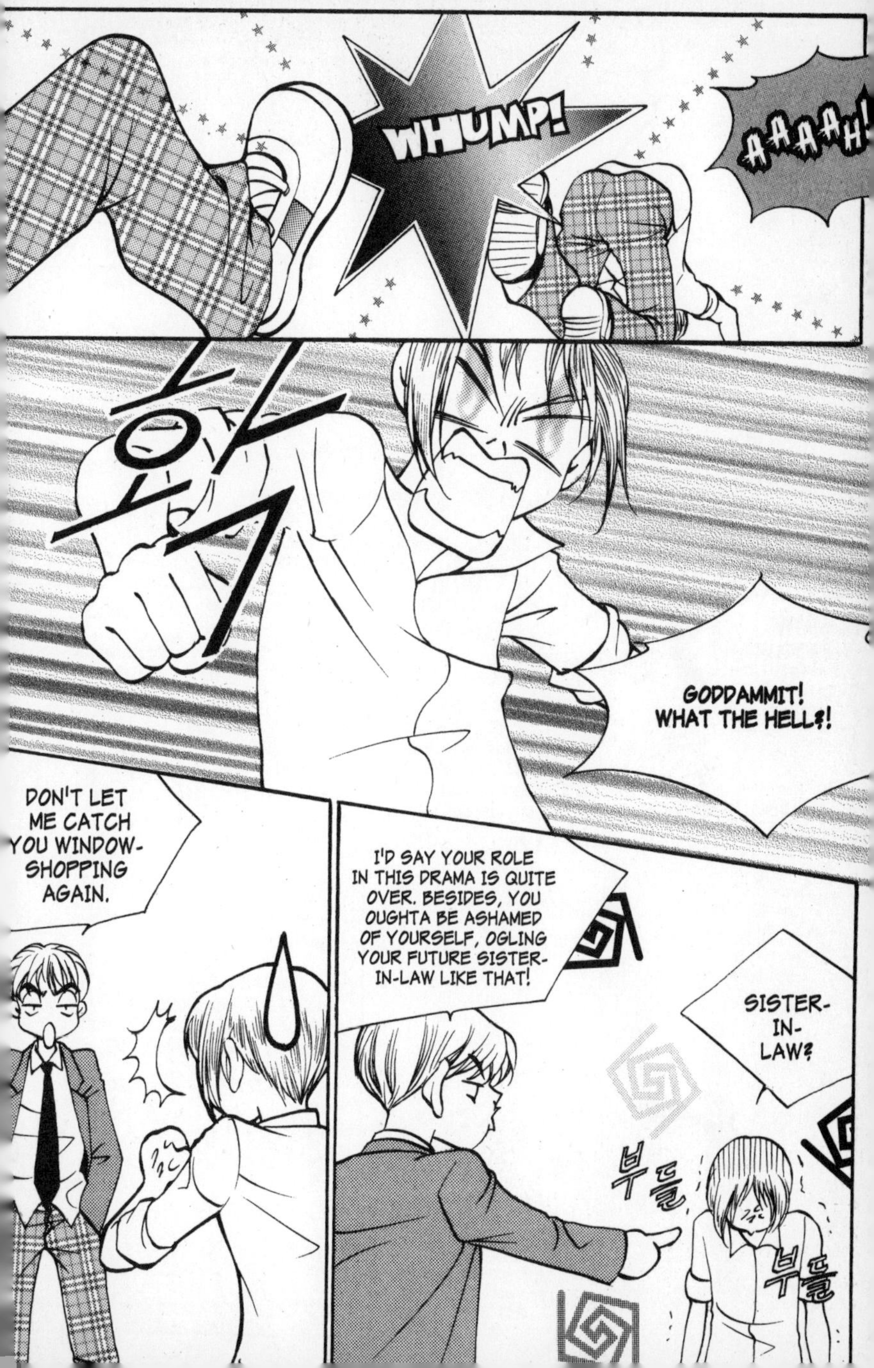
WHUMP!
AAAAH!
GODDAMMIT! WHAT THE HELL?!
DON'T LET ME CATCH YOU WINDOW-SHOPPING AGAIN.
I'D SAY YOUR ROLE IN THIS DRAMA IS QUITE OVER. BESIDES, YOU OUGHTA BE ASHAMED OF YOURSELF, OGLING YOUR FUTURE SISTER-IN-LAW LIKE THAT!
SISTER-IN-LAW?
부들
부들

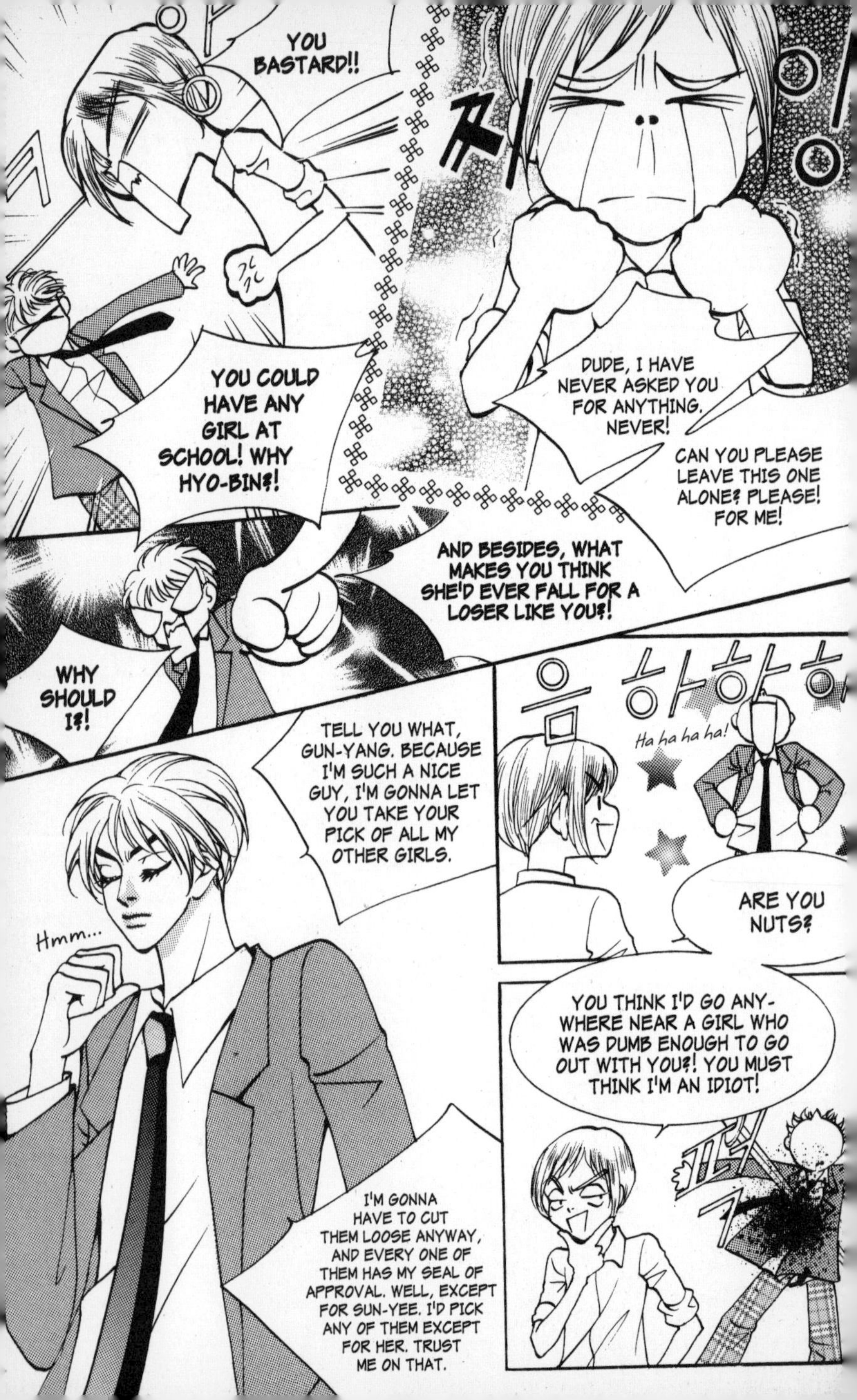
YOU BASTARD!!
YOU COULD HAVE ANY GIRL AT SCHOOL! WHY HYO-BIN?!
DUDE, I HAVE NEVER ASKED YOU FOR ANYTHING. NEVER!
CAN YOU PLEASE LEAVE THIS ONE ALONE? PLEASE! FOR ME!
AND BESIDES, WHAT MAKES YOU THINK SHE'D EVER FALL FOR A LOSER LIKE YOU?!
WHY SHOULD I?!
TELL YOU WHAT, GUN-YANG. BECAUSE I'M SUCH A NICE GUY, I'M GONNA LET YOU TAKE YOUR PICK OF ALL MY OTHER GIRLS.
Hmm...
I'M GONNA HAVE TO CUT THEM LOOSE ANYWAY, AND EVERY ONE OF THEM HAS MY SEAL OF APPROVAL. WELL, EXCEPT FOR SUN-YEE. I'D PICK ANY OF THEM EXCEPT FOR HER. TRUST ME ON THAT.
음 하하하
Ha ha ha ha!
ARE YOU NUTS?
YOU THINK I'D GO ANY-WHERE NEAR A GIRL WHO WAS DUMB ENOUGH TO GO OUT WITH YOU?! YOU MUST THINK I'M AN IDIOT!

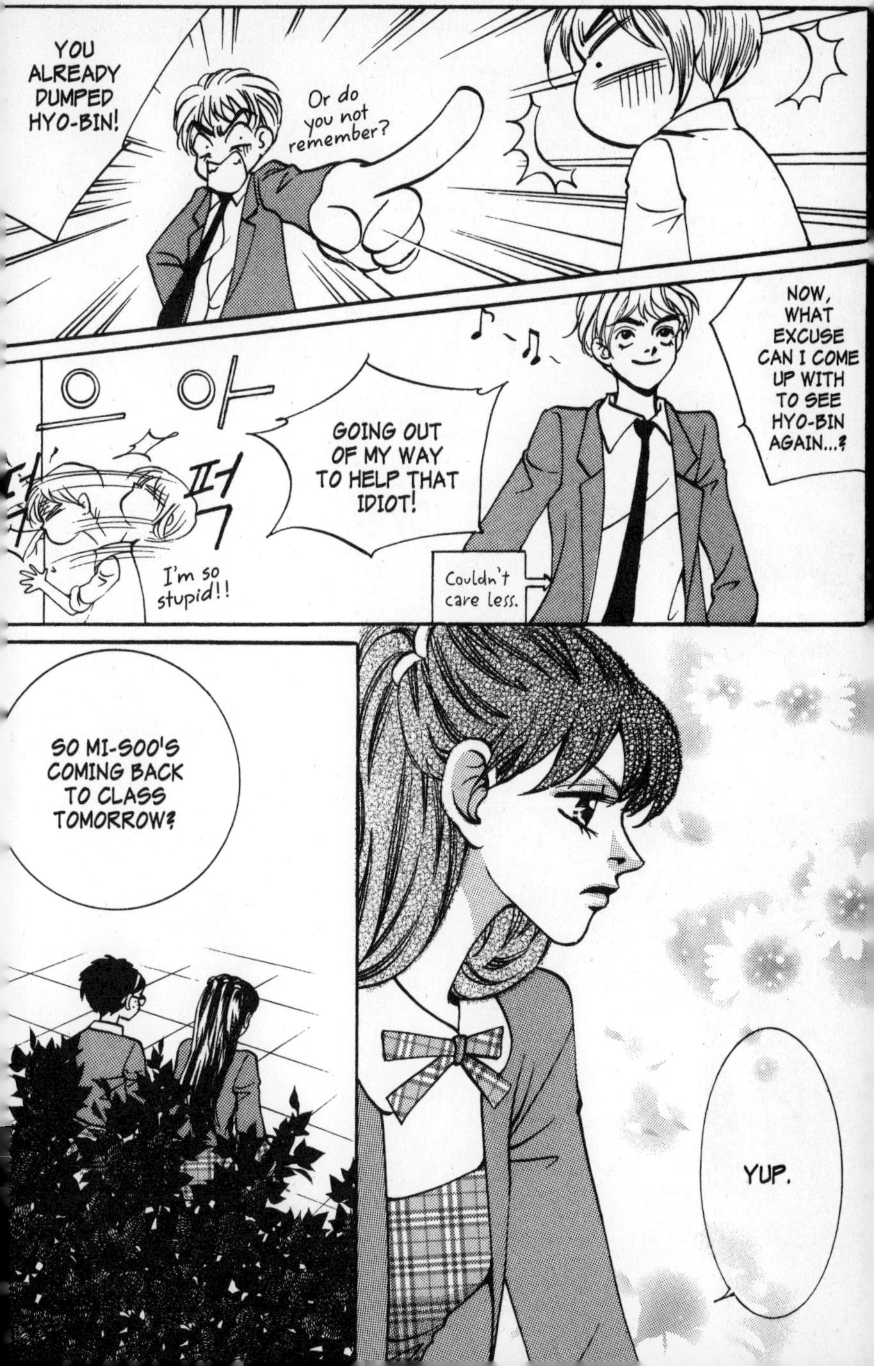

YOU ALREADY DUMPED HYO-BIN!
Or do you not remember?
으아
퍽
I'm so stupid!!
GOING OUT OF MY WAY TO HELP THAT IDIOT!
Couldn't care less.
NOW, WHAT EXCUSE CAN I COME UP WITH TO SEE HYO-BIN AGAIN...?
SO MI-SOO'S COMING BACK TO CLASS TOMORROW?
YUP.

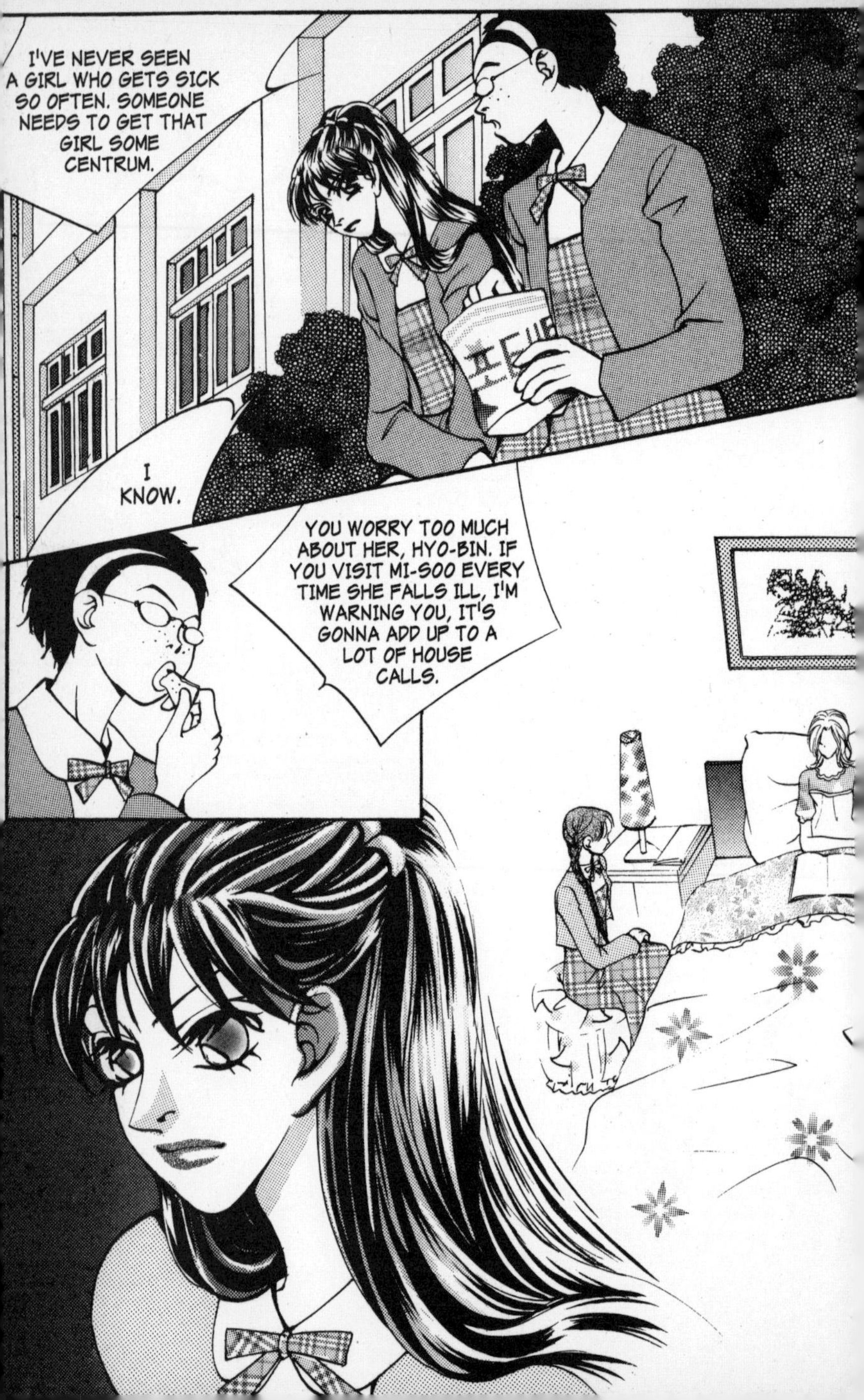
I'VE NEVER SEEN A GIRL WHO GETS SICK SO OFTEN. SOMEONE NEEDS TO GET THAT GIRL SOME CENTRUM.
I KNOW.
YOU WORRY TOO MUCH ABOUT HER, HYO-BIN. IF YOU VISIT MI-SOO EVERY TIME SHE FALLS ILL, I'M WARNING YOU, IT'S GONNA ADD UP TO A LOT OF HOUSE CALLS.

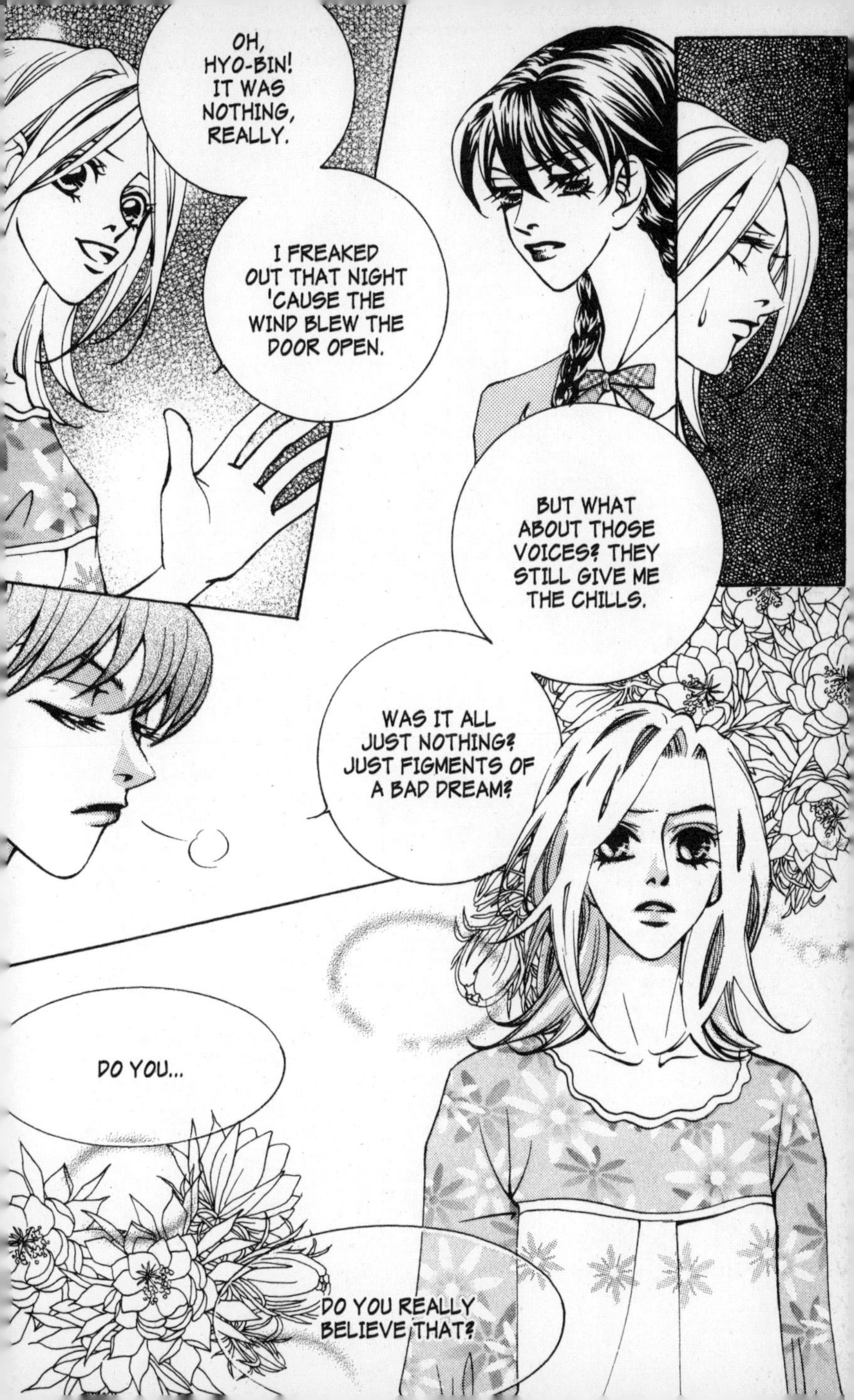
OH, HYO-BIN! IT WAS NOTHING, REALLY.
I FREAKED OUT THAT NIGHT 'CAUSE THE WIND BLEW THE DOOR OPEN.
BUT WHAT ABOUT THOSE VOICES? THEY STILL GIVE ME THE CHILLS.
WAS IT ALL JUST NOTHING? JUST FIGMENTS OF A BAD DREAM?
DO YOU...
DO YOU REALLY BELIEVE THAT?

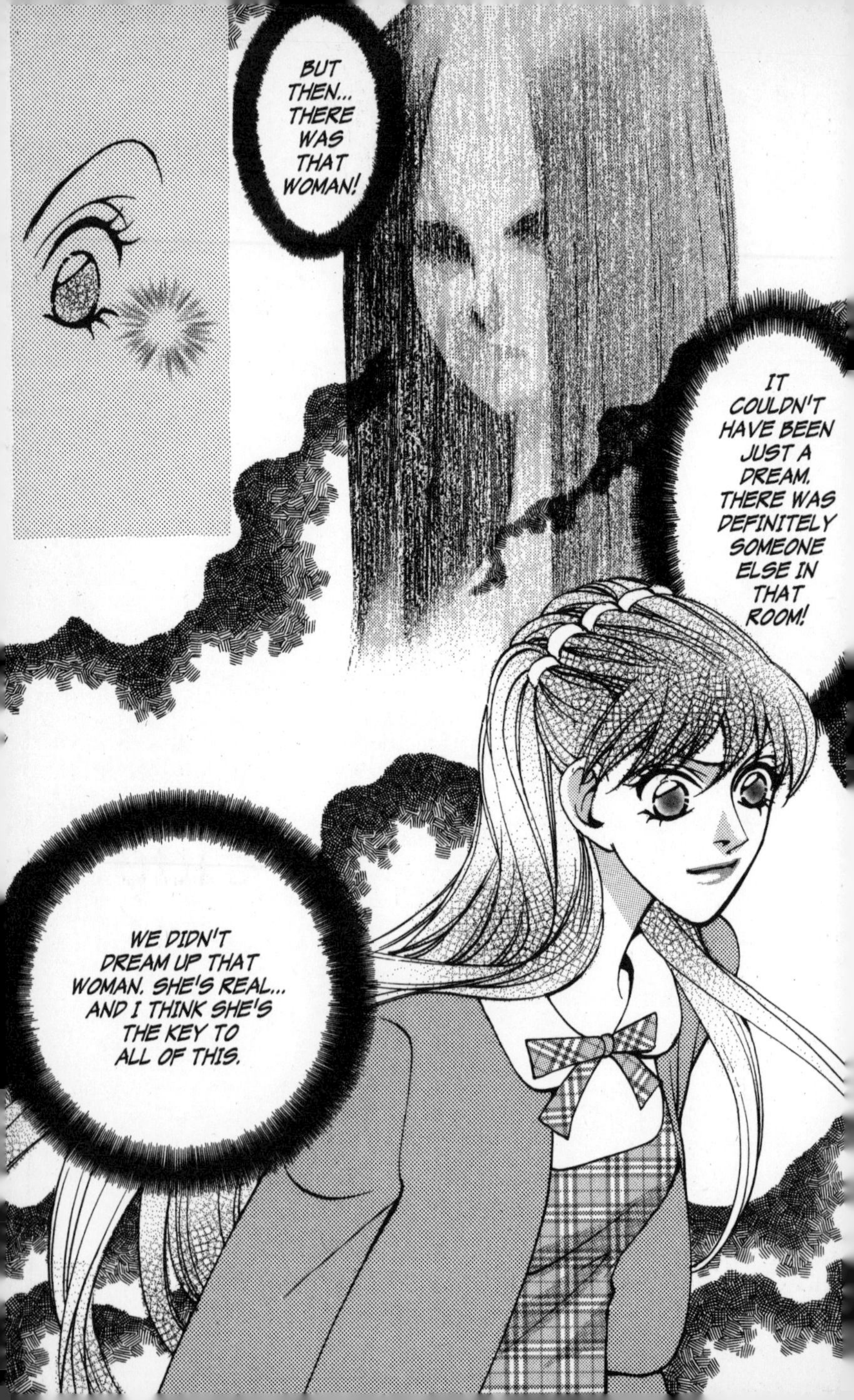
BUT THEN... THERE WAS THAT WOMAN!
IT COULDN'T HAVE BEEN JUST A DREAM. THERE WAS DEFINITELY SOMEONE ELSE IN THAT ROOM!
WE DIDN'T DREAM UP THAT WOMAN. SHE'S REAL... AND I THINK SHE'S THE KEY TO ALL OF THIS.

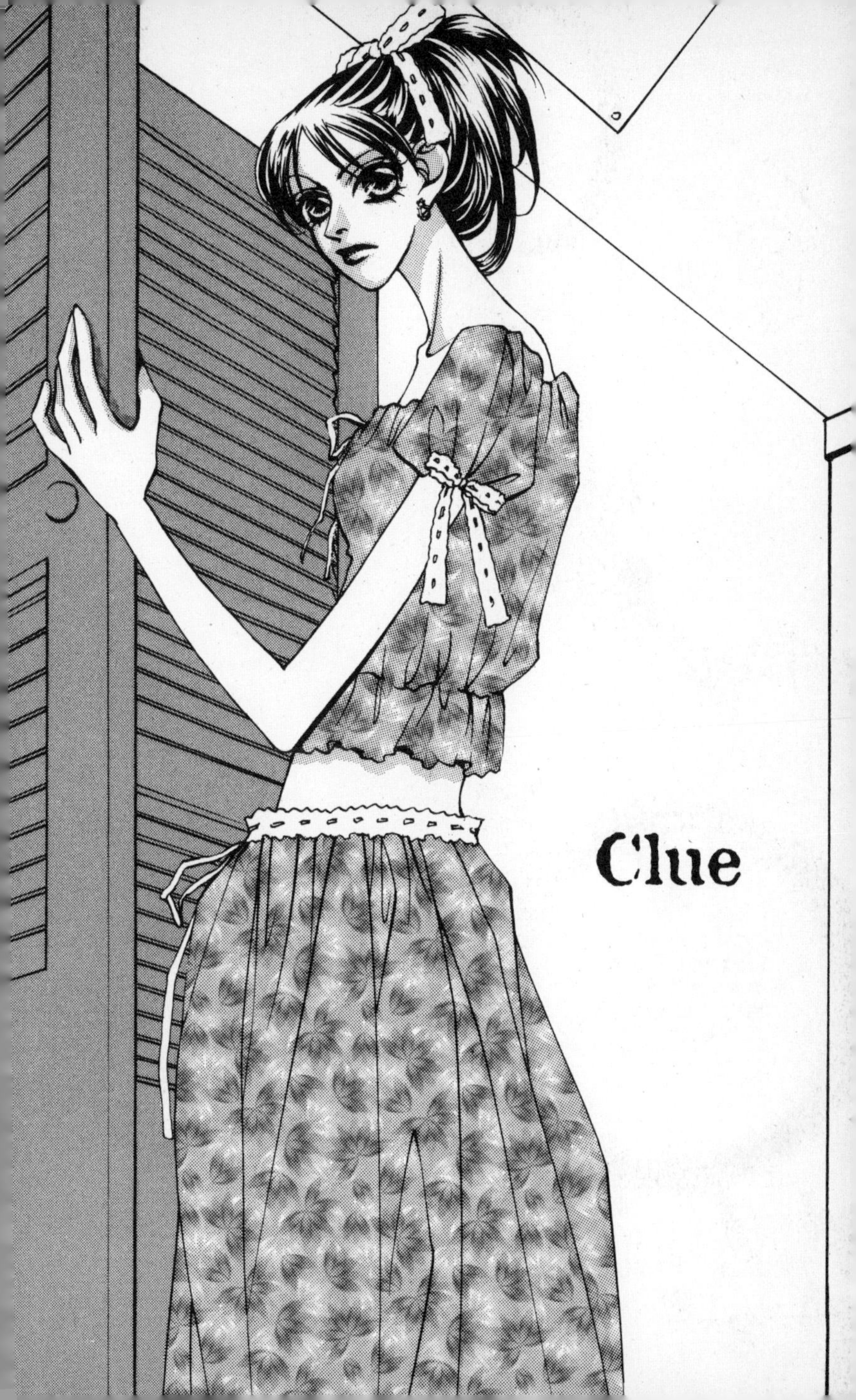
Clue

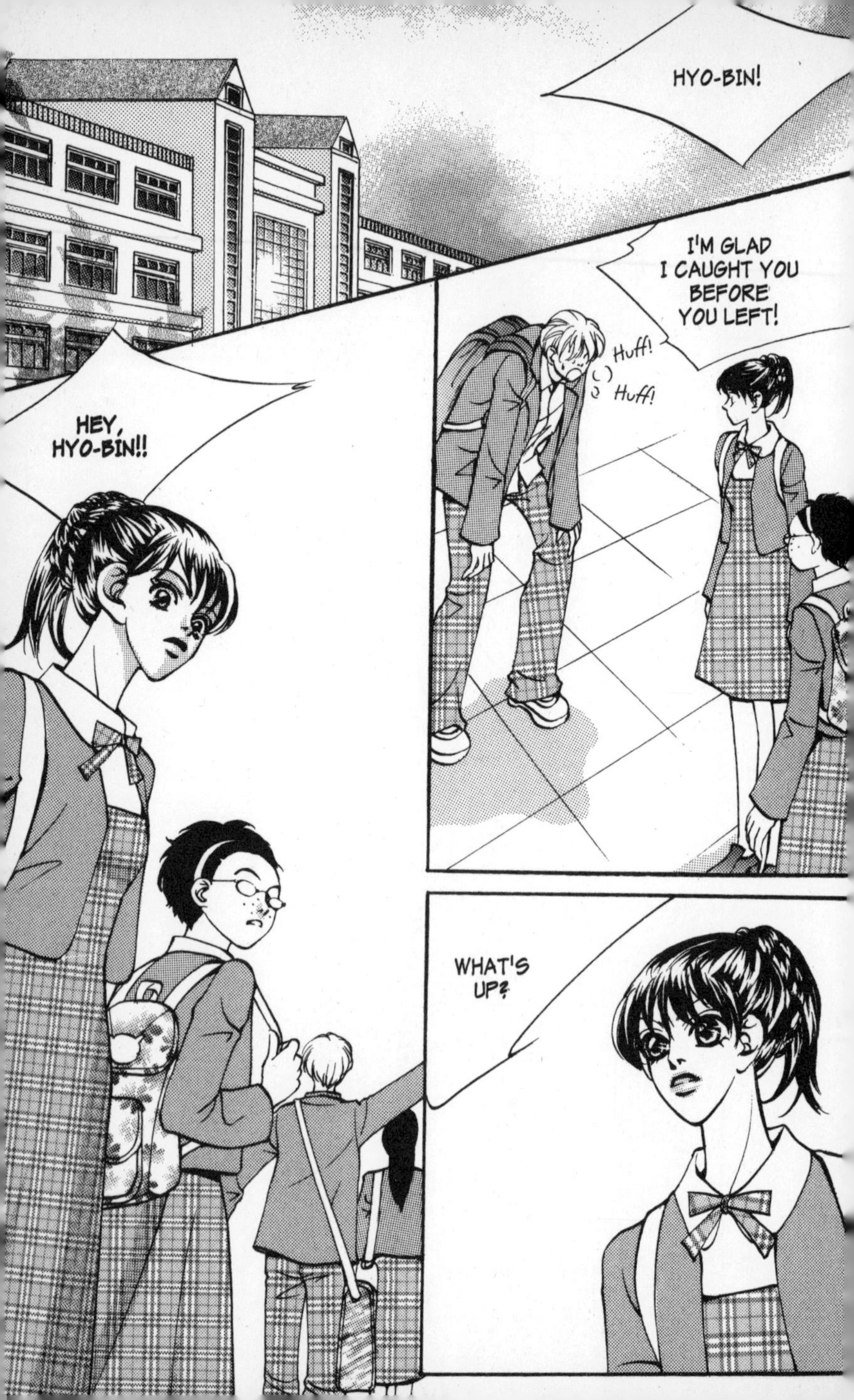
HYO-BIN!
HEY, HYO-BIN!!
I'M GLAD I CAUGHT YOU BEFORE YOU LEFT!
Huff!
Huff!
WHAT'S UP?

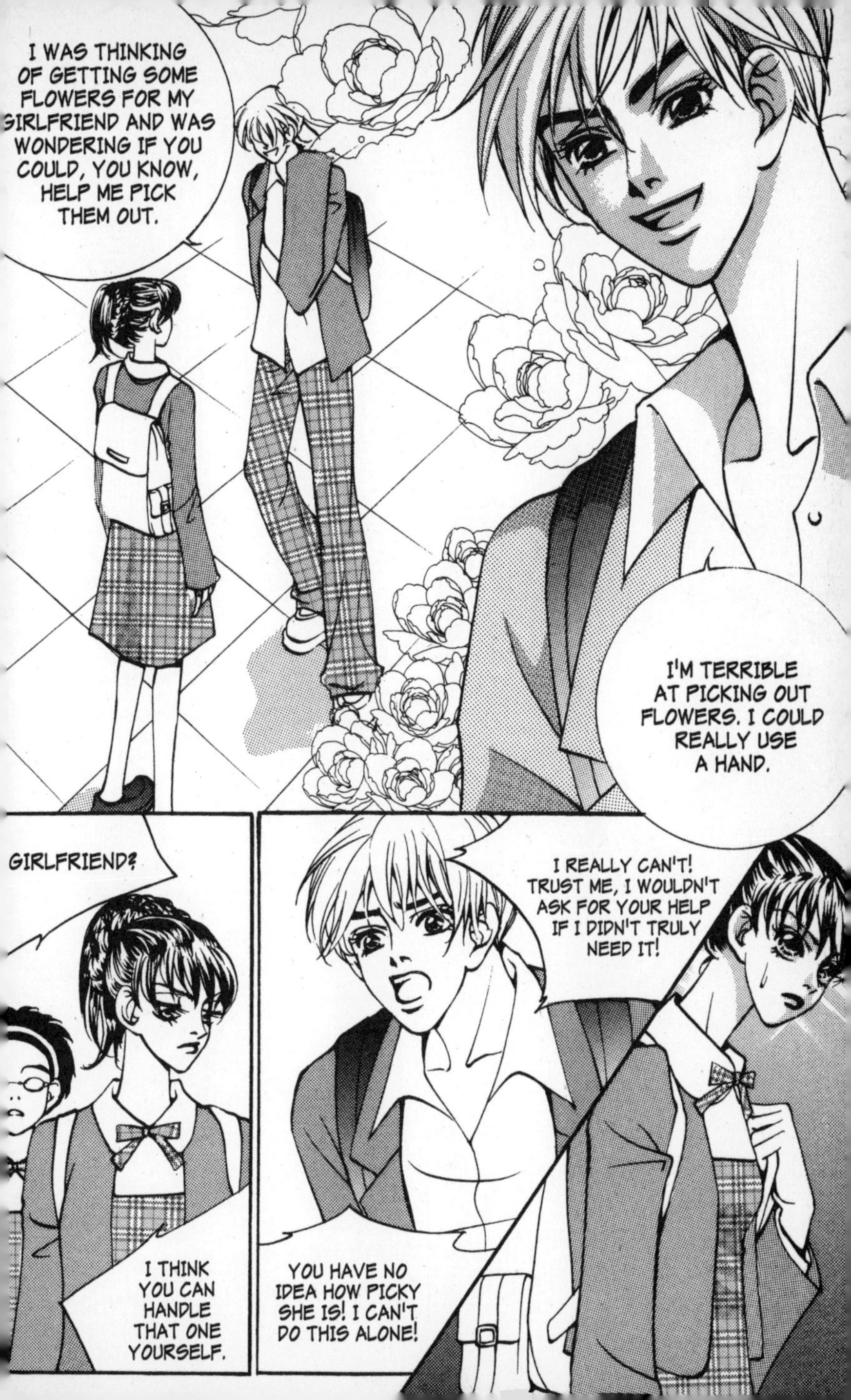
I WAS THINKING OF GETTING SOME FLOWERS FOR MY GIRLFRIEND AND WAS WONDERING IF YOU COULD, YOU KNOW, HELP ME PICK THEM OUT.
I'M TERRIBLE AT PICKING OUT FLOWERS. I COULD REALLY USE A HAND.
GIRLFRIEND?
I THINK YOU CAN HANDLE THAT ONE YOURSELF.
I REALLY CAN'T! TRUST ME, I WOULDN'T ASK FOR YOUR HELP IF I DIDN'T TRULY NEED IT!
YOU HAVE NO IDEA HOW PICKY SHE IS! I CAN'T DO THIS ALONE!

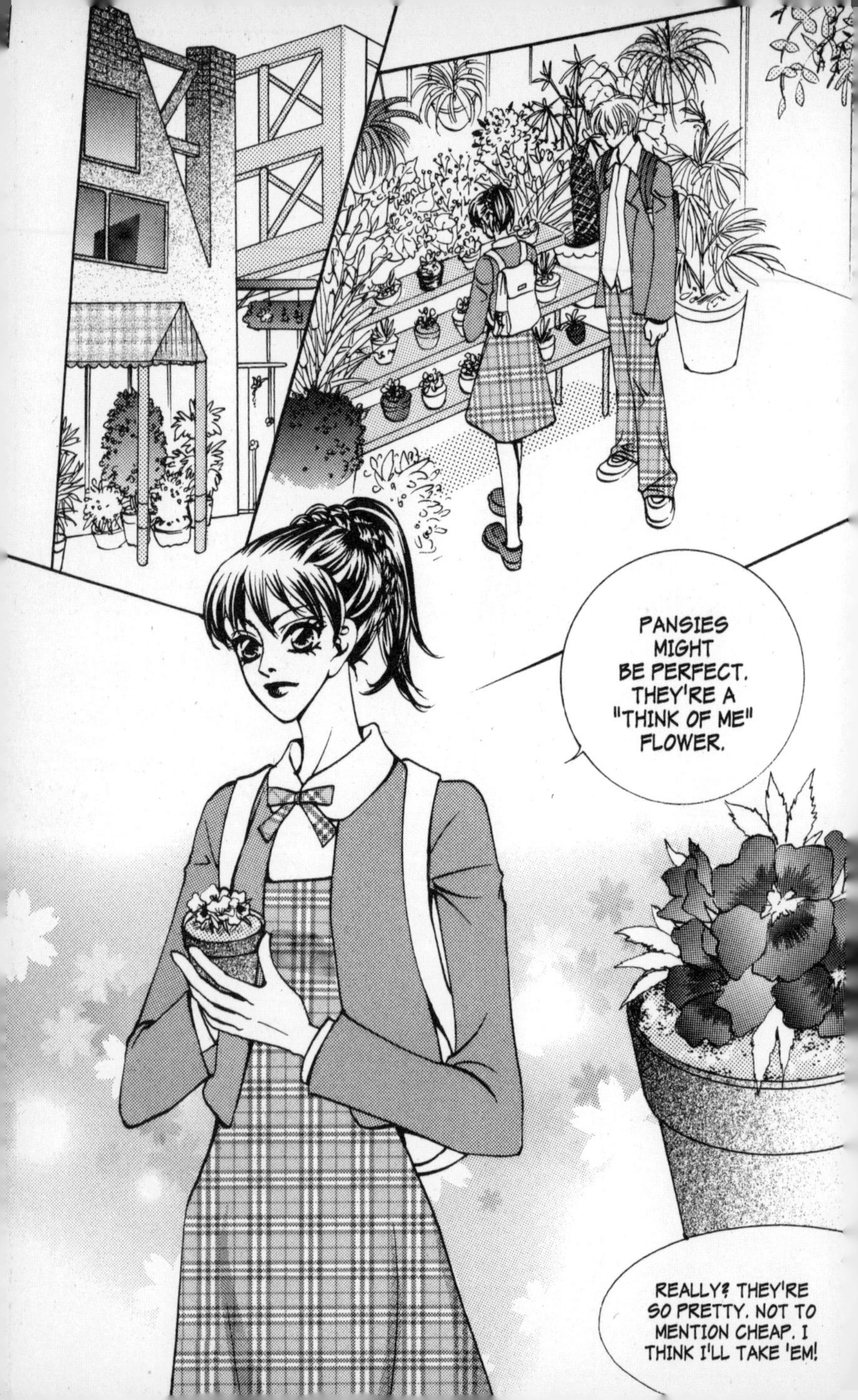
PANSIES MIGHT BE PERFECT. THEY'RE A "THINK OF ME" FLOWER.
REALLY? THEY'RE SO PRETTY. NOT TO MENTION CHEAP. I THINK I'LL TAKE 'EM!

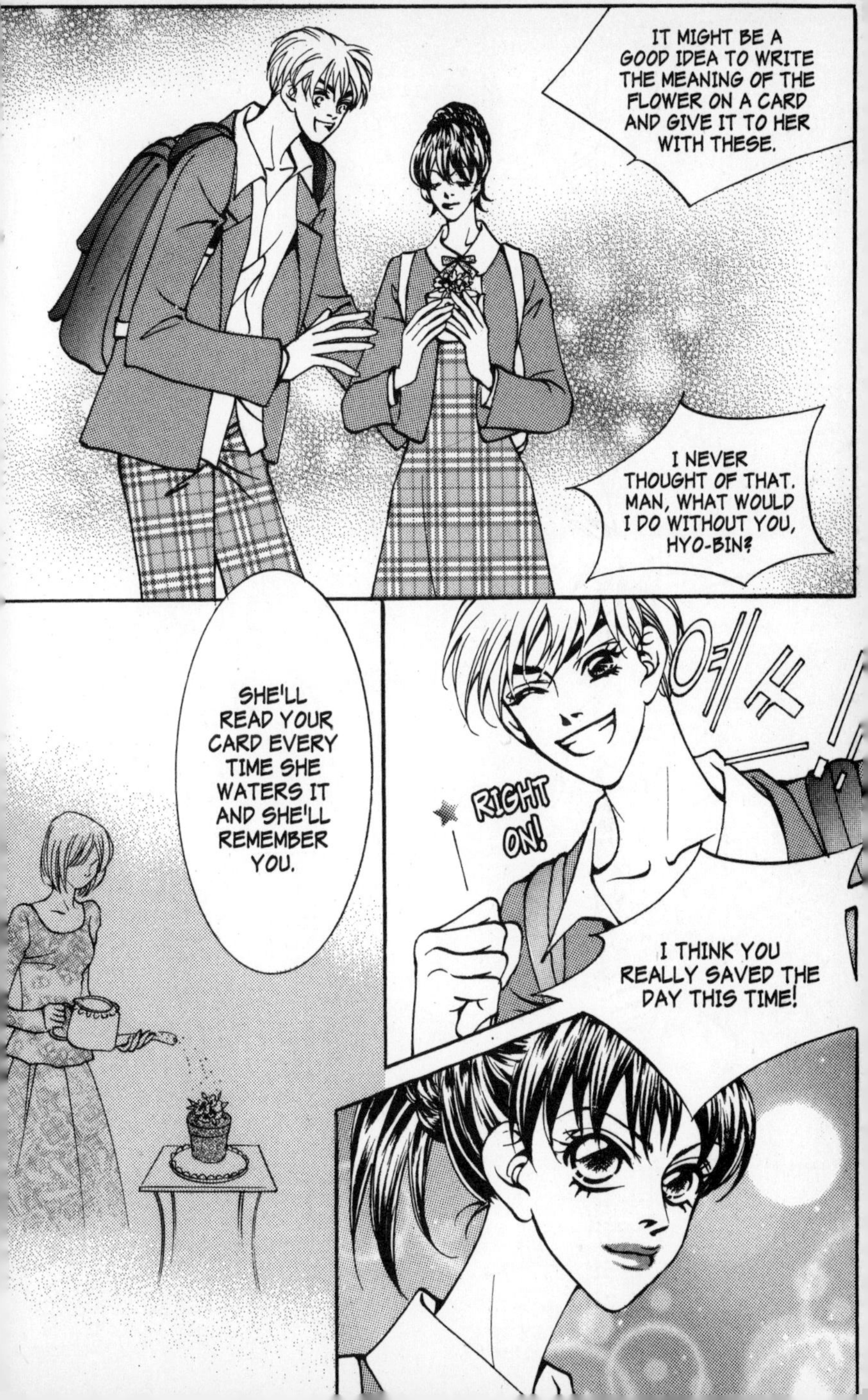
IT MIGHT BE A GOOD IDEA TO WRITE THE MEANING OF THE FLOWER ON A CARD AND GIVE IT TO HER WITH THESE.
I NEVER THOUGHT OF THAT. MAN, WHAT WOULD I DO WITHOUT YOU, HYO-BIN?
SHE'LL READ YOUR CARD EVERY TIME SHE WATERS IT AND SHE'LL REMEMBER YOU.
RIGHT ON!
I THINK YOU REALLY SAVED THE DAY THIS TIME!

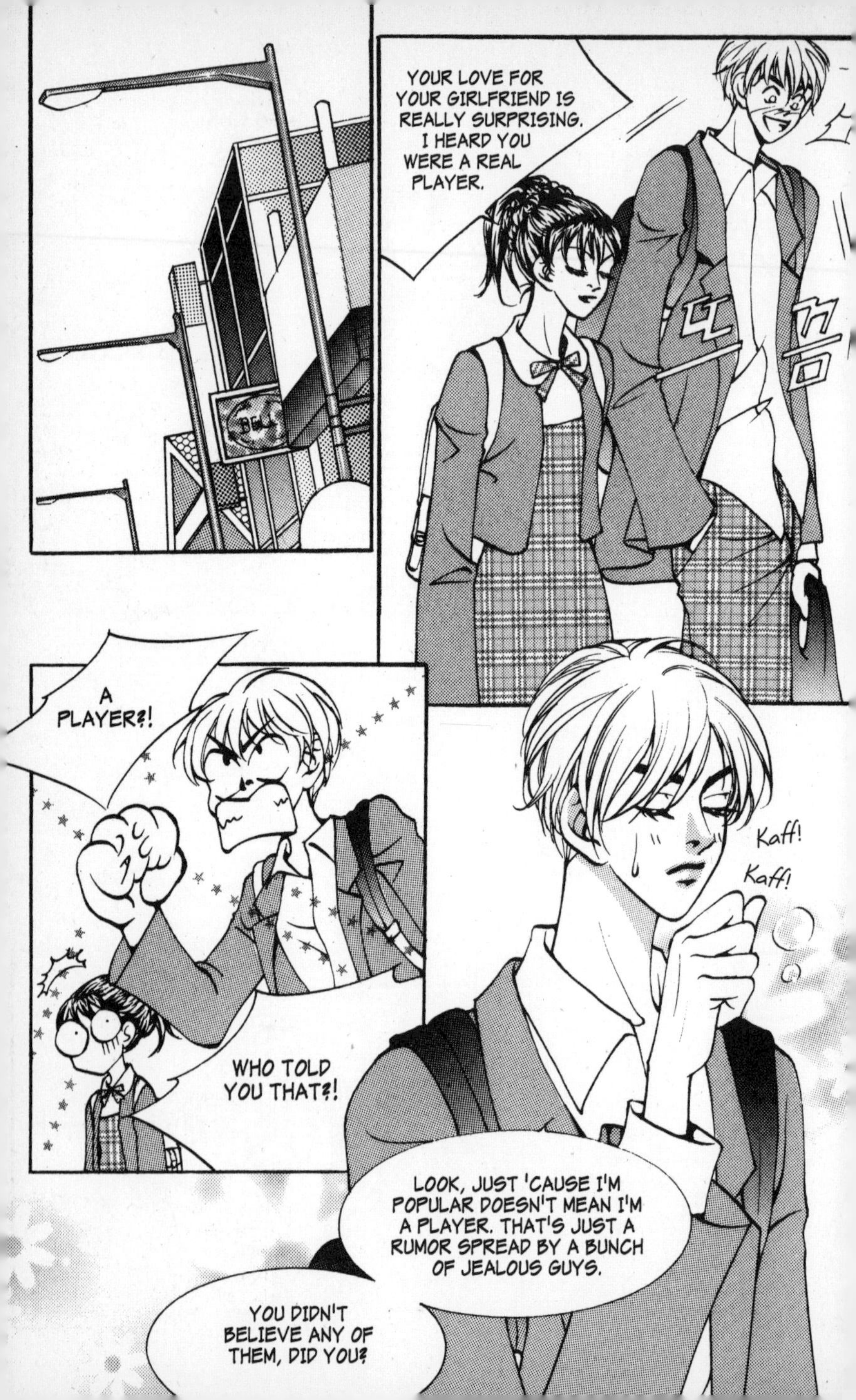
YOUR LOVE FOR YOUR GIRLFRIEND IS REALLY SURPRISING. I HEARD YOU WERE A REAL PLAYER.
A PLAYER?!
WHO TOLD YOU THAT?!
Kaff!
Kaff!
LOOK, JUST 'CAUSE I'M POPULAR DOESN'T MEAN I'M A PLAYER. THAT'S JUST A RUMOR SPREAD BY A BUNCH OF JEALOUS GUYS.
YOU DIDN'T BELIEVE ANY OF THEM, DID YOU?

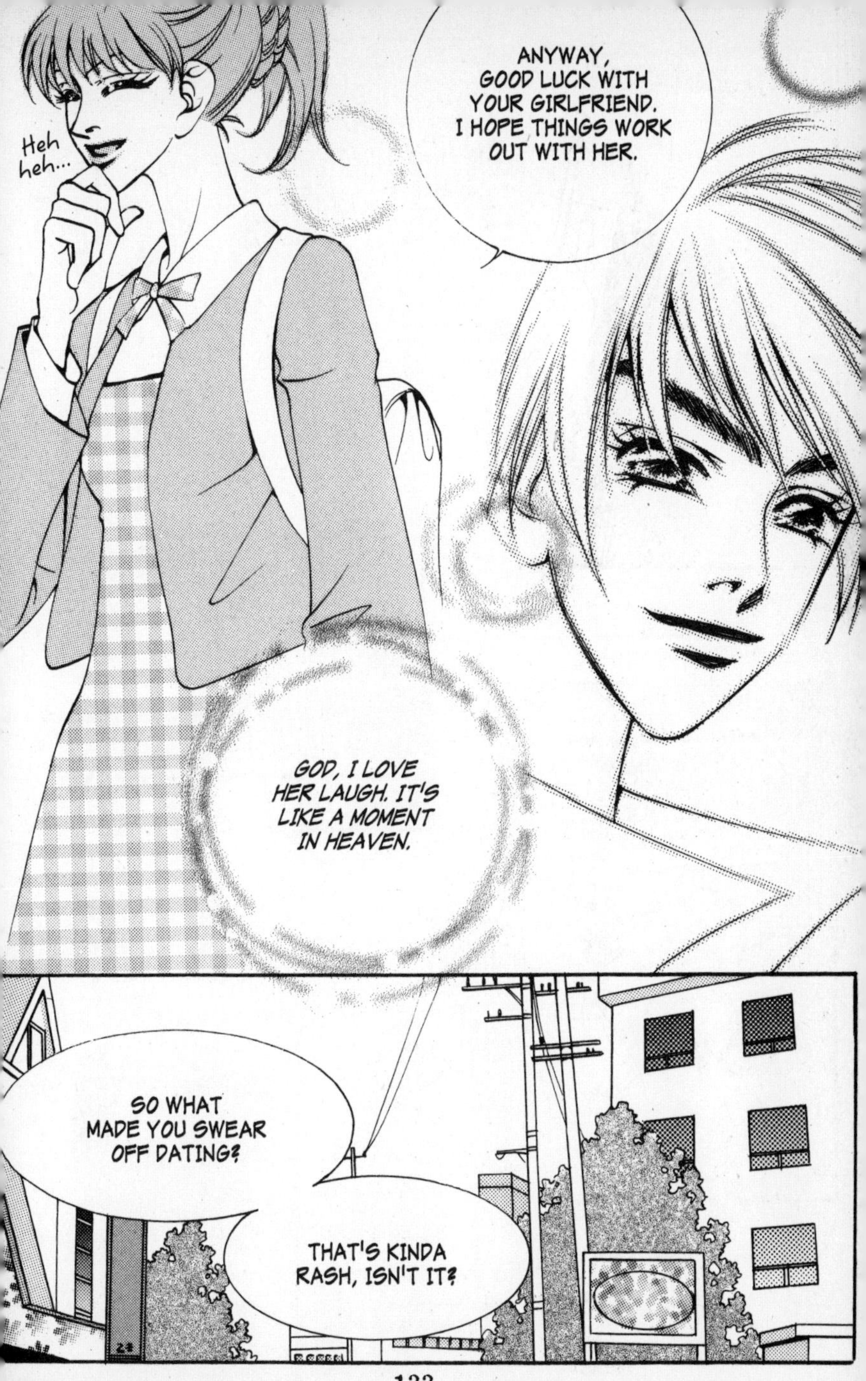
Heh heh...
ANYWAY, GOOD LUCK WITH YOUR GIRLFRIEND. I HOPE THINGS WORK OUT WITH HER.
GOD, I LOVE HER LAUGH. IT'S LIKE A MOMENT IN HEAVEN.
SO WHAT MADE YOU SWEAR OFF DATING?
THAT'S KINDA RASH, ISN'T IT?

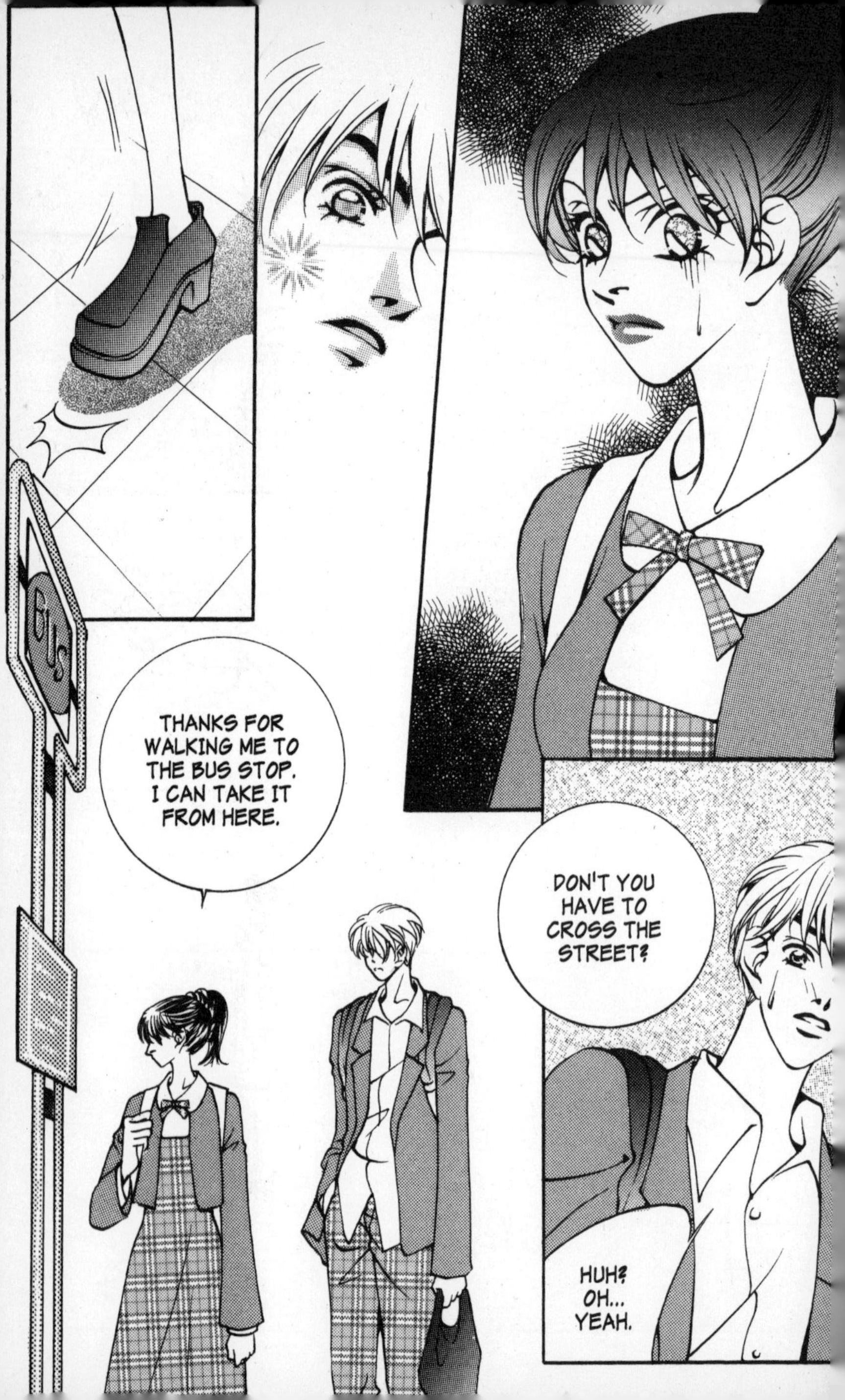
BUS
THANKS FOR WALKING ME TO THE BUS STOP. I CAN TAKE IT FROM HERE.
DON'T YOU HAVE TO CROSS THE STREET?
HUH? OH... YEAH.

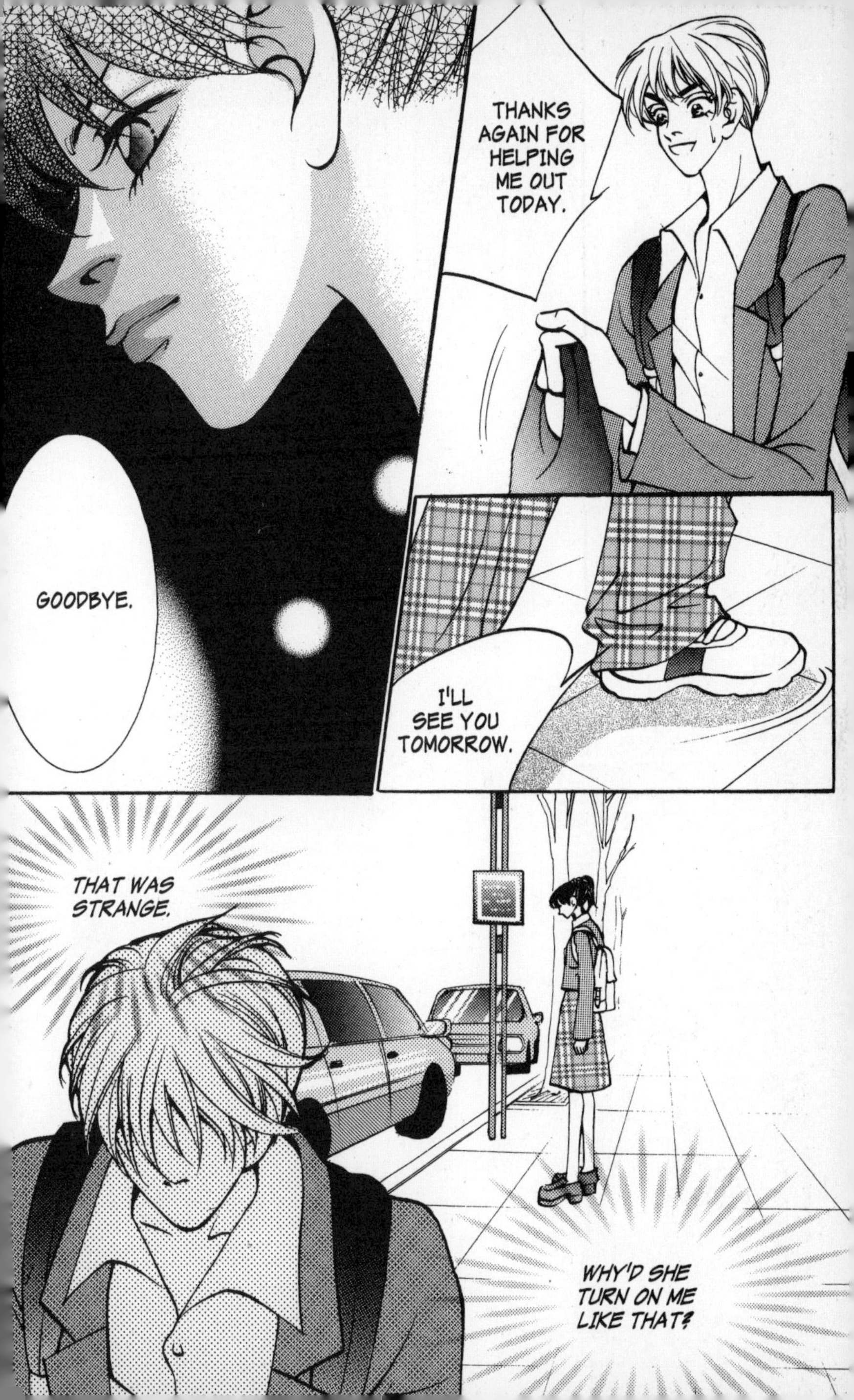
GOODBYE.
THANKS AGAIN FOR HELPING ME OUT TODAY.
I'LL SEE YOU TOMORROW.
THAT WAS STRANGE.
WHY'D SHE TURN ON ME LIKE THAT?

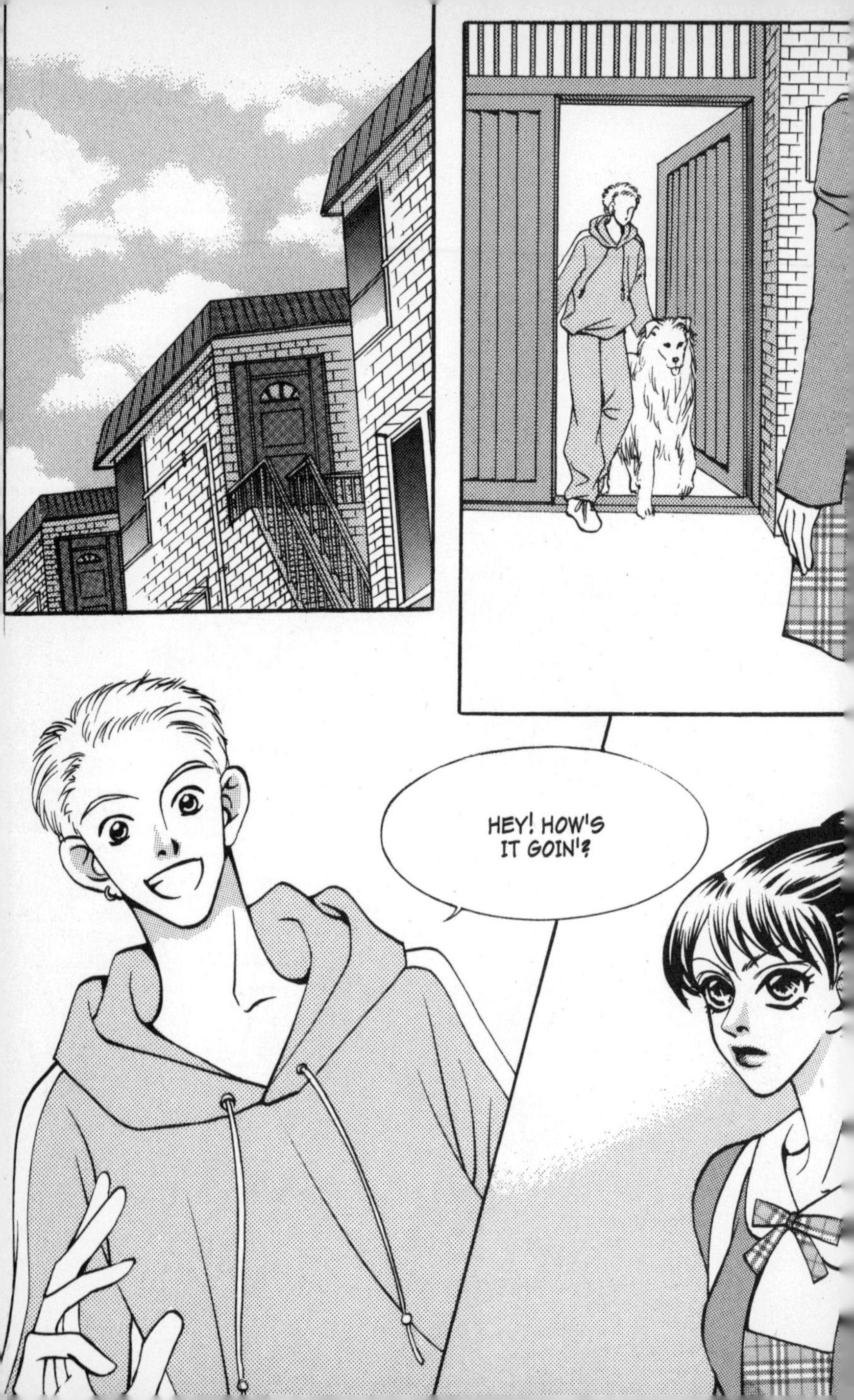
HEY! HOW'S IT GOIN'?

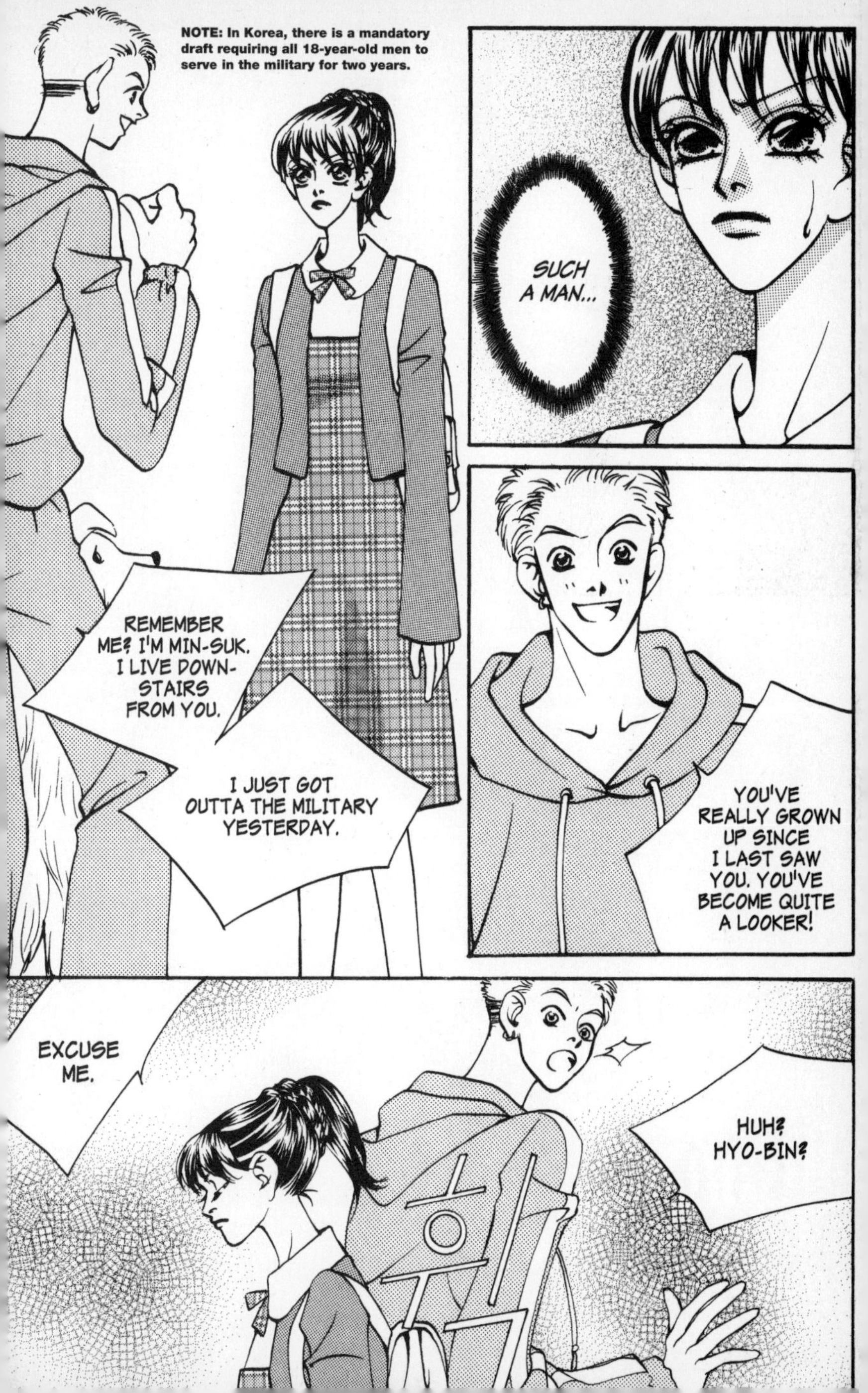
NOTE: In Korea, there is a mandatory draft requiring all 18-year-old men to serve in the military for two years.
REMEMBER ME? I'M MIN-SUK. I LIVE DOWN-STAIRS FROM YOU.
I JUST GOT OUTTA THE MILITARY YESTERDAY.
SUCH A MAN...
YOU'VE REALLY GROWN UP SINCE I LAST SAW YOU. YOU'VE BECOME QUITE A LOOKER!
EXCUSE ME.
HUH? HYO-BIN?

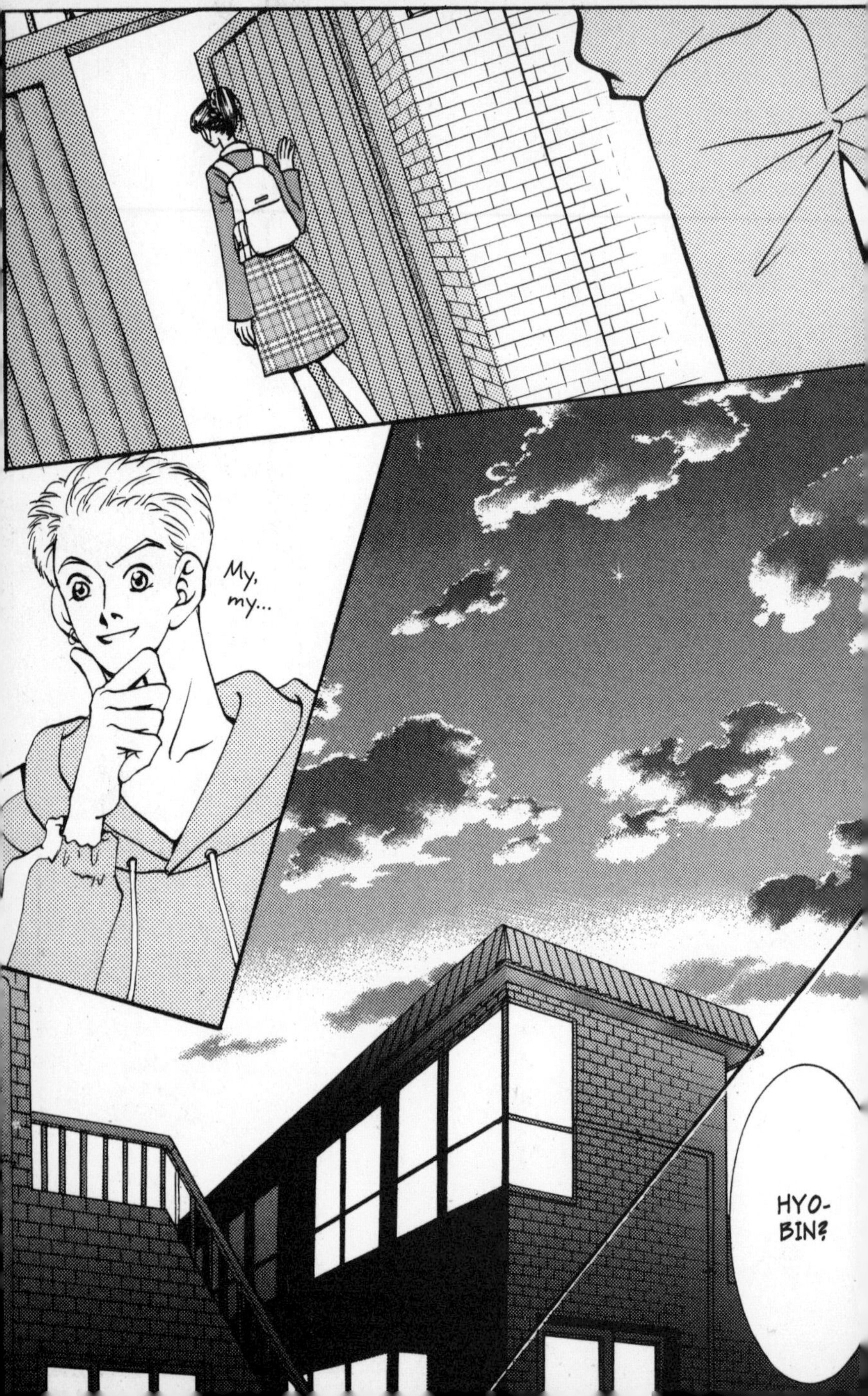
My, my...
HYO-BIN?

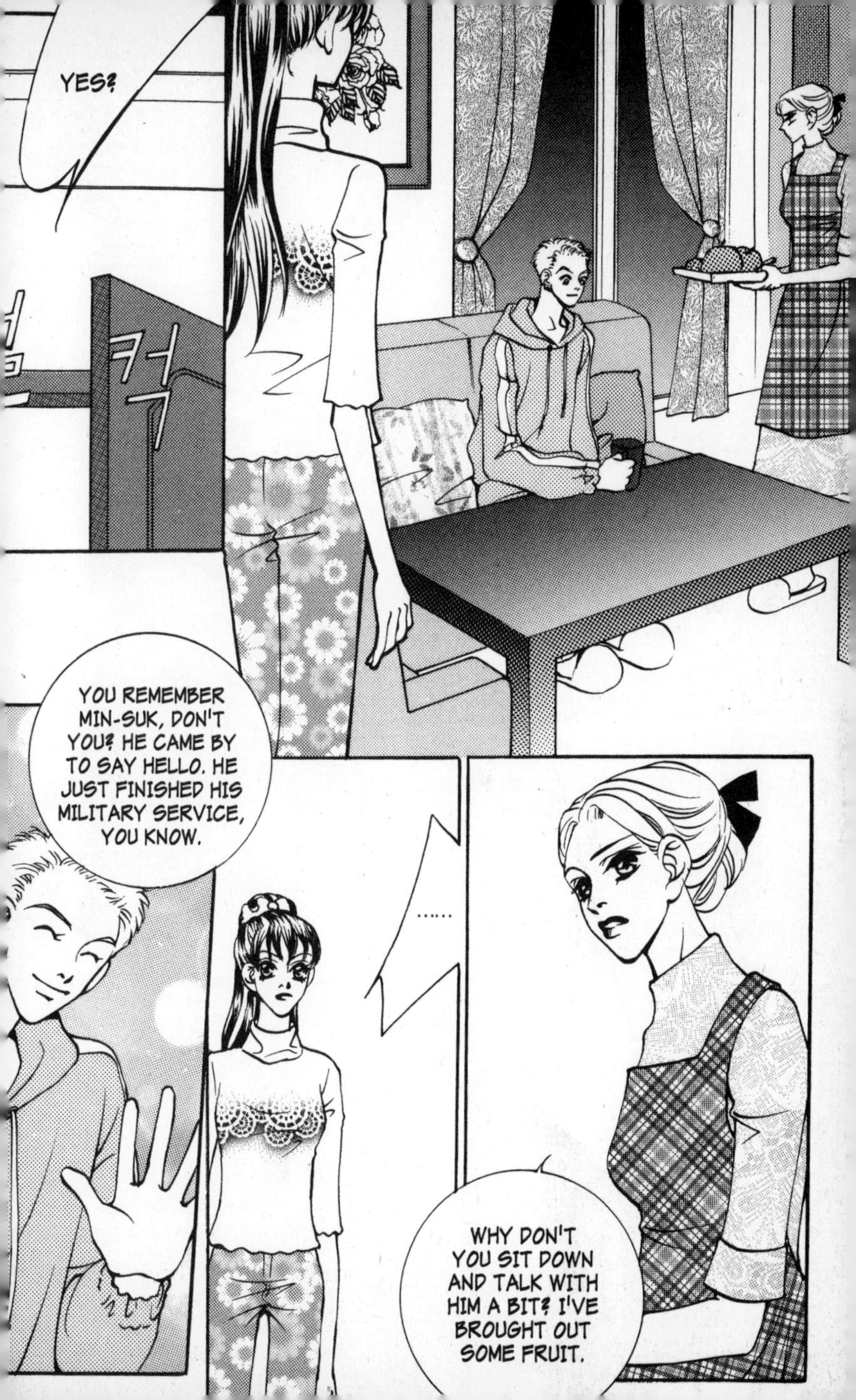
YES?
YOU REMEMBER MIN-SUK, DON'T YOU? HE CAME BY TO SAY HELLO. HE JUST FINISHED HIS MILITARY SERVICE, YOU KNOW.
......
WHY DON'T YOU SIT DOWN AND TALK WITH HIM A BIT? I'VE BROUGHT OUT SOME FRUIT.

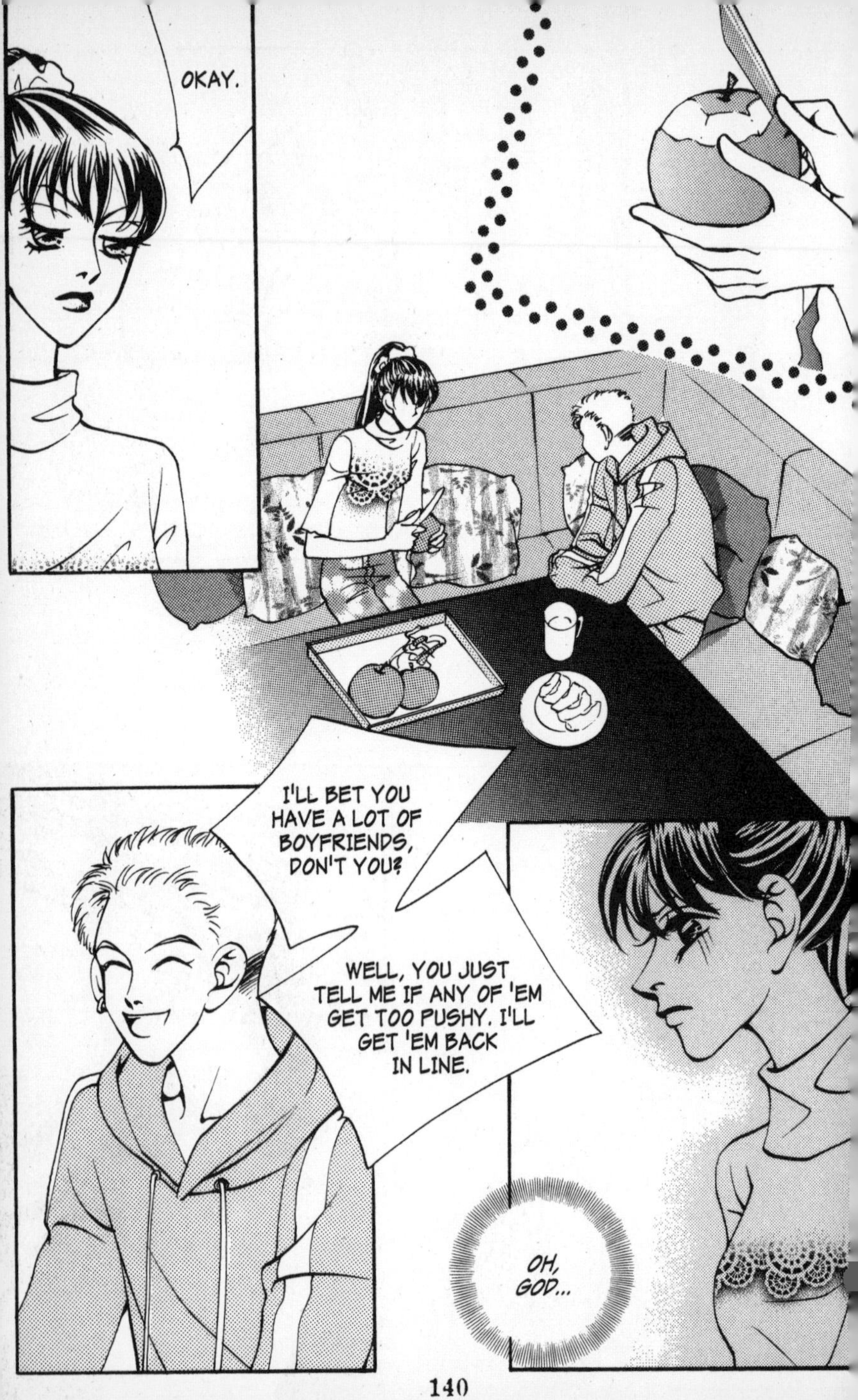
OKAY.
I'LL BET YOU HAVE A LOT OF BOYFRIENDS, DON'T YOU?
WELL, YOU JUST TELL ME IF ANY OF 'EM GET TOO PUSHY. I'LL GET 'EM BACK IN LINE.
OH, GOD...

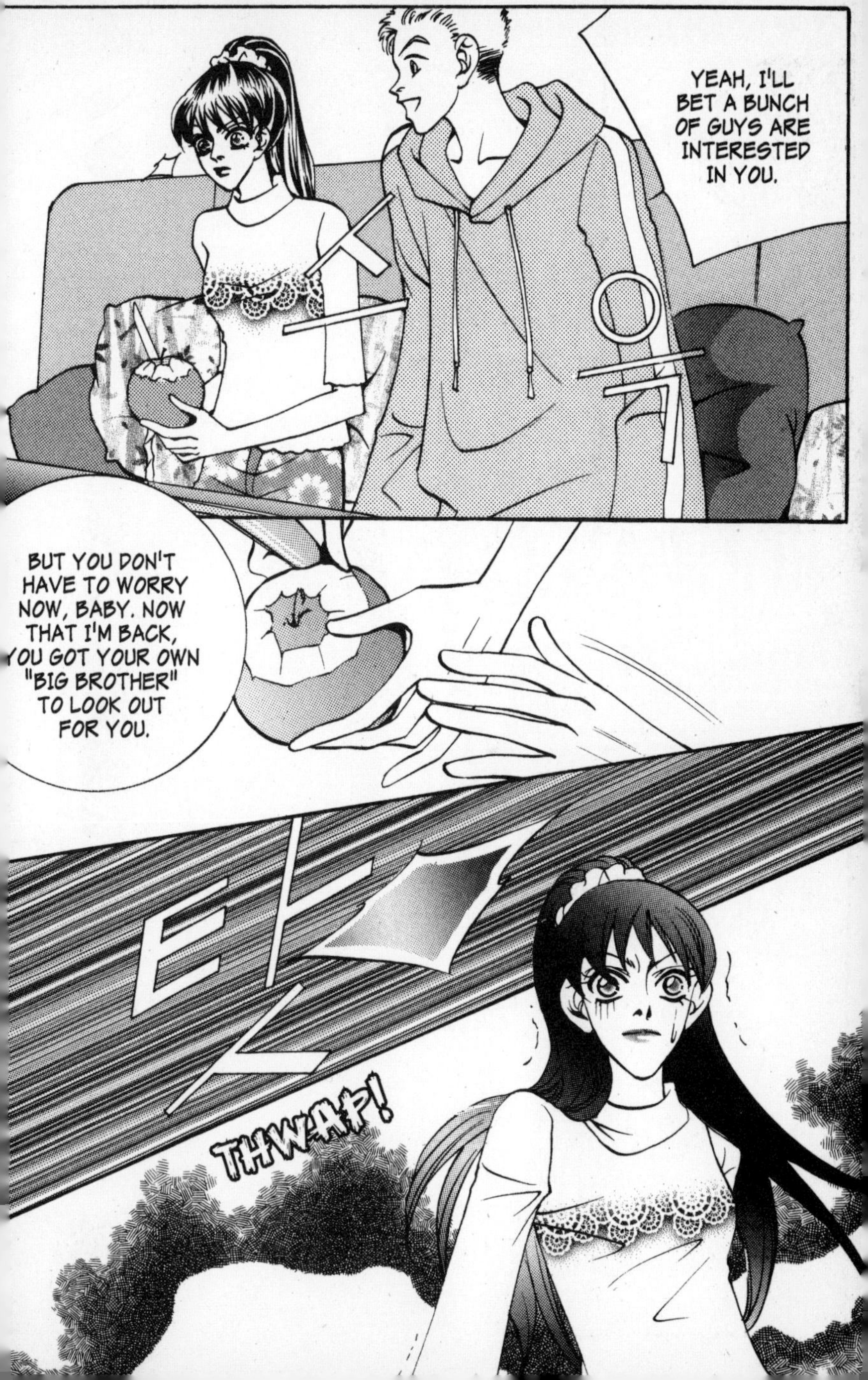
YEAH, I'LL BET A BUNCH OF GUYS ARE INTERESTED IN YOU.
BUT YOU DON'T HAVE TO WORRY NOW, BABY. NOW THAT I'M BACK, YOU GOT YOUR OWN "BIG BROTHER" TO LOOK OUT FOR YOU.
THWAP!

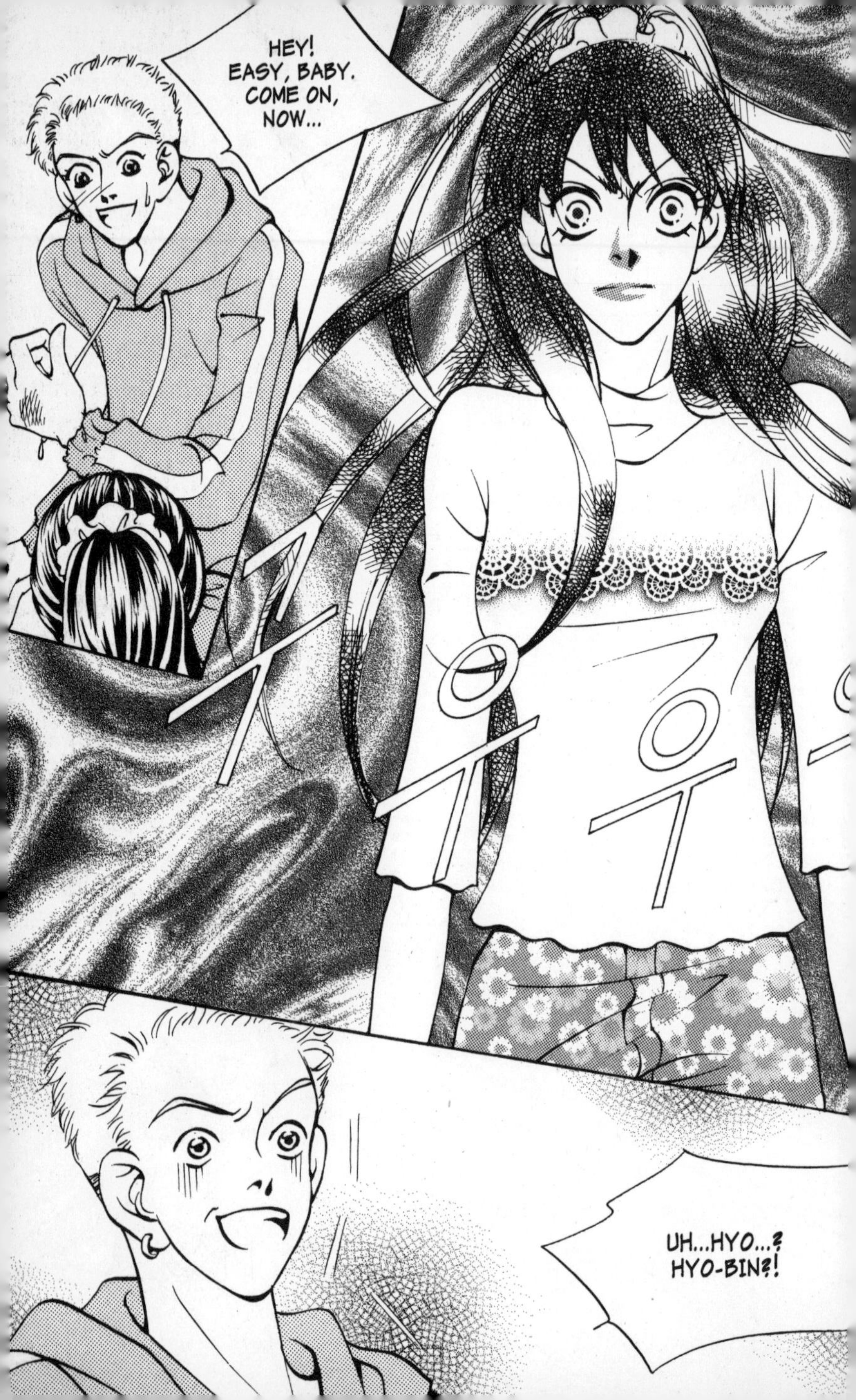
HEY! EASY, BABY. COME ON, NOW...
UH...HYO...? HYO-BIN?!

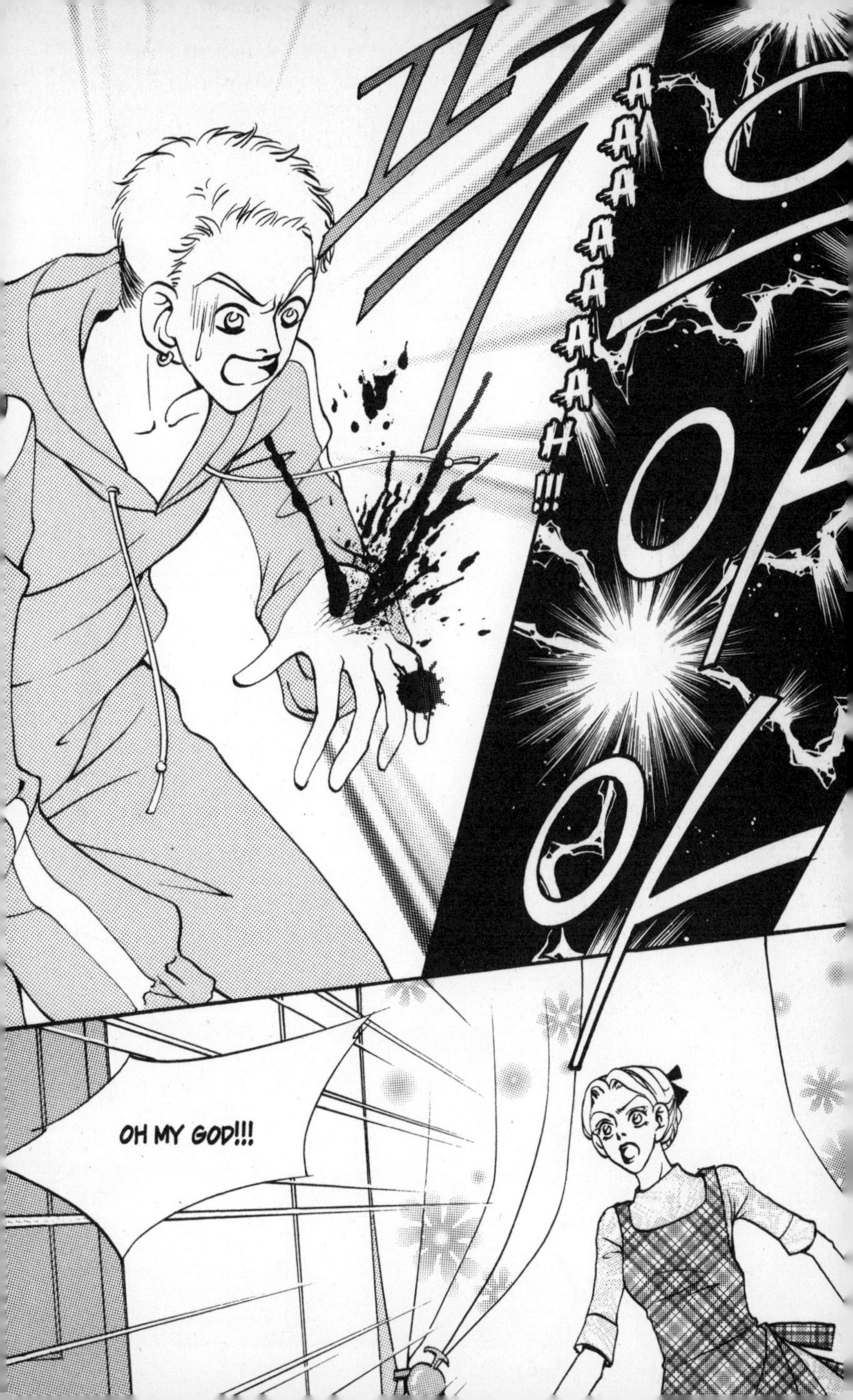
AAAAAAAH!!!
OH MY GOD!!!

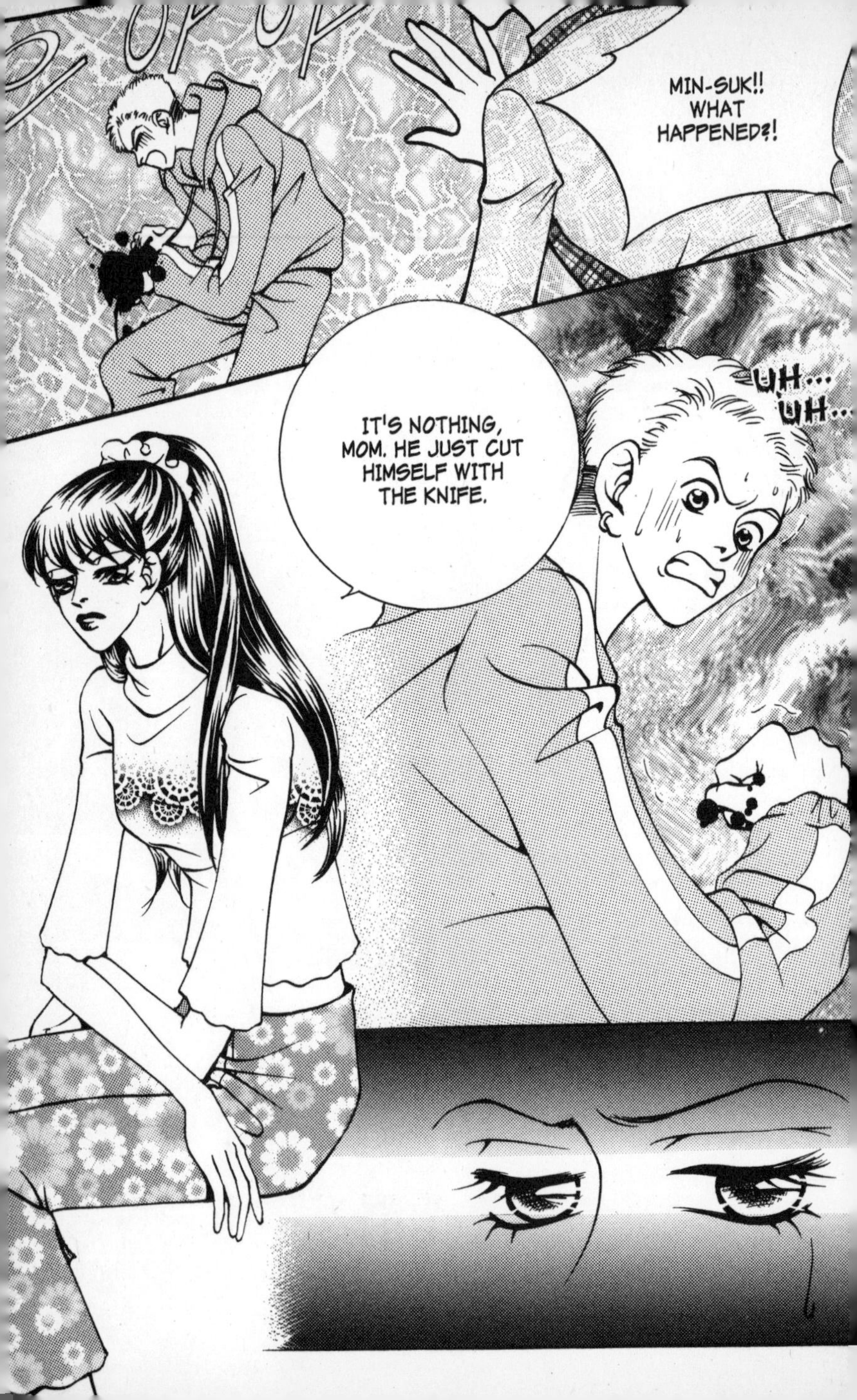
MIN-SUK!! WHAT HAPPENED?!
IT'S NOTHING, MOM. HE JUST CUT HIMSELF WITH THE KNIFE.
UH... UH...

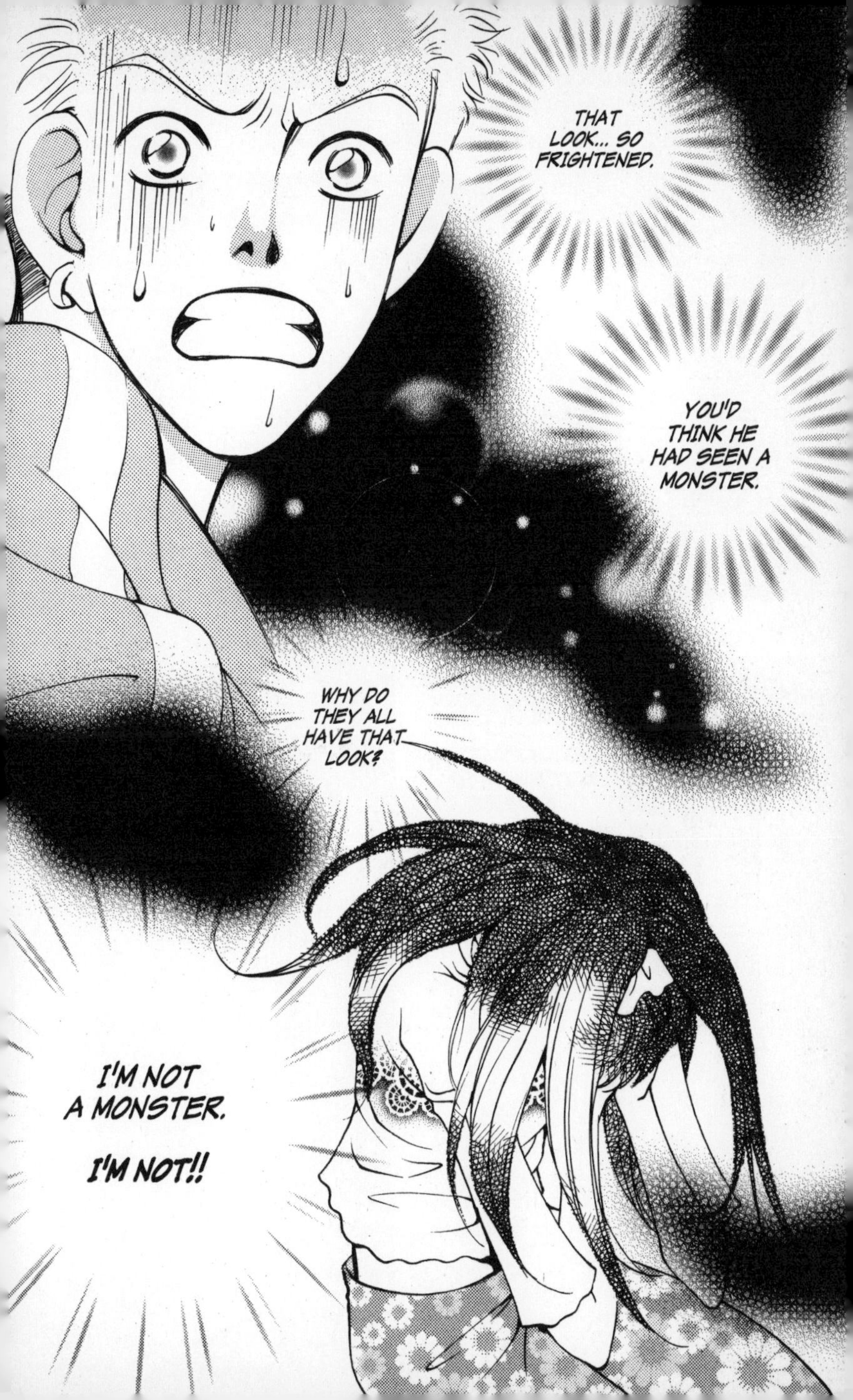
THAT LOOK... SO FRIGHTENED.
YOU'D THINK HE HAD SEEN A MONSTER.
WHY DO THEY ALL HAVE THAT LOOK?
I'M NOT A MONSTER.
I'M NOT!!

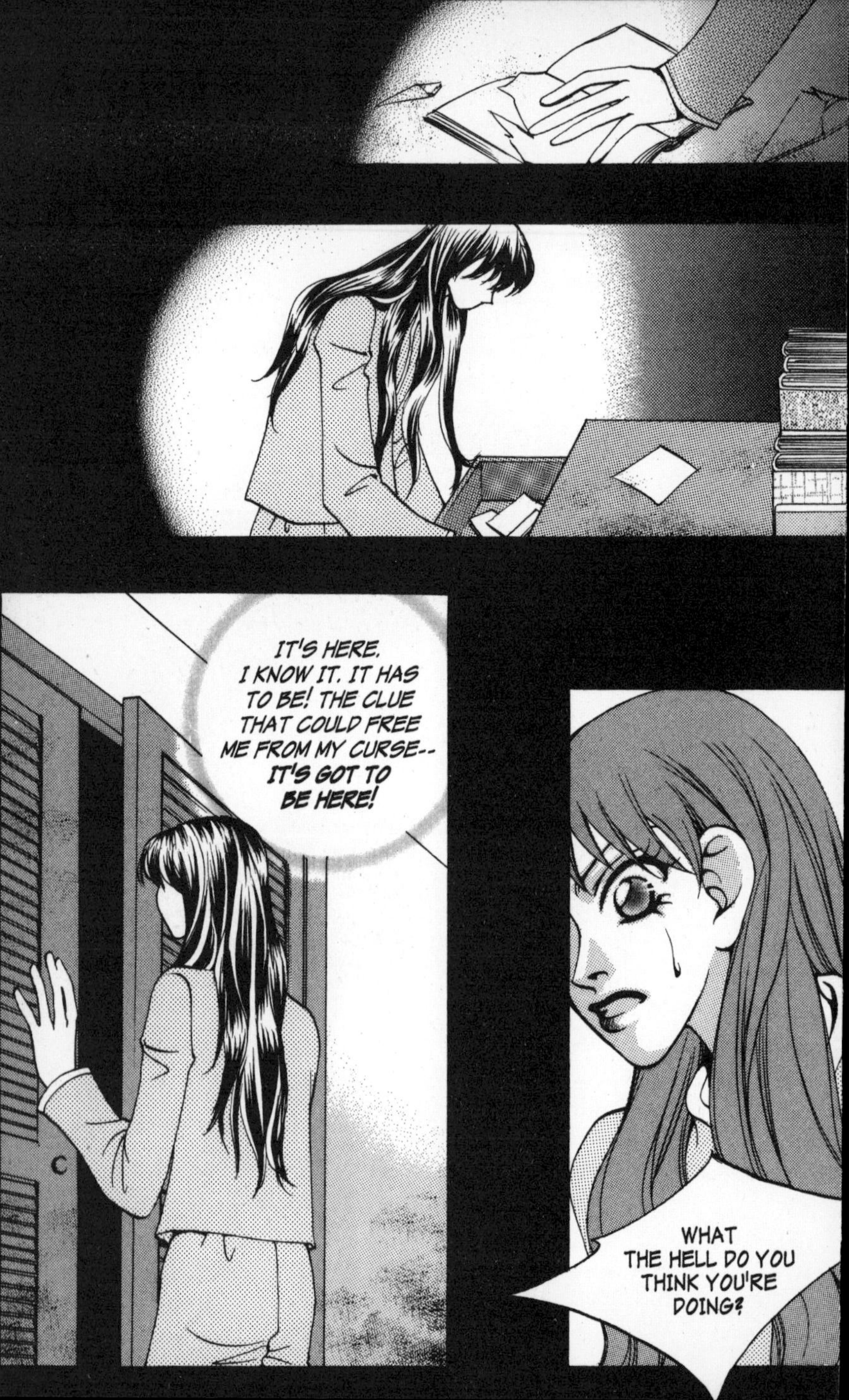
IT'S HERE. I KNOW IT. IT HAS TO BE! THE CLUE THAT COULD FREE ME FROM MY CURSE-- IT'S GOT TO BE HERE!
WHAT THE HELL DO YOU THINK YOU'RE DOING?

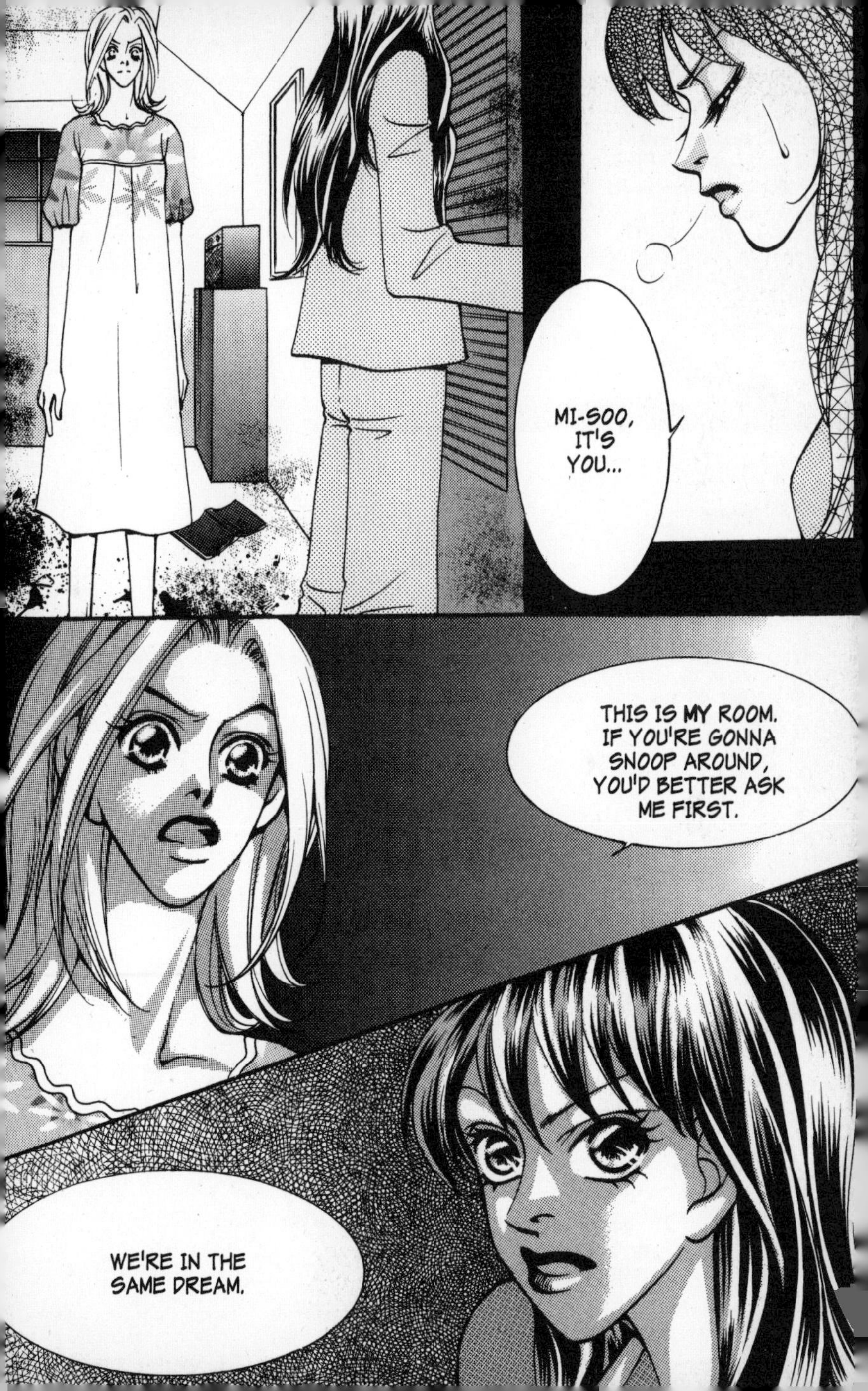
MI-SOO, IT'S YOU...
THIS IS MY ROOM. IF YOU'RE GONNA SNOOP AROUND, YOU'D BETTER ASK ME FIRST.
WE'RE IN THE SAME DREAM.

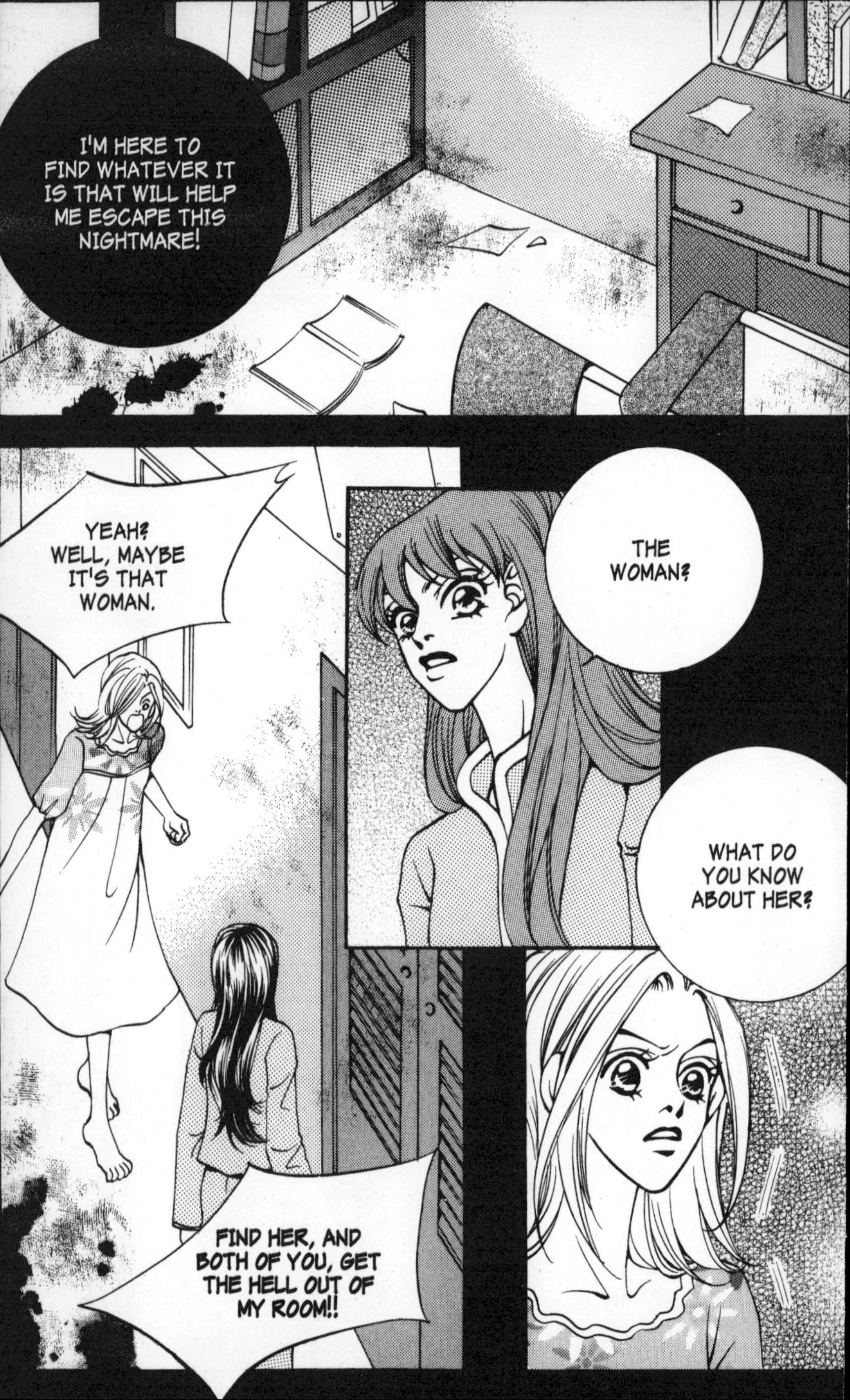
I'M HERE TO FIND WHATEVER IT IS THAT WILL HELP ME ESCAPE THIS NIGHTMARE!
YEAH? WELL, MAYBE IT'S THAT WOMAN.
THE WOMAN?
WHAT DO YOU KNOW ABOUT HER?
FIND HER, AND BOTH OF YOU, GET THE HELL OUT OF MY ROOM!!

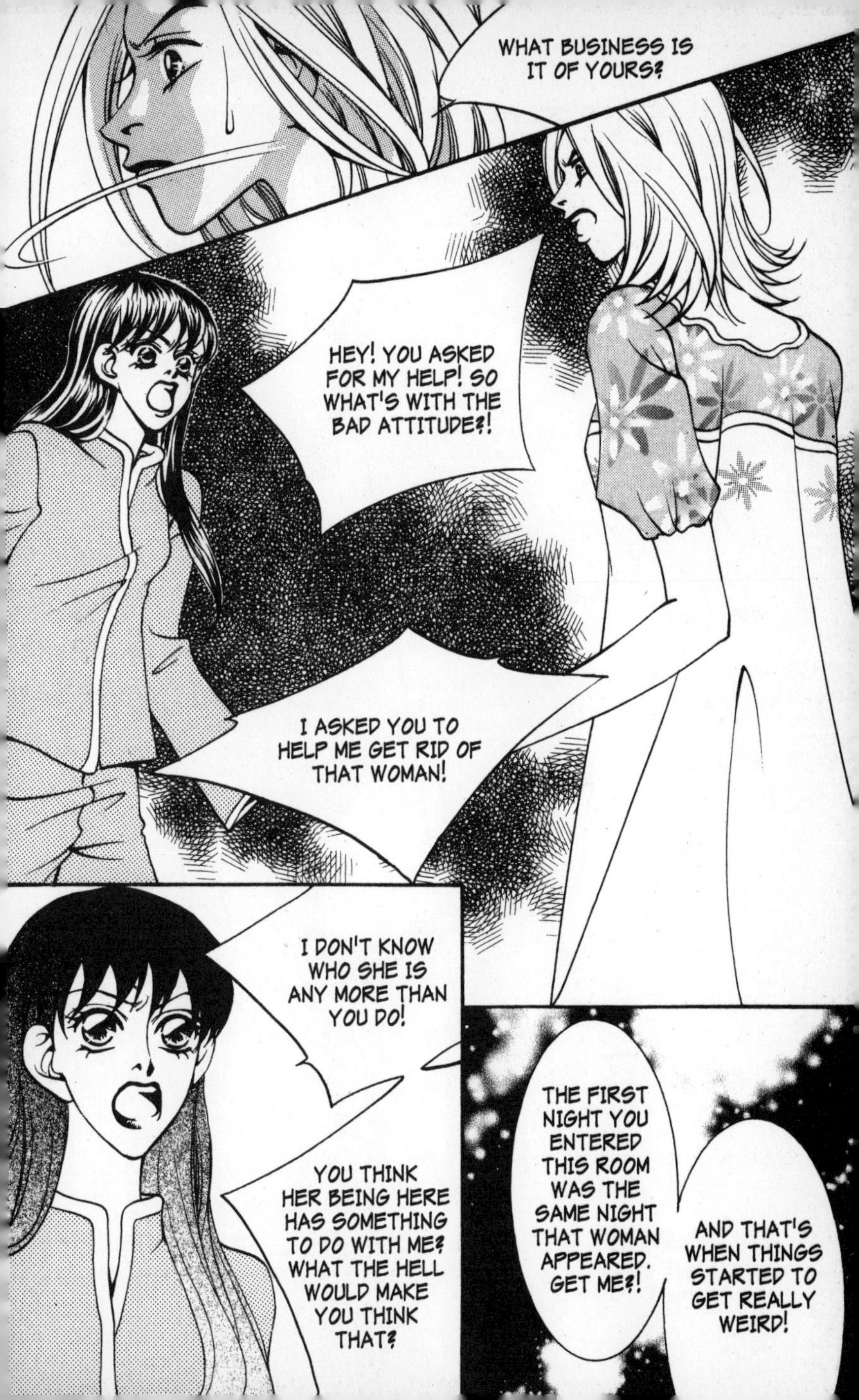
WHAT BUSINESS IS IT OF YOURS?
HEY! YOU ASKED FOR MY HELP! SO WHAT'S WITH THE BAD ATTITUDE?!
I ASKED YOU TO HELP ME GET RID OF THAT WOMAN!
I DON'T KNOW WHO SHE IS ANY MORE THAN YOU DO!
YOU THINK HER BEING HERE HAS SOMETHING TO DO WITH ME? WHAT THE HELL WOULD MAKE YOU THINK THAT?
THE FIRST NIGHT YOU ENTERED THIS ROOM WAS THE SAME NIGHT THAT WOMAN APPEARED. GET ME?!
AND THAT'S WHEN THINGS STARTED TO GET REALLY WEIRD!

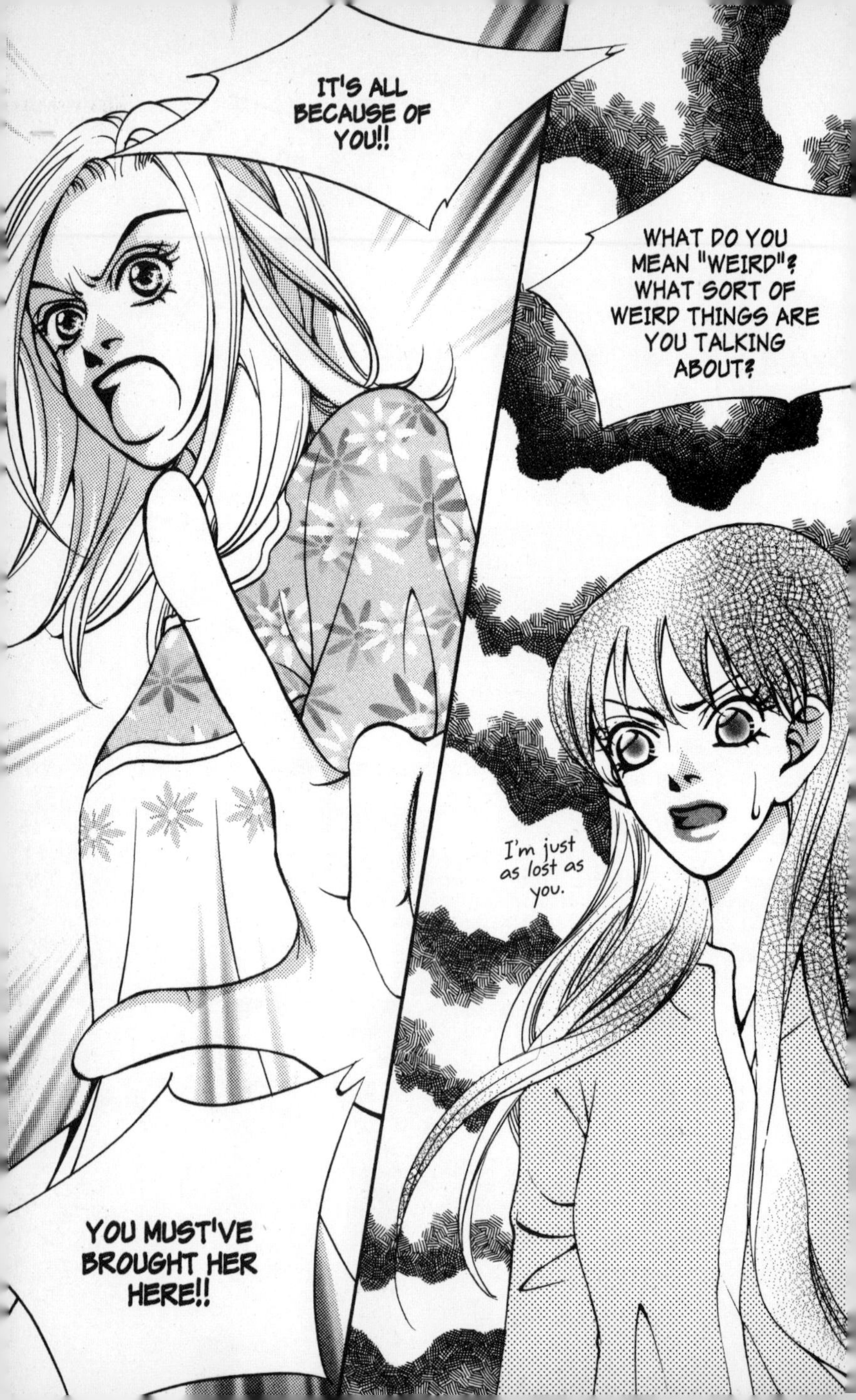
IT'S ALL BECAUSE OF YOU!!
YOU MUST'VE BROUGHT HER HERE!!
WHAT DO YOU MEAN "WEIRD"? WHAT SORT OF WEIRD THINGS ARE YOU TALKING ABOUT?
I'm just as lost as you.

She

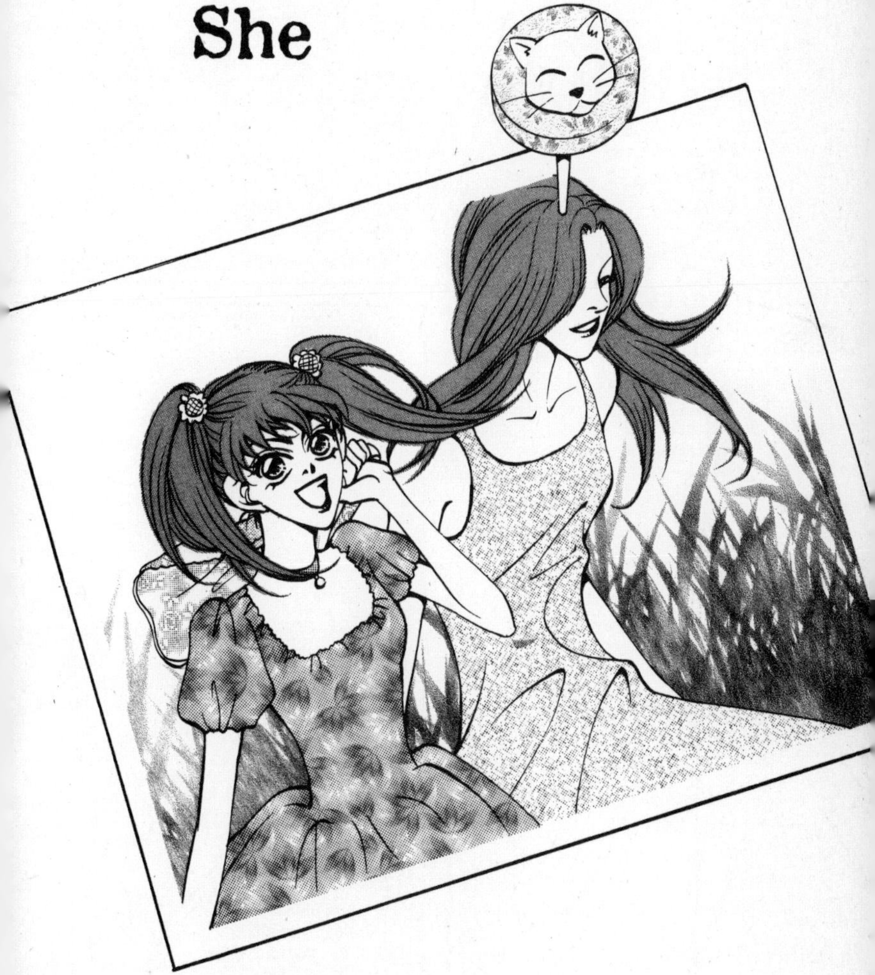

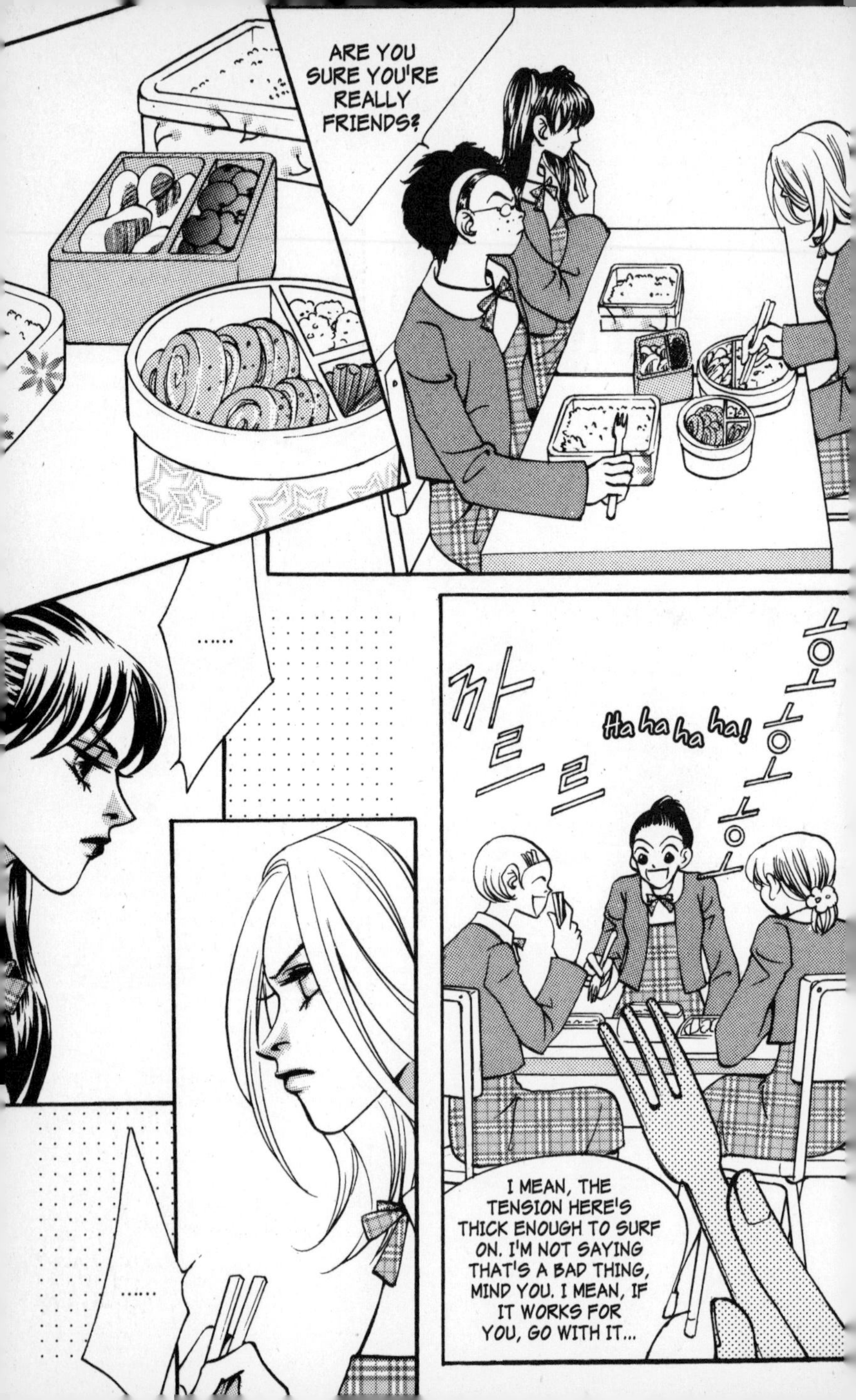

ARE YOU SURE YOU'RE REALLY FRIENDS?
......
......
까르르
Ha ha ha ha!
I MEAN, THE TENSION HERE'S THICK ENOUGH TO SURF ON. I'M NOT SAYING THAT'S A BAD THING, MIND YOU. I MEAN, IF IT WORKS FOR YOU, GO WITH IT...

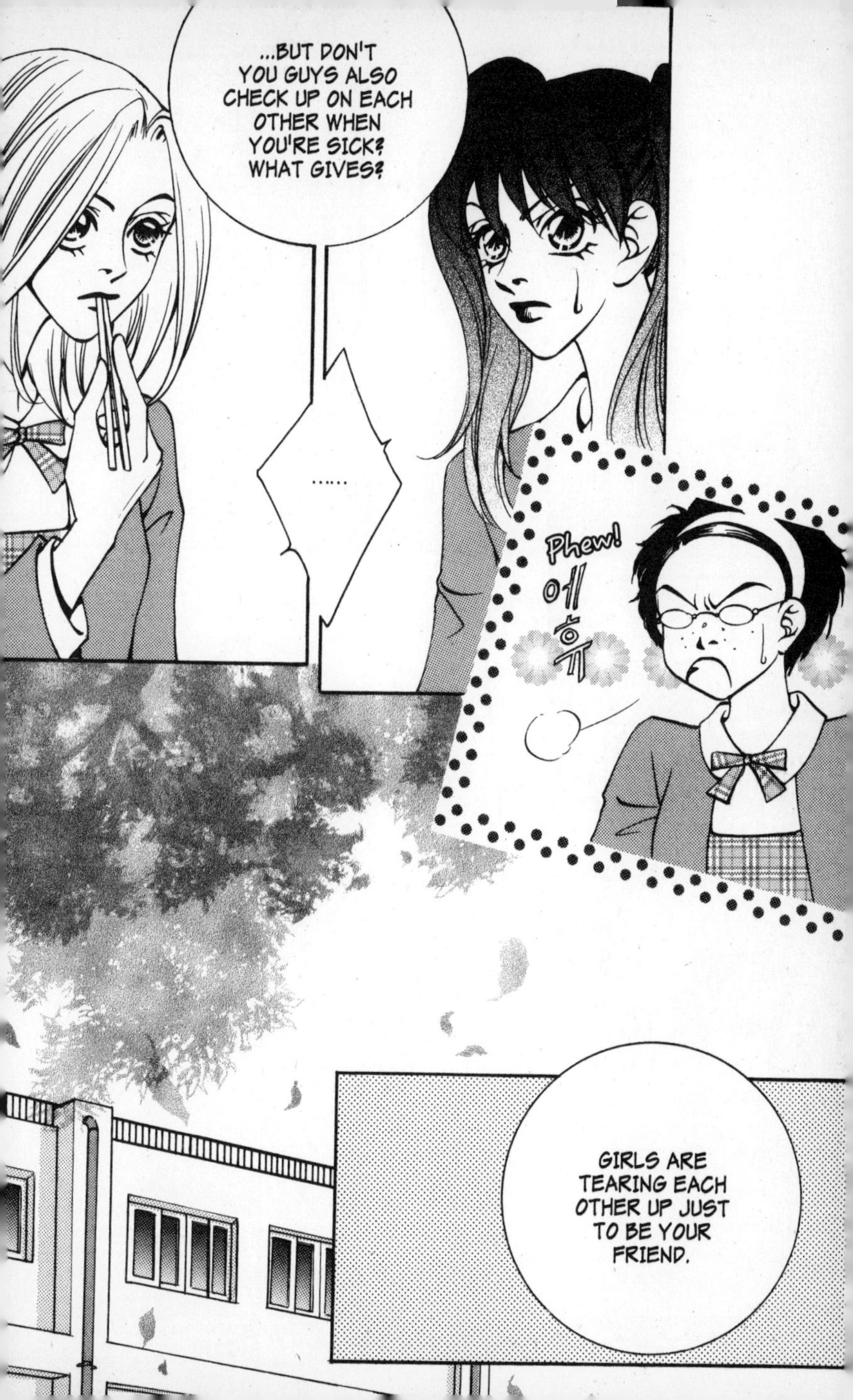

...BUT DON'T YOU GUYS ALSO CHECK UP ON EACH OTHER WHEN YOU'RE SICK? WHAT GIVES?
......
Phew!
에휴
GIRLS ARE TEARING EACH OTHER UP JUST TO BE YOUR FRIEND.

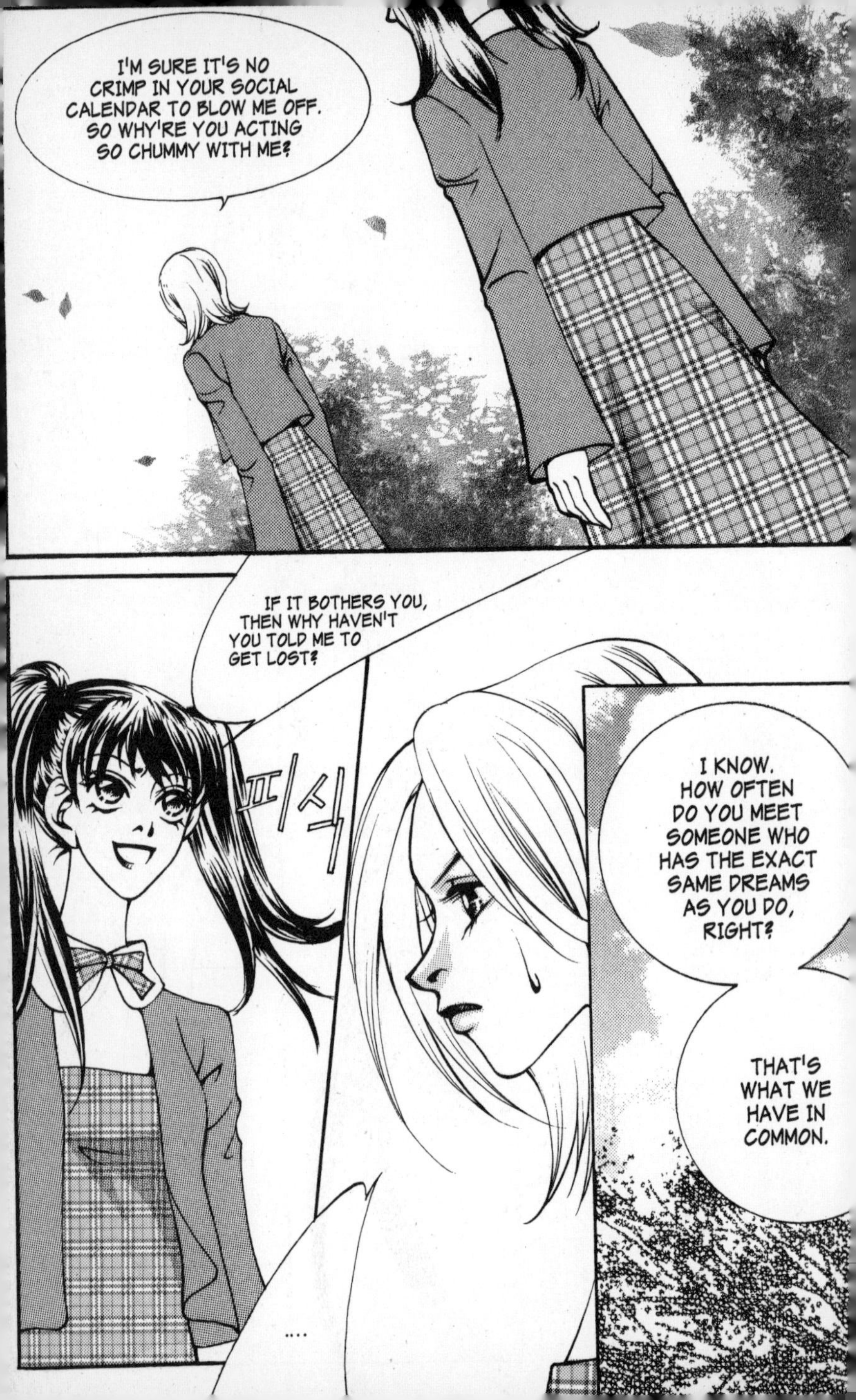
I'M SURE IT'S NO CRIMP IN YOUR SOCIAL CALENDAR TO BLOW ME OFF. SO WHY'RE YOU ACTING SO CHUMMY WITH ME?
IF IT BOTHERS YOU, THEN WHY HAVEN'T YOU TOLD ME TO GET LOST?
피식
....
I KNOW. HOW OFTEN DO YOU MEET SOMEONE WHO HAS THE EXACT SAME DREAMS AS YOU DO, RIGHT?
THAT'S WHAT WE HAVE IN COMMON.

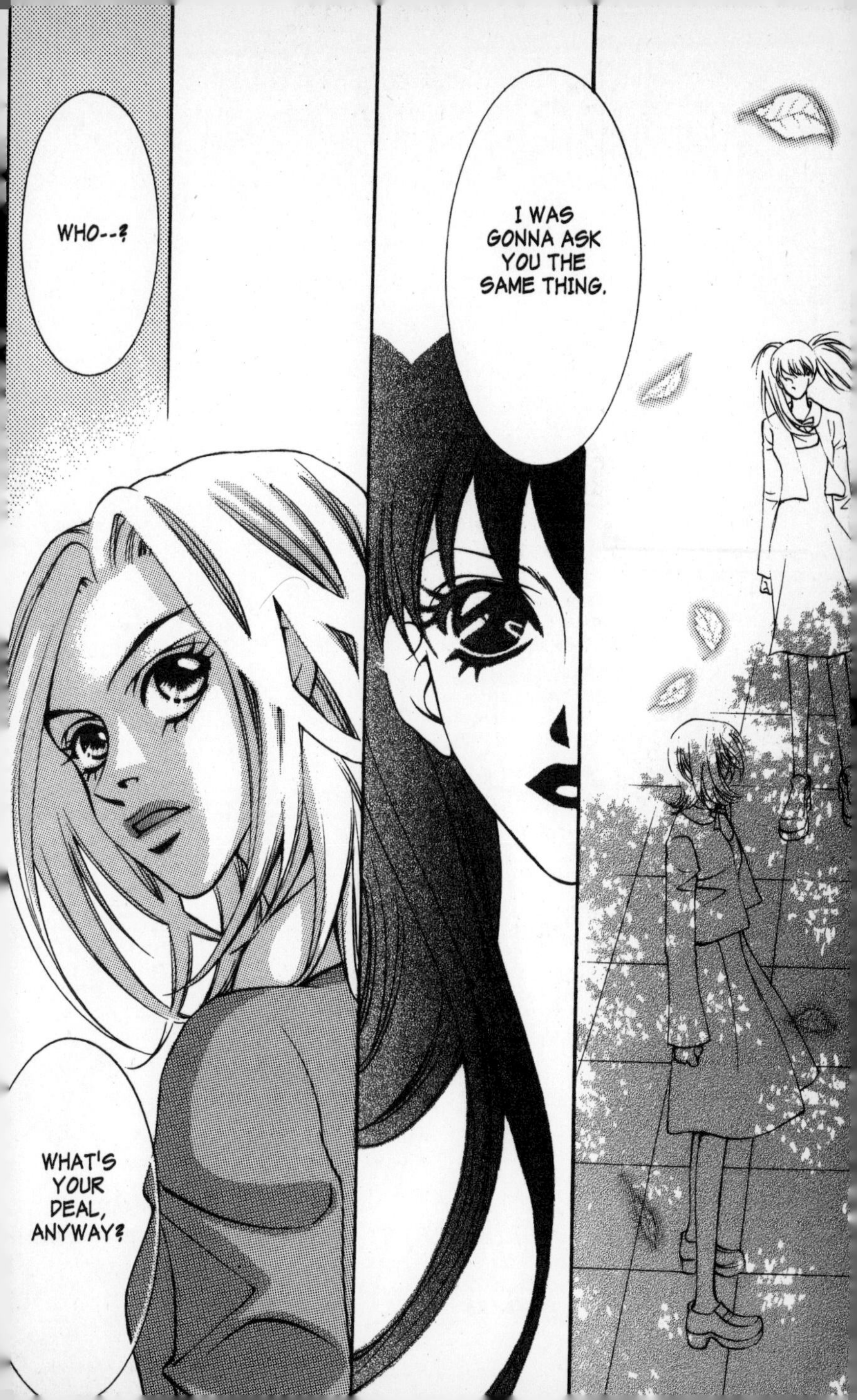
WHO--?
I WAS GONNA ASK YOU THE SAME THING.
WHAT'S YOUR DEAL, ANYWAY?

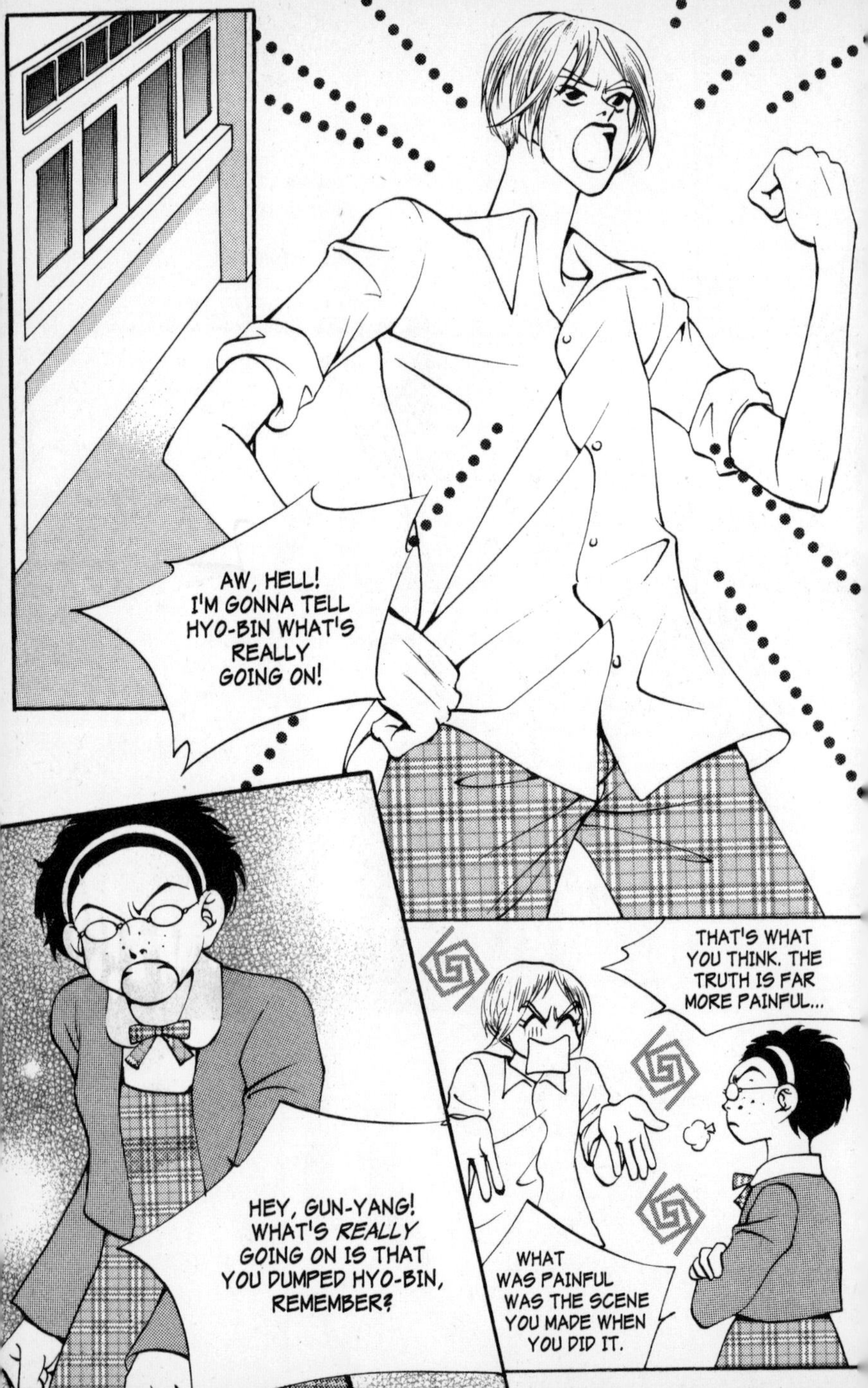
AW, HELL! I'M GONNA TELL HYO-BIN WHAT'S REALLY GOING ON!
HEY, GUN-YANG! WHAT'S *REALLY* GOING ON IS THAT YOU DUMPED HYO-BIN, REMEMBER?
THAT'S WHAT YOU THINK. THE TRUTH IS FAR MORE PAINFUL...
WHAT WAS PAINFUL WAS THE SCENE YOU MADE WHEN YOU DID IT.

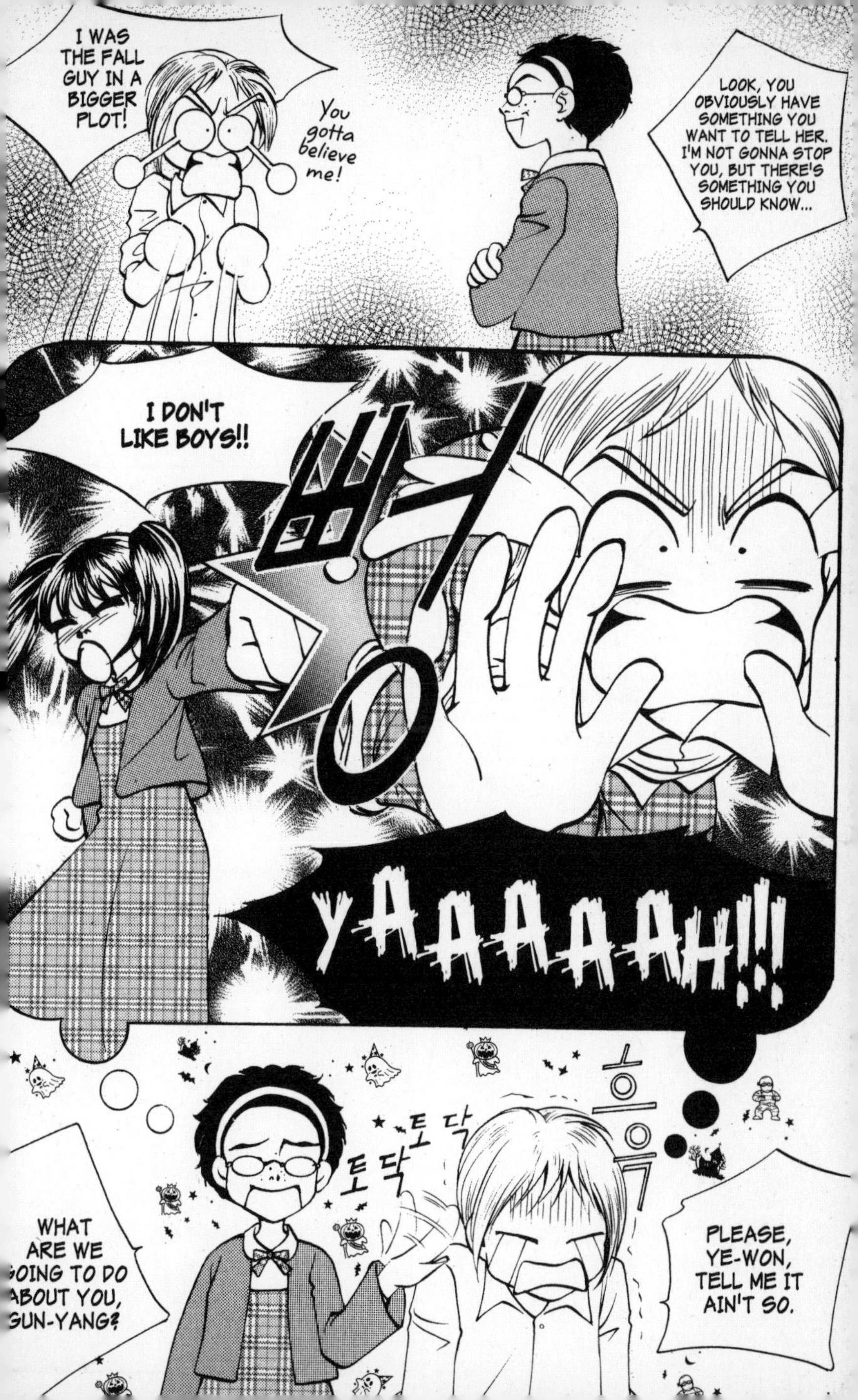
I WAS THE FALL GUY IN A BIGGER PLOT!
You gotta believe me!
LOOK, YOU OBVIOUSLY HAVE SOMETHING YOU WANT TO TELL HER. I'M NOT GONNA STOP YOU, BUT THERE'S SOMETHING YOU SHOULD KNOW...
I DON'T LIKE BOYS!!
YAAAAAH!!
WHAT ARE WE GOING TO DO ABOUT YOU, GUN-YANG?
토닥 토닥
PLEASE, YE-WON, TELL ME IT AIN'T SO.

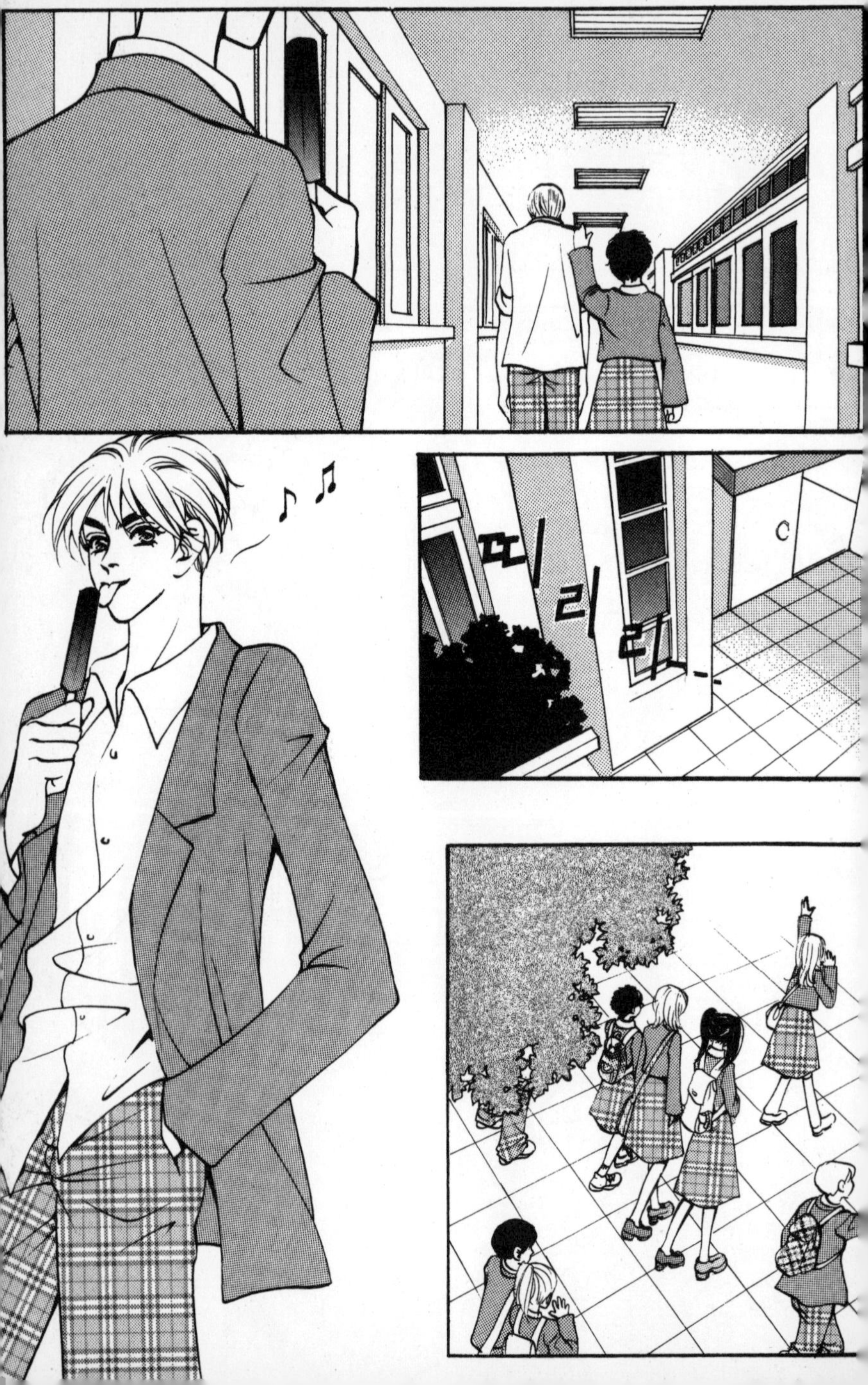
♪ ♫
띠리리--

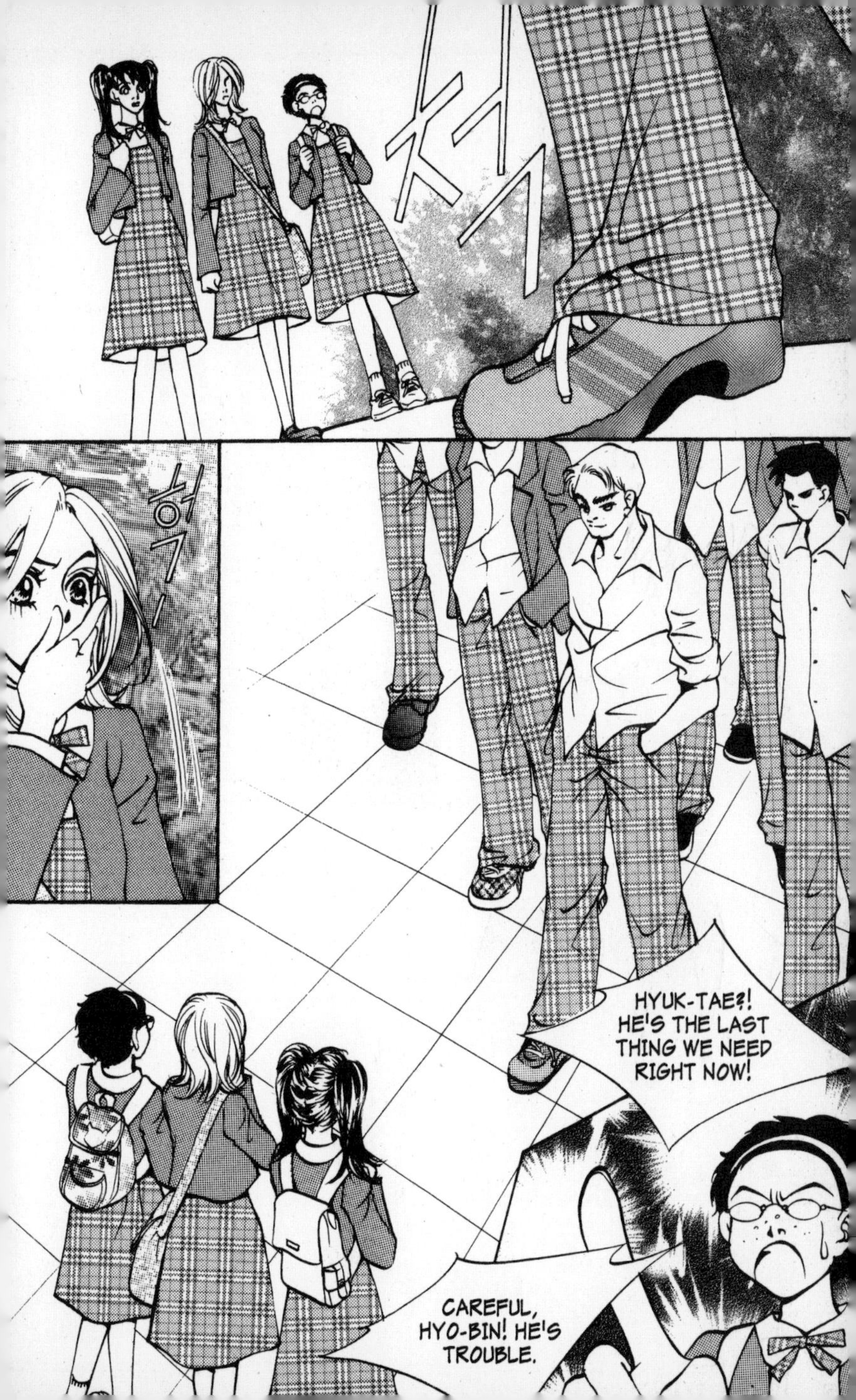
HYUK-TAE?! HE'S THE LAST THING WE NEED RIGHT NOW!
CAREFUL, HYO-BIN! HE'S TROUBLE.

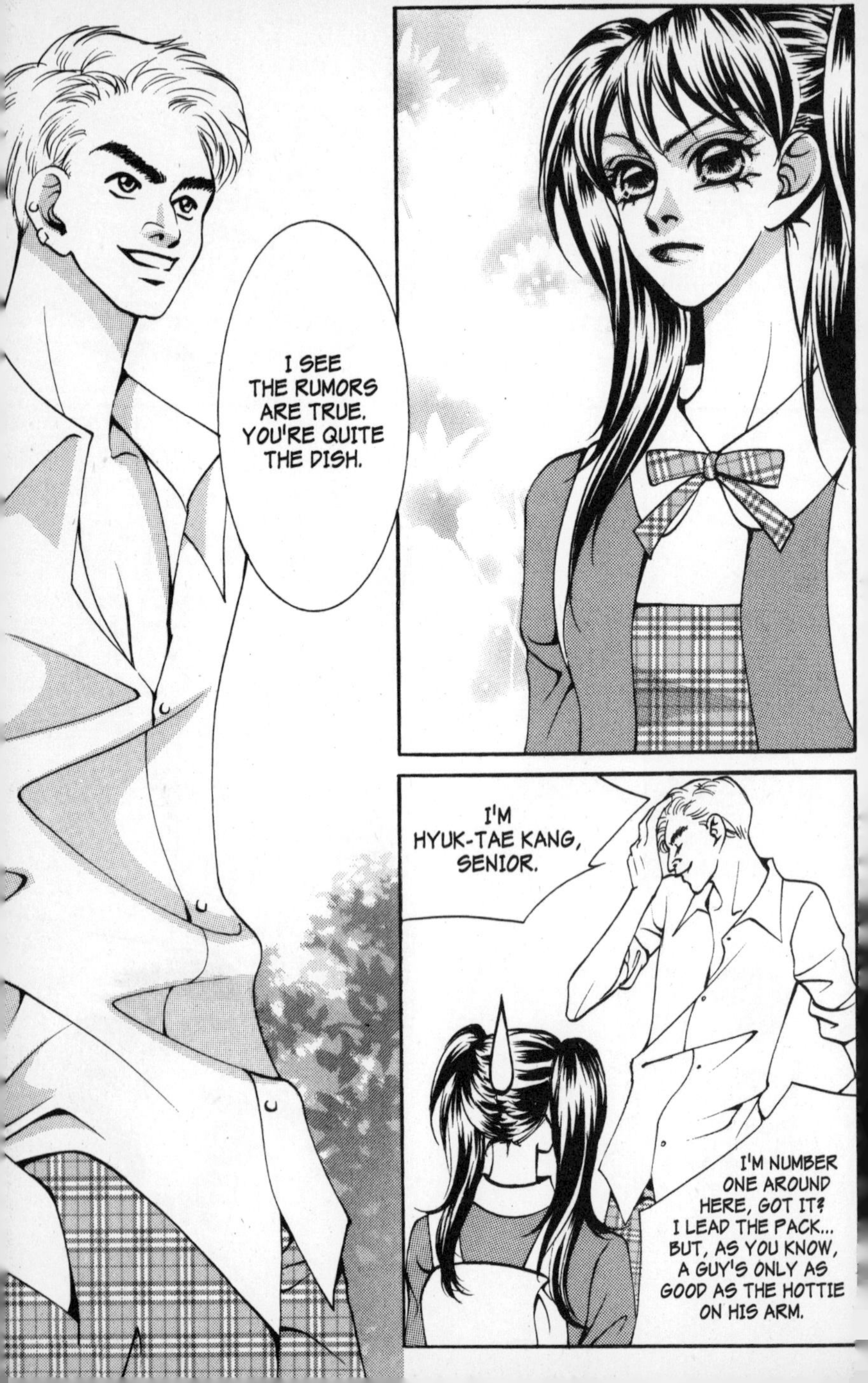
I SEE THE RUMORS ARE TRUE. YOU'RE QUITE THE DISH.
I'M HYUK-TAE KANG, SENIOR.
I'M NUMBER ONE AROUND HERE, GOT IT? I LEAD THE PACK... BUT, AS YOU KNOW, A GUY'S ONLY AS GOOD AS THE HOTTIE ON HIS ARM.

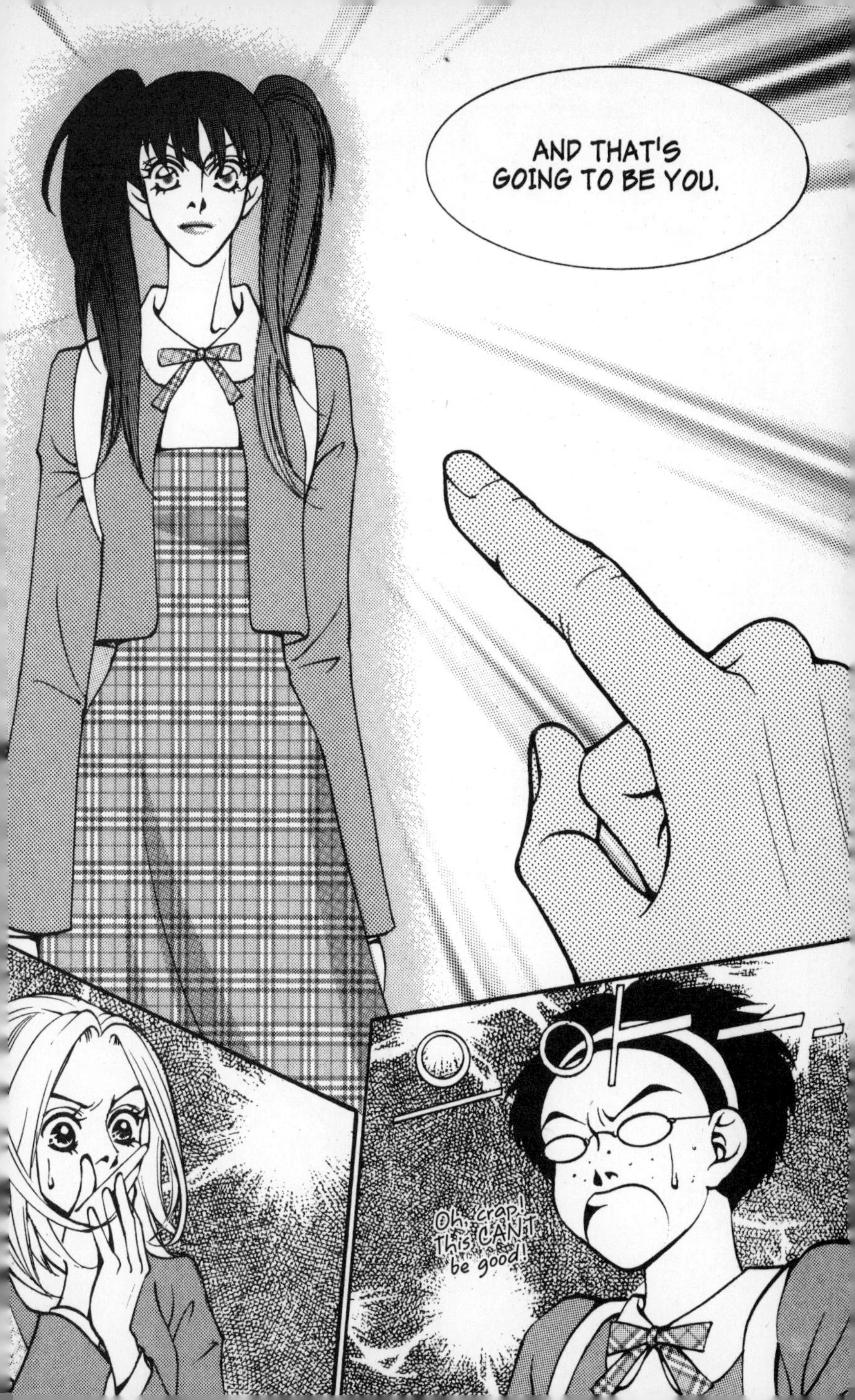
AND THAT'S GOING TO BE YOU.
Oh, crap! This CAN'T be good!

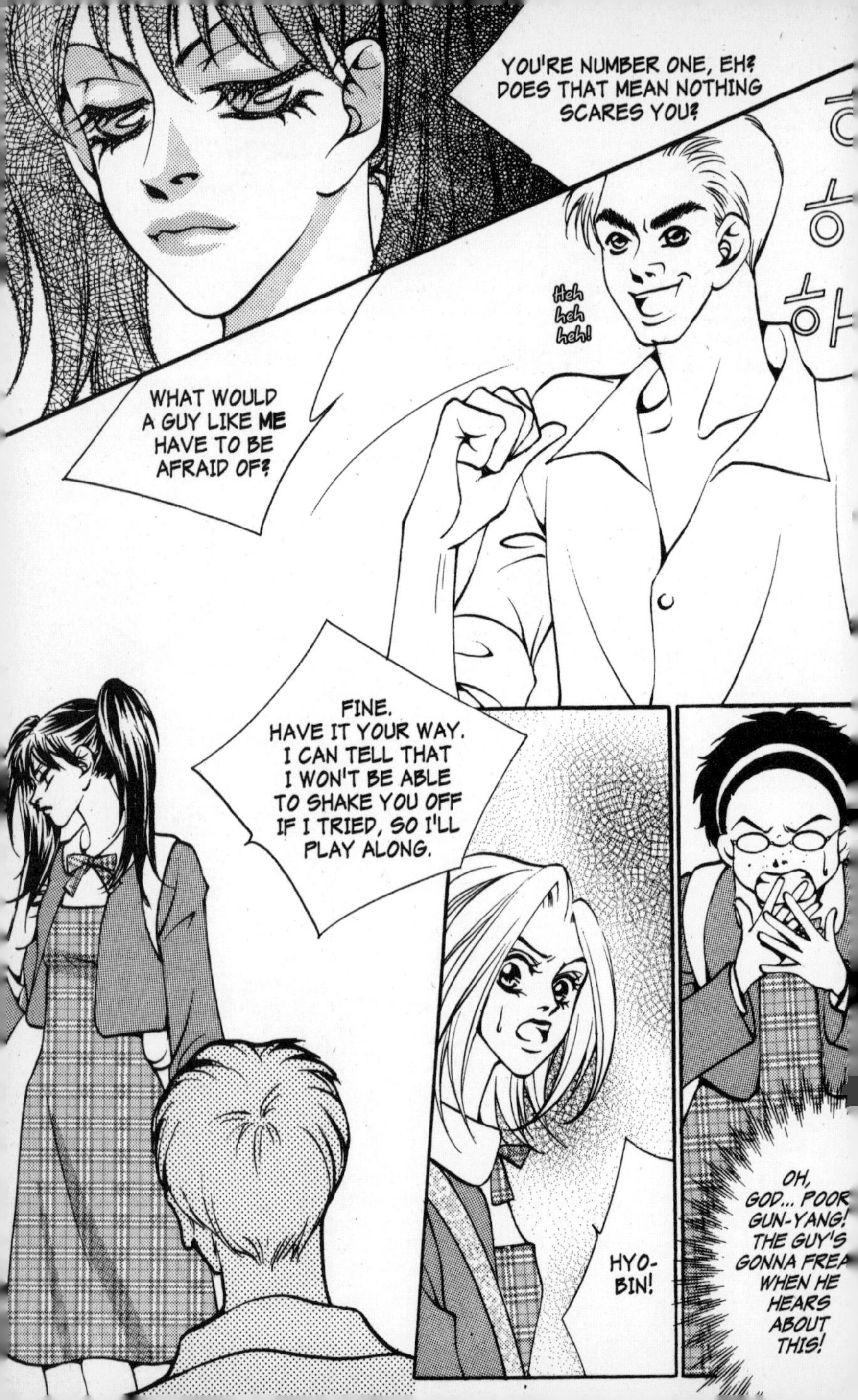

YOU'RE NUMBER ONE, EH? DOES THAT MEAN NOTHING SCARES YOU?
Heh heh heh!
흥하
WHAT WOULD A GUY LIKE ME HAVE TO BE AFRAID OF?
FINE. HAVE IT YOUR WAY. I CAN TELL THAT I WON'T BE ABLE TO SHAKE YOU OFF IF I TRIED, SO I'LL PLAY ALONG.
HYO-BIN!
OH, GOD... POOR GUN-YANG! THE GUY'S GONNA FREA WHEN HE HEARS ABOUT THIS!

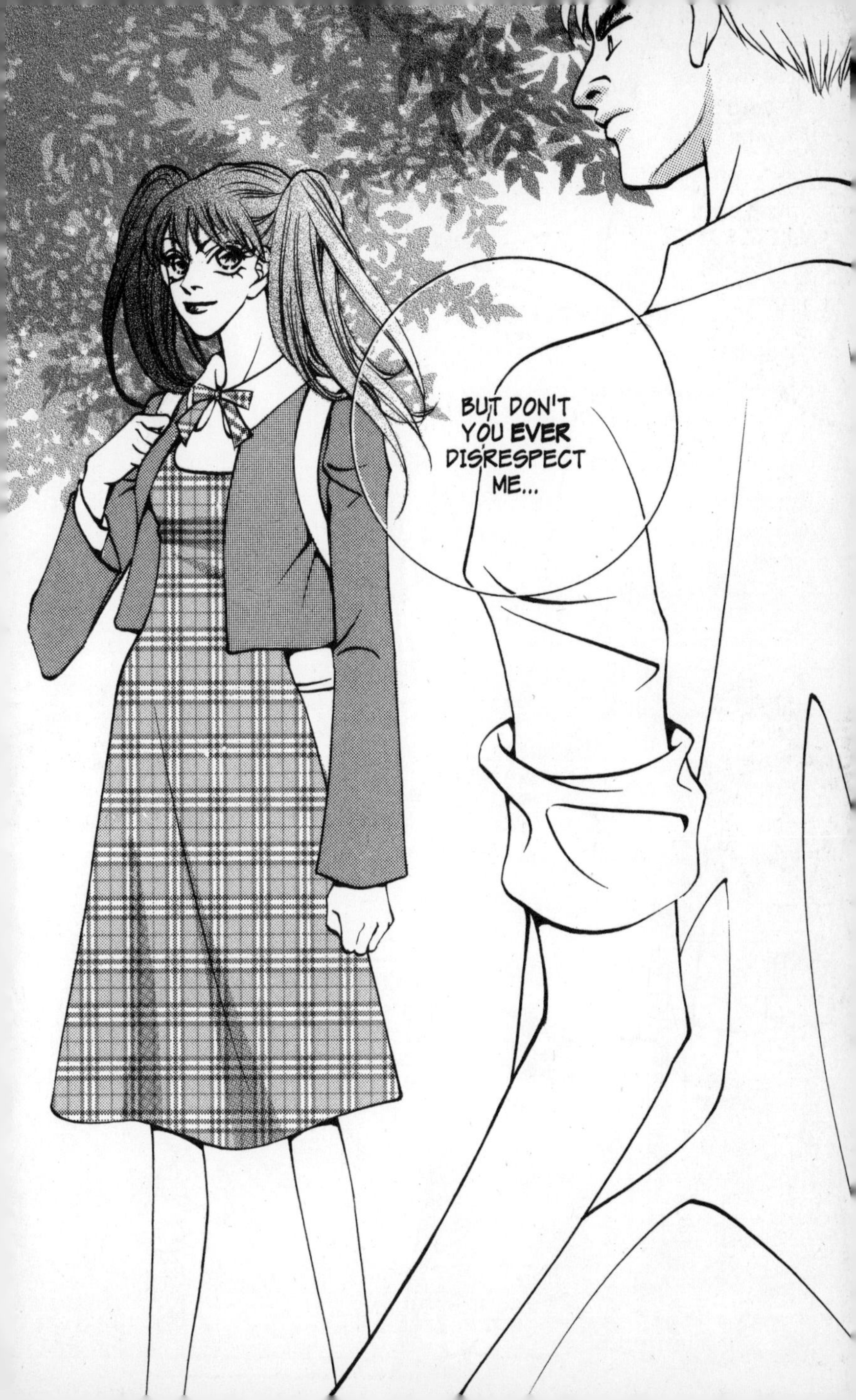
BUT DON'T YOU EVER DISRESPECT ME...

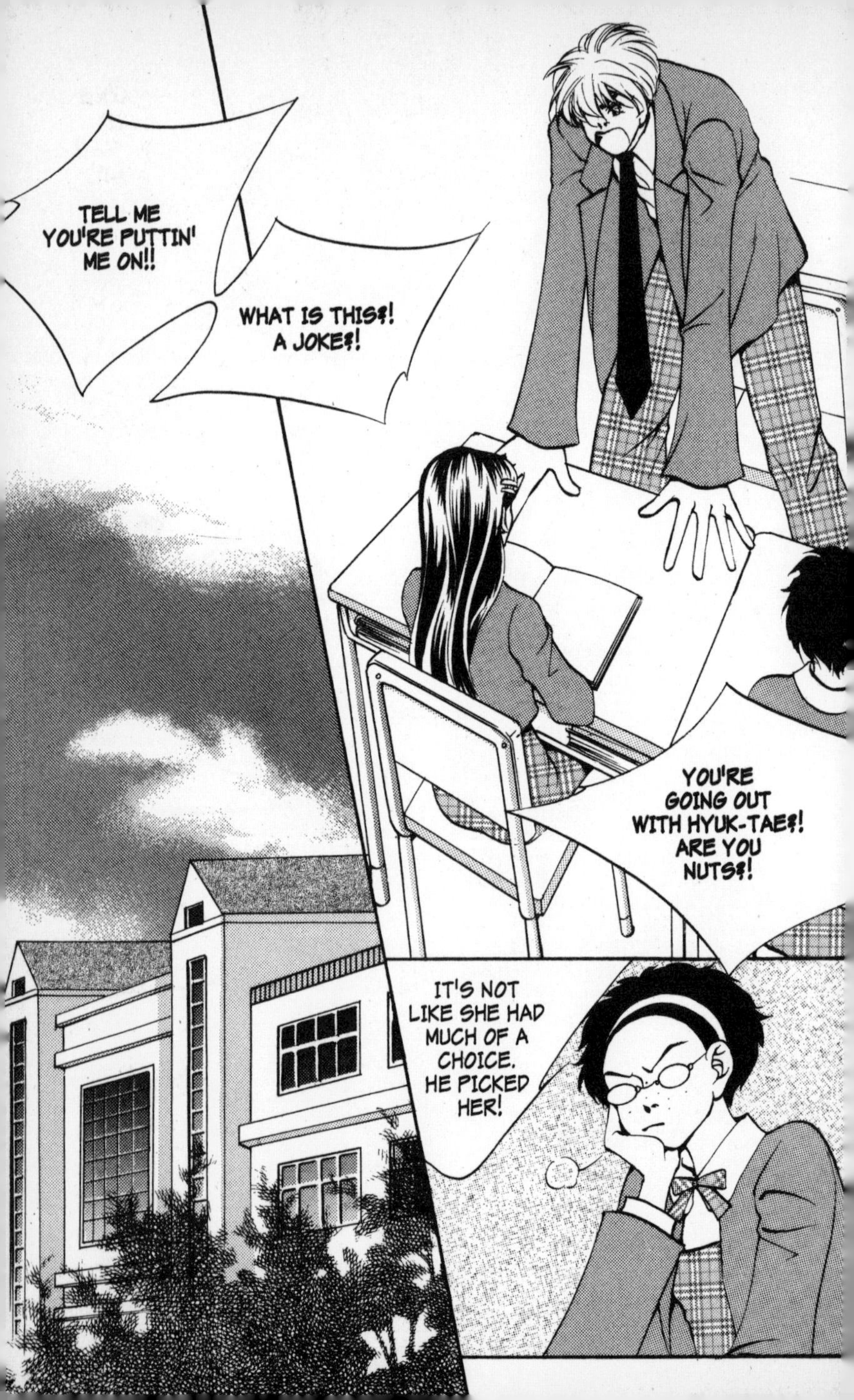
TELL ME YOU'RE PUTTIN' ME ON!!
WHAT IS THIS?! A JOKE?!
YOU'RE GOING OUT WITH HYUK-TAE?! ARE YOU NUTS?!
IT'S NOT LIKE SHE HAD MUCH OF A CHOICE. HE PICKED HER!

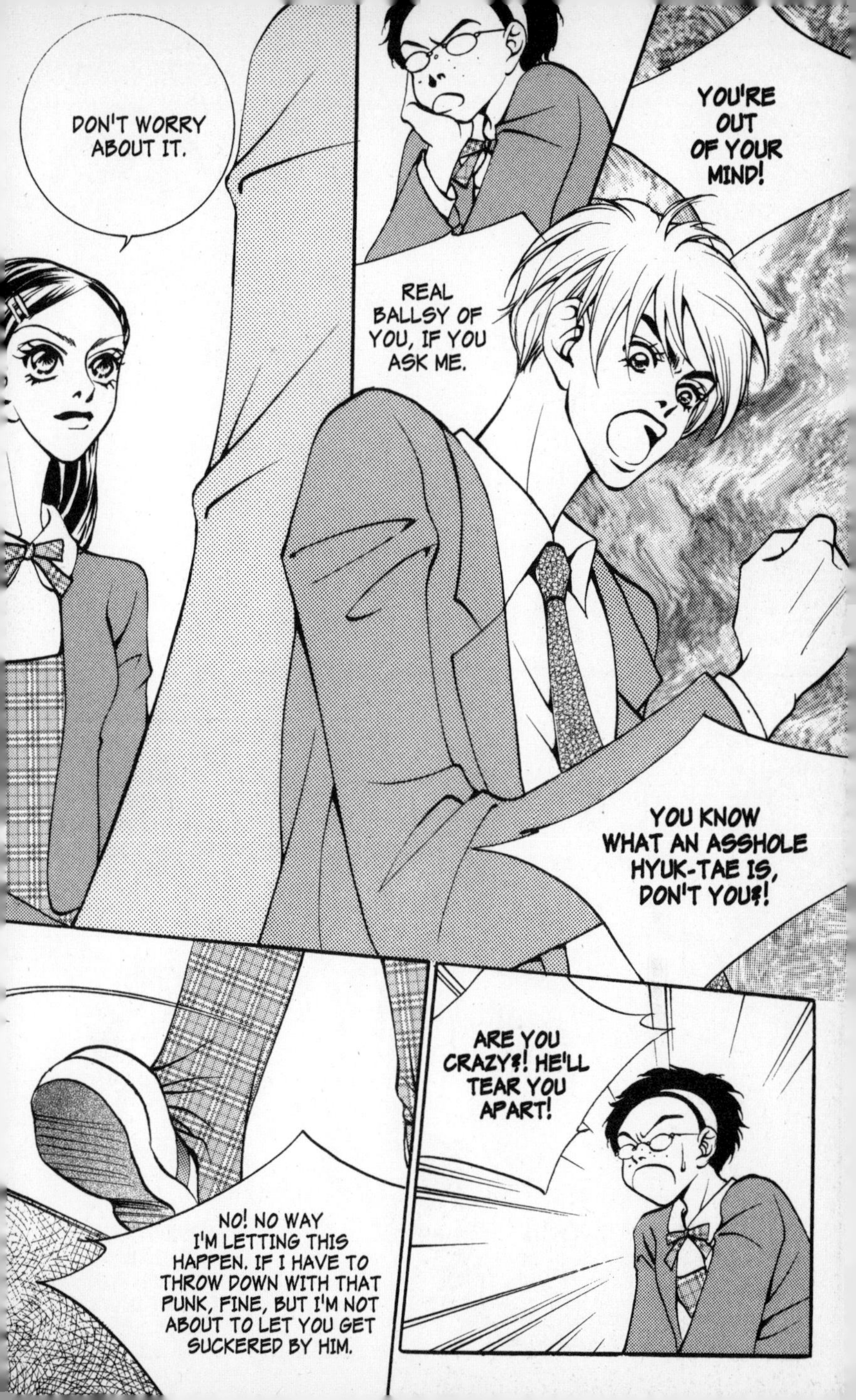
DON'T WORRY ABOUT IT.
YOU'RE OUT OF YOUR MIND!
REAL BALLSY OF YOU, IF YOU ASK ME.
YOU KNOW WHAT AN ASSHOLE HYUK-TAE IS, DON'T YOU?!
NO! NO WAY I'M LETTING THIS HAPPEN. IF I HAVE TO THROW DOWN WITH THAT PUNK, FINE, BUT I'M NOT ABOUT TO LET YOU GET SUCKERED BY HIM.
ARE YOU CRAZY?! HE'LL TEAR YOU APART!

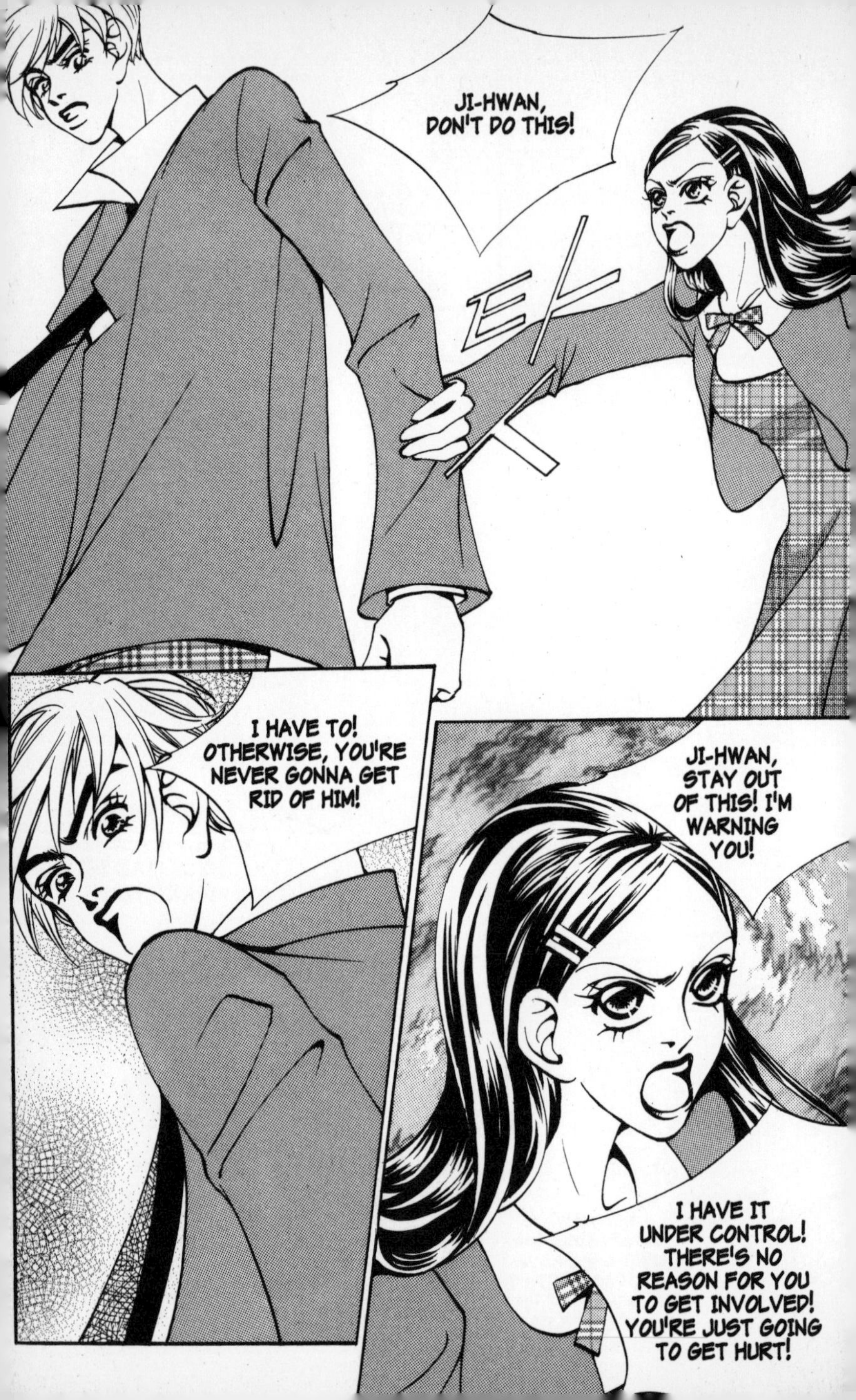
JI-HWAN, DON'T DO THIS!
I HAVE TO! OTHERWISE, YOU'RE NEVER GONNA GET RID OF HIM!
JI-HWAN, STAY OUT OF THIS! I'M WARNING YOU!
I HAVE IT UNDER CONTROL! THERE'S NO REASON FOR YOU TO GET INVOLVED! YOU'RE JUST GOING TO GET HURT!

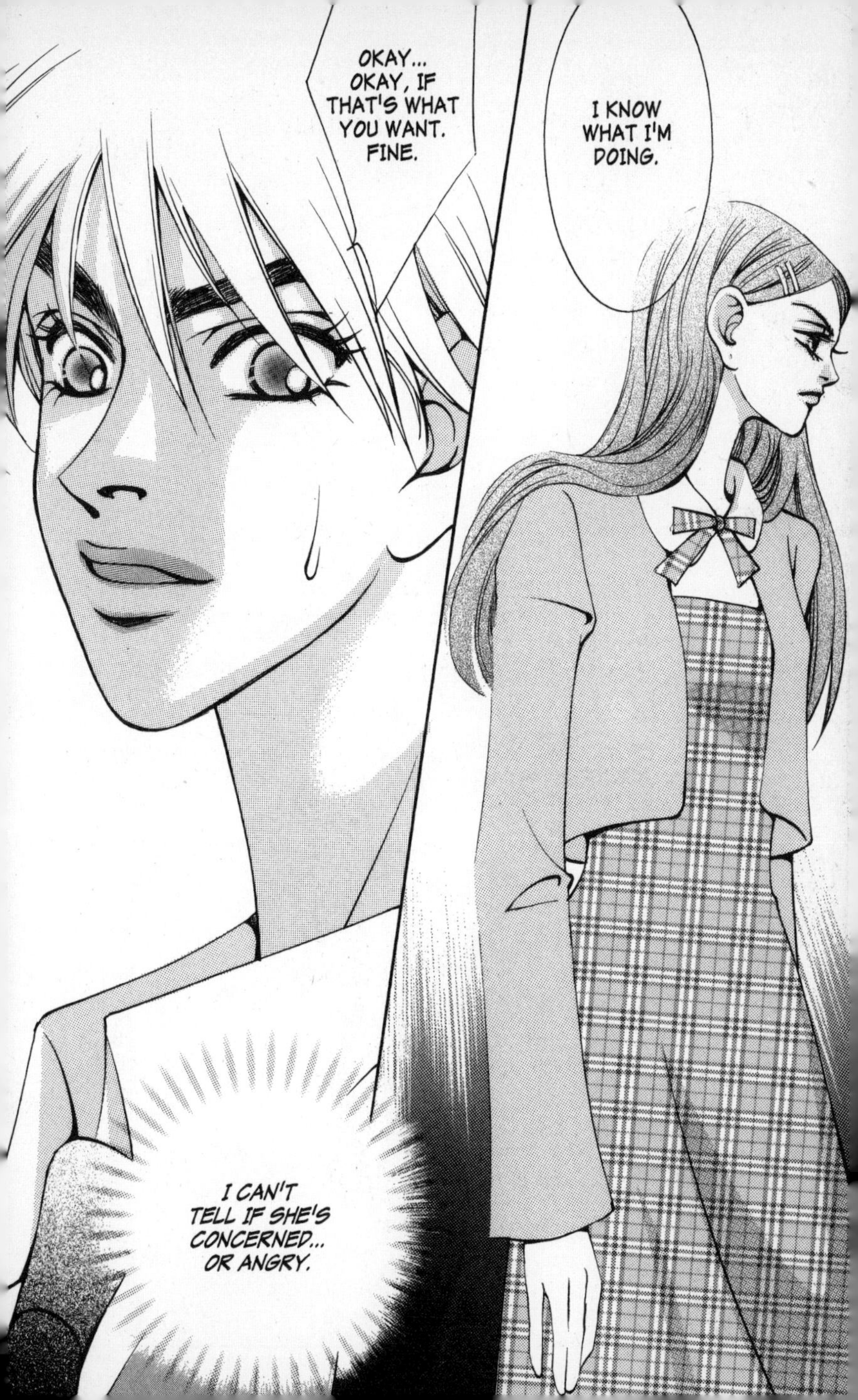
OKAY... OKAY, IF THAT'S WHAT YOU WANT. FINE.
I CAN'T TELL IF SHE'S CONCERNED... OR ANGRY.
I KNOW WHAT I'M DOING.

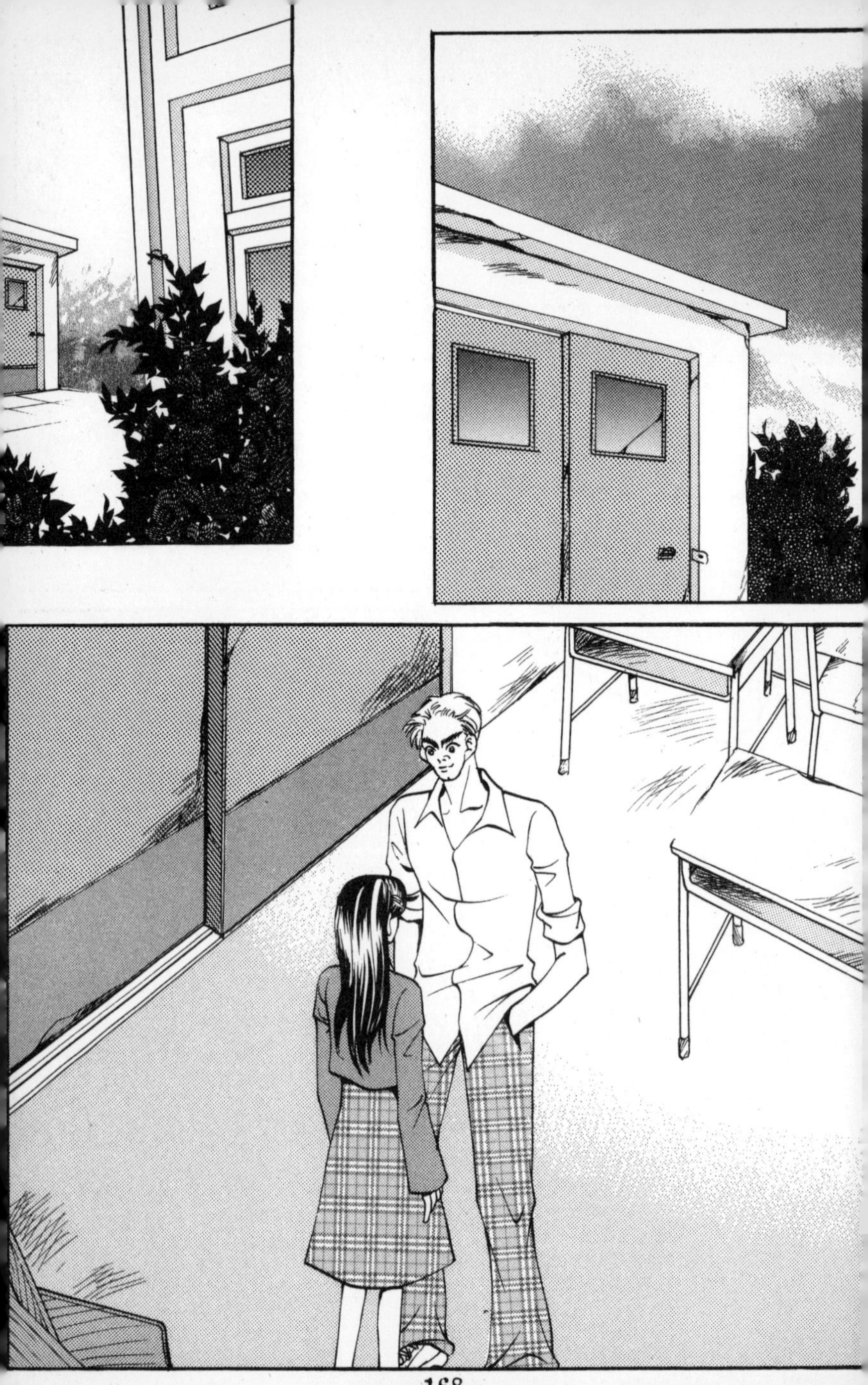

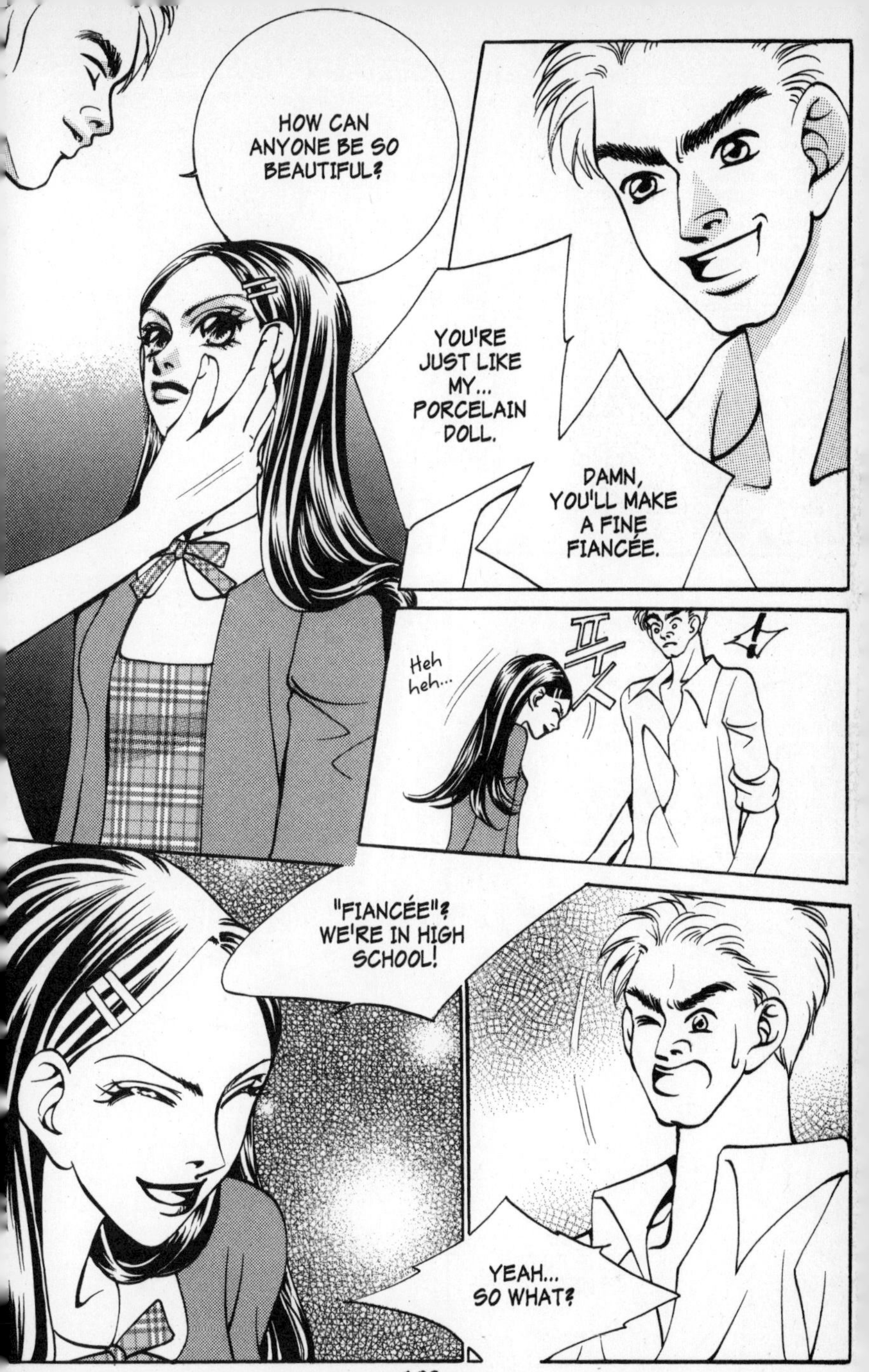
HOW CAN ANYONE BE SO BEAUTIFUL?
YOU'RE JUST LIKE MY... PORCELAIN DOLL.
DAMN, YOU'LL MAKE A FINE FIANCÉE.
Heh heh...
"FIANCÉE"? WE'RE IN HIGH SCHOOL!
YEAH... SO WHAT?

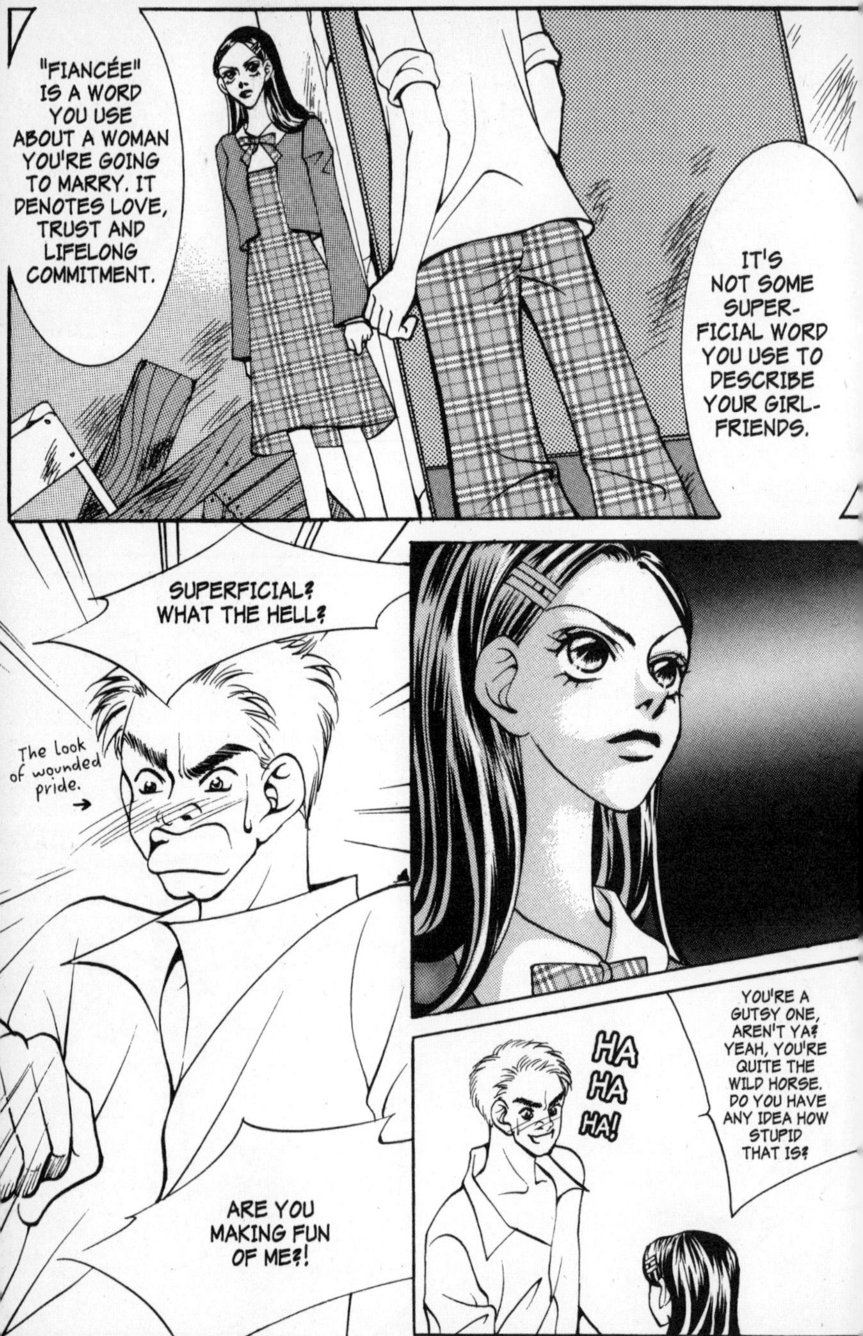
"FIANCÉE" IS A WORD YOU USE ABOUT A WOMAN YOU'RE GOING TO MARRY. IT DENOTES LOVE, TRUST AND LIFELONG COMMITMENT.
IT'S NOT SOME SUPER-FICIAL WORD YOU USE TO DESCRIBE YOUR GIRL-FRIENDS.
SUPERFICIAL? WHAT THE HELL?
The look of wounded pride.
ARE YOU MAKING FUN OF ME?!
HA HA HA!
YOU'RE A GUTSY ONE, AREN'T YA? YEAH, YOU'RE QUITE THE WILD HORSE. DO YOU HAVE ANY IDEA HOW STUPID THAT IS?

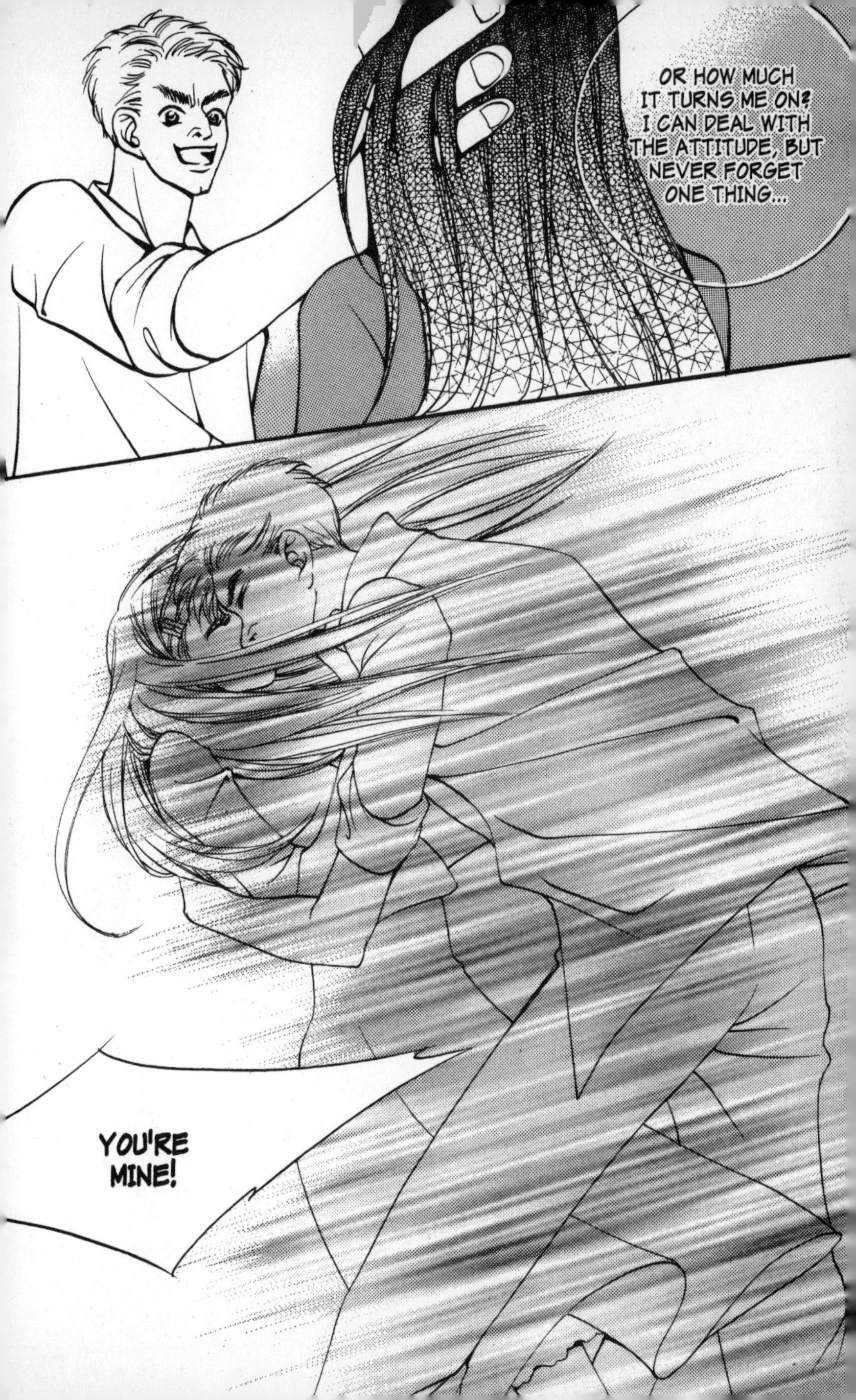
OR HOW MUCH IT TURNS ME ON? I CAN DEAL WITH THE ATTITUDE, BUT NEVER FORGET ONE THING...
YOU'RE MINE!

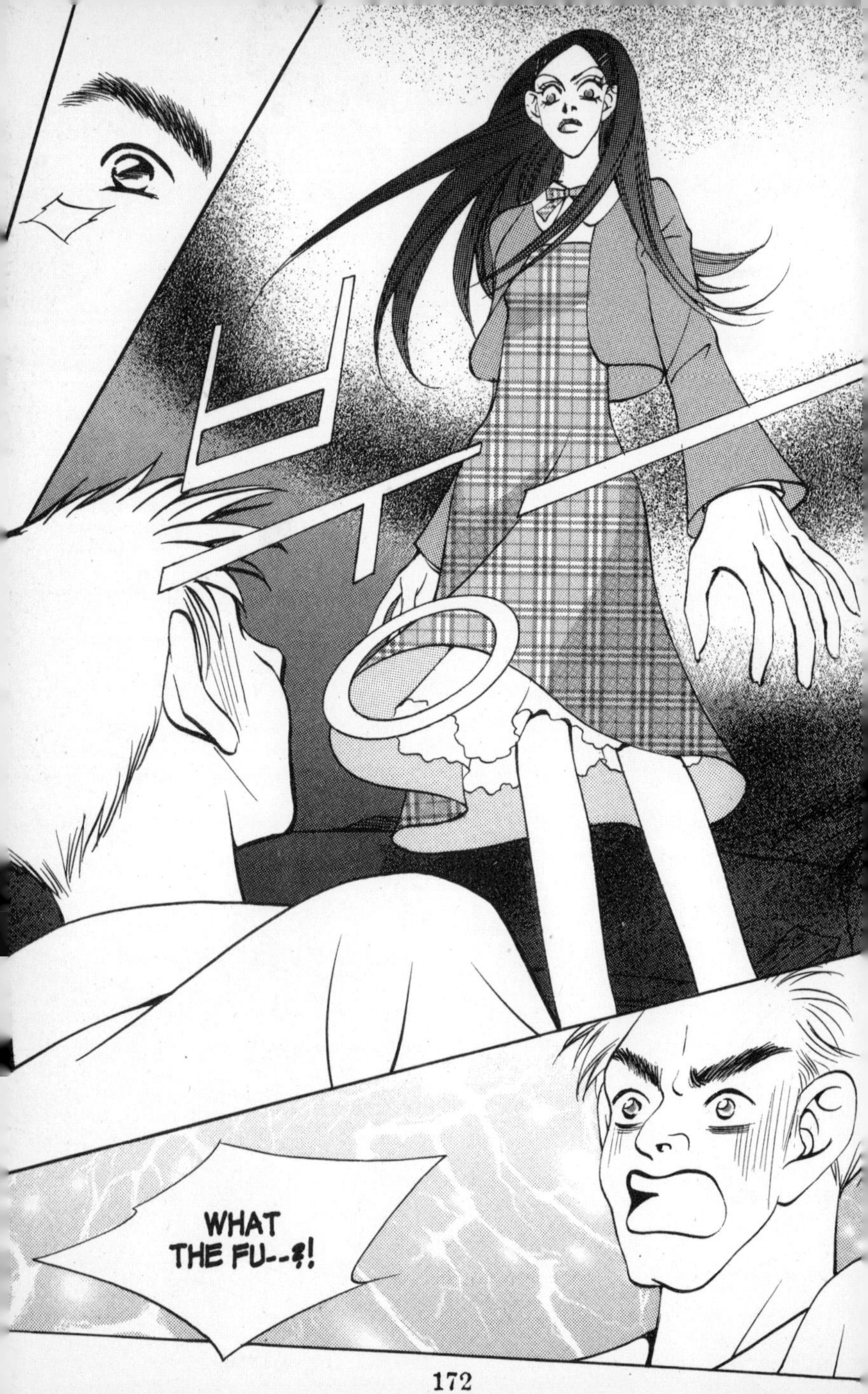
WHAT THE FU--?!

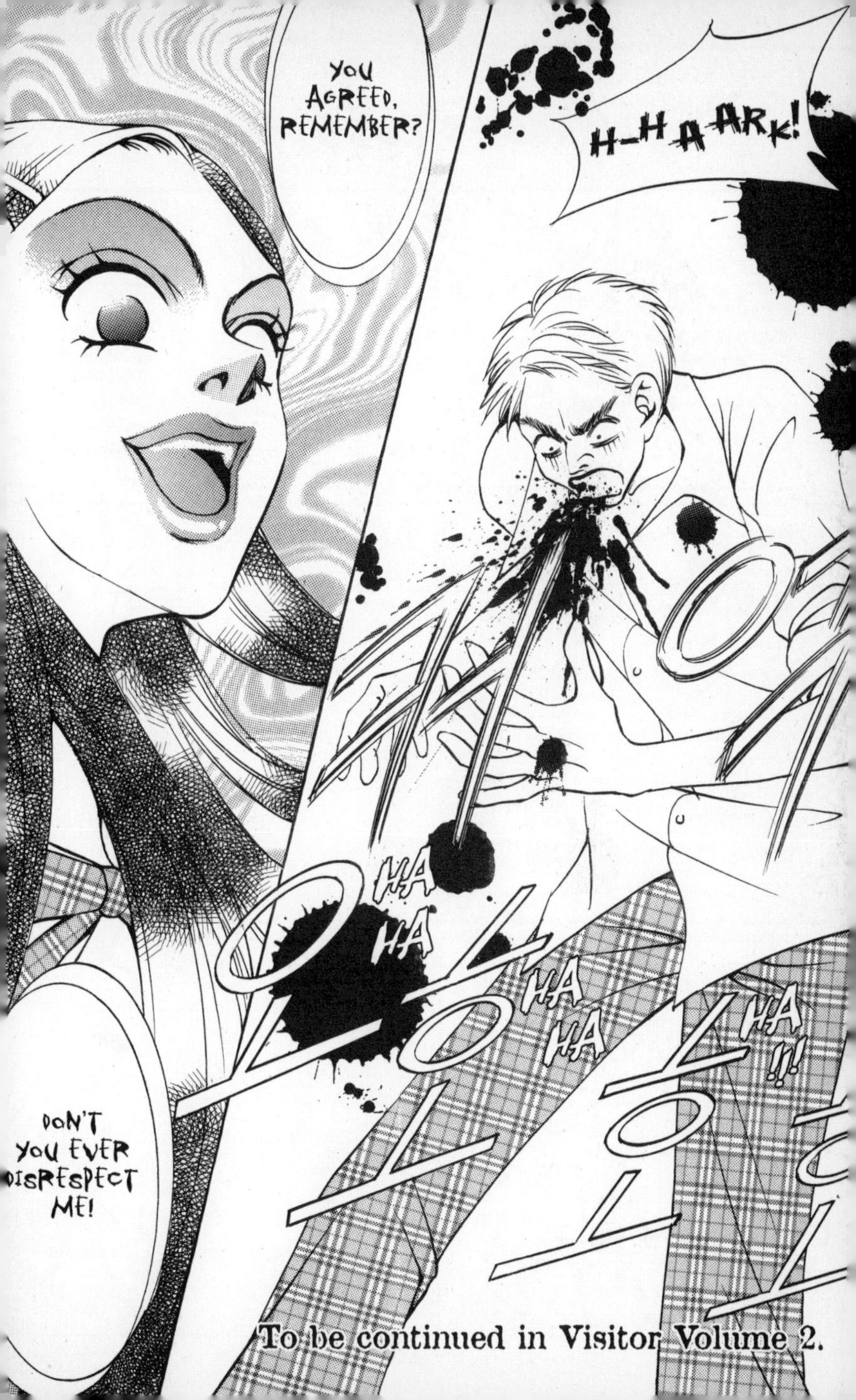
YOU AGREED, REMEMBER?
DON'T YOU EVER DISRESPECT ME!
H-HAARK!
HA HA
HA HA
HA!!
To be continued in Visitor Volume 2.

☆ AUTHOR'S POSTSCRIPT ☆

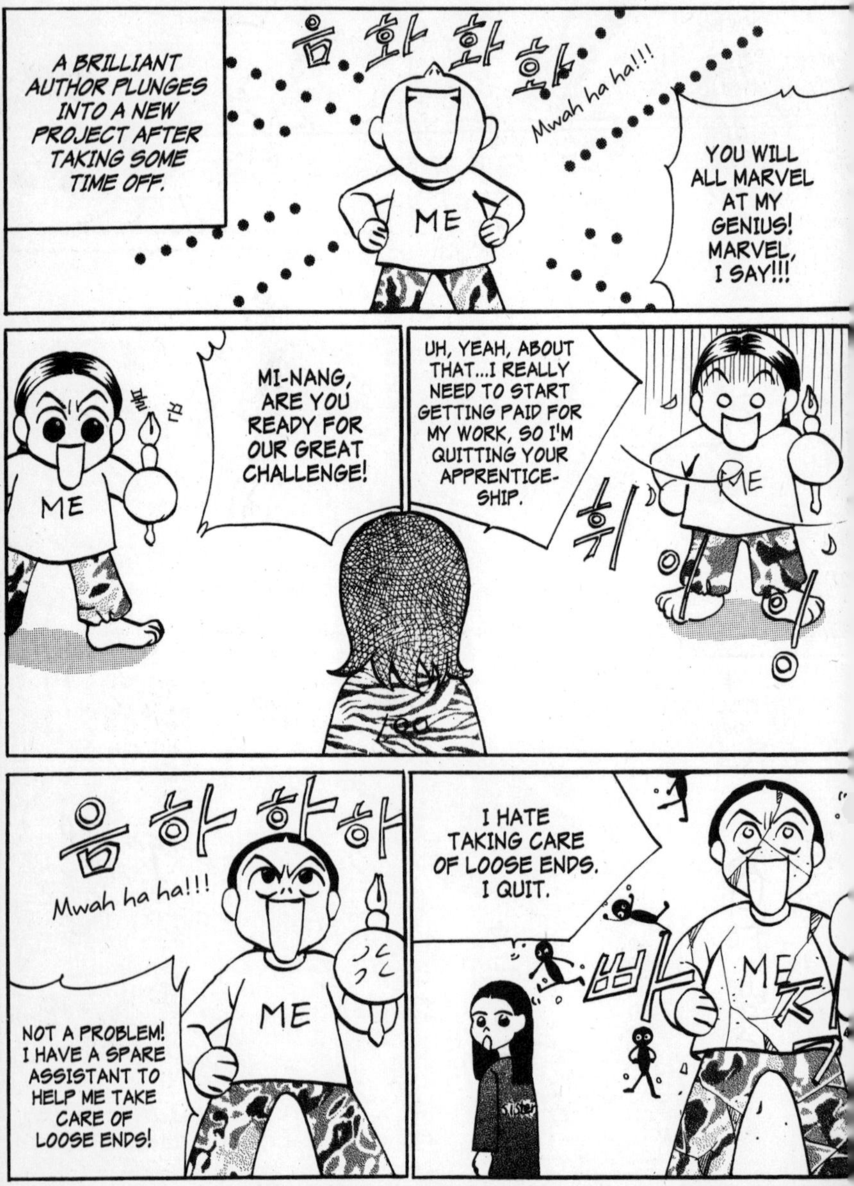

A BRILLIANT AUTHOR PLUNGES INTO A NEW PROJECT AFTER TAKING SOME TIME OFF.
Mwah ha ha!!!
YOU WILL ALL MARVEL AT MY GENIUS! MARVEL, I SAY!!!
MI-NANG, ARE YOU READY FOR OUR GREAT CHALLENGE!
UH, YEAH, ABOUT THAT...I REALLY NEED TO START GETTING PAID FOR MY WORK, SO I'M QUITTING YOUR APPRENTICESHIP.
음하하하
Mwah ha ha!!!
NOT A PROBLEM! I HAVE A SPARE ASSISTANT TO HELP ME TAKE CARE OF LOOSE ENDS!
I HATE TAKING CARE OF LOOSE ENDS. I QUIT.

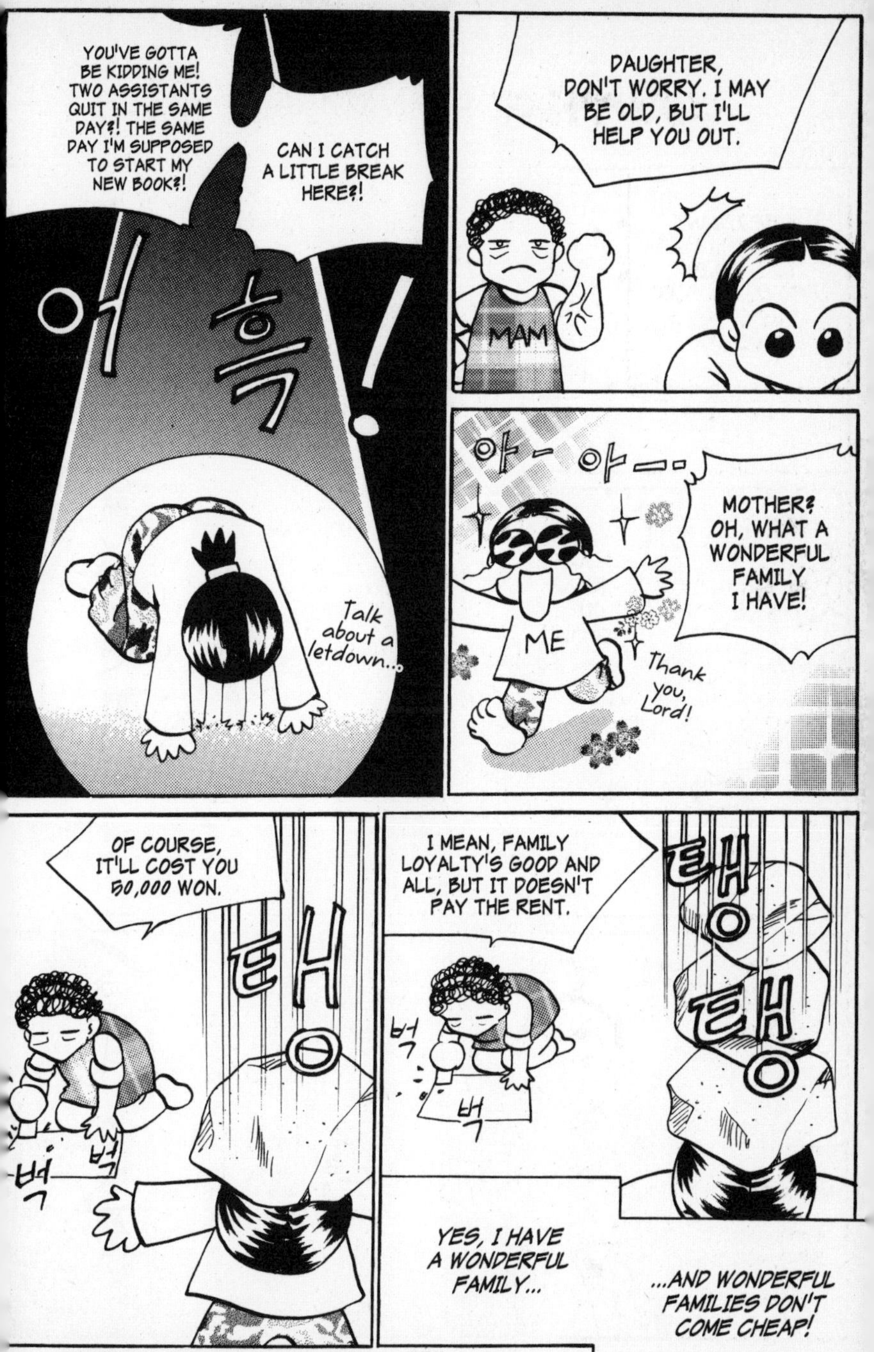
YOU'VE GOTTA BE KIDDING ME! TWO ASSISTANTS QUIT IN THE SAME DAY?! THE SAME DAY I'M SUPPOSED TO START MY NEW BOOK?!
CAN I CATCH A LITTLE BREAK HERE?!
Talk about a letdown...
DAUGHTER, DON'T WORRY. I MAY BE OLD, BUT I'LL HELP YOU OUT.
MAM
MOTHER? OH, WHAT A WONDERFUL FAMILY I HAVE!
ME
Thank you, Lord!
OF COURSE, IT'LL COST YOU 50,000 WON.
I MEAN, FAMILY LOYALTY'S GOOD AND ALL, BUT IT DOESN'T PAY THE RENT.
YES, I HAVE A WONDERFUL FAMILY...
...AND WONDERFUL FAMILIES DON'T COME CHEAP!

NOTE: 50,000 won is about $50.

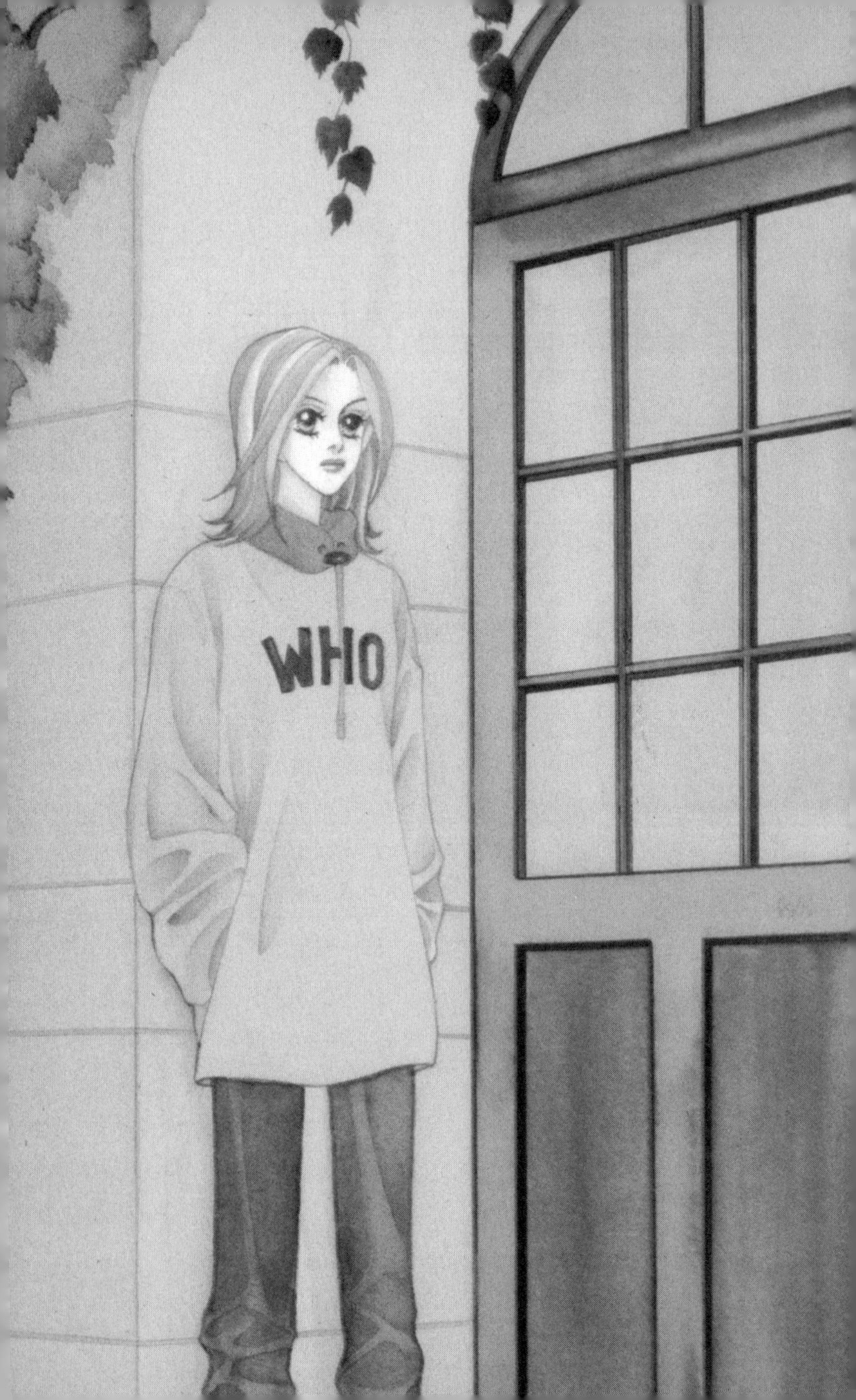
WHO

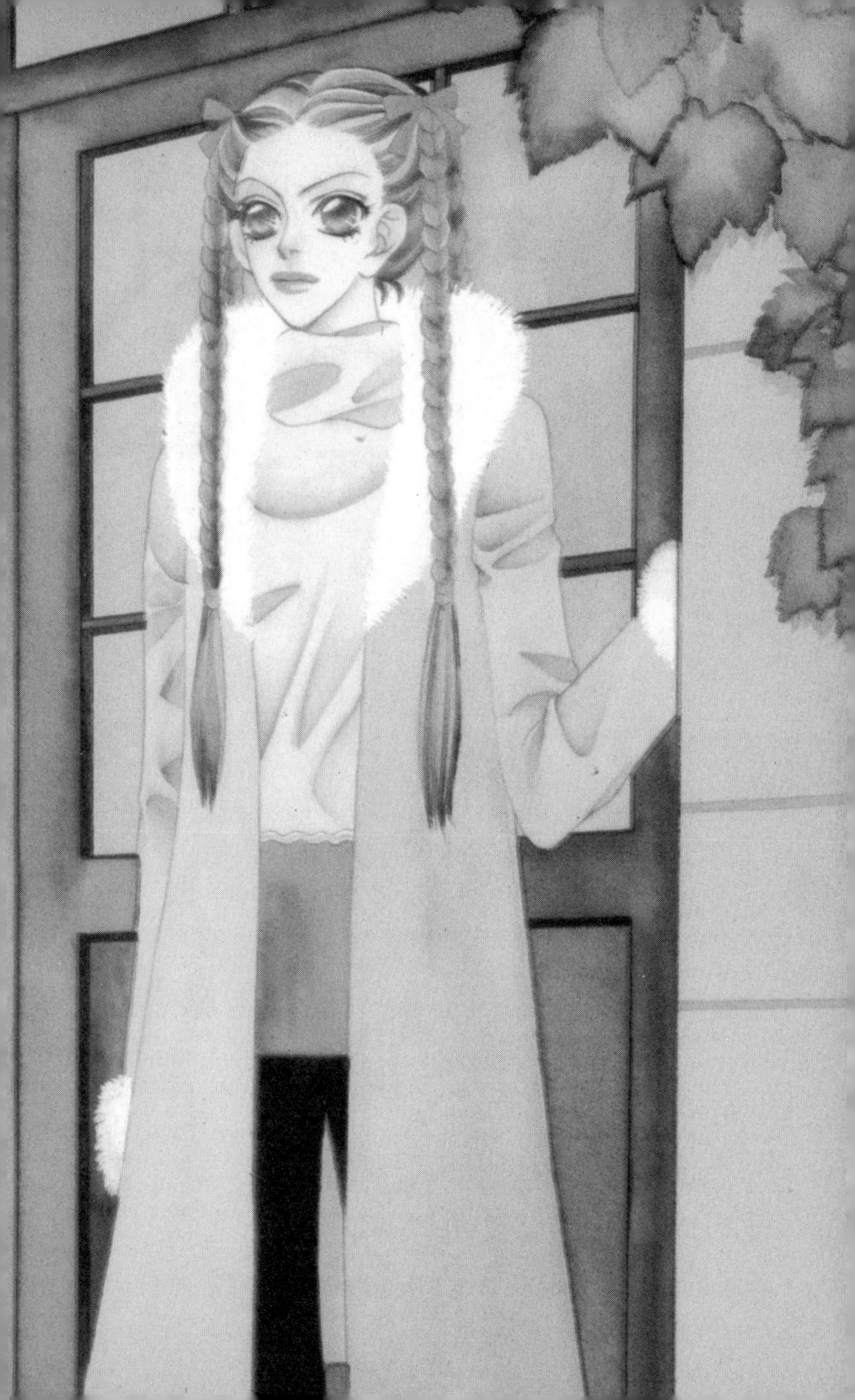

In the next volume of

VISITOR

It's a strange thing, memory. We take the moments recalled in our minds as history, and believe, with no incertitude, that they are real. However, a memory is something that cannot be touched. They obey no physical laws, nor do they function with any sense of dependability or order. One moment you may recall something with vivid clarity, and the next it may be gone from your mind.

Imagine, if you will, a trip to an unfamiliar place. You enter and look around, only to find that the place isn't new, and although you cannot recall having passed through its halls before, people greet you with familiar recognition. While this scenario is alarming in and of itself, imagine now that the place is a hospital, and the people are doctors. They look at you with concern in their eyes and speak of sisters you never knew you had and appointments that you have no recollection of making. Slowly, the situation shifts from alarming to sinister...

Welcome to the life of Hyo-Bin Na, and welcome to Volume 2 of Visitor.

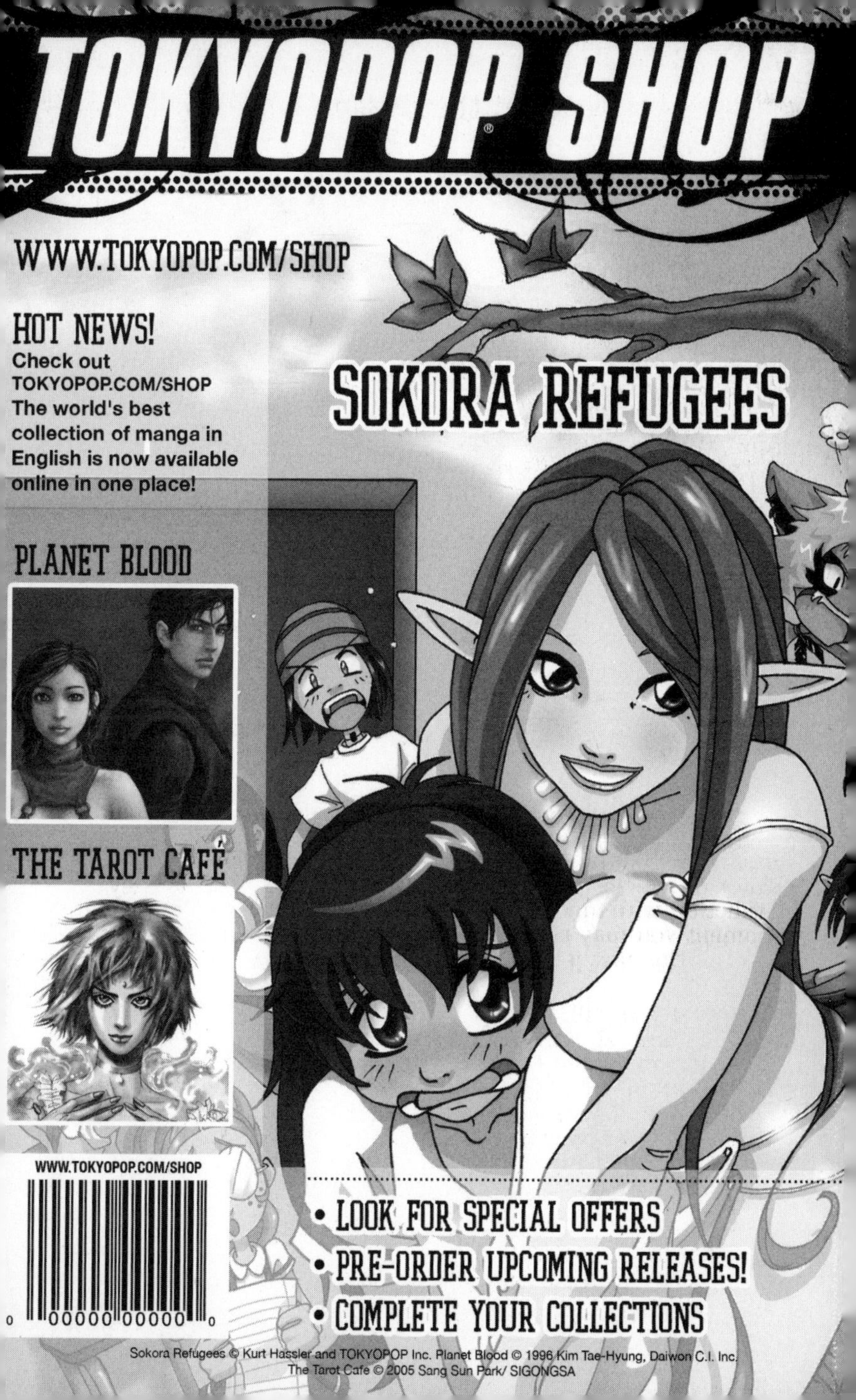

TOKYOPOP® SHOP
WWW.TOKYOPOP.COM/SHOP
HOT NEWS!
Check out TOKYOPOP.COM/SHOP The world's best collection of manga in English is now available online in one place!
SOKORA REFUGEES
PLANET BLOOD
THE TAROT CAFÉ
WWW.TOKYOPOP.COM/SHOP
• LOOK FOR SPECIAL OFFERS
• PRE-ORDER UPCOMING RELEASES!
• COMPLETE YOUR COLLECTIONS
Sokora Refugees © Kurt Hassler and TOKYOPOP Inc. Planet Blood © 1996 Kim Tae-Hyung, Daiwon C.I. Inc.
The Tarot Cafe © 2005 Sang Sun Park/ SIGONGSA

EVIL NEVER DIES...
BUT EVIL STUFF DOES!

FROM THE
WINNERS OF
TOKYOPOP'S FIRST
RISING STARS OF
MANGA™
COMPETITION

VAN VON HUNTER™

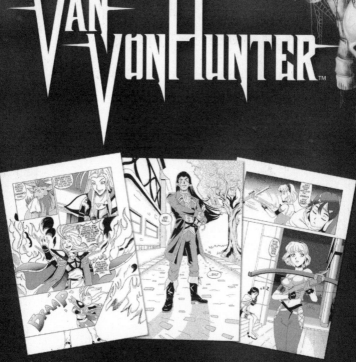

In the dark ages long ago, in a war-torn land where tranquility and harmony once blossomed, tyranny ruled with a flaming fist! At last, a hero arose to defeat the evildoers and returned hope to the people and peace to the countryside. Now...the sinister forces are back with a vengeance, and in their hour of direst-est need, the commoners once again seek a champion to right wrongs and triumph over villainy! Unfortunately, they could only get the mighty warrior Van Von Hunter, Hunter of Evil...Stuff!

Together with his loyal, memory-challenged sidekick, Van Von Hunter is on a never-ending quest to smite the bad guys—and believe us, they're real bad!

Preview the manga at:

www.TOKYOPOP.com/vanvonhunter
www.VanVonHunter.com

TEEN
AGE 13+

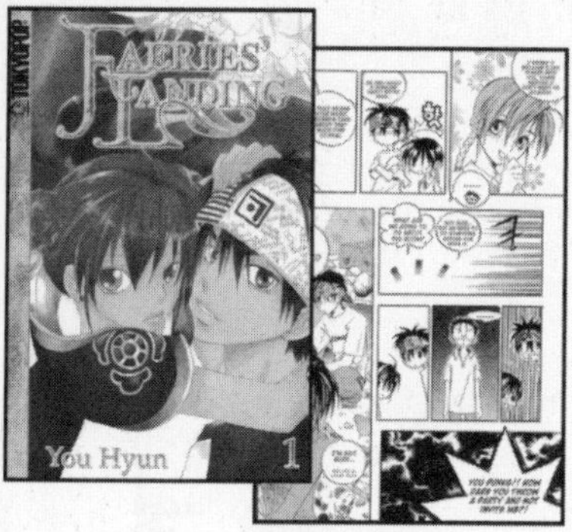
TOKYOPOP
Faeries' Landing
You Hyun
1

BY YOU HYUN

FAERIES' LANDING

Following the misadventures of teenager Ryang Jegal and Fanta, a faerie who has fallen from the heavens straight into South Korea, *Faeries' Landing* is both a spoof of modern-day teen romance and a lighthearted fantasy epic. Imagine if Shakespeare's *A Midsummer Night's Dream* had come from the pen of Joss Whedon after about a dozen shots of espresso, and you have an idea of what to expect from You Hyun's funny little farce. Bursting with sharp wit, hip attitude and vibrant art, *Faeries' Landing* is guaranteed to get you giggling.
~Tim Beedle, Editor

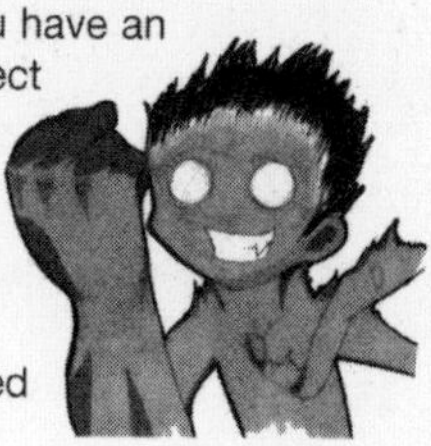

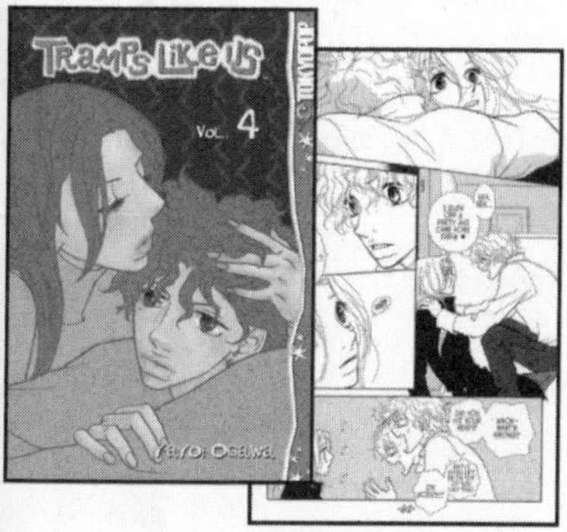
Tramps Like Us
Vol. 4
TOKYOPOP
Yayoi Ogawa

BY YAYOI OGAWA

TRAMPS LIKE US

Yayoi Ogawa's *Tramps Like Us*—known as *Kimi wa Pet* in Japan—is the touching and humorous story of Sumire, a woman whose striking looks and drive for success alienate her from her friends and co-workers...until she takes in Momo, a cute homeless boy, as her "pet." As sketchy as the situation sounds, it turns out to be the sanest thing in Sumire's hectic life. In his quiet way, Momo teaches Sumire how to care for another being while also caring for herself...in other words, how to love. And there ain't nothin' wrong with that.
~Carol Fox, Editor

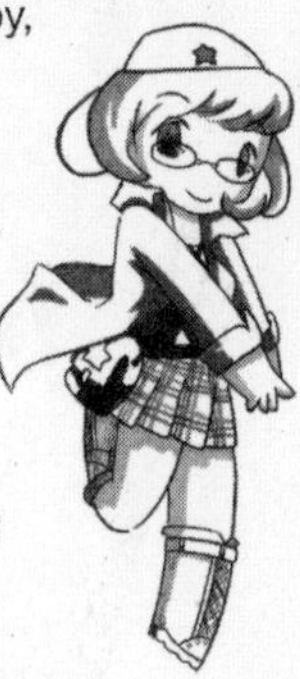

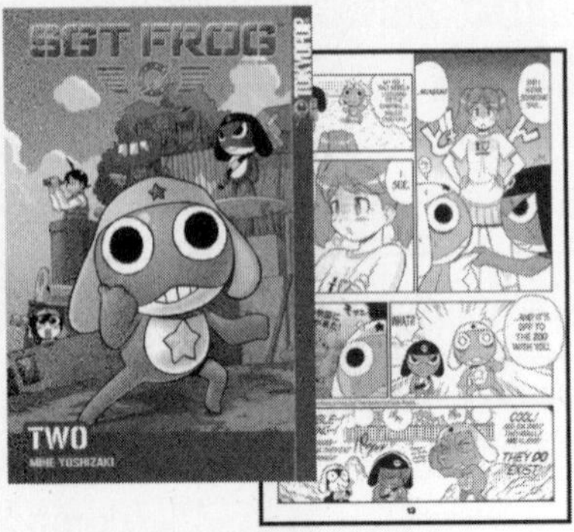
SGT FROG
TOKYOPOP
TWO
MINE YOSHIZAKI

BY MINE YOSHIZAKI

SGT FROG

Sgt. Frog is so absurdly comical, it has me in stitches every time I edit it. Mine Yoshizaki's clever sci-fi spoof showcases the hijinks of Sergeant Keroro, a cuddly looking alien, diabolically determined to oppress our planet! While some E.T.s phone home, this otherworldly menace has your number! Abandoned on Earth, Keroro takes refuge in the Hinata home, whose residents quickly take advantage of his stellar cleaning skills. But between scrubbing, vacuuming and an unhealthy obsession with Gundam models, Keroro still finds time to plot the subjugation of humankind!

~ Paul Morrissey, Editor

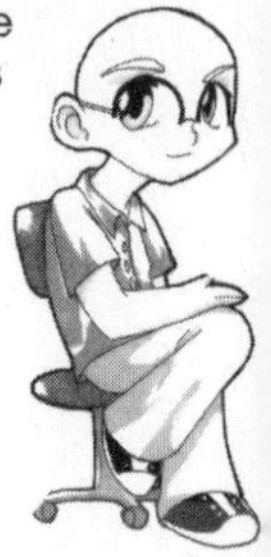

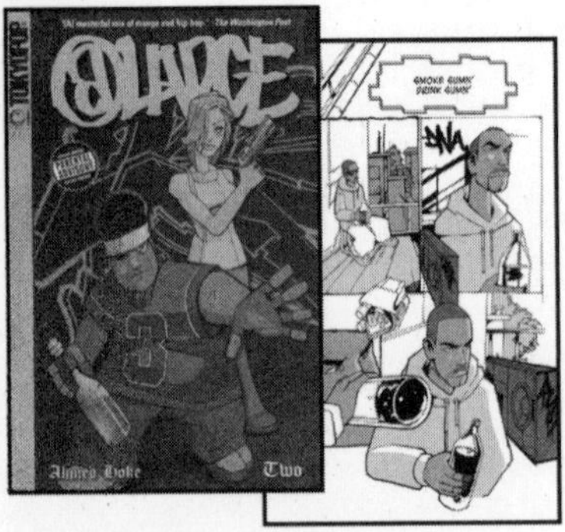
TOKYOPOP
Ahmed Hoke
Two

BY AHMED HOKE

@LARGE

Ahmed Hoke's revolutionary hip-hop manga is a groundbreaking graphic novel. While at first glace this series may seem like a dramatic departure from traditional manga styles, on a deeper level one will find a rich, lyrical world full of wildly imaginative characters, intense action and heartfelt human emotions. This is a truly unique manga series that needs to be read by everyone—whether they are fans of hip-hop or not.

~Rob Valois, Editor

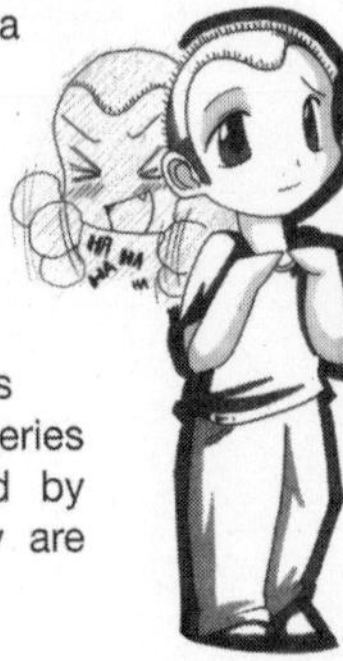